CHINA'S SEARCH FOR SECURITY

Andrew J. Nathan ✺ Andrew Scobell

CHINA's SEARCH FOR SECURITY

Columbia
University
Press ✺
New York

Columbia University Press
Publishers Since 1893
New York   Chichester, West Sussex
cup.columbia.edu
Copyright © 2012 Andrew J. Nathan and Andrew Scobell

The authors and Columbia University Press wish to thank Robert S. Ross
for permission to use material that originally appeared in this book's first
edition, *The Great Wall and the Empty Fortress*.

Library of Congress Cataloging-in-Publication Data
Nathan, Andrew J. (Andrew James)
    China's search for security / Andrew J. Nathan and Andrew Scobell.
        p.   c.m
    Includes bibliographical references and index.
    ISBN 978-0-231-14050-8 (cloth : alk. paper) — ISBN 978-0-231-51164-3
(ebook)
    1.   China—Foreign relations—1949– 2.   National security—
China.   I.   Scobell, Andrew.   II.   Title.

    JZ1734.N37   2012
    355'.033551—dc23
                                                            2012009156

Columbia University Press books are printed on permanent and durable
acid-free paper.
This book is printed on paper with recycled content.
Printed in the United States of America
c 10 9 8 7 6 5 4 3 2 1

Cover images: Alamy   Cover design: Lisa Hamm
Book Design: Lisa Hamm

Frontispiece: China and Its Neighbors

Dedicated to the memory of our fathers

Paul S Nathan, 1913–2009

Charles L. Scobell, 1926–2009

CONTENTS

PART III

PART IV

PART V

ABBREVIATIONS

ANZUS	Australia, New Zealand, United States Alliance
ARATS	Association for Relations Across the Taiwan Strait
ASEAN	Association of Southeast Asian Nations
CCP	Chinese Communist Party
CENTCOM	U.S. Central Command
CIA	U.S. Central Intelligence Agency
CLSG	central leading small group
CMC	Central Military Commission
DPP	Democratic Progressive Party
DPRK	Democratic People's Republic of Korea
EEZ	Exclusive Economic Zones
FBI	U.S. Federal Bureau of Investigation
GDP	gross domestic product
IAEA	International Atomic Energy Agency
ICBM	intercontinental ballistic missile
IMF	International Monetary Fund
KEDO	Korean Peninsula Energy Development Organization
KMT	Kuomintang, Nationalist Party
MOOTW	Military Operations Other Than War
MR	military region
MSG	Military Strategic Guidelines

NATO	North Atlantic Treaty Organization
NCO	noncommissioned officer
NGO	nongovernmental organization
NPC	National People's Congress
NPT	Nuclear Nonproliferation Treaty
NSC	U.S. National Security Council
ODA	official development assistance
PACOM	U.S. Pacific Command
PAP	People's Armed Police
PBSC	Politburo Standing Committee
PLA	People's Liberation Army
PRC	People's Republic of China
ROC	Republic of China
ROK	Republic of Korea
SASTIND	State Administration for Science, Technology, and Industry for National Defense
SCO	Shanghai Cooperation Organization
SDF	Self-Defense Forces
SEATO	Southeast Asia Treaty Organization
SEF	Straits Exchange Foundation
TAR	Tibet Autonomous Region
TRA	Taiwan Relations Act
UDHR	Universal Declaration of Human Rights
UN	United Nations
UNCLOS	United Nations Convention on the Law of the Sea
WHO	World Health Organization
WTO	World Trade Organization

INTRODUCTION

China's Search for Security grew out of a previous work called *The Great Wall and the Empty Fortress*, which was published in 1997.[1] We set out to produce a revised and updated edition of that book, but China's position in the world has changed so much that we ended up with what is almost entirely a new book. The analytical approach remains the same: we look at China's security problems from the Chinese point of view in order to analyze how Chinese policymakers have tried to solve them. The basic conclusion also stands: China is too bogged down in the security challenges within and around its borders to threaten the West unless the West weakens itself to the point of creating a power vacuum.

In other respects, however, China's position in the world has changed. In 1997, it was a vulnerable country, fielding a foreign policy that was mainly defensive and aimed at preventing domestic instability, avoiding the loss of historically held territories such as Taiwan and Tibet, and reconstructing strained relations with potentially threatening powerful neighbors such as Japan, Russia, and India. It had no major interests or significant means of influence in parts of the world beyond its immediate periphery. It was not an actor of consequence in Europe, North or South America, Africa, or the Middle East.

But the 1997 book predicted that things would change, saying, "China is the largest and economically most dynamic newly emerging power in the history of the world. It intends to take its place in the next century as a great power."[2] That century has arrived, and China has fulfilled its intention. *Great power* is a vague term, but China deserves it by any measure: the extent and strategic location of its territory, the size and dynamism of its population, the value and growth rate of its economy, its massive share of global trade, the size and sophistication of its military, the reach of its diplomatic interests, and its level of cultural influence. It has become one of a small number of countries that have significant national interests in every part of the world—often driven by the search for resources—and whose voice must be heard in the solution of every global problem. It is one of the few countries that command the attention, whether willingly or grudgingly, of every other country and every international organization. It is the only country widely seen as a possible threat to U.S. predominance.

It is easy to forget that China's rise was what the West wanted. Richard Nixon laid the groundwork for the policy of engagement by arguing in 1967, "[W]e simply cannot afford to leave China forever outside the family of nations, there to nurture its fantasies, cherish its hates and threaten its neighbors. There is no place on this small planet for a billion of its potentially most able people to live in angry isolation."[3] He launched the engagement policy with his historic visit to China in 1972. Every American president since then has stated that the prosperity and stability of China are in the interest of the United States.

Engagement was a strategy designed to wean China from Mao Zedong's pursuit of permanent revolution by exposing the country to the benefits of participation in the world economy. Over the course of three decades, the West opened its markets, provided loans and investments, transferred technology (with a few limits related to military applications), trained Chinese students, provided advice on laws and institutions, and helped China enter the World Trade Organization (WTO) (although negotiating hard over the conditions of China's entry; see chapter 10). American and more generally Western support had incalculable financial and technological value to China, and it is not an exaggeration to say that Western support made China's rise possible.

Seldom has the admonition "be careful what you wish for" been so apt. At home, China did abandon Maoist radicalism, but it did not democratize. Instead, economic growth strengthened the one-party dictatorship's hold on power. Abroad, China took its place as a full player in the global system with a stake in the status quo, as the engagers intended. But now Americans wonder whether a strong China poses a strategic threat.

Thirty-five years of rapid economic growth were bound to produce some shift in relative power just by bulking up Chinese resources. But China's rise turned out to be all the more dramatic because of its competitors' weaker trajectories. While China surged, the Soviet Union collapsed, and the successor Russian government struggled to define an international role. Japan stagnated economically and vacillated between accepting security dependence on the U.S. or taking more responsibility for its own defense. India engaged less deeply than China with the world economy and focused most of its security energy on its nearby enemy, Pakistan. While China cultivated mutually cooperative relations with any country that was willing, the U.S. vitiated the advantages of its status as the world's only superpower with a series of wars and confrontations that weakened rather than strengthened its global influence. For all these reasons, the shift in China's relative power has been more striking than it otherwise might have been.

These developments have given rise to two interlinked debates over Chinese foreign policy. First, is China an aggressive, expansionist power with enough resources to overwhelm its neighbors and create a "Chinese century" in which China will "rule the world," or is it a vulnerable power facing numerous, enduring security threats?[4] We argue controversially that vulnerability remains the key driver of China's foreign policy. That is why the subtitle of the previous book, *The Great Wall and the Empty Fortress: China's Search for Security*, takes its place as the title of this new volume. The main tasks of Chinese foreign policy are still defensive: to blunt destabilizing influences from abroad, to avoid territorial losses, to moderate surrounding states' suspicions, and to create international conditions that will sustain economic growth. What has changed is that these internal and regional priorities are now embedded in a larger quest: to define a global role that serves Chinese interests but also wins acceptance from other powers.

We add that last qualifying phrase because defining a role for a rising great power is not a unilateral process. A decade ago it was largely a matter for China itself to determine how to provide for its own security (except for its management of the Taiwan issue, on which the U.S. asserted a right to limit Chinese options; see chapter 4). But as China's core interests evolve from regional to global, they intersect more and more with those of the other major powers, leading to greater possibilities for both cooperation and conflict. As China's influence increases, so do other powers' efforts to channel or constrain that influence. Rising power brings not only new scope for action, but new checks. China will have to define its role through interactions that are inevitably contentious with other actors and that may turn conflictual, which makes it more important than ever to understand what drives Chinese foreign policy.

That is why we start in chapter 1 with the fundamentals of geography and demography—where China is on the map, who lives there, how its population is distributed, and who its neighbors are. The relevance of these facts is emphasized by the approach to foreign policy analysis called "geo-strategic" or "classical realism," which says that the world does not look the same from every point on the map. The Chinese are not where we are, they are not who we are, and we have to look at their situation to understand their actions. China is not special in the fact that geography matters; what is special for China—as for every other country—are the specifics of its geopolitical situation.

Chapter 1 also takes account of culture and ideology. People think and talk about their national situation and national interests in terms that are meaningful and understandable to them. We need to know the concepts they use in order to understand the discourse. Paying attention to culture does not mean cultural relativism: a country's core security interests are intelligible to an analyst from any culture. But to understand how they are being talked about requires a process of interpretation.

The causal path from facts on the ground to policy outputs runs through actors and institutions—the people who make policy and the institutions within which they do so. These people and institutions are discussed in chapter 2. Sometimes the connection is straightforward. Sometimes it is distorted by cognitive factors (misinformation, miscalculation), perceptual factors (erroneous guesses about others' motives), and value commitments (preferences for values besides security) or by institutional habits and struc-tures, domestic political needs, and leadership shortcomings. Thus, we may sometimes fail to find an interest-based explanation that makes sense of a particular element of foreign policy. When that happens, we turn to other factors to explain why China—like other countries—sometimes adopts policies that apparently do not serve its national interests. As we show, this happened relatively rarely in China even during the Mao period and has happened rarely since then. Chinese foreign policy has usually made sense as part of a search for security. Why Chinese policy should more often be more interest based than some other countries' policies is a question we explore in several places, especially in the first four chapters.

CHINESE FOREIGN POLICY AND INTERNATIONAL RELATIONS THEORY

The second debate occasioned by the rise of China is whether its policy-making processes are driven more by culture, nationalism, and resentment over a "century of humiliation" or more by a realistic calculus that seeks to match available resources to concrete security goals. On this question, we lean, again controversially, to the position that Chinese foreign poli-cymaking is more often than not rational. To be sure, China's behavior can be puzzling at first glance. Why did China formally ally itself with the Soviet Union in 1950, then split with it ten years later? Why did it move from antagonism to rapprochement with the U.S. in 1971? Why does China pursue disputes with Japan over historical issues at certain times and not at others? Why did China seek to promote unification with Taiwan by counterproductively building up a missile threat to the island from the early 1990s onward and threatening to use military force if Taiwan were to "secede"? Why does China cooperate with "rogue states" such as North Korea, Sudan, Iran, and Burma? What were Beijing's aims in forming the Shanghai Cooperation Organization (SCO)? What are its territorial ambitions in the South China Sea?

Every decision, no doubt, has a back story—bureaucratic politics, misperception, international signaling—that we are usually not going to know because it is confidential. But such actions and policies also make larger patterns that we as observers are able to discern. We find that the puzzles of Chinese foreign policy most often yield answers through the insights of a theory called "realism," which suggests that foreign policy is driven by national self-interest—in turn meaning strategic and economic advantage, or what we call "security" in this book. For all its vastness and resources, China has extensive vulnerabilities throughout its security environment, a theme we develop in chapter 1. Because of rapid social change and ethnic diversity, it is insecure within its own borders; around its periphery, it has a history of wars with many of its neighbors (Korea, Japan, Taiwan, Vietnam, India, Russia); in each neighboring region, it faces factors of instability; and in the regions beyond Asia, China's economic security is subject to forces beyond its control. The theory of realism says that these challenges set the agenda for Chinese foreign policy.

The political science field of international relations also presents two other useful perspectives on how to understand the drivers of a country's foreign policy: *constructivism*, the theory that a state's interests as well as its strategies to achieve these interests are constructed through actors' use of perceptions, values, and ideas to understand and react to their situations; and *institutionalism*, a theory that emphasizes how states, once they engage themselves in institutional arrangements (such as treaties and international organizations), become constrained by these sets of rules in patterns of "complex interdependence" as a result of the benefits they gain from using such prearranged channels to work with other states toward common goals. We also draw occasionally from a fourth theory in the field, *liberalism*, which draws attention to the role of a country's domestic interest groups in making foreign policy. But the theory does not tell us much about China because, as we argue in chapter 2, most foreign policy issues in China are managed by a small elite with little interference from other political institutions and social forces. Foreign economic policy is a partial exception, where domestic interests help shape foreign economic policy to a greater extent than in other fields (chapter 10). Of course, the role of social interests in Chinese foreign policy may grow in the future. We use these theoretical traditions to nuance our mostly realist analysis in the belief that the various approaches are not mutually exclusive.

Realism tells us that security is the ability to maintain effective control over one's own political regime, economy, way of life, borders, and population. The means for achieving security are various kinds of power. The Western literature on Chinese foreign policy pays attention to five elements of Chinese power: military power;[5] economic power (including trade, investment, access to markets, access to resources, and foreign exchange holdings);[6] interdependence–power (China's impact on the environment, public health, and other global issues beyond its own borders);[7] diplomatic power (China's role in such settings as the United Nations [UN] Security Council, in the talks over Korea, and in negotiations that involve Iran,

Sudan, and other problem states);[8] and soft power (the influence of Chinese values and of China's political and economic models, international interest in Chinese culture and language, and so on).[9] For their part, Chinese analysts use a notion of "comprehensive national power," which has various components and which they tend to assess as a package.[10] We pay attention to all these elements of power throughout the book and discuss three of them in detail in part IV.

We agree with constructivists that security is a dynamic rather than a static concept. In China's complex environment, the decision makers' concept of their nation's security interests must adapt to changing information and opportunities. In the 1950s, Chinese leaders took the U.S. as their main enemy, and in the 1960s the USSR; in the 1970s, they positioned themselves as leading the Third World against two hegemons in the search for a world of peace and stability for development; then in the 1990s they seemed again to see the U.S. as the main threat to their security; and now, at a time when the U.S. is perhaps more unilateralist in its behavior and has more military forces near China than ever, they seem to believe that the two countries can find a way to balance one another and cooperate to achieve mutual interests.

Constructivism says that policy decisions are influenced by the leaders' perceptions and values and the institutions through which they make and implement decisions. In chapter 2, we look at ideas and institutions involved in making foreign policy, including factional and bureaucratic politics and central–local relations.[11] We find that an important feature of Chinese foreign policymaking is that it is centralized and coordinated, allowing even imperfect human institutions to pursue realist policies more often than not.

Realism argues that any two powers whose security interests intersect (which can happen in terms of territory or in terms of economic interests or in terms of power-projection potential) can become caught in a dynamic that Robert Jervis has identified as the "security dilemma."[12] The dilemma occurs when one country's attempt to increase its ability to protect itself diminishes the security of the other country by changing the relative balance of power. This dynamic may easily come into play in the Sino–American relationship as China's rise in its own region intensifies the intersection of its security perimeter with long-established American positions throughout Asia and as China's economic outreach under conditions of globalization brings it into increasing interaction with the already established economic presence of the U.S. and its European and Japanese allies in many parts of the world.

Yet institutionalist scholars have pointed out that even while competition increases, states can also experience "gains to cooperation" in the international system.[13] As an example, the growth of the Chinese economy has benefited the U.S. economy by providing a market for American goods, supplying cheap, high-quality consumer products, and soaking up U.S. government debt, among a multitude of ways. Cooperation on public health and environmental issues similarly creates mutual benefit. To be more than fleeting, gains have to be institutionalized in the form of international agreements and organizations. The China–America relationship illustrates these dynamics: engagement enmeshed China in a series of institutions that it has come to value for their benefits. China's record of compliance with many international regimes (trade, investment, arms control) has moved from nonexistent to strong in the course of a few decades; in other regimes, China is engaged but lags in compliance (intellectual property protection, human rights). The theory of institutionalism is compatible with realism because cooperation may increase an actor's power and security. It is compatible with constructivism because actors have to perceive the opportunities for gain, create or learn the rules, and establish the domestic and international bureaucracies needed to harvest the gains—a set of processes scholars refer to as "learning" or "socialization."

Cooperative gains in turn, however, can generate new frictions over the distribution of costs and benefits. How much American interference does China have to accept in order for its products to meet American health and safety standards? And are such standards fair? How much stake does each side have in the other's management of foreign exchange rates when the two are doing a huge volume of trade? What does China give up in informational autonomy when it cooperates with the World Health Organization (WHO) to fight this or that contagious disease? Who pays what portion of the cost of halting global climate change? Such frictions can be intense but need to be placed in perspective as part of the process of cooperating.

Military interests may also converge, as in the case of the shared U.S. and Chinese interest in the denuclearization of Korea. Yet the Korea example also suggests that such overlaps are seldom as encompassing or protracted as the compatibilities in economic, public-health, or global-order issues. Although neither China nor the U.S. wants a nuclear Korea, they vie for long-term predominance on the peninsula. So cooperation on a near-term goal is limited by different preferences about how that goal is to be achieved and by a divergence of interests in the shape of the ultimate outcome.

When geostrategic conflicts of interest are difficult and intense, they tend to find parallel expression as cultural conflicts, a point important to constructivists. A good example of this dynamic has occurred in China–Japan relations. Most scholars of this relationship consider it puzzling that Sino–Japanese relations are as bad as they are and usually explain the puzzle by referring to history and culture or to nationalism seen as an ungovernable collective emotion or as a creature of political entrepreneurs.[14] The more realism-centered explanation that we offer in chapter 5 is that these two militarily powerful and geographically close countries have overlapping, competitive core security interests in the East China Sea, the Senkaku Islands, the Sea of Japan, the Korean Peninsula, the Russian Far East, the Taiwan area, and the broader Pacific as well as with respect to the security of sea lanes through the South China Sea and beyond. Neither has a solid defense against the other, and both stand to lose in the event of military conflict. These enduring geostrategic facts have generated a long history of distrust and contention. In chapter 5, we interpret conflicts over history textbooks and visits to religious shrines as expressions of this underlying security dilemma, thus combining realist and constructivist perspectives.[15]

According to the theory of realism, as power expands, ambitions expand with it.[16] But power cannot expand infinitely because power is relational: the other side always has some way to resist. This relationship makes it meaningless to say in the abstract how much power China (or any other actor) has. One needs to evaluate Chinese power in relation to the power of potential allies and adversaries and with an eye to the usability of power in particular situations. The bare fact that China's power is expanding does not tell us where it will expand (Southeast Asia? Central Asia? Africa? Latin America?) or how (militarily? economically?) or how it will be used. For example, as Thomas Christensen has shown, even though the Chinese military remains inferior to the American military, it has the capability to pose serious challenges to U.S. armed forces operating in the western Pacific.[17] However, economists have argued that even though China as of

April 2010 held nearly a trillion dollars in U.S. Treasury bills and other dollar-denominated assets, it could not use this resource to cause serious damage to the American economy because the attempt to do so would exact too high a cost on China itself. So power is not fungible: it can be exerted only in specific ways based on a country's geostrategic position, assets, and vulnerabilities as well as on the assets and deployments of those against whom it is being used.

THE GREAT WALL AND THE EMPTY FORTRESS

The earlier book from which this one stems, *The Great Wall and the Empty Fortress*, refers in its title to two elements of the Chinese strategic tradition that are still worth noticing.

The Great Wall is an extensive network of battlements and fortifications along the northern edge of China's demographic heartland. Various parts of the network were constructed by different dynasties over the centuries— one of a number of strategies adopted by different rulers to protect the heartland from invasions by Central Asian horse-mounted armies.[18] The Great Wall is in part a symbol of weakness because it signals susceptibility to invasion, but also in part a symbol of strength because it represents the economic and cultural superiority of the land within the wall and its productive denizens' ability to deter invasion with feats of engineering and vigilance.

Today's invaders are more likely to be department store buyers, venture capitalists, tourists, and foundation officers than mounted nomads, but China is no less concerned to control their influence. The methods of protection are now more virtual than physical—among them a nonconvertible currency, regulatory obstacles to full foreign access to the domestic economy, repression of independent civil society organizations that have foreign connections, active police surveillance of foreigners and foreign-connected Chinese, and the so-called Great Firewall that restricts the Chinese Internet's access to the international Internet.

Geographically as well, China still lies open to invasion or dismemberment, even though no country currently shows an appetite for such an adventure. Traditional invaders had the advantages of mobility, concentrated force, and explosive violence. But if they breached the northern fortifications, they faced decades of resistance before they could conquer the whole of China, and then they were able to stabilize their rule only by assimilating themselves to Chinese civilization, as did the dynasties of the Yuan (1271–1368) and the Qing (1644–1911). No foreigners after the Manchus (the ethnic group that established the Qing dynasty) have conquered China. China ceased to be vulnerable to invasion not because it had strong enough border defenses to keep out a determined aggressor, but because it threatened to bog down the invader so badly that neither the nineteenth-century Western imperialists nor the twentieth-century Japanese militarists could take over the country. We show in chapter 3 that under Mao this quagmire threat was sufficient to deter both the U.S. and the Soviet Union.

Today, Chinese policymakers continue to be more concerned with defending their territory than with expanding it. China maintains a near-seas navy, strong border troops, nationwide anti-aircraft capabilities, and a nuclear deterrent. As we detail in chapter 11, these assets are deployed to defend China's territorial holdings and its unresolved territorial claims. Even the posture of Chinese nuclear forces is deterrent rather than coercive. But we also discuss whether China is building the capability for force projection in the future and, if so, for what contingencies.

The previous book used the "empty fortress," like the Great Wall, as a symbol of mixed weakness and strength. In a famous chapter in the *Romance of the Three Kingdoms* (chapter 95), a great fourteenth-century novel about second- and third-century civil wars, the strategist Zhuge Liang is outnumbered in the defense of a walled city. He lowers the military banners, orders his troops to hide, opens the gates, and sunbathes on the ramparts in view of the enemy army. Seeing him so unconcerned, they conclude that the city must be well defended and that Zhuge[19] is trying to entice them into an ambush. So they decamp without attacking.

The ancient story symbolizes Chinese strategists' ability to magnify limited resources, appear stronger than they are, and deter enemies from attack or subversion while biding their time to build up power. Even after China's rise, that reading of the symbol remains relevant today. China's power is real, but foreigners are prone to evaluate the country as even more formidable than it really is. In comparison, the U.S. has a vastly larger economy and stronger military, with true global reach. Japan has a better-financed, more technologically advanced military. India, with a similar-size population and territory, albeit a smaller gross domestic product (GDP), has a more advantageous geostrategic position and a better-equipped navy and air force. And the European Union (EU) has a large population, a continental strategic position, a larger GDP, and more advanced technology. Why is it that, except for the U.S., these other powers languish, relatively speaking, in the global shadows, generating neither the respect nor the fear that China does?

One reason, which we explore in chapter 1, is China's uniquely sensitive geostrategic position, at the hinge between Eurasia and the Pacific, with a decisive role in six complex and important regional subsystems that we label *Northeast Asia, continental Southeast Asia, maritime Southeast Asia, Oceania, South Asia,* and *Central Asia.* A second reason is, however, the ability of China's foreign policy leadership to control information and perception sufficiently to create a mystique of strength. Their skill at doing so has some disadvantages, such as drawing attention to China as America's primary potential rival. But its advantage is to produce more deference from other countries than China's objective power resources warrant.

China's power, however, if sometimes overhyped, is no illusion. It was not China's weakness but its burgeoning strength that the late leader Deng Xiaoping instructed his colleagues to hide when he gave the four-character instruction, "taoguang yanghui" (Hide our light and nurture our strength). After Deng's death in 1997, China continued his reassurance strategy—telling other countries that its foreign policy goals are limited, seeking resolution or postponement of territorial disputes with most neighbors, acceding to more and more treaties on arms control, human rights, and the environment. Are these cooperative gestures signals of China's maturation into a status quo power that supports the global rules of the game? Or are they tactics to lull others into complacency while China builds up its capabilities to challenge the system? We grapple with these issues in chapter 13.

In the end, we doubt that China's leaders today have a fixed blueprint for the future. They will define a global role for China depending not only on their own goals and behavior, but also on how others around the world interact with them. That means that we can afford to be optimistic in believing that there are no inevitable conflicts of geostrategic interest between China and the West, but we must also be realistic in acknowledging that pathways to cooperation in international affairs are found only through friction and contention, if they are found at all.

The ancient Chinese military handbook *The Thirty-Six Stratagems* ends with the following quip: "Of the thirty-six stratagems, running away is the best." But China is not going to run away, and we cannot run away from it. It is going to continue to be there, and the rest of the world will have to deal with it. The purpose of this book is to understand what drives Chinese policy—to analyze the world as much as possible as Beijing policymakers analyze it. The attempt to understand Chinese policy from the viewpoint of China's place in the world should be read as neither approval nor disapproval of that policy. Our analysis should be equally useful for those who want to accommodate Chinese goals, for those who want to frustrate them, and for those who seek just to understand them.

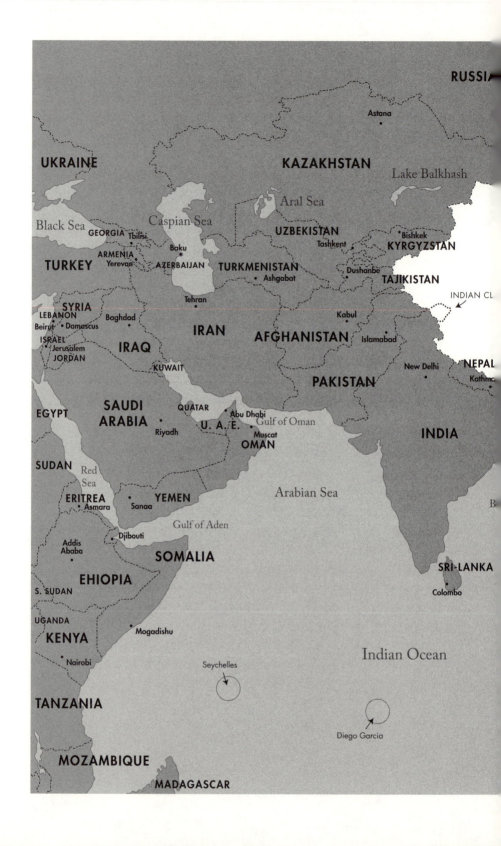

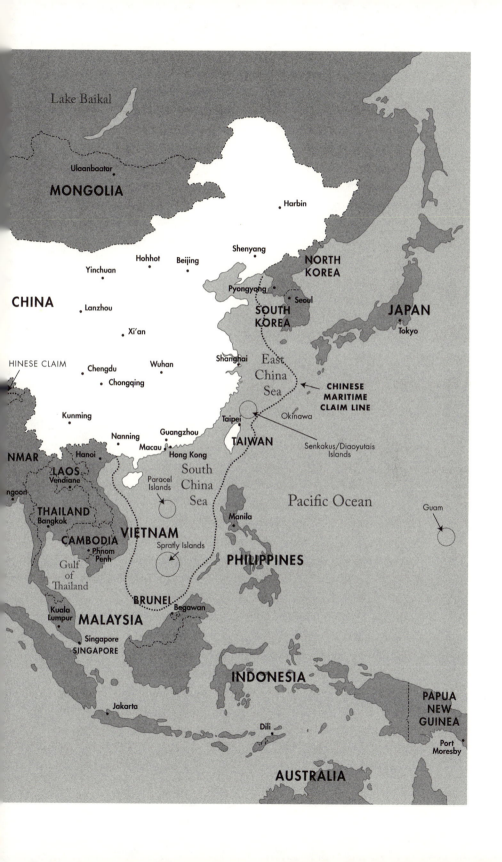

PART I

INTEREST AND IDENTITY IN
CHINESE FOREIGN POLICY

1

WHAT DRIVES CHINESE FOREIGN POLICY?

Vulnerability to threats is the main driver of China's foreign policy. The world as seen from Beijing is a terrain of hazards, stretching from the streets outside the policymaker's window to land borders and sea lanes thousands of miles to the north, east, south, and west and beyond to the mines and oilfields of distant continents.

These threats can be described in four concentric circles. In the *First Ring*—across the entire territory China administers or claims—the Chinese government believes that domestic political stability is placed at risk by the impact of foreign actors and forces. The migrant workers and petitioners who crowd the streets of Beijing and other major cities have been buffeted by the forces of the global economy, and their grievances have become issues in the West's human rights criticisms of China. Foreign investors, managers, development advisers, customs and health inspectors, tourists, and students swarm the country—all with their own ideas for how China should change. Foreign foundations and embassies give grants and technical support to assist the growth of nongovernmental organizations (NGOs).

Along the coast to the east lie maritime territories, large swathes of which Beijing claims but does not control and which are disputed by its neighbors. These territories include islands and adjacent waters in the East China and South China seas. The most significant island is Taiwan, seat of the Republic of China (ROC). Located a hundred miles off the coast, Taiwan is a populous, prosperous, and strategically located island that China claims but does not control. The island has its own government and military force, formal diplomatic recognition from twenty-odd states, strong defense ties with the U.S., and political and economic relations with Japan and other countries around the world. To the far west, dissidents in Tibet and Xinjiang receive moral and diplomatic support and sometimes material assistance from fellow ethnic communities and sympathetic governments abroad.

Although no country is immune from external influences—via migration, smuggling, and disease—China is the most penetrated of the big countries, with an unparalleled number of foreign actors trying to influence its political, economic, and cultural evolution, often in ways that the political regime considers detrimental to its own survival. These themes are further explored in this chapter and chapter 10.

At the borders, policymakers face a *Second Ring* of security concerns, involving China's relations with twenty immediately adjacent countries arrayed in a circle from Japan in the east to Vietnam in the south to India in the southwest to Russia in the north. No other country except Russia has as many contiguous neighbors. Numbers aside, China's neighborhood is uniquely complex. The contiguous states include seven of the fifteen largest countries in the world (India, Pakistan, Russia, Japan, the Philippines, Indonesia, and Vietnam—each having a population greater than 89 million); five countries with which China has been at war at some point in the past seventy years (Russia, South Korea, Japan, Vietnam, and India); and at least nine countries with unstable regimes (including North Korea, the Philippines, Myanmar/Burma,[1] Bhutan, Nepal, Pakistan, Afghanistan, Tajikistan, and Kyrgyzstan). China has had border disputes since 1949 with every one of its twenty immediate neighbors, although most have been settled by now.

Every one of these Second Ring neighbors is a cultural stranger to China, with a gap in most cases larger than that which the U.S., Europe, India, and Russia face with their immediate neighbors. Although Japan, Korea, and Vietnam borrowed some parts of their written and spoken languages and some Confucian beliefs from China, they do not consider themselves in any sense Chinese. The other neighboring cultures—Russian, Mongolian, Indonesian, Indian, and others—have even less in common with China. None of the neighboring states perceives that its core national interests are congruent with China's. All the larger neighbors are historical rivals of China, and the smaller ones are wary of Chinese influence.

Complicating the politics of the Second Ring is the presence of Taiwan (which is also part of the First Ring). The overriding goal of its diplomacy, as we discuss in chapter 8, is to frustrate China's effort to gain control. In doing so, it seeks support from other countries within and beyond the Second Ring. Taiwan is thus a major problem for Chinese diplomacy and counts as a twenty-first political actor on China's immediate periphery.

Finally, the Second Ring includes a twenty-second actor whose presence poses the largest single challenge to China's security: the U.S. Even though the U.S. is located thousands of miles away, it looms as a mighty presence in China's neighborhood, with its Pacific Command headquarters in Honolulu; its giant military base on the Pacific island of Guam (6,000 miles from the continental U.S., but only 2,000 miles from China); its dominating naval presence in the South and East China Seas; its defense relationships of various kinds around China's periphery with South Korea, Japan, Taiwan, the Philippines, Vietnam, Thailand, India, Pakistan, Afghanistan, and Kyrgyzstan; and its economic and political influence all through the Asian region. If the vast distances that separate the United States from China prevent China from exerting direct military pressure on it, the same is not true in reverse.

All in all, China's immediate periphery has a good claim to be the most challenging geopolitical environment in the world for a major power. Except for China itself, Russia faces no contiguous country that is anywhere near its own size; its demographic and economic heartland in the European part of the country is buffered from potential enemies by smaller states; it has invaded its neighbors more often than it has been invaded by them; and it has not been attacked by a direct neighbor since the Russo–Japanese War of 1904–1905. Even more striking is the comparison of China's situation with that of the U.S., a country that has only three immediate neighbors, Canada, Mexico, and Cuba, each much smaller, and that is separated by oceans from all other potential enemies.

Also unlike the U.S., China seldom has the luxury of dealing with any of its twenty-two neighbors in a purely bilateral context, a fact that brings into play a *Third Ring* of Chinese security concerns, consisting of the politics of six nearby multistate regional systems. Beijing's policies toward North Korea affect the interests of South Korea, Japan, the U.S., and Russia; its policies toward Cambodia affect the interests of Vietnam and Thailand

and often those of Laos—as well as the interests, again, of the U.S.; its policies toward Burma affect India, Bangladesh, and the nine states that are comembers with Burma in the Association of Southeast Asian Nations (ASEAN)—and again, the U.S. Because of such links, China can rarely make policy with only one state in mind and can almost never make policy anywhere around its periphery without thinking about the implications for relations with the U.S. The map of Asia is too crowded for that.

This Third Ring of Chinese security consists of six regional systems, each consisting of a set of states whose foreign policy interests are interconnected. The memberships of some of the systems overlap. The six systems are Northeast Asia (Russia, the two Koreas, Japan, China, and the U.S.), Oceania (Australia, New Zealand, Papua New Guinea, Fiji, twelve Pacific island microstates, China, and the U.S.), continental Southeast Asia (Vietnam, Cambodia, Laos, Thailand, Burma, China, and the U.S.), maritime Southeast Asia (Vietnam, Malaysia, Singapore, Indonesia, Brunei, the Philippines, China, and the U.S.), South Asia (Burma, Bangladesh, India, Nepal, Bhutan, Pakistan, Sri Lanka, the Maldive Islands, Russia, China, and the U.S.), and Central Asia (Russia, Kazakhstan, Kyrgyzstan, Tajikistan, Uzbekistan, Turkmenistan, Afghanistan, China, and the U.S.) (see frontispiece map). The aggregate number of states in the six systems is forty-five.[2]

China is the only country in the world that is physically part of such a large number of regional systems. (If the U.S. and Russia are engaged in even greater numbers of regional systems, it is not by the dictates of geography, but by choice.) Some issues are pervasive across all six systems (for example, China faces the U.S. presence in all of them, and in all systems its neighbors are wary of its rising influence), whereas some are distinctive to particular systems (such as the North Korean nuclear weapons issue in Northeast Asia and Islamic fundamentalism in Central, South, and maritime Southeast Asia). Each system presents multifaceted diplomatic and security problems.

These first three rings of security—from the domestic to the regional—thus present a foreign policy agenda of extreme complexity, which absorbs most of the resources China is able to devote to foreign and defense policy. Yet these three rings cover only about one-quarter of the globe's surface if one leaves out the vast watery region dotted with the microstates of Oceania. The rest of the world—including eastern and western Europe, the

Middle East, Africa, and North and South America—belongs to an outer, or *Fourth Ring*, of Chinese security.

China has entered this farthest circle in a big way only since the late 1990s and has done so not in pursuit of general power and influence, but, as we argue in chapter 7, to serve six specific needs: for energy resources; for commodities, markets, and investment opportunities; for diplomatic support for its positions on Taiwan and Tibet; and for support for its positions on multilateral diplomatic issues such as human rights, international trade, the environment, and arms control. Not only its goals but its tools of influence in the Fourth Ring are limited: they are commercial and diplomatic, not military or, to any significant extent so far, cultural or political.

To be sure, China's weight in this wider global arena is enhanced by its demographic and geographic size, its trajectory of economic growth, its independence of the U.S., and its status as a permanent member of the UN Security Council. But in contrast to the U.S., Europe, and even to some extent Russia, and in common with regional powers such as Japan, India, Brazil, and Turkey, China seldom endeavors proactively to shape the politics of distant regions to its own preferences. Instead, it must deal with whomever it finds in power, and if that regime is overthrown, it seeks relations with its successor. China has arrived in the Fourth Ring as a dramatically new presence, but not in the role of what we would call a global power—at least not yet.

Within each of the four rings, China's foreign policy agenda is seldom its policymakers' free choice, as can sometimes be the case when the strongest powers take an initiative to oust a government or force a peace settlement in a region far from their own shores. Chinese foreign policy instead responds defensively to a set of tasks imposed by the facts of demography, economics, geography, and history.

DEMOGRAPHY: HUGE, POOR, CONCENTRATED, AGING, AND ETHNICALLY DIVERSE

The problematic nature of China's situation begins with its demography. China's territory is about the same size as that of the U.S., but at 1.3 billion its population is more than four times as large. Three-quarters of the population is concentrated on about one-quarter of the territory, leading to intense pressure on both urban and rural living space. The demographic heartland is located in a 600-mile band along the eastern and southern coasts, with an outcropping along the Yangtze River reaching onto the Chengdu Plain in Sichuan (see the map showing the demography of China). It is roughly the size and shape of the American East Coast from Massachusetts to Florida, including Pennsylvania, West Virginia, and Alabama, but contains five and a half times as many people as those states. The most heavily populated eighteen of China's thirty-three province-level units have a combined population of 957 million, more than the cumulative populations of China's eight most populous neighbors, not counting India.

The heartland produces 83 percent of the country's GDP. It contains sixteen of the world's twenty most polluted cities. Population is so dense that 70 percent of China's rivers and lakes are said to be polluted, and the World Bank estimates that pollution reduces the value of China's GDP by as much as 12 percent annually.

Even after decades of stellar economic growth, China's people are relatively poor. In 2009, the country ranked 128 out of 227 in GDP per capita. Moreover, income is unevenly distributed: a strong share of the increased wealth has gone to a new class of the rich and ultrarich. Many urban residents are dissatisfied because of job insecurity, low wages, unpaid benefits, and land disputes. Rural residents — 57 percent of the population by official government classification — resent their second-class political and economic status. An estimated 160 million rural people have migrated temporarily to the cities to do factory and construction work. Facing all these dissatisfied social groups, the government needs to improve incomes and welfare benefits to maintain political stability, but it can do so only gradually because of the huge cost.

For the longer term as well, the demographic structure of the heartland population is full of latent threats. Because the regime enforced a policy of one child per family starting in the late 1970s, there are now more old people and fewer young people than in a normal population distribution. By 2040, retired people will make up nearly one-third of the population, worse than the ratio in Japan today, and the number of children and elderly will nearly equal the number of working-age men and women. The burden on the working population will hold back economic growth and may create a

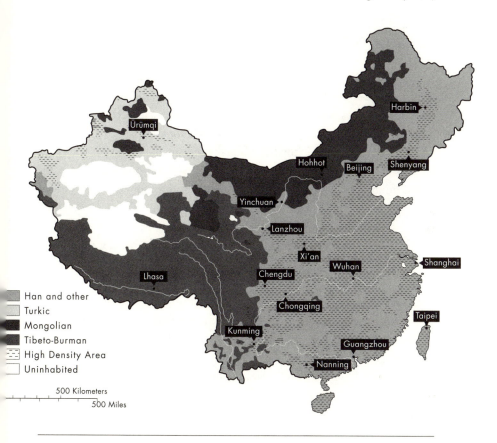

Han and other
Turkic
Mongolian
Tibeto-Burman
High Density Area
Uninhabited

500 Kilometers
500 Miles

THE DEMOGRAPHY OF CHINA

shortage of military manpower. Even if the government were now to relax the one-child policy, as it has begun to do, the shortage of people in the reproductive ages will continue to create a shortage of children, causing the population to peak at about 1.5 billion around 2030 and then decline. As this happens, India will overtake China as the country with the world's largest population and will enjoy the economic benefits of more workers and a lower ratio of dependents. China's population-planning program also produced an imbalanced sex ratio because some families aborted female fetuses or in some cases even killed or abandoned baby girls. By 2030, China is expected to have 25–40 million surplus males, with unknowable consequences for social stability.

Above and beyond the heartland towers a second China, remote and high, stretching as far as 1,500 miles farther to the west. The western thirteen of China's provinces occupy three-quarters of China's land surface but contain only a little more than one-quarter of its population and produce less than one-fifth of its GDP. These provinces contain most of China's mineral resources and the headlands of its major rivers. Most of this area is mountainous or desert, and most of its people are poor.

Even though China's fifty-five officially recognized national minorities constitute only about 8 percent of the country's total population, several of the minorities living in the West have weak commitments to the Chinese state, strained relations with the central government, and active cross-border ties with ethnic kin in neighboring countries. This is especially true of two groups: the Tibetans, who live not only in the Tibet Autonomous Region, but also in parts of four other contiguous provinces; and the Uyghurs, who form the largest population group in the vast region of Xinjiang. These two populations occupy the extensive buffer area that has historically protected the heartland from the political storms of Inner Asia. Beijing nominally gives what it calls "autonomy" to 173 minority-occupied areas ranging from province-size regions such as Tibet and Xinjiang to counties, but these areas are in fact controlled by ethnically Chinese (that is, Han) administrators and military garrisons. The government invests major resources to assure its control over this far-flung domain, a topic we explore further in chapter 8.

ECONOMICS: FROM AUTARKY TO GLOBALIZATION

China made a strategic turn from autarky to globalization in the 1980s and 1990s that fundamentally altered its relations with the outside world. The turnabout generated new power resources but also new security challenges.

China traditionally was an economic world unto itself. The premodern economy did not support power projection beyond the borders, nor did it require initiatives in international trade or diplomacy. It produced little that could be sold abroad, needed little that was produced abroad, saved no money to invest abroad, and offered no skills to attract investors from abroad. After World War II, when other parts of Asia that started out with agrarian economies and Confucian cultures similar to China's registered growth rates of 8–10 percent a year by producing consumer goods for the West, China did not have the same option of export-led development. For one thing, levels of global trade were too small both in absolute terms and as a proportion of world gross national product to accommodate China. Second, even had international markets been more inviting, China's entry into them was barred by a trade embargo which the West imposed at the start of the Korean War and which it maintained later as part of the effort to drive a wedge between China and the Soviet Union (see chapter 3). The Soviet Union for its part—China's ally in the 1950s—was recovering from World War II and gearing up its defense forces for the Cold War. It could give China only limited, although crucial, assistance, and this assistance came to an end with the Sino–Soviet split in 1960. For all these reasons, China in the 1960s and 1970s was the one major country whose domestic economy was completely isolated from the international economic system.

China's leaders had to look inward for a solution to the country's economic problems. To get the country to develop self-reliantly, Mao Zedong and his colleagues devised a strategy modeled on Stalinism but with a number of unique features. They created large communes with no private ownership of land, restricted the migration of rural residents to the cities, used ideological campaigns instead of material incentives to mobilize human energies, and applied political terror and indoctrination to make people accept low living standards. The population found itself organized into work units—communes, factories, offices, and schools—that controlled all aspects of daily life. The ruling party deterred opposition by mobilizing mass persecutions of designated "class enemies." This totalitarian model produced industrialization at a rapid pace, but at a huge human cost.

Mao left his successors to face a crisis that was both economic and political. China had made itself self-sufficient in nearly all resources and technologies but lagged twenty to thirty years behind world technical standards, with low labor and capital productivity. Living standards did not exceed the levels of the 1930s. Most Chinese lived in cramped quarters with poor food and clothing, few comforts, and no freedoms. Japan, South Korea, Taiwan, and Hong Kong enjoyed levels of GDP per capita that were five to seventeen times greater than China's. Chinese in the post-Mao era were no longer willing to tolerate frozen living standards in pursuit of a grotesque utopia. Pro-reform policymakers reckoned that the economy had to grow at 6 to 10 percent a year to improve living standards enough to prevent an economic and social breakdown, nor, they thought, could China protect itself militarily or diplomatically with such a weak economy.

When Deng Xiaoping came to power in late 1978, he therefore announced a policy of "reform and opening." "Reform" meant liberalizing the domestic economic and administrative systems; "opening" meant abandoning autarky in relations with the rest of the world. The two were linked. Opening gave China access to foreign markets, investment, and technology; reform made room for more efficient, competitive enterprises that could survive the encounter with the world market.

The embrace of globalization enhanced China's security in some ways and threatened it in others. Rapid economic growth helped the regime survive as it relaxed totalitarian controls, although it was not the only factor. The plunge into the world economy generated the financial resources needed to modernize the military and created the technological infrastructure to support a modern military. And economic clout translated into diplomatic clout and soft power (chapter 10).

At the same time, the embrace of globalization required China to compromise its autonomy in numerous ways. In the First Ring, globalization opened China to penetration by foreign people, media, institutions, ideas, norms, and values. It required China to alter its domestic legal, administrative, banking, and judicial systems; subjected China to deep surveillance and adverse judgment by and pressure from foreign organizations and governments; and created sharp competition for state enterprises in their own markets. Globalization generated disruptive changes throughout Chinese society, including the rise of a new middle class, the growth of economic inequality, and the influx of foreign ideas and values.

In the Second Ring and Third Ring, China needed peace and stability in order to pursue economic ties. It abandoned antiregime movements it had supported in neighboring countries, normalized ties with neighbors with whom it had broken either state-to-state relations (South Korea, Singapore, Malaysia, Indonesia) or party-to-party relations (Vietnam), and resolved most of its boundary disputes. It worked to develop economic complementarities with neighboring states—in some cases involving resource extraction and in others involving the development of global supply chains in which intermediary products produced in neighboring countries were shipped to China for assembly. China engaged with—in some cases helped create—regional security institutions such as the SCO in Central Asia, the Six-Party Talks on Korea, ASEAN+3 in Southeast Asia, and the ASEAN Regional Forum in the Pacific region. We discuss these developments further in chapters 5 and 6.

In the Fourth Ring, China joined and in large part complied with most of the international regimes by which states regulate their interactions in the interdependent world of today. It joined the WTO, signed the main arms control and disarmament treaties, and ratified the main international human rights treaties, and joined other treaties and organizations (chapters 10 and 12).

China came through the reform and opening process with a net strengthening of both the regime's and the country's security, but it did so by giving up much of the autonomy it had exercised under Mao. To enjoy the benefits of globalization, it subjected itself to international rules. To be sure, China abides by the rules in differing degrees depending on how compliance with any given set of international norms suits its security needs. In some cases, compliance is substantive; in other cases, it is formal. In some cases, China seeks to reinforce existing rules; in other cases, it tries to use its place at the table to change those rules. But overall it has become a status quo power in a system designed by the West.[3]

AT THE HINGE BETWEEN THE GREAT POWERS

A country's geographical position is less malleable than its economic strategy, but it too produces a distinctive combination of security advantages and vulnerabilities. The great gift bestowed on the People's Republic of China (PRC) by geography was its strategic location as a vast territory on the mainland of Asia located between the spheres of influence of the two Cold War superpowers. This position gave it special prominence in international politics throughout the period of the Cold War and beyond.

In Europe, except for a few small neutrals, every country was on one side or other of the Cold War line and was threatened by one but not the other of the two superpowers. Asia was divided as well between the Soviet and American blocs. Two countries were divided across the middle, Korea and Vietnam. China alone aligned permanently with neither of the two superpowers. For a decade, it stood on the Soviet side but then broke away. Without formally joining the Western camp, it tilted to the West after 1971. It became what theorists call a "weak pole" in the international system, giving North Vietnam and North Korea a way to balance against the Soviet Union and for a time giving Cambodia and Burma an alternative to alignment with either of the two superpowers.[4]

As the only major country at the intersection of the two camps, China found itself in the uniquely influential yet also dangerous position of being alternately wooed and threatened by both. When China allied with the Soviet Union, the U.S. responded with a strategy of pressure designed to break the alliance. When China shifted out of the Soviet camp, the Soviets responded with similar pressures. Any expansion of China's influence—for example, in Korea and Vietnam—brought it into conflict with the sphere of influence of either the Soviet Union or the U.S. China is the only country to have been threatened with nuclear attack by both superpowers—the only country that had to deter and defend itself from both.

The only development more dangerous to China than superpower rivalry during the Cold War would have been superpower collusion. That possibility took shape in the late 1950s when the American "wedge strategy" to separate China from Russia led the Soviets to push for coexistence (chapter 3).[5] Had the Soviet–American duopoly that Chinese strategists feared ever taken shape, it would have exposed China to potential *diktat* in any area the superpowers wished.

China did not seek to overcome its isolation by joining existing blocs or constructing its own. It instead sought to encourage fluidity and multipolarity wherever it could. From 1958 onward, Chinese diplomacy aimed at countering emergent U.S.–Soviet cooperation on arms control, European stability, and the Middle East. China's diplomacy in Africa, the Middle East, and Latin America aimed at breaking rather than constructing alignments. Mao once said, "The world is in chaos, the situation is excellent." But his diplomatic goal was not literally chaos, which might have threatened China in other ways, but loosening the superpower vise that constricted his freedom of maneuver.

The ability to seesaw between the two powers, however, eventually enabled China, alone among all countries during the Cold War, to extract security benefits from the U.S.–Soviet rivalry by creating and manipulating a "strategic triangle" during the period from 1972 to 1989 (chapter 3). And when the Soviet–American military confrontation eased starting in the mid-1980s, China was able to deal on favorable terms with both former enemies at once.

This orientation continues today. Of all the large powers, China is the most free to maneuver, shift alignments, and flexibly pursue national interest. This freedom of maneuver magnifies its importance to other major powers and its influence over smaller states. Its size and situation continue to make it "a critical independent factor in the balance of world forces."[6]

AN EXPOSED GEOGRAPHICAL POSITION

The downside of China's geographical position is its exposure in all directions to instability, pressure, and even invasion.

Potentials for conflict are everywhere around China's periphery. Its nearly 14,000 miles of land borders are the longest in the world. The 4,000-mile boundary with the Soviet Union was for twenty-five years the longest unfriendly frontier in the world. At one point, nearly 1.5 million troops were ranged closely along the two sides of this line, and some on the Soviet side were armed with nuclear weapons. The two sides began to demilitarize the border and restore local cross-border trade in the late 1980s. But the breakup of the Soviet Union gave rise to a new set of neighbors that was in some ways even more complicated than before: Russia plus five Central Asian states (three of them directly contiguous to China) and a Mongolia set free from Russian domination and committed to democracy and relations with the West. The new states' internal troubles have the potential to weaken Chinese control of Tibet, Xinjiang, and Inner Mongolia, and their foreign policies create tension with China over ethnic, trade, and security issues.

Along the eastern and southern sides of the Chinese landmass are sea borders ranging for 9,000 miles. All along this coastline, the Han heartland lies exposed. Set back from the coast by distances ranging up to only about 600 miles, most of the heartland consists of fertile, well-watered low-land plains and valleys that grow wheat and rice. Only a small part of the heartland is protected by coastal mountains from seaward attack. When Japan invaded in 1937–1938, it occupied most of this area in a year of fighting; in today's era of precision-guided munitions, ballistic missiles, satellite technology, and nuclear weapons, the heartland's population is even more exposed to attack.

Most of China's borders are easier to invade than to defend. The long coastline was invaded repeatedly in the nineteenth and twentieth centuries. The inland border regions are mountainous and cold, difficult to garrison and defend, and open to subversion by outside powers who might appeal to the resident ethnic minorities. Facing the U.S., Russia, Japan, and India, China's defenders do not benefit from the presence of buffer states on most of the likely invasion routes.

During the twentieth century, China engaged in military conflicts with Japan, the U.S., South Korea, India, Russia, Vietnam, and Taiwan. Even though relations have improved greatly with each, in the long view all remain potential military rivals. The armies of these seven states rank in the top twenty-five of world armies by size. China's army, even though it is the biggest in the world, suffers a net two and a half to one disadvantage of troop strength compared to the aggregate militaries of its six main regional neighbors, even leaving aside the more distant U.S., which is likely to get involved in almost any conflict that involves China. By way of comparison, the U.S. enjoys a more than three to one manpower advantage in troop strength over the combined armed forces of its immediate neighbors Mexico, Canada, and Cuba, with whom military conflict is in any case almost unthinkable today.

The PRC inherited a variety of territorial disputes along the entire length of its land and sea borders. During the 1960s, it concluded boundary treaties with Mongolia, Burma, Bhutan, Sikkim (subsequently annexed by India), Nepal, Pakistan, and Afghanistan. In the 1990s, it signed boundary treaties with Laos, Tajikistan, Kyrgyzstan, Kazakhstan, and Russia. In 2004, it resolved the last details of its formerly disputed borders with Russia. China still has unresolved boundary or territorial disputes with Bhutan, North Korea, Vietnam, Indonesia, India, Japan, Malaysia, the Philippines, and Brunei.

Even though war today looks unlikely, Chinese defense planners can never rule out the possibility of war at almost any location along China's long borders. China's potential battlegrounds are not overseas, but on its own administered or claimed territory. This strategic situation is the opposite of that faced by American defense planners, whose home territory is so far from all conceivable enemies that invasion is not a concern in defense planning. The vulnerability to invasion was the reason why for decades Beijing's planners left undeveloped the southern coastal provinces of Guangdong and Fujian, with their combined populations of 50 million at the time, in the expectation that China's own air force would have to bomb them in the event of an invasion by the U.S. or the Nationalist Party (Kuomintang, KMT). After the 1965 Gulf of Tonkin Incident increased tensions between the U.S. and North Vietnam, Mao Zedong decreed with the Third Front policy the removal of already-developed industrial projects and infrastructure from urban concentrations in the North and Northeast to remote mountain valleys in the West and Southwest. From 1965 to 1971, two-thirds of state industrial investment was spent to disperse and hide industrial assets so the enemy could not destroy them from the air. Productivity dropped, and transport costs rose, imposing huge costs on the already struggling economy.[7]

China is surrounded by smaller countries that fear Chinese domination. Throughout the Cold War, China had neither the strategic power to coerce its neighbors nor the dynamic economy to attract them. Thailand moved closer to China when it lacked strong support from the U.S., and North Vietnam did so when it lacked strong support from the Soviet Union, but these alignments were temporary, based on expediency rather than on long-term common interests. China has enjoyed formal alliances with only two of its neighboring countries, the Soviet Union and North Korea, and long-term alignments with two others, Pakistan and Burma. Of these four relationships, the one with the Soviet Union turned to enmity, and the defense treaty was not renewed. The defense commitment to North Korea was weakened by China's opening to the U.S. and by the establishment of diplomatic and trade relations with South Korea. Pakistan and Burma remain China's friends, but both are troubled states, diplomatic liabilities as much as assets. For the rest of its neighbors, fear of China has not yet been fully counterbalanced even today by the kinds of forces that sometimes draw nations together—common economic or security interests or cultural sympathies.

Finally, geography leaves China more exposed than any other major power to damage from global climate change. The densely populated North China Plain, which uses a great deal of water for industry, agriculture, and daily living, has suffered since the early 1980s from a water shortage, and that shortage is growing steadily more severe. In response, the government in 2002 started to build the massive South–North Water Transfer Project, comprising three separate canal systems totaling more than 2,000 miles in length. As global warming proceeds, the North will need even more irrigation to help crops survive, yet northern aquifers are on track to dry up within thirty years. At the same time, climate change will reduce the flow in the southern rivers that Beijing looks to as its source of water for the North by melting the Tibetan glaciers that feed the rivers. Climate change will also increase the frequency and severity of droughts, floods, and cyclones, threatening farmers and the residents of poorly built cities. Along the coast, Chinese scientists estimate, a twelve-inch rise in sea level would inundate more than 31,000 square miles of coastal lowlands, an area far greater than the area expected to be similarly impacted in the U.S., India, Korea, or Japan.[8]

HISTORY: FROM EMPIRE TO MULTIETHNIC NATION-STATE

Of all the features of China's geopolitical situation we have described, only one can truly be called permanent, the location in Asia. Yet the significance even of being in Asia has never been fixed. Asia was once outside the European-based world system; in the nineteenth century, it became part of it; in the age of globalization, it has become an economic and strategic pole of its own. The map of Asia evolved with the rise and decline of colonialism, the start and end of the Cold War, and the coalescence and splitting of nations. Five territories—Annam, Cochin China, Tonkin, Cambodia, and Laos—became French Indochina in the nineteenth century, then split into four states in the 1950s, and became three countries after the unification of Vietnam in 1975. Indonesia and Malaysia were created from princedoms, sultanates, and tribal territories by Dutch and British colonialists and then survived as states in the postcolonial era, making some adjustments in their own boundaries and creating their own national myths. After the Bolshevik Revolution, the Russian Empire became a union of fifteen soviet-socialist republics, and in the 1990s the Asian part of the Soviet Union was replaced by Russia and five independent Central Asian states. As technology shrank the world in the twentieth century, America became part of geopolitical Asia, with alliances and troops in the region and with extensive economic and cultural ties.

The boundaries and populations that Chinese policymakers have to defend—the entity known as "China"—is likewise not a fixed or natural object, but an uneasy amalgam of lands and peoples created by history. In ancient times, the term *zhongguo*, today translated as "China," meant "the states of the central plain," referring to various cities, states, and regions in what is now central China. Only later did this word come to mean the Middle Kingdom or what we think of today as China.[9] The first unified Chinese state, the Qin (221–206 B.C.E.), occupied a territory only about a quarter of the size of today's country. Over centuries, the primary Chinese ethnic group, who referred to themselves as "Han," took shape from various regional cultures and expanded from the central plain by conquest and migration to the south, west, northwest, and northeast, incorporating the territories of ethnic groups living around them and assimilating many of the inhabitants. The Han territory in turn was conquered five times by Inner Asian nomads, who made themselves part of China and thus expanded it. By the early nineteenth century, under the conquest dynasty of the Manchus (the Qing dynasty, 1644–1911), China was larger than ever before or since.

Traditional China did not see itself as a nation-state or even as an empire with separate subject peoples, but rather as the center of civilization. In Chinese eyes, other kingdoms and tribes were more or less civilized depending on how close they were to the Han people culturally and politically. The Koreans and Vietnamese were the most civilized among the non-Han because they followed Confucian ethics and used Chinese characters as their written languages. Others were less so. China's cultural and political influence stretched from the core provinces through more remote southern and western provinces, to garrisons in territories dominated by non-Han peoples, to northern and northwestern tribes and kingships extending as far as the edges of Tashkent and Samarkand in present-day Uzbekistan, to a penumbra of other societies with their own governments, such as Korea, Vietnam, Burma, and Nepal, and finally to barbarians so remote that some of them were mythical.

Toward all peoples, the Qing practiced a policy of "impartial benevolence." They viewed fights among barbarians of different degrees of closeness to China as adjustments of relations among cultural inferiors, not as the transfer of territory from one empire to another. So in the nineteenth century Beijing did not perceive a threat to its security in growing British influence over its own tributary states of Nepal, Sikkim, and Tibet. The supremacy of Chinese moral and cultural influence seemed intact, and Britain was too small and far away to be seen as a rival. Beijing was also willing to grant special rights to non-Chinese authorities around the periphery to administer and tax trade and to discipline their own people living in Chinese territory, as in the Sino–Kokand accord of 1835. This type of arrangement fit into the Qing worldview, but it also later provided precedents for extraterritoriality—the application of Western rather than Chinese law—in the Western-dominated treaty ports.[10]

In the nineteenth century, Chinese dominance in the regions farther from the capital became insecure. In the Northeast, the Qing dynasty's Manchurian homeland had come to be inhabited mostly by Han Chinese, had been incorporated into the regular administrative system in the form of three provinces (today Heilongjiang, Jilin, and Liaoning), but was threatened by Russian and Japanese pressure. In the West, Qing garrisons maintained a tenuous supremacy in Xinjiang, where Chinese settlers were recent arrivals among a host of oasis states and nomadic tribes. Here China was but one of many cultural influences, political forces, and trading partners, no more important than India, Persia, or Russia. Tibet was formally still part of China but had coalesced into a loosely constructed theocratic state as recently as the eighteenth century and maintained informal ties across the Himalayas to Nepal, Sikkim, and parts of India. A rising British India in the South and a rising Russia in the North promoted their influence there at Chinese expense. Only in Inner Mongolia, where nomadic tribes were overwhelmed by Chinese settlers, did the Qing exercise firm control of the border regions.

When the military forces of the expanding Western powers reached the perimeter of the Chinese Empire, they forced China to define its physical borders in Western conceptual terms, starting with the Treaty of Nerchinsk in 1689. This meant giving up claims to varying kinds and degrees of paramountcy over parts of Central Asia and Siberia, outer Mongolia, Korea, the Ryukyu Islands, Vietnam, and Burma—and even in a sense over Russia and Britain themselves, for although the Chinese emperor had at one time unsuccessfully demanded that both countries' envoys kowtow to him as vassals, now China had to recognize them not just as equals, but as victors in war. China ceded Hong Kong to Britain in perpetuity, then leased away additional territory to enlarge the colony, ceded Macao to Portugal, and ceded other pieces of territory to Russia, Japan, French-ruled Indochina, British Burma, and British India. The most difficult legacy of territorial loss was Taiwan. This island was incorporated into the Chinese Empire in 1683, then ceded as a colony to Japan in 1895, then returned to Chinese control under the Nationalist regime in 1945. But after 1949, when the Communist Party took over the mainland, Nationalist-ruled Taiwan remained separate, posing a major continuing problem for PRC diplomacy (chapter 8).

The PRC denied the legitimacy of many of these Qing territorial losses, leading to territorial disputes with all of its neighbors, most of which have been settled by now. All of China's remaining unrealized territorial claims—the island of Taiwan, 45,000 square miles of territory in three parcels disputed with India, smaller border claims with other neighbors, and several sets of islands in the East China and South China seas—are based in this history of one-time possession or exploration. In Beijing's official rhetoric, maps, and history books, we see no signs of preparations to lodge claims to additional irridenta. In this sense, China is not an "expansionist" power with elastic territorial ambitions. Its claims appear fixed. Nevertheless, those claims are large and important, and Beijing has been consistently assertive about them, especially when it perceives challenges (chapters 5, 6, 8). If the concept of "China" undergoes any further historical evolution, it most likely will involve the loss of territory (potentially, for example, Taiwan), not the addition.

Besides defining its borders, modern China had to define its citizens' legal status. In 1909, it adopted its first law of nationality, defining as "Chinese" the children of Chinese fathers anywhere in the world. This principle of jus sanguinis (determining nationality status by bloodlines) was consistent with traditional thinking about the meaning of being Chinese, but it placed China at odds with most countries' modern view of citizenship as a territorial rather than an ethnic concept and put China in the position of treating other countries' ethnically Chinese citizens as Chinese subjects. Despite claiming the Overseas Chinese as citizens, China found itself unable to extend protection to them. Chinese were victims of racial riots and the Chinese Exclusion Acts in nineteenth-century America and of discrimination in Japan and Southeast Asia. Claiming as citizens tens of millions of ethnic Chinese concentrated in Southeast Asia and scattered throughout the rest of the world was ultimately more a liability than an asset.[11]

The PRC began to extricate itself from this dilemma in 1955, when Premier Zhou Enlai announced at the Afro–Asian Conference at Bandung, Indonesia, that Overseas Chinese should voluntarily adopt the citizenship of their host country and give up Chinese citizenship. During the 1950s, China reached agreements with North Vietnam and Indonesia that renounced the principle of dual nationality. The same model was applied in the 1970s when China normalized relations with other countries in Southeast Asia. In 1980, it resolved the problem once and for all with a new nationality law under which Chinese who take citizenship abroad automatically lose their citizenship in China.

Within China's borders as well, the comfortable ambiguity of tradition on the subject of ethnicity was replaced by problematic clarities. In premodern times, the emperor's subjects included people of many tribes, religions, and ethnic or subethnic groups. Broader labels such as *Mongol*, *Tibetan*, and *Kyrgyz* actually covered people from scores of culturally distinct groups.[12] The Han "Chinese" majority itself was a mix of people with a broad spectrum of physical characteristics, speaking eight major and many minor dialects that are as different from one another as Italian and French and treating one another with varying degrees of subethnic prejudice.[13]

Modern social thought, influenced by Darwinism, wanted sharper definitions of ethnic and national identity. Late-nineteenth-century nationalists intent on overthrowing the Manchus were the first to create a clear sense of Han ethnicity by labeling the Manchus as "alien." They defined the Chinese state that came out of the 1911 revolution as multiethnic, thus creating a national (or civic) identity that incorporated several distinct ethnic identities. The first flag of the new Chinese republic in 1912 accordingly consisted of five differently colored stripes symbolizing a unified state of five "races," as they were called at the time (Han, Manchu, Mongol, Tibetan, and Muslim).

But the PRC soon decided that it had more than five ethnic groups among its citizens. The new regime in the 1950s assigned anthropologists to count and classify the people. It eventually officially recognized fifty-five national minorities (who by virtue of recognition became eligible for certain political and cultural privileges) plus the majority Han. The process was more administrative than scientific: some once-extant groups that had adopted Han identities were resurrected and given government assistance to revive or even create minority-group languages and rituals, and certain actually existing cultural communities were folded into the fifty-five accepted categories or classified as part of the majority Han.[14]

In any case, the classifications stuck, and the idea of dual national and ethnic identities continues to shape the Chinese state's relations with its citizens and the outside world. Several of the officially recognized national minorities are sizable groups with developed cultures, occupying strategically important territories and maintaining connections with non-Chinese populations across China's borders. They include the Tibetans; the group of interrelated Muslim peoples, mostly Uyghur, Kazakh, and Kyrgyz, who live primarily in Xinjiang; the Mongolians, who make up a significant part of the population of the Inner Mongolian Autonomous Region; the Koreans who live on China's border with North Korea; and the Dai, who occupy parts of China across from Burma, Laos, and Vietnam. Only after 1949 did the central government begin to have the ability to impose tight control over these regions. Local populations have resisted Han rule in a variety of ways, violent and nonviolent, sometimes threatening national security on strategic borders. Control over the minority regions is an interstate issue because of the native populations' ethnic and political ties across national borders (chapter 8).

CULTURE: A REPERTOIRE OF OPTIONS

As China's leaders manage their security problems — bestowed by demography and geography, shaped by economics, and inherited from history — they possess a range of options for action. Some analysts see culture, ideology, and nationalism as factors that limit possible strategies of action. We see these forces more loosely, as shaping not so much the actions themselves as the ways in which the actions are framed, understood, and justified.

Culture is a repertoire of possible patterns of behavior, some more and some less relevant to a particular problem that actors face at a given time. Habits of behavior, inherited attitudes and beliefs, and memories of how things used to be done provide in their aggregate a series of precedents for nearly any pattern of action that social actors select. They do not tell an actor exactly what to do, but they help him interpret his adversaries' and allies' interests and actions in order to decide how to act.

For example, scholars have described Chinese culture as both peaceful and warlike.[15] The country was created by conquest, both when the Han invaded neighbors' territory and when Inner Asian neighbors conquered the Han. China conquered but was ultimately expelled from Vietnam and Korea; its settlements but not its rule extended into what later became Russia and the Central Asian republics. It expanded when there was population pressure on the land and room to expand. It stopped when it met insurmountable geographic obstacles or was turned back by other armed peoples. In the twentieth century, Chinese troops fought mostly in civil wars or near the country's borders in wars that were primarily defensive. Chinese society has been violent internally when weak government, economic disorder, or social dislocation has made violence attractive, but peaceful when it has been well governed and prosperous. For Chinese, as for Americans and others, violence is apparently not a matter of culture, but of need and opportunity. Like any other people, the Chinese are capable of both peace and war, and cultural precedent does not tell us which they will prefer.

Chinese culture similarly contains elements of both realism and moralism. Chinese view the historical epic *The Three Kingdoms* as a template for thinking about the role of human relations in international affairs. The legend tells of the struggles among three rulers who sought to reunify China in 168–265 C.E. The tales are told by village storytellers, enacted in operas and movies, and illustrated in almanacs, calendars, and pictures posted on doors. Some of the heroes have become gods worshiped in temples. Every literate Chinese has read the novelized version written by Luo Guanzhong in the late 1300s. Chinese diplomats and military officers often describe their maneuvers in terms of these stories. The very language is full of references to it.

The opening line of the book states the theme of balance of power realism: "Empires wax and wane; states cleave asunder and coalesce." In a world in which power is evanescent, the book glorifies the use of "stratagems" (*ji*), deceptions designed to win battles against greater forces, if possible without placing one's own forces at risk. In the "borrowed arrows stratagem," for example, the military adviser Zhuge Liang is ordered to prepare a hundred thousand arrows within three days for a coming military action—an apparently impossible mission. He mystifyingly does nothing for three days. Then on the third evening he sends twenty boats filled with straw across the river in a fog. The frightened enemy shoots the straw full of arrows, and Zhuge brings them back to camp to use in the coming action. In the "defecting with a secret stratagem," also called the "personal injury stratagem," a loyal general purposely accepts a cruel beating at the hands of his own commander to create the pretext for him to defect to the enemy's side so he can spy on it. Stories like this praise mirrors-within-mirrors deceit. People with steel nerves and quick wits disarm others' suspicions, only to betray them. Leaders lose their power because they trust others. Intended treacheries are secretly perceived and turned against their perpetrators.

But the cynicism in this classic work is counterbalanced by a stress on loyalty and legitimacy. Perhaps its best-known scene is the "Peach Garden oath," where two of the main heroes pledge fealty to one of the contenders for power, Liu Bei. Nothing shakes their commitment through the rest of the book, and the novel is full of inspiring examples of self-sacrifice for the common mission. Liu Bei inspires devotion not because he is the most able general—in fact, that distinction belongs to the evil Cao Cao—but because he is the legitimate heir to the empire and therefore morally worthy. That is why he can recruit an adviser such as Zhuge Liang, who has a supernatural understanding of what the Chinese consider the decisive forces in war and politics: *shi*, *di*, and *shi* (time, place, and the correlation of forces). Both realism and idealism are strains in Chinese culture, and neither one automatically provides the key to understanding a given policy decision.

Chinese tradition emphasizes the importance of giving and getting "face," or favorable personal recognition. Face has long been a central consideration in interpersonal relations in China. At the same time, the exchange of face can be a practical bargaining tool. The norm of face can be used instrumentally to warn other countries not to shame Chinese leaders by demanding humiliating compromises, lest tension escalate and cooperation become difficult. If China can convince its counterpart that its flexibility is constrained by concern for face, it can force the counterpart to moderate its demands. This strategy is particularly useful for the weaker party in negotiations, which China has often been in its dealings with the West.

But China is not always equally sensitive to giving face to others. By citing the principle that "he who tied the knot should untie it," China can sometimes extract humiliating concessions from a negotiating adversary. Face may be given afterward as a reward for diplomatic cooperation. Even China's legendary diplomatic hospitality can be used to demonstrate cultural superiority. When a foreign head of state visits China, Chinese television shows the deferential visitor being graciously received by the Chinese leader and nodding appreciatively as the leader lectures him on the principles of international relations. All this affirms China's importance. If the foreign visitor says anything negative, the state-controlled Chinese media do not report it. Face is a traditional value that has been usefully adapted to modern diplomacy.

The problem of when and how cultural explanations apply also extends to the idea of China as a "middle kingdom," whose identity requires neighboring smaller powers to accept a hierarchical relationship. To be sure, imperial China regulated its relations with other states partly by a tribute system, under which some foreign rulers were treated as vassals of the emperor. Historians have argued that this precedent affects Chinese ways of acting in the modern world of nation-states. Because traditional foreign policy was Sinocentric, assimilative, normative, ideological, personalistic, and hierarchical, nineteenth-century China had trouble adapting to the European-organized multistate system, which was egalitarian, nonideological, and contractual.[16] Mao's worldview, too, often seemed Sinocentric as the leaders of pro-Mao Communist parties from around the world trooped to China to receive audiences and pay symbolic tribute. During the period of the strategic triangle, China allowed itself to be courted by the Americans as if they were students coming to learn strategy at the knee of the master. As the triangle faded in the 1980s, China continued to talk about its ties with other countries less in terms of practical cooperation than in terms of the partner's friendliness and acceptance of Chinese norms.

Yet the tribute system was only one form of traditional relations between the center and the periphery.[17] In the heartland, government was bureaucratic. Toward and beyond the northern and western frontiers, one found a mix of military governors-general, Manchu Banner (tribal) garrisons, *jasaks* (hereditary princes), khans, hakim beys (governors), *aksakals* (representatives), tribute-paying theocratic and tribal rulers, and, even farther beyond, a few states that were linked to China as tributaries of Beijing's tributaries, as Sikkim and Ladakh were of the Dalai Lama. Relations with Inner Asia were often pragmatic and egalitarian.[18] Dealings with maritime Asia were conducted according to what scholars have called a "maritime subculture" that was commercial, exploratory, and intellectually realistic.

The tribute system was a way of thinking about political relations that served Chinese interests and those of some of its partners for a certain period of time. Like the Five Principles of Peaceful Coexistence or the "new security concept" today, Sinocentrism was an idea sufficiently malleable that it could facilitate trade and legitimate a range of diplomatic practices.[19] The maritime subculture provided precedents of pragmatic egalitarianism that China can draw on when it needs to. We have to analyze present realities to explain when and how Sinocentric elements have remained useful in Chinese diplomatic practice and when and how they have not.

IDEOLOGY AND INTERESTS: COMPATIBLE MOTIVES

Ideology also expresses, explains, and justifies policy rather than determining what it will be. Chinese foreign policy is not deduced from formulas but, in our view, responds to interests. The broad concepts and values in terms of which the leadership understands its interests and explains its methods give insight, when properly interpreted, into their goals and methods, however.

Among the most long-standing tenets of Chinese foreign policy are the Five Principles of Peaceful Coexistence: mutual respect for sovereignty and territorial integrity, mutual nonaggression, noninterference in internal affairs, equality and mutual benefit, and peaceful coexistence. The government first enumerated these principles in 1954 when China was trying to reach out to the non-Communist countries of Asia. At that time, the principles were intended to strengthen relations with neutral countries such as India and Burma and to mollify Southeast Asian governments who were fighting Communist insurgencies and worried about the fifth-column potential of Chinese minorities within their borders. After the Cold War, the Five Principles, with no change in wording, served a new purpose, offering an alternative to the American conception of a new world order in which international regimes and institutions would limit the rights of other sovereign states to pursue policies at variance with American interests and values. China's alternative design for the world at that time stressed—and continues today to stress—the sovereignty of all states, large and small, Western and non-Western, rich and poor, democratic and authoritarian, each to run its own system as it sees fit, whether its methods suit Western standards or not. The language is moralistic, but the policy behind the words is interest based: to join with others against American ambitions to control other countries' behavior.

China says it "never seeks hegemony." This principle dates from the 1960s, when *hegemony* was a code word for Soviet expansionism. In the late 1970s and the 1980s, China extended the concept to Vietnam's domination of Cambodia and Laos. Chinese officials use the term today to refer to one-sided American efforts to enforce its will on other countries in such matters as trade practices, weapons proliferation, and human rights. By saying it will not seek hegemony, China both sets itself in opposition to certain American policies and seeks to assure its smaller neighbors that its own economic development and growing military might will not turn it into a regional bully. But this is a policy of realism because bullying would create an incentive for local powers to band together to restrict China's rise.

Since the 1980s, China has said that it pursues "an independent foreign policy of peace." This formula uses ethical language, but represents a realist interest. Independence means that China does not restrict its freedom of maneuver in relation to the other major powers; peace means that it seeks regional—and increasingly global—stability so that it can concentrate on economic development.

China's official position on most disputes around the world is that they should be solved by peaceful negotiations. This has been China's view on the struggle between Israel and the Arabs, the conflicts in the former Yugoslavia, the conflicts in the Sudan, the India–Pakistan dispute over Kashmir, the war between Iran and Iraq in the 1980s, Iraq's invasion of Kuwait in 1990, the North Korean nuclear weapons crisis, the Iranian nuclear weapons crisis, and so on. At the UN, China has usually refrained from voting or voted an abstention on resolutions that mandated sanctions or armed interventions to reverse invasions, end civil wars, or stop terrorism (so-called Chapter VII resolutions). In most cases, China has preferred nonintervention because it sees such interventions as expanding U.S. power, it does not have the power to lead or profit from such interventions itself, and it needs good relations with whoever is in power in each of the countries involved in the disputes. Instead of vetoing such interventions, however, it has usually abstained or cast no vote in order to avoid angering countries that favor intervention.

Deng Xiaoping in 1989 counseled that China should not create unnecessary antagonisms with foreign powers, but should "taoguang yanghui" (hide our light and nuture our strength). Deng's successor Jiang Zemin expressed a similar idea with his policy of *"zengjia xinren, jianshao mafan, fazhan hezuo, bugao duikang"* (enhance trust, reduce friction, develop cooperation, and avoid confrontation). In the late 1990s, Chinese leaders introduced the idea of a "new security concept" under which countries should "rise above one-sided security and seek common security through mutually beneficial cooperation."[20] In the early 2000s, China introduced the slogan "peaceful rise" (later "peaceful development"), under which "the people of all countries should join hands and strive to build a harmonious world of lasting peace and common prosperity."[21] All these ideas articulate morally commendable principles while also advancing the long-standing Chinese practical interest in dissuading other powers from banding together to hamper China's rise and justifying resistance to American unilateralism.

Some tenets that no longer suit China's needs have been abandoned, such as Mao's call for worldwide revolution. But as the foregoing list of examples suggest, many key themes in Chinese foreign policy rhetoric have endured as China's international role has evolved. They have done so for several reasons. First, in contrast to states with globe-spanning interests, China is still mainly a regional power. Only in Asia does China face the sorts of dilemmas America faces everywhere: between conflicting long- and short-term interests, economic and political needs, the incompatible demands of friendly states, historical friendships and new alignments, and old principles and new realities. But in more distant regions such as the Middle East, Africa, and Latin America, a few simple principles reflect Chinese interests most of the time. To oppose great-power intervention and defend sovereignty and equality among states is not only high-minded but also represents China's real security interest in regions where it cannot intervene itself and opposes intervention by other states. The farther one gets from China's borders, the easier it is for China to match rhetoric with interests (chapter 7).

Second, a weaker power strengthens its bargaining position when it insists on the inviolability of its principles. To the extent that Beijing can persuade other capitals that it never changes its mind, foreign diplomats shy away from raising issues Beijing has labeled closed. Even if concessions have to be made, the claim that they are not concessions preserves an appearance of power, which is itself an element of power.

Third, even when there are inconsistencies and trade-offs in Chinese policy, it is easy to hide them from view under the cloak of rhetoric because a handful of top leaders and professionals run Chinese diplomacy (see chapter 2). The Cultural Revolution (1966–1976) brought to the fore a group of leaders and diplomats who changed both foreign policy rhetoric and practice, but only for a short time. Even after domestic dissent appeared in the late 1970s, foreign policy has not been a major issue of debate. Dissident and off-the-record views differ from official ones chiefly in more openly acknowledging China's ambition to be a major power in the twenty-first century.

Fourth, ideology helps the Chinese leaders provide the public with easily understood explanations of what they are doing in world affairs. For both domestic and foreign consumption, officials have explained foreign policy decisions in terms of a limited list of "core interests" (*hexin liyi*). For example, a white paper called "China's Peaceful Development," issued in 2011, includes these core interests: "state sovereignty, national security, territorial integrity and national reunification," as well as "China's political system," "overall social stability," and "sustainable economic and social development."[22] Moral principles such as peace and development or mutual respect and equality among states provide an easily grasped summary of a complex foreign policy.

In short, the fact that China's foreign policy is so often consistent with its rhetoric does not mean that the policy derives deductively from the principles. Instead, the principles draw their meaning in specific circumstances and their ongoing utility from their service to national interests. They are open to interpretation as interests require, even to the point of disguising policy U-turns. Rhetoric and strategy in Chinese foreign policy are ultimately as consistent as they are because both respond to China's evolving geopolitical situation.

NATIONALISM: SECURITY AND IDENTITY

Like culture and ideology, nationalism is a strong presence in Chinese foreign policy discourse, similarly shaping and expressing the understanding of China's security interests without placing much constraint on the policymakers' decisions about how to pursue those interests.

Every nationalism is unique. In contrast to the usually self-confident American nationalism of Manifest Destiny, Chinese nationalism is powered by feelings of historical humiliation and wounded national pride, which contemporary policymakers often cultivate and manipulate to advance their agendas. Nationalism gained salience from the experience of imperialism and the perceived tenuousness of China's territorial, cultural, and, in some minds, even racial survival. The push over more than a century to regain and consolidate national sovereignty gave foreign policy a strong nationalist bent. In order to "save China," political leaders had to answer the question of what was worth saving.

In a world of political and economic modernity, was China in any sense a great civilization? Was there something in its way of life that should be preserved, or was the search for wealth and power merely about protecting a piece of territory? Would the Chinese have to sacrifice everything that made them different in order to enter the path to development opened by the West? Such issues were reflected in the nineteenth-century debate over the limits of reform and in the intellectual revolution of the early twentieth century when contending groups of thinkers struggled over whether to save China through liberalism, fascism, or Marxism.

Chinese nationalism is built on a contradiction: if the nation's problems are perceived as coming from outside, so are all the possible solutions. It was Western betrayal of China's interests at the peace negotiations ending World War I that sparked the 1919 May Fourth Movement to save China by making its culture more like that of the West. The three leading contenders throughout the twentieth century to solve China's search for a modern political form—liberal democracy, corporatist authoritarianism, and communism—came from the West. All the formulas to modernize China—rule of law, science and technology, Christianity—were Western. In an age of iconoclasm and revolution, what was Asian or traditional was rejected as backward. Where Chinese had traditionally thought of outside cultures as pale versions of their central culture, with its power to transform and civilize others, now the creative forces in China got their power from reacting against while also absorbing elements from a more powerful outside culture.

In 1949, Mao Zedong declared, "China has stood up." With his "Sinification of Marxism," he claimed to have combined a national identity with a global one—emulating one of the key claims of Confucianism—and to have forged a world-class model of thought and society that was at the same time distinctively Chinese. If the nineteenth-century German philosopher G. F. W. Hegel had once declared Asia to be outside of history because nothing important happened there, now in Mao's vision the center of world history had moved to China. China was forging practices that would transform all humankind. But Mao's death initiated a new period of debate over the cultural roots of his tyranny and the changes that would have to be made to put China back on the road to modernity.

As China joined the world decisively under Deng Xiaoping, the disagreement between those who favored and those who opposed Westernization (often referred to respectively as "liberals" and "conservatives") became once again the fundamental cleavage in Chinese politics. In 1988, an officially produced television documentary series, *Elegy for the Yellow River* (*Heshang*), used language almost identical to that of late-nineteenth-century reformers to declare that China's inward-looking, land-bound civilization was moribund and that China would have to "join the blue sea" of Western culture in order to escape disintegration.[23] The authors of *Elegy* went into exile in the aftermath of the pro-democracy demonstrations of spring 1989. The issue of cultural identity was taken over by conservative leaders who were concerned about cultural subversion by the West. Attacking what they alleged were American schemes to promote "peaceful evolution" and "bourgeois liberalization," they tried to promote a nationalistic mix of Confucian and Sino–Marxist values.

With the fading of the Chinese Communist Party's (CCP) utopian ideals, nationalism remains the party's most reliable claim to the people's loyalty, in part because of nationalism's protean character and diverse interpretations. As the only important value still shared by the regime and its critics, nationalism unites Chinese of all walks of life no matter how uninterested they are in other aspects of politics. Schoolchildren learn about Treaty Ports and concessions (foreign-governed areas in Chinese cities), foreign leaseholds and spheres of interest, extraterritoriality (by which foreigners in China charged with crimes were judged under foreign laws by foreign judges), "most-favored-nation" clauses that required China to extend low-tariff treatment to all its trading partners regardless of whether they did the same in return,[24] and foreign control over the Chinese customs, salt, and postal administrations. The problem of cultural identity infuses every aspect of China's foreign relations, including policies toward military security, foreign trade and investment, human rights, international academic collaboration, tourism, and the treatment of foreign news in the domestic press. The memory of "national humiliation" has been a strong element not only in rhetoric, but in Chinese perceptions of strategic realities.[25] Many Chinese see themselves as a nation beleaguered, unstable at home because insecure abroad and vulnerable abroad because weak at home. To them, it seems that China is always ready either to fly asunder or to be torn apart. China's very vulnerability engenders an urge not only to be secure in the world, but to take a turn at being a great power, capable of contending with any competitor in Asia.

CHINA'S GRAND STRATEGY

Geography and history set the agenda for Chinese foreign policy. The policy's first objective is to restore and maintain territorial integrity: to maintain domestic political stability; block outside support for separatist movements in Tibet, Xinjiang, and the Inner Mongolian Autonomous Region; reclaim Taiwan; defend maritime claims in the East China and South China seas; and, in short, defeat subversion and deter intervention or invasion on all fronts. This objective requires improving the capacity for internal security, working the global diplomatic scene to prevent Taiwan from expanding its international space and to cut off support for separatist forces in Tibet and Xinjiang, and improving the military capacity to deter threats from nearby armies and the U.S.

A second goal is to prevent the domination of the Asian region by others while expanding Chinese influence among neighbors. On the one hand, if China's location at the center of Asia surrounds it with potential enemies and involves it in complicated rivalries, it also gives it great influence in the most dynamic region of the world. Should another nation dominate the region, it might bring pressure on China in many ways. On the other hand, policies that are too assertive may alarm China's neighbors into thinking that China itself seeks to dominate Asia. A careful mix of military capability, economic power, and diplomatic involvement is needed to influence neighbors without pushing them into a hostile reaction.

Third, Chinese foreign policy seeks to create a favorable international environment for its economic growth. China favors stable world markets, opposes trading blocs, and works for access to foreign markets and foreign sources of energy and other commodities.

Finally, China seeks a voice in the shape of the evolving global order. Its rise has coincided with a period of growth in the international regimes governing trade, finance, nonproliferation, public health, environmental policy, human rights, and more. In all these areas—as well as in the use of the UN Security Council's powers to authorize military interventions on behalf of international peace and security—China's interests give it distinctive preferences, which are seldom identical with those of the other major powers. China's diplomats use both trade-offs and "soft power" to generate cooperation with like-minded states and influence the way these rules evolve (see chapters 7 and 12).

China pursues these goals with a mixture of power and weakness. If size and extended borders render the country vulnerable, they are also advantageous in deterring invasion. The vast hinterland provides room to fall back and defend in depth. That is a major reason why China was not colonized during the era of imperialism. Population is also a mixed liability and asset. Merely by being so numerous, the Chinese affect the fates of the rest of the world whatever they do—when they emigrate, when they purchase grain on world markets, when they build roads and drive cars. Because of China's demographic size, no global problem can be solved without it.

China's economy is on track to become the world's largest by around 2030, if not sooner. This position gives the country global influence and provides a strong basis for a sophisticated military machine, but it also makes China heavily dependent on global markets and resources for its prosperity and stability. Chinese spokesmen worry that talk of China's economic rise also encourages the rise of "China threat" theory. They insist that China is and will continue to be a poor, developing country. To be sure, China's GDP per capita of $6,600 (in U.S. dollars) in 2009 still ranked only 128th out of 227 countries in the world. Yet by quality-of-life measures, the Chinese population is more educated, healthier, and better skilled than bare income figures suggest. The fact is that China is in different senses both poor and rich. By entering the world economy, China has both gained the ability to influence others and opened itself to economic influence from others.

A nation's influence consists not only of strategic and economic power, but also of the "soft power" of values and ideas. China's opening to the world has reduced the mystique that the Chinese "way of socialism" once enjoyed in the West. In exchange, the success of the Chinese model— "market authoritarianism" or the "Beijing consensus"—has given Chinese diplomats a respectful hearing throughout the developing world and in the West's boardrooms. But China remains vulnerable to international criticism over the regime's violations of human rights, which reveal the illegitimacy of the Chinese political model to many of the country's own people.

In the post–Cold War era, the four rings of China's security are more closely linked than ever before. Beijing has come to realize that internal stability is increasingly vulnerable to international events and that China's international influence depends on its ability to maintain stability at home. As China's 2006 defense white paper observed, "Never before has China been so closely bound up with the rest of the world as it is today."[26] In the first decade of the twenty-first century, "thinking locally demands acting globally" has become the unofficial mantra guiding the PRC's diplomacy. This mantra has required a more proactive and global foreign policy.

China's location in the heart of Asia, the complexity of its regional environment, its abundance of difficult neighbors, its location between American and Russian spheres of influence—all the attributes that define the difficulties of China's geopolitical position—also contribute to its strategic importance and its ability to achieve foreign policy goals. Despite its power liabilities, it has taken advantage of its situation to turn itself into one of the major world actors. China is a large developing country, but it is in a different diplomatic class from other large developing countries such as India, Brazil, and Indonesia.

For now, China frames the assertion of its existential interests in the language of cooperation, seeking to reassure its neighbors and the major powers of its willingness to cooperate and to respect their interests. At the same time, it integrates into the world system to gain advantage, with a long-term possibility of working to change the system to suit its own values, political model, and vision of the world. The possibilities exist for both cooperation and conflict with the rest of the world. China's role remains to be defined by its interactions with its neighbors and by theirs with it. Its security needs are not logically incompatible with the interests of its neighbors and the other major powers, but neither will these interests automatically mesh.

2

WHO RUNS CHINESE FOREIGN POLICY?

A country's search for security is shaped by the vision, skills, and information embedded in its leadership and policymaking institutions. In the case of the PRC, the institution that has shaped foreign policy most decisively has no formal existence: the post of supreme leader. So far this position has been occupied by only four men: Mao Zedong (ruled 1949–1976), Deng Xiaoping (the dominant leader 1978–1992), Jiang Zemin (in office 1989–2002), and Hu Jintao (term of office 2002–2012). A fifth leader, Xi Jinping, has been selected to succeed Hu Jintao in 2012 for what is anticipated to be two five-year terms.

The leader's personal vision shaped the substance of China's search for security in each period—the willingness to endure isolation under Mao, the plunge into globalization under Deng, the push to reassure other powers under Deng, Jiang, and Hu, and under all four leaders an attentiveness to balance of power and a willingness to use force if other methods of asserting China's interests failed. The institution of the supreme leader has also given Chinese foreign policy some of its operational characteristics—consistency of strategic vision, the ability to enforce sacrifices upon certain institutions and individuals, and the capacity to change course dramatically without negotiating with other centers of power.

Over time, the role of the leader has changed. Each successive chief has been weaker politically than the previous one, forced to be more of a consensus seeker, and each has faced a progressively more complex foreign policy agenda. The other parts of China's foreign policymaking system have grown larger, more bureaucratic, more institutionalized, and more professional. Today the policy center still consists of a small, authoritarian, party–state–army elite that has the advantages of compactness and insulation from other government institutions, media, and civil society. Yet compared to the past, the makers of foreign policy confront more complex and vocal social constituencies that have more to lose or gain from foreign policy decisions than previously because of the impact of globalization on their daily lives and that know more about foreign policy than in the past because of the liberalization of the official media. The policy elites today sometimes find themselves hedged in by public attitudes they have helped to create, which set limits not so much on the substance of decisions as on how they must be presented.

The top foreign policy decision makers are well-vetted and long-experienced cadres of the Communist system. They have been promoted through career tracks that have socialized them well to the rules of the system, so much so that they sometimes have trouble striking out in new policy directions. They work within decision-making procedures—both formal channels and informal consultations—that are clearer and more stable than they were in the past, but that are often cumbersome and stovepiped, with a weak capability for crisis response. The leaders are served by a well-resourced intelligence apparatus, but they suffer from information overload and selective analysis. China has the policy advantages and disadvantages of an authoritarian state. It can sustain strategic policies in a disciplined way over long periods of time, but it suffers the risk that leaders unchecked by independent institutions will make large mistakes and have difficulty correcting them.

FORMAL AND INFORMAL STRUCTURES OF POWER

China's formal government structure does not provide for the post of supreme leader.[1] The Chinese Constitution, modeled on the 1936 Soviet Constitution created by Stalin, says that "all power in the People's Republic of China belongs to the people." Theoretical state sovereignty is accordingly concentrated in the institution that notionally represents the people, the National People's Congress (NPC), which is made up of around three thousand delegates, who meet for a couple of weeks once a year and whose powers are exercised between meetings by the Standing Committee. The state structure is unitary: the Constitution provides for neither separation of powers nor federalism. Instead, the NPC appoints the premier, who heads the State Council (i.e., the cabinet), whose job is supposed to be to execute policy set down by the ruling party, the CCP, and by the NPC. The NPC also appoints the officials of the judicial branch and holds the power to interpret and supervise implementation of the Constitution, to amend it, or even to replace it. A great deal of territorial power has been delegated from the central government down to the provinces, municipalities, counties, and townships, but the center never gives it away permanently. Local budgets are controlled from the top either by financial allocations or by delegated taxing powers.

Also recognized in the formal structure is the leadership of the state apparatus by the CCP, an elite party whose membership in 2011 was about 80 million, around 6 percent of the nation's population. The party, according to Marxist theory originally the political vanguard of the working class, now has members in all walks of society and is the dominant channel to political power. It appoints personnel throughout the government, army, economy, and cultural and educational establishments. It decides on major policies and transmits these policies for implementation to the state apparatus (i.e., government agencies). Its own constitution makes its highest organ the Central Committee, a body with a membership that varies in the range of two hundred to four hundred. But the Central Committee meets only once or twice a year, mainly to hear reports. Its powers are actually exercised by the Political Bureau (Politburo), consisting of twenty-odd top leaders who meet about once a month, and by an even more select body called the Politburo Standing Committee (PBSC), which consists of the five to eleven most powerful leaders (always an odd number), who meet once a week and pass on all the important decisions in both domestic and foreign policy. The party's top official is the general secretary.

In keeping with the idea—rooted in both Chinese and Marxist traditions—that the citizens have no real conflicts of interest among themselves,[2] the formal structure is designed to avoid any kind of pluralism. CCP ideologists state that the people's historic decision to vest power in the ruling party, effected by the CCP's victory in the revolutionary war of

1946–1949, is irreversible, so there is no need for multiparty competition for power. (Eight small "democratic parties" exist but do not compete.) When elections are held, except in scattered cases at the village level, they do not foster competition but allow the masses to chose leaders approved by the party, albeit sometimes from among multiple candidates.

Because China is such a huge country, power does not work in practice quite the way it works on paper. Four of China's thirty-three province-level units have populations larger than the largest European nation, Germany; 216 of China's 2,861 counties have populations larger than seven American states; and China has twenty cities of more than 5 million in population compared to one in the U.S. (New York). As a result, the system assigns great responsibilities and correspondingly great powers to the party chiefs at each level of government, who are told to make everything work as best they can in whatever way they think best.

At any level of government, the local party secretary directly or indirectly runs everything—the police, the courts, the local-level people's congresses, the population-planning bureaucracy, the Propaganda Department and local media, the agricultural bureau, industry, commerce, and the rest. The center's ultimate control is enforced by awarding promotion to those officials who meet its priorities, of which the most important in recent years have been to grow the economy, to keep the increase of population within planning targets, and to prevent the outbreak of social protest. This model of concentrated local control, which some scholars call "de facto federalism," means that power is both decentralized and centralized: it is decentralized to local leaders who exercise authority within their jurisdictions, but it is centralized because these local officials' careers are controlled by the ruling party's personnel system, which rewards officials whose performance meets the center's demands.

This system of concentrated local power responsive to central priorities largely determines how Chinese officials deal with security problems in the First Ring, including demonstrators and dissidents throughout the country, dissatisfied ethnic minority populations in places such as Tibet and Xinjiang, as well as foreign foundations, NGOs, journalists, and travelers gathering information and promoting change. Outside analysts sometimes see local diversity in human rights and environmental practices or in openness to foreign business as a sign of policy disagreements within the regime, but it is closer to the truth to say that all local party secretaries share the same priorities—development and social order—and simply pursue them in different ways depending on local conditions and their own skills.

Policymaking for the Second, Third, and Fourth rings beyond China's borders is reserved to the central authorities—and with respect to important decisions to a small circle among them. Just as a village party chief takes ultimate responsibility for all problems in the village, so for global issues the three large foreign policy bureaucracies—the CCP, the state, and the military—bring their biggest problems to Zhongnanhai, the complex of offices in the heart of the old imperial palace complex in Beijing where the Politburo and its Standing Committee meet.

THE LEADER'S CHANGING ROLE

If in America all politics is local because issues find their ultimate resolution with the voters, so in China all important politics is ultimately court politics because the difficult issues find their way up the system to the top. But the character of court politics has changed over time.

In the person of Mao Zedong, the system produced a dictator who often ignored the Central Committee and Politburo and made decisions unilaterally, frequently in the dark of night, half-asleep, based on quirky sources of information and shifting, delphic rationales.[3] The other leaders were often puzzled about Mao's goals, but he enforced his decisions with a mix of power resources. Official position was one such resource. Mao was head of state, a mainly ceremonial post he relinquished in 1959 to the second-ranking leader, Liu Shaoqi. He was also CCP chairman, a position he retained until his death that allowed him to control personnel appointments not only in the party itself, but throughout society and the economy. The chairmanship also gave him control of the mass media, education, arts, culture, and ideology through the party Propaganda Department. To honor Mao, the post of chairman was abolished after his death, and subsequent party heads were given the title *general secretary*.

Mao's most important formal source of power, however, was the chairmanship of the Central Military Commission (CMC), a job he gripped tightly throughout the power struggles of the 1950s and the Cultural Revolution of the 1960s and 1970s. In the capital, he controlled the physical security of his rivals in the central leadership by controlling the central guard corps and the Beijing garrison. In the provinces, his command of the military enabled him to dictate the course of the Cultural Revolution. With the trump card of physical force, Mao stood down the opposition of his top military officers to the Cultural Revolution in 1967 and prevented his comrade-in-arms Lin Biao from conducting a coup against him in 1971.

Equally important were Mao's informal sources of power. His authority reflected not only his long history in the party—he was present at its creation in 1921, and in 1934–1935 he led the Long March—but also his reputation as the leader of the revolution, founder of the army, and creator of China's form of Marxism–Leninism. During the great famine of 1959–1961, when China sustained an estimated 45 million deaths chiefly because of Mao's misguided economic policies, the CCP managed to hold onto power in part because of Mao's status as a demigod. Even as the peasants died from hunger, they believed that Mao could do no wrong and that he would rescue them. It was therefore just when he caused the regime's greatest crisis that his colleagues could least afford to purge him.[4] Similarly, when Mao's intraparty victims came back to power after his death to consolidate their power as his heirs, they felt it necessary to say that Mao's "contributions to the Chinese revolution far outweigh[ed] his mistakes."[5] By reaffirming in words many of the practices they abandoned, they preserved their claim to Mao's hand-me-down charisma. The endless game of maintaining supremacy also depended on attributes of character. Mao's deviousness, will power, and ruthlessness seemed to cow even the former bandits and warriors who made up his circle of followers and rivals.[6]

When Mao died in 1976, his successor, Hua Guofeng, and allies in the military and the Beijing guard corps arrested Mao's more radical followers (the so-called Gang of Four, who included Mao's wife, Jiang Qing) and, after an interlude, passed power to Deng Xiaoping in late 1978. In formal terms, Deng's highest civilian post after his return to power was vice premier, and after 1989 his only formal position was honorary chairman of the Chinese Bridge Playing Association. His authority came first from his prestige and personal connections throughout the party, army, and bureaucracy dating back to the CCP's earliest years. Second, Deng's power, like Mao's, was based on his control of the military. From 1981 to 1989, he held the post of CMC chairman. This source of power became decisive in

1989 when Deng overruled other leaders and mobilized military units to suppress democracy demonstrators in Beijing. Third and most important, other senior leaders who were Deng's potential rivals vested authority in him because they believed that China needed to adopt the kinds of pragmatic policies he had been associated with—and punished for—during the Mao period. Although there were debates throughout the Deng period over the pace of reform, he sustained the consensus by policy zigzags and by initiating occasional purges of his own lieutenants (such as Hu Yaobang and Zhao Ziyang) when they went too far.[7]

Unlike Mao, Deng ruled with considerable consultation in the narrow circle of top power holders. Balancing the more conservative views of senior contemporaries such as Chen Yun and the more reformist views of some of his own followers, such as Zhao Ziyang, Deng remained the indispensable man, the ultimate arbiter for decisions in both domestic and foreign policy—policy areas that became increasingly interlinked by virtue of his decision to take the Chinese economy global (see chapter 10). To deal with the growing complexity of the issues involved in going global, Deng restored and built up the foreign policy apparatus—the professional diplomatic service, academic institutes, and bodies of experts in trade disputes, foreign exchange, intellectual property rights, arms control, human rights, and similar areas.

Deng endured some foreign policy failures (such as the inability to rein in Vietnamese challenges to Chinese interests in the late 1970s; see chapter 6) and suffered some setbacks (such as the Tiananmen crisis and the failure to be admitted to the WTO on his watch; see chapters 12 and 10, respectively). However, by and large his colleagues considered his policies successful as long as China's economy and global influence grew. Deng guided China's 1979 normalization of relations with the U.S. and the 1989 normalization of relations with the Soviet Union (see chapter 3). Above all, he led the process of China's immersion in globalization through a series of decisions first to open Special Economic Zones, then to open the entire coastal area to foreign investment and trade, and finally, in 1992, to place the policy of opening to the outside world beyond political debate with a series of forceful statements made during his so-called Southern Tour. With this last act, Deng set in concrete China's commitment to globalization as a way to build national power. His role then faded as illness encroached, and he passed away in 1997 at the age of ninety-two.

As Deng's influence waned, that of Jiang Zemin grew.[8] Elevated by Deng to the position of CCP general secretary during the crisis of 1989, Jiang spent a significant part of his thirteen years in office consolidating power. With the deaths of most of the senior leaders of Deng's generation and the retirements of Jiang's own main cogenerational rivals by 1997, Jiang was able to exercise unchallenged authority for the remaining years of his term as general secretary until 2002. It was Jiang, for example, who made the ultimate decisions on China's negotiating stance on WTO membership[9] and who articulated the strategy of maintaining smooth relations with the U.S. under the slogan "Enhance trust, reduce friction, develop cooperation, and avoid confrontation."

The personal nature of power under Mao and Deng generated activity by faction leaders below the top leader who wished to influence policy.[10] As with the man at the top of the system, so too the power resources of the faction leaders at levels below him included institutional position, personal connections, attractive or fearsome attributes of character, and the rhetorical ability to define ideological orthodoxy. Some factions dwelt in the leader's court and drew power from access to him; others centered in the military, the bureaucracy, or regional governments and rooted their influence in the corresponding bureaucratic resources. Factions took shape through networks of people who had personal connections (*guanxi*) based on long associations and personal trust. Senior leaders contended for power by adopting ideological and policy positions that served the needs of their power bases. Some stressed ideological purity, others the practical needs of their institutions. When the supreme leader was vigorous, the factions fought for his ear. When he was weak or chose not to intervene, other senior leaders tried to take control over policy.

Foreign policy was not usually the central issue in factional conflicts. It was a realm unfamiliar to most of the Communist leaders and, especially under Mao, one that usually affected their power interests less than domestic issues. Despite factionalism, the supreme leader had his way on most foreign policy issues, imposing a consistent style and strategy across a range of decisions.[11] Many of Mao's senior colleagues at first opposed intervening in the Korean War, but they united quickly behind him once he decided to do so. Mao's choice to break with the Soviet Union in the early 1960s faced hardly any dissent at top levels of the leadership. The chairman was personally responsible for launching the two 1950s Taiwan Strait crises that risked war with the U.S. and for initiating the policy of rapprochement with the U.S. in 1971–1972.

In a similar way, it was Deng Xiaoping who decided on China's open-door policy in the late 1970s, normalization of relations with the U.S. in 1979, the 1979 incursion into Vietnam, rapprochement with the Soviet Union in the 1980s, the "one-country two-systems" policy for reunification of Hong Kong and Taiwan, and the agreement with Great Britain on the return of Hong Kong to China. PRC foreign policies may not always have been correct, but under Mao and Deng they were usually the product of a coherent vision and were carried out with discipline.

However, every major factional struggle drew foreign policy issues to some extent into its vortex. All of Mao's early conflicts with party rivals over revolutionary strategy involved the question of how closely to follow orders from the Soviet-controlled Communist International (Comintern). The first major power struggle after 1949 led to the purge and death in 1954 of a top leader, Gao Gang, who had tried to cultivate close relations with Stalin independently of Mao. Mao's purge of Peng Dehuai in 1959 was also based in part on the charge that Peng wanted closer relations with Moscow. As a count against Peng, this charge may have been unjustified, but it sent a message to other colleagues who were thinking of questioning the wisdom of splitting from the Soviet Union. When Mao purged Liu Shaoqi and other orthodox party leaders in the Cultural Revolution, he accused them not only of domestic deviations, but of conciliatory leanings toward the West. The power struggle between Mao and Lin Biao in 1970–1971 embroiled Lin in resistance to Mao's opening to the U.S., and after Lin's death he was charged, justly or not, with favoring capitulation to the Soviet Union.

When the leader was weak, factional struggles might not only refer to foreign policies but affect them as well. When Mao was incapacitated late in his life, the faction led by his wife attacked its rivals for their association with U.S.–China rapprochement and a conciliatory Taiwan policy, thus forcing the government to adopt a temporary hard line toward the U.S. Even after the radicals were defeated, the power struggle between Deng Xiaoping and Mao's designated successor, Hua Guofeng, froze policy toward the U.S. for a time until Deng gained power. Not until 1978 did Deng establish the authority needed to make compromises over Taiwan and thus normalize relations with the U.S. Setbacks to Deng's power after the 1989 Tiananmen incident were associated with a temporary hardening of policies on trade with the U.S., arms transfers, human rights, and Hong Kong, among other areas. Deng's illness in 1995–1997 contributed to the hardening of PRC policies toward Taiwan, human rights, and trade.

For foreigners, negotiating with Beijing under Mao and Deng had advantages and disadvantages. The considerations that shaped policy were either hidden in plain sight in the leader's speeches and the official newspaper or were so private that even intelligence agencies could not discover them. From demonstrators in the streets to diplomats in conference rooms, the nation maintained unanimity behind a seemingly rigid ideology. But a Malraux, a Kissinger, or an Edgar Snow might be ushered into Mao's or Deng's presence to hear disquisitions marked by candor and flexibility. An enemy such as Nixon might be received as a friend, or a friend such as Khrushchev might be received as an enemy. China's diplomats presented poker faces of discipline and secrecy during negotiations. But in the presence of the great leader or his authorized representative—under Mao, this representative was normally Premier Zhou Enlai—everything might be negotiable. Even so, any policy changes would be cloaked in public claims of doctrinal consistency. Once reached, an agreement could be relied on.[12]

GROWING INSTITUTIONALIZATION

Mao's foreign policy apparatus was rudimentary. His decisions were implemented by a small staff under Zhou Enlai, the premier and sometime foreign minister. After receiving a phone call or written instruction from Mao, Zhou frequently handled even small details of policy personally. There is no record that Zhou had independent foreign policy views, but his urbane style often led foreign negotiators to view him as a voice of moderation. He negotiated all the arrangements for the 1971 visit to China of an American ping-pong team, which opened the way for Henry Kissinger and later Richard Nixon. Even on his deathbed, Zhou continued his diplomatic work, receiving a Romanian delegation and holding discussions on policy toward Taiwan.[13] Zhou sometimes had to work with a severely diminished staff. During the Cultural Revolution, Mao disbanded the few foreign policy institutes China had, called home all but one of its ambassadors, and sent most of the foreign policy establishment to the countryside to be reeducated by the peasants.

One of Deng Xiaoping's goals starting in the early 1980s was to create greater institutionalization in party and government processes so that the political chaos of the Mao years would not recur. Under Deng's guidance, limits on the length of political leaders' terms of office began to be observed; leaders retired from office before they died and did not interfere in politics after retirement; the NPC and the CCP's Central Committee met on schedule every year; new leaders were chosen by consultation among the outgoing leaders; the military ceased to exercise a voice in the succession to civilian posts; decision making in various spheres was supported by the work of staff in specialist agencies; a division of labor developed within the leadership over who had the right to propose decisions in which policy areas; and the PBSC chaired by the general secretary collectively cleared important decisions.[14]

Jiang Zemin both benefited from and paid a price for the institutionalization begun by Deng. He benefited because he could draw real power from his formal positions as general secretary, head of state, and chair of the CMC. Even though he had no prior credibility as an ideologist, economic decision maker, or military strategist, his official posts gave him the right to speak in each of these areas. He had to fight less than Mao or Deng to defend his power in the factional arena because by this time lines of authority were better defined and terms of office more reliable. In other ways, Jiang was hampered by institutionalization: he could exercise final say only after consulting with other leaders in their areas of responsibility, and he had to step down from office when his term was over—which he did with apparent reluctance in a three-step process lasting from 2002 to 2004—and accept a successor, Hu Jintao, whom he had not chosen himself, but whom Deng had put in place as heir apparent early in Jiang's term.

More than any of his predecessors, Hu Jintao worked within an apparatus that routinely required a great deal of coordination with other powerful, trusted, and expert actors. He could not decide issues arbitrarily or purge other leaders, the way Mao did, or intervene unpredictably in the policymaking domains assigned to others. as Deng did. But because he held the same triad of positions as Jiang Zemin—party general secretary, head of state, and chair of the CMC—he exercised the crucial prerogatives of setting agendas, leading discussions, and summarizing the results of meetings, which gave him the dominant influence over the course of foreign policy.

The Politburo and the PBSC are the levels at which major foreign policy decisions are most likely to be integrated with one another and with domestic policy decisions. It was at this level that policymakers dealt with such issues as the negative impact of the Great Leap Forward on relations with the Soviet Union (chapter 3) and the need to relax domestic ideology in order to implement Deng Xiaoping's open-door economic policy (chapter 10). When the U.S. and China were negotiating the agenda for Richard Nixon's pathbreaking visit to China in 1972, the Politburo issued the negotiating instructions for Chinese diplomats. In 1995, when the Clinton administration, in the face of China's warnings to the contrary, allowed Taiwan's leader Lee Teng-hui[15] to visit the U.S., a meeting of the Politburo decided on China's response, which included missile exercises in the East China Sea and the Taiwan Strait, the withdrawal of the Chinese ambassador to the U.S., and the suspension of high-level U.S.–China diplomatic and military contacts.

Below the Politburo and the PBSC are the central party Secretariat and the General Office. There are also four departments that help the leaders set policy for specific aspects of foreign and domestic affairs. The Propaganda Department (in 1998 officially renamed in English the Publicity Department) governs the domestic and foreign work of the propaganda apparatus, which includes the media, the educational sector, and the cultural establishment. The United Front Work Department oversees policy related to nongovernmental persons and groups in Taiwan, Hong Kong, and Overseas Chinese circles as well as relations with people at home and abroad classified as intellectuals, members of national minorities, and representatives of religious communities. The International Department (formerly International Liaison Department) manages party-to-party relations with political parties abroad, which was a central element of Chinese foreign policy during the years of high Maoism, but a less central element today. There is also the Organization Department, which is in charge of personnel matters.

The major mechanism for debating, coordinating, and recommending policies in specific issue areas is a type of ad hoc body called a "central leading small group" (CLSG, *zhongyang lingdao xiaozu*). Such groups existed in the past to implement orders from the top rather to than make decisions. Today they are venues for the top leaders to consult, reach consensus, and recommend policies to the Politburo for final approval. Like the Principals Committee or the Deputies Committee of the U.S. National Security Council, CLSGs are committees of ranking decision makers created to coordinate policy among bureaucracies. They operate on assignment from the Politburo and are reshuffled as the Politburo deems necessary. A highly ranked person—the general secretary himself or another member of the PBSC—chairs each group; a person of ministerial rank administers the group's work; and the heads of relevant cabinet-level offices are normally members of each CLSG.

Several CLSGs are known currently to operate within the domain of international relations:[16]

The Foreign Affairs CLSG (Zhongyang waishi gongzuo lingdao xiaozu) is normally chaired by either the general secretary or the premier. The senior staff person for the committee is normally the vice premier or state councillor in charge of foreign affairs (vice premier and state councillor are cabinet ranks above the rank of minister). The working group includes a high-level military representative. As the coordinating institution (or "mouth") for the whole foreign affairs bureaucratic system, this group coordinates the foreign affairs–related work of a mix of party and state agencies: the International Liaison Department; the Ministries of Defense, Foreign Affairs, Commerce, and Culture; the party central's Foreign Affairs Office, the party central's news office, and the General Staff Department of the People's Liberation Army (PLA).

The State Security CLSG (Zhongyang guojia anquan lingdao xiaozu) is normally chaired by the general secretary and includes among its members the PBSC member in charge of state security and public-security affairs, the senior military intelligence officer, and representatives from the State Council offices on Taiwan affairs and Hong Kong and Macao affairs. This CLSG coordinates work across the fields of security, foreign affairs, and defense.

The Overseas Propaganda CLSG (Zhongyang duiwai xuanquan lingdao xiaozu) is normally chaired by the PBSC member in charge of propaganda work and includes the heads of the party's Propaganda and United Front Work departments and the leaders of the party central's news office, the party's Xinhua News Agency, the official party newspaper (*People's*

Daily), and the Ministry of Culture. The same group meets under another label as the CLSG in charge of domestic propaganda.

The Taiwan Work CLSG (Zhongyang dui Tai gongzuo lingdao xiaozu) is normally chaired by the general secretary and includes the PBSC member who supervises agencies working on the Taiwan issue. It includes a high-ranking military representative. This small group coordinates the Taiwan-related work of the Ministry of State Security, the State Council Taiwan Affairs Office, the PLA General Staff's intelligence department, and the Association for Relations Across the Taiwan Strait.

The Hong Kong and Macao Affairs CLSG is run by a PBSC member and includes relevant United Front Work Department, State Council, and military representatives.

The Finance and Economics CLSG is chaired by either the general secretary or the premier and includes top party and cabinet officials supervising domestic and international economic affairs.

The Energy CLSG was established in 2006 to coordinate management of domestic and foreign energy strategy. It is chaired by the premier and includes a range of senior officials whose agencies are involved in or affected by energy security.

The Foreign Affairs CLSG superficially resembles the U.S. National Security Council (NSC), but there are important contrasts. The Foreign Affairs CLSG's scope of work is defined more narrowly than the scope of issues that the NSC coordinates, with a range of related issues delegated instead to the other CLSGs that have responsibilities related to foreign affairs. Unlike the NSC, the Foreign Affairs CLSG makes decisions rather than just pooling advice from other agencies. But where the NSC has full-time staff to help it enforce decisions down the bureaucracy, the CLSG does not. After it makes decisions, state agencies under the State Council are supposed to implement them.

Within the State Council, a Foreign Affairs Office under the premier coordinates the work of the various state agencies involved in foreign affairs, including four ministries. The Ministry of Foreign Affairs manages diplomacy and staffs embassies and consulates. The Ministry of Commerce concentrates on trade issues, such as conflicts regarding protection of intellectual property rights, accusations of Chinese protectionism, and policy toward multilateral economic institutions, including the Asia–Pacific Economic Cooperation (APEC) forum and the WTO. The Ministry of State

Security handles espionage and counterespionage, diplomatic security, and border control, combining many of the functions of America's Central Intelligence Agency (CIA) and Federal Bureau of Investigation (FBI). The Ministry of National Defense is a front for the CMC, lacking the staff and functions of a full ministry. Its job is to represent the military in the cabinet (State Council) and in dealings with foreigners.

Other cabinet-level ministries and commissions conduct negotiations on specific foreign policy issues, as is the case in the U.S. and other governments. The Ministry of Finance, for example, has been China's primary representative to the International Monetary Fund (IMF). The Ministry of Education administers the policy of sending students abroad and receiving foreign students in China. The Ministry of Public Security handles police functions relating to foreigners, from crime solving to fire safety and traffic control. The Ministry of Culture has a Department of Cultural Relations with Foreign Countries. The State Commission on Science and Technology controls allocation of foreign currency among civilian and military industries for importing advanced technology. Below the cabinet, other government agencies that have foreign policy roles include the People's Bank of China, the State Administration of Foreign Exchange, the State Statistical Bureau (which has the right to approve surveys conducted by foreigners in China), and the bureaus that administer policies regarding customs, travel and tourism, aviation, foreign experts employed by Chinese agencies, and so on.

This system often achieves enviable consistency in the articulation and application of policy across different policy bureaucracies. On important matters on which the center has spoken, Chinese officials and policy intellectuals are briefed and disciplined. People at all levels know what the policy is and are motivated to comply with it whether they agree or disagree with it because the political system does not reward disobedience or dissent. This compliance allows China to pursue a more strategic foreign policy than most other countries across the broad span of issue areas and policy actors as well as over time. But the high centralization of power also creates some span-of-control problems. Although officials up and down the line are well informed on what the policy is, there are not enough hours in the day for the people who have real power to make sure that all the bureaucracies below them implement policy in the way they intend. Classic examples of this problem have included the failure of military-run enterprises to comply with nonproliferation commitments made by central officials,[17] local officials' toleration of intellectual property rights violations,[18] and human rights violations carried out by security authorities that embarrassed the foreign ministry and the justice ministry.[19]

Lamarckian evolution, long discredited in biology, functions with important effect in the world of policy. A change in behavior (such as deciding to join the WTO) induces a change in physiology (staffing up the bureaucracy with experts on WTO rules and procedures), which induces a change in DNA (those experts become a constituency with distinctive beliefs and values, who push a set of policies within the system).[20] Although the initial impulse to get involved in such an issue area may be only instrumental, some degree of socialization to international norms occurs through the creation of an expert staff in the bureaucracy, which in turn affects not only the technical bureaus themselves, but to some extent, through them, the decision makers at the top.[21] In this way, the process that international relations theorists refer to as "social learning" among states takes place as governments gain both the capability and the propensity to negotiate over and selectively comply with new international regimes.[22] Other policy areas in which this phenomenon occurred in the Chinese system in the post-Mao period included nonproliferation and arms control, human rights, intellectual property rights, international commercial dispute resolution, international environmental regulation, international public health, UN affairs, and product safety regulation. In all these areas, Deng Xiaoping's shift to a policy of global engagement required China to participate in the relevant international regime; participation in such a technical field required expertise; experts were trained and brought into the government; and once in the government, the experts gained some degree of influence because only they knew how to work the particular international system in which they were experts. Seldom, if ever, however, has the siren song of emerging international norms trumped national interest in the final calculations made by the decision makers at the top.

INTELLIGENCE

The outer ring of the Chinese foreign policy establishment consists of research institutes, think tanks, and intelligence agencies that provide the leaders with information and ideas.²³ The Chinese Academy of Social Sciences has numerous area studies institutes studying all parts of the world from the angles of politics, economics, history, religion, and culture. In addition, at least twenty-five think tanks in Beijing are devoted to analyzing international affairs. Specialized research institutes serve the Foreign Ministry, the State Council, the CCP's CMC, the Ministry of National Defense, and the PLA's General Staff. Some institutes, such the China Institute for Contemporary International Relations, seem to serve more than one master. Although formally under the auspices of the Central Committee's Foreign Affairs Office, this institute, which is one of the largest and oldest foreign policy think tanks, also maintains close ties to the Ministry of State Security. Each provincial government runs a social sciences academy that includes international relations in its field of studies. The governments of Shanghai, Guangzhou, Xiamen, Harbin, and other major cities have also established foreign policy institutes. Think tank staff are often sent to Chinese embassies abroad. They visit foreign universities and research centers to give lectures and conduct interviews, spend time as visiting scholars overseas, attend foreign academic conferences, and participate with experts from other countries in "Track II" dialogues (policy-related dialogues among persons with government connections but without current governmental responsibilities). These analysts prepare reports for government agencies, informing the Chinese leadership of the latest thinking overseas on issues affecting Chinese security. Many research organizations provide periodic reports to the Politburo.

The Chinese government also posts around the world a large staff of journalists, who prepare reports on the same subjects covered by embassy personnel and think tanks. Most Chinese journalists work for the official Xinhua News Agency, the China News Service, or a government or party newspaper such as the *People's Daily*. Most of them are party members. Abroad as at home, reporters write not only for publication, but also for classified, "internal" news bulletins that circulate among ranking party and government officials. In most foreign countries, Chinese reporters are allowed to base themselves more widely and travel more freely than diplomats.

Like all major powers, China has a sophisticated overseas covert intelligence system. Because it is secret, our knowledge of it is limited. Most of the few cases in which the U.S., Japan, and other countries have apprehended Chinese spies have involved efforts to transfer sensitive information on advanced technologies with potential military use. Such cases suggest that the Chinese security agencies focus in part on technological information. They develop relationships with some Chinese going abroad for long-term visits or permanent residence, expecting that a portion of them will develop careers in fields dealing with national security or sensitive technology and will one day provide classified information to the Chinese government.

The U.S. congressional Cox Commission in 1999 issued a report alleging extensive and effective espionage operations by China in the U.S. Some commentators charged that the commission's claims were unsubstantiated, and botched prosecutions by U.S. law enforcement agencies, as in the 1999 case against Taiwan-born scientist Wen Ho Lee, gave the impression that the threat of Chinese espionage might be overhyped. But it is likely that Beijing is indeed engaged, as the U.S. intelligence community believes, in widespread and aggressive espionage operations in the U.S. to acquire military and dual-use technology.[24] In the 2000s, there were increasingly frequent reports of extensive Chinese hacking into Western government, company, and NGO computer networks. It was hard to prove where the hacks came from, but many must have represented attempts to obtain information or discover weak spots that could be attacked in case of cyber war. The hacking went both ways: Beijing authorities claimed that their computers were also frequently attacked by outsiders.

China's experts on U.S. affairs seem to have achieved a good understanding of the American political system after about twenty years' effort. American goals and methods in international affairs used to puzzle Chinese analysts because the country's pluralist system works so differently from China's. Here is a system in which the chief executive is selected not by a deliberate promotion process within the ruling elite, but by an unpredictable, uncontrollable public process that often brings inexperienced people to power; a system in which political parties with significantly different international strategies alternate in power or sometimes divide power during the time in office of a given administration, leading to puzzling inconsistencies and changes of direction in national strategy; a system in which no single center seems to be in charge of matters of high importance to national security because the Congress or the courts — sometimes individual congressional representatives or judges — have the power to intervene in matters of consequence; a system in which ideology often seems to hold sway over pragmatic national interest as policymakers labor to sell their policies to a skeptical public. The key to good intelligence in deciphering these puzzles has not been the discovery of secrets, but an understanding of the complex signals emitted by a pluralistic political system. By training an impressive cadre of U.S. experts—many in American graduate schools—and through a long process of interaction with Washington policymakers, the Chinese leaders have developed the necessary body of advisers to give them a reasonable understanding of U.S. policy and its drivers. Their views of American goals and methods are discussed further in chapter 4.

As in most countries, intelligence agencies also focus on identifying and assessing threats to the state. China's intelligence system seems adept at information gathering but less skillful at interpretation and analysis. From *The Tiananmen Papers*, a body of secret documents related to the 1989 Tiananmen incident, we get the impression that a great deal of raw intelligence goes to the top, more than the senior leaders can conceivably read, although they may sample it on important topics.[25] At the time of any international crisis or shift in U.S. China policy, squads of information collectors from Chinese media, think tanks, and government agencies fan out internationally to collect a vast quantity of evidence, most of which must be redundant. People working on Chinese human rights issues have become used to pervasive Chinese surveillance and harassment of their Internet traffic and phone calls not only within China, but outside it.

Assessments, however, may sometimes succumb to information pathologies, which appear to work differently depending on whether the threat is domestic or foreign. When monitoring and assessing domestic threats, intelligence organs may be pressured to downplay the full extent of a problem, a pressure that may paradoxically be greater the more the agency realizes the seriousness of the stakes. For example, intelligence agencies appear to have been caught off guard by the scope of the unrest in Tibetan areas in March 2008 and the intensity of outrage among Uyghurs in Xinjiang in July 2009. The reason for the lapse may lie in the agencies' unwillingness to deliver assessments that embarrass local authorities or contradict current thinking among the leaders. Disaffected Tibetans and Uyghurs are always officially depicted as constituting "a small handful" of troublemakers who have foreign links and do not enjoy broad support in their communities. This view may also be reflected in internal reporting. To suggest that disaffection is deeply rooted and widespread would challenge the official belief that economic development in areas populated by ethnic minorities is the answer to the problem. Moreover, it is easier to blame foreign instigators for the unexpected scope and intensity of domestic dissent than to say that government policies have failed.

The reverse may be true in the case of foreign threats, where the intelligence community has reasons to play up challenges. For example, articulating the means and mechanisms by which the U.S. may appear to threaten China requires little encouragement. For Chinese intelligence professionals, the assumption of a U.S. threat to the PRC is not only politically astute, but also representative of actual beliefs. It is easy to interpret the uncoordinated words and actions of diverse actors in the complex U.S. political scene as elements of a coordinated scheme to weaken China. For example, proclamations about human rights and democracy are not interpreted as expressions of American idealism, but as methods for meddling in China's internal affairs and undermining CCP rule.

Outside the circle of expert advisers and policy professionals, the regime has little interest in or access to critical or original views. The only public dissent the government tolerates is the occasional expression of strong nationalism, the loudness of which the government seems to be able to modulate depending on whether it needs more or less background noise of that type for its diplomacy. The lack of independent opinion arguably does no harm as long as the government's policy is working. But when the policy is unwise, the echo-chamber effect robs the country of a chance to consider alternatives.

THE ROLE OF THE MILITARY

The PLA—the collective name given to China's army, navy, air force, and missile forces—is the third pillar of the regime's authority along with the CCP and the state. It not only protects the country against external enemies but helps defend the regime against internal threats (chapter 11). The CCP came to power as an armed rather than a civilian force by winning a civil war rather than an election. Its claim to legitimacy is rooted in that victory. Mao's regime after 1949 continued to rely on the army, first to establish and then to maintain control. When the Cultural Revolution brought the country near chaos, Mao called out the military in 1967. The PLA not only restored order but also took over the administration of every major institution and every level of government from the county level up to the provincial level through so-called revolutionary committees. After Mao's death, military leaders supervised the arrest of his radical heirs, backed Hua Guofeng as Mao's immediate successor, and then a couple of years later supported the rise of Deng to power. Deng used the PLA to save the regime during the Tiananmen crisis of 1989.[26] Domestic security remains a key mission of the Chinese military. In all these ways, the PLA is truly a "party army," not neutral among political contenders, but loyal to a specific ruling group. The Chinese system is best characterized not as a "party–state," as it is often called, but as a "party–army–state" in which the military is an integral part of the regime.

The military's relations with the civilian authorities strike a balance seldom seen elsewhere. A bedrock principle of CCP ideology is that "the party controls the gun." Military officers sit as symbolic but not powerful presences in the party Central Committee and the NPC. The army holds two seats in the Politburo, enough to exchange information but not to influence outcomes. Since the Deng period, no military officers have been appointed to the most powerful decision-making body, the PBSC. Senior officers serve in the relevant CLSGs, where they provide information and coordinate actions, but so far as we know, they do not tend to use these positions to lobby for a distinct institutional point of view. Except when summoned, the PLA intervenes little in civilian affairs. Unlike some armies, the PLA does not promote an ideology of its own such as corporatism or military nationalism. It has remained loyal to the civilian regime's conception of socialism as this conception has evolved under successive leaders. It promulgates the party's ideology in its ranks through a hierarchy of political commissars. The PLA used to raise much of is own budget from farms and enterprises. In 1998, Jiang Zemin decided to divest the PLA of these independent sources of income, a decision apparently taken with the military leadership's concurrence.[27] Since then, military expenditures have been allocated by the state, including some significant allocations outside the official defense budget. In all these ways, the Chinese political system is characterized by civilian control.

Yet in its own area of responsibility, the PLA operates with a high degree of autonomy. Once overall defense expenditures have been set by the state, military officials decide how to spend the money among competing needs.

Civilian leaders lay down a vision of likely enemies and probable foci of future world tension, but the military decides how to equip and train itself for future contingencies, handles military tensions with other countries, and conducts military diplomacy. The civilian leaders decide when to go to war, but the military manages the war. Such a division of labor stands in sharp contrast to the way the U.S. system works, in which civilians in White House, the Pentagon, the intelligence community, and the Congress play key roles in deciding how war will be prepared for and how it is fought.

The crucial channel for high-level civilian control over the military is a narrow one: the chairmanship of the CMC. There are formally two such commissions, one within the party apparatus and, since 1982, another one within the state. In reality, they are the same body. The commission's chairmanship has been occupied successively by Mao, Hua Guofeng, Deng, Jiang, and Hu. The CMC's civilian leader appears to have few civilian staff to advise him on his work in the commission (except that Hua, Jiang, Hu, and Xi Jinping served as CMC vice chairs in their capacities as heirs apparent); rather, he is assisted by a staff in uniform, beginning with the generals who serve as CMC vice chairs and moving down the ranks from there.

Under Mao and Deng, the civilian–military imbalance may have been less important because both of them had served in the military, understood the military technology of their day, and commanded deep personal loyalty among the officers. Later CMC chairs, however, have had no military background, and at the same time China's strategic problems and military technology have become more complex. The later chairmen have therefore been increasingly captive to the PLA for expertise in military matters. The civilian chair's chief tool of influence has been his jealously guarded control of senior promotions. Mao frequently purged and replaced top military officers. Deng, Jiang, and Hu consolidated power by rotating their own appointees into positions as commanders of the central staff departments, service arms, military regions, and the central guards bureau that handles security for the top leaders. This process generated some degree of personal loyalty to them in the most senior ranks. The incoming party leader, Xi Jinping, is the son of a one-time Communist guerilla leader and served as secretary for a senior military official in his twenties, giving him slightly deeper roots in the military than Jiang Zemin or Hu Jintao.

Despite the thinness of civilian control over military matters, party leaders have been able to make the major decisions of war and peace. It was Mao who decided to intervene in Korea in 1950, to develop nuclear weapons in 1955, to launch a war with India in 1962, and to ambush Soviet troops in early 1969. Deng Xiaoping decided on the Chinese invasion of Vietnam in 1979 and on the naval clash with Vietnam in the Spratly Islands in 1988.[28] Jiang Zemin gave the green light for Chinese missile tests and military exercises in the Taiwan Strait in 1995–1996.

Civilian control seemed to fray only during the Cultural Revolution, after Mao had placed the army in administrative control of the whole country and labeled the army's chief, Lin Biao, as his "designated successor." In October 1969, Lin issued the so-called No. 1 Order, which put the PLA on heightened alert against possible imminent attack by the Soviet Union. He reportedly issued this directive without Mao's knowledge, which contributed to Lin's estrangement from the chairman. Lin Biao may have contemplated a military coup in 1971—or at least Mao believed a Lin family coup was in the works—but it never materialized. The October 1976 arrest of the Gang of Four was carried out by a group of military and civilian officials who did not seize power themselves but pledged their loyalty to Mao's successor at the time, Hua Guofeng.[29]

It is less clear who made decisions for military force in a long list of lesser incidents, including naval clashes with Vietnam in the South China Sea in 1974, 1992, and 1994 and with the Philippines in 1995, 1996, and 1997; the collision between a Chinese fighter plane and an American EP-3 surveillance aircraft in 2001 in the vicinity of Hainan Island; an unannounced antisatellite test in January 2007; Chinese harassment of the USNS *Impeccable* in 2009; and a variety of clashes and near clashes with Japanese and American ships at various times in the East China Sea, around the Diaoyutai (Senkaku) Islands, and elsewhere. These decisions were quite possibly made within the military chain of command without input from civilian decision makers. Moreover, China's behavior during some of these incidents showed that civilian authorities had difficulty getting control of crises once they were in the hands of the military. In 2001, for example, a stovepiped command-and-control structure apparently made it difficult for the top leaders to get information and make decisions on a timely basis about the collision between the Chinese fighter and the American surveillance aircraft and the latter's subsequent emergency landing on Hainan Island.

The delay caused the crisis with the U.S. to drag on for weeks. Chinese officers have created diplomatic kerfluffles on some occasions when they used threatening language that was out of tune with the civilian leadership's emphasis on "peaceful development" and "the new security concept."[30]

PLA officers are not unlike military officers elsewhere in being nationalistic, suspicious of adversaries, hawkish, and politically conservative, but they operate on a longer leash than soldiers in many other countries. The old structures of civilian control may no longer be robust enough to coordinate China's military actions with its diplomatic strategy at a time when the army's capabilities are expanding and its regional role is growing. In the trend of institutionalization in the making of foreign policy in general, civilian control of the military lags behind.[31]

THE ROLE OF PERSONALITY

The less institutionalized the policymaking process, the more difference is made by the leader's beliefs and style. Mao Zedong's quirks and convictions had a decisive impact on Chinese foreign policy in the first two and a half decades of the regime, as explored further in chapter 3. How Deng Xiaoping and Jiang Zemin shaped policy toward the U.S., globalization, and other issues is discussed throughout the book.

Hu Jintao was sixty years old when he acceded to the leadership in 2002.[32] Born in Shanghai, he was trained as a hydropower engineer in China's elite technical university, Tsinghua. He served in a series of technical and provincial posts and in the politically influential Communist Youth League in Beijing. In December 1988, he was assigned to serve as party secretary in Tibet. Unfortunately for him, Lhasa convulsed in riots a few months later, and Hu had to order his subordinate, the local government chairman, to declare martial law. Deng Xiaoping in 1992 selected him ahead of all the competing cadres of his generation to serve in the PBSC, apparently as a reward for his loyalty to the organization. Affable and cautious, Hu held onto his slippery perch as heir apparent for ten years and duly succeeded Jiang Zemin in 2002.

Hu was viewed by his colleagues in the top leadership as a good listener and a consensus builder. His "work style" was considered "democratic" in Chinese Communist terms: he was businesslike, thoughtful, and uninterested in empty show—all in contrast to the way Jiang Zemin was perceived. Although different from Jiang in style, Hu did not depart from Jiang's foreign policy line in substance. He set out to sustain the previous leader's achievements—stable relations with the U.S. and successful navigation of the white-water pace of globalization. As China's challenges evolved during his time as leader, Hu led the country to a more extended and assertive international presence, not only in Asia but in Africa, South America, and the Middle East. Although his strategy at times posed difficult choices—among them how to frame policies toward Taiwan, Japan, the U.S., human rights, and the global trade and financial systems—analysts discerned no indications of serious dissent in Beijing's policy circles. Hu apparently guided the collective leadership to consensus around decisions that bore his personal stamp.

The elite's consensus choice of Xi Jinping to succeed Hu in 2012 signaled the intention to give China a more assertive international voice. Xi is a large man with the build of a football player, and he is married to a popular folk singer who worked in a PLA entertainment troupe. His father was an early guerilla fighter in the Communist Revolution and a senior party leader of Mao's generation. When the father lost his post in Mao's purges, Xi was sent to the countryside to "learn from the peasants" in a poverty-stricken agricultural commune. His size and strength helped him to survive the grueling life of agricultural labor. He was the champion of wrestling matches with the farmers and was renowned for his ability to carry a shoulder pole of twin 110-pound buckets of wheat for several miles across mountain paths. On his local government's recommendation, Xi got into Tsinghua University as a "peasant–worker–soldier student." As noted earlier, he briefly served a senior military leader who had once been a subordinate of his father's.

Unlike Hu Jintao, Xi served for much of his career in one province, Fujian, where he rose from deputy mayor of a city in 1985 to provincial governor in 2000. There he gained a reputation as populist, pushy, and results oriented. His superiors evaluated him as "modest, full of ideas, hard-working, unpretentious; insists on eating meals in the city government cafeteria, washes his own clothes, refuses excessive banqueting, has warm relations with Party committee and city government staff." During his governorship, he tried to make the province attractive for investors from Taiwan, which is directly across the Taiwan Strait, and many of whose people speak one of the Fujian dialects. He urged his subordinates to practice "limited government" and to take an attitude of "public service." He hectored provincial cadres for laziness, careerism, and caution in a manner said to be similar to that of former premier Zhu Rongji, who was known for being confrontational with his subordinates and producing results. "Many of our civil servants still think they are running a planned economy," Xi said at one meeting. "Whenever there's a problem they seek to add more staff and introduce more government structures." On another occasion, he accused provincial officials of spending all their time chasing promotions and engaging in alliance building: "These guys may manage to fall into a few better jobs. But as our efforts [to improve government efficiency] build steam, they will fall by the wayside."[33]

In the 2000s, Xi moved from Fujian to the top party posts in Zhejiang and then Shanghai. His appointments as a member of the PBSC in 2007, PRC vice president in 2008, and CMC vice chair in 2010 signaled that he had been chosen as heir apparent to Hu Jintao, to take office as general secretary in fall 2012 and as head of state in spring 2013. In keeping with the ground rules of the CCP personnel system, Xi is a decade younger than Hu, so he is scheduled to succeed to the general secretary post at the age of fifty-nine.

During his anticipated two five-year terms in office, Xi will try to guide China to the rank of second or even first economy in the world; to the status of a middle-level economy on a per capita basis; to an approximate diplomatic parity with the U.S. as a major power in a multipolar world; and to a military position where China can deter or defeat intervention in any of the territories that China claims, including Taiwan, and play a role in protecting its economic interests overseas. Just as Hu Jintao had the right kind of personality to represent China in the 2000s during its low-keyed period of "peaceful rise," so Xi Jinping has been chosen to speak for a China that is expected to be increasingly powerful and assertive in the second decade of the twenty-first century.

PART II

SECURITY CHALLENGES AND STRATEGIES

3

LIFE ON THE HINGE

China's Russia Policy During the Cold War and After

China's foreign policy during the Cold War (conventionally dated 1946–1991) shifted dramatically more or less every decade. Upon coming to power, the new government's chairman, Mao Zedong, announced his decision to "lean to one side," allying China with the Soviet Union and isolating it from the West. Eleven years later, in 1960, however, Mao split with the Soviet Union, positioning China between the two superpowers as dual enemies. In 1972, by inviting Richard Nixon to China, he activated what came to be called the "strategic triangle," in which China was the swing player between the two superpowers. After another ten years, Mao's successor, Deng Xiaoping, announced in 1982 an "independent foreign policy of peace," under which China distanced itself from both superpowers without severing ties with either. In 1989, Deng "normalized" relations with Moscow, which led eventually to closer cooperation with post-Communist Russia, even while Beijing also intensified its ties with the West through globalization.

Such unstable alignments may seem to challenge our thesis that foreign policy is largely a response to geostrategic conditions. After all, factors such as geography and demography change slowly. If geostrategic realism makes sense, then policy should evolve slowly, too. In addition, China's leaders—especially Mao—articulated the rationale for China's policy shifts in strong ideological terms, which they doubtless believed. Yet the puzzle of frequent policy change can best be resolved by focusing on the shifting strategies of the two superpowers as they struggled to leverage China to their own advantage and China's responding efforts to preserve its autonomy. The intensity of superpower competition over China was in turn due to a permanent feature of China's situation that we noted in chapter 1: its hinge position between the Eurasian continent and the Pacific Ocean and thus, in the Cold War, between the camps of the East and the West.

Ever since the age of European expansion, China had lain on the strategic frontier, where global forces tried to control it but failed. From the seventeenth to the twentieth centuries, when European powers colonized much of the world, they established beachheads around the edges of China but did not conquer the vast hinterland. During World War II, Japan occupied parts of northern, eastern, and southern China, but only with difficulty and only for about six years. In the post–World War II era, the American informal empire in Asia reached its limit at the edge of China. After the defeat of the American-allied KMT in the Chinese civil war that followed World War II, Washington withdrew to a new Free World "defensive perimeter" that ran, as Secretary of State Dean Acheson famously said in a January 1950 speech, "along the Aleutians to Japan and then to the Ryukyus . . . [and] from the Ryukyus to the Philippine Islands"—in other words, a perimeter that excluded not only China, but also Korea and Taiwan.[1] Meanwhile, the Soviet Union under Stalin tried to extend its influence over China, but—as we detail in this chapter—was unable to turn China into a reliable ally. As in previous centuries, China remained independent even when it was weak.

Both Cold War superpowers presented potential threats to China, but of the two the Soviet Union was the closer and more demanding. Moscow needed Chinese cooperation to realize its strategic vision, whereas the Americans cared chiefly to deny the Chinese asset to the Soviets. The twists and turns of Chinese policy during the Cold War evolved as a series of attempts first to live within the embrace of the Soviet Union and then to fend it off, against the background of U.S. policies that were purposely designed to intensify those very conflicts between the communist powers. In this way, for three and a half decades the Soviet threat, first potential and then actual, was the pivot of Chinese foreign policy. By focusing on China's relations with the Soviet Union, we can review the history of PRC foreign policy from the beginning to the end of the Cold War.

When the Cold War ended and the Soviet Union collapsed, the U.S. rather than Russia became China's primary security threat. Chinese policymakers seized the opportunity to put Sino–Russian relations on a cooperative footing that they hoped would serve Chinese interests for a long time to come.

LEANING TO ONE SIDE, 1949–1958

Mao Zedong announced in June 1949, shortly before the Communist victory in the civil war, that China "must lean either to the side of imperialism or to the side of socialism. Sitting on the fence will not do, nor is there a third road."[2] As his forces moved south, they engaged in what he called "sweeping the courtyard before welcoming guests," carrying out a series of sometimes violent moves against Western diplomats and missionaries that made the point that new China would accept relations with the West only on equal terms. These incidents forced the U.S. State Department to abandon a plan it was considering to establish diplomatic relations with the PRC.[3] In February 1950, Beijing signed a Treaty of Friendship, Alliance, and Mutual Assistance with Moscow, and eight months later, in October 1950, China intervened in the Korean War, which led to direct combat between Chinese and U.S. military forces.

This series of events not only set U.S.–China antagonism in stone for the next two decades but left two legacies that are still unresolved today. President Harry S. Truman's interposition of the U.S. Seventh Fleet in the Taiwan Strait in response to the outbreak of the Korean War created a problem that would almost certainly otherwise not still exist more than half a century later—the "Taiwan issue" (chapters 4 and 8). Also still unresolved over six decades later is the peace in Korea. Although fighting ended with an armistice in 1953, a peace treaty has yet to be signed, and there is still no formal diplomatic recognition of North Korea by South Korea or the U.S. Protracted tensions and serial crises continue on the peninsula (chapter 5).

Historians have debated whether the U.S. lost a chance in the late 1940s to build a cooperative relationship with the PRC. Late in World War II and during the Chinese civil war, there was some fluidity in the CCP's orientation to foreign powers. Likewise, Washington was disillusioned with

Chiang Kai-shek on one side of the civil war, and Moscow was often disloyal to the CCP on the other. Washington sent the U.S. Army Observer Group (the Dixie Mission) to Yan'an, and Zhou Enlai sent some private probes to U.S. ambassador John Leighton Stuart, but these feelers did not change the basic facts. The CCP correctly viewed Washington as committed to anticommunism, and Washington correctly perceived the CCP as committed to socialism and antagonistic to Western privileges in China. It is difficult to imagine that under those conditions the two countries could have formed an alliance or even an alignment. At most, China might have put itself into a more equidistant relationship between the two powers, as it eventually did a little more than two decades later. Events instead led to a sharp polarization of relations between Beijing and Washington.

Mao's tilt to the Soviet Union had four motives. First was the need to consolidate his shaky regime. The new government had to extend its authority over large parts of China where it had had no presence before, including the Southeast and the South, the island of Hainan, and the vast inland frontier areas of Tibet and Xinjiang. KMT troops in the South were still resisting the Communist takeover. KMT forces based in Taiwan conducted air raids on the mainland and carried out a blockade of Shanghai. The Communist forces had to take over and run broken systems of civil administration, education, transportation, and finance, even as they made ready to carry out a social revolution. Rural areas were rife with bandits, landlord militias, and other groups hostile to the new regime. Most landlords, businesspeople, and intellectuals viewed the Communists with a combination of hope and suspicion. The CCP launched a series of violent, costly internal campaigns aimed at winning the support of sympathetic sectors and destroying opponents, including the land-reform campaign (1948–1953) to smash the power of the landlords and rich peasants and to win the support of the poor peasants; the "suppression of counterrevolutionaries" campaign (1950–1952) to crush enemies of the party; and the Three-Anti and Five-Anti campaigns of the early 1950s to discipline party cadres and capitalists, respectively, for corruption and cheating the state. The huge Anti-Rightist Campaign of the late 1950s severely punished at least half a million intellectuals, sending them to prison, internal exile, or menial jobs in their original units.

The Soviet Union provided the most obvious model and useful advice for dealing with such a wide range of domestic political challenges, all the more so as the CCP leaders had looked to Moscow for inspiration since the founding of their party in 1921. The PRC set up a Soviet-style governing structure that provided for overall control by the CCP (chapter 2). It patterned its constitution, adopted in 1954, on the 1936 Soviet Constitution adopted under Stalin. It learned from the Soviets how to set up a central party apparatus to run a government rather than a war; how to manage government ministries; how to create a system of courts, procurators, police, and jails; how to embed political security functions into factories, universities, offices, and other work units; how to set up Soviet-style mass organizations; and how to use the network of newspaper reporters around the country as a supplementary intelligence service. Even the mere fact of the Soviet alliance showed the party's domestic enemies that the regime had powerful international support. Soviet socialism appeared, however briefly, to be the key to the national salvation that Chinese had long sought.

A second reason to lean to one side was the need for defense against an American strategy of "containment and isolation" that had begun to take shape even before the end of the Chinese civil war. In Japan, the U.S. started as early as 1948 to reverse its original intent to disarm its former enemy. Now Washington aimed to rebuild Japan's military potential so it could serve as an ally in the emerging Cold War. The so-called reverse course included canceling reparations, negotiating a Mutual Defense Treaty, establishing U.S. bases on Japanese territory, and constructing a major American naval and air base on the island of Okinawa, which the U.S. kept under its direct control until the island's reversion to Japanese sovereignty in 1972. The complex of American bases remains on Okinawa to this day.

The U.S. ringed China with threats on every side. The CIA provided millions of dollars in covert support and military training for Tibetan guerrillas resisting the imposition of Chinese rule. The U.S. government conducted or assisted covert activities against China from Taiwan, Thailand, Burma, and Laos. After the Korean War ended, the U.S. created a web of treaty arrangements covering much of Asia, including the Southeast Asia Treaty Organization (SEATO), which joined the U.S., Thailand, the Philippines, Pakistan, Australia, New Zealand, France, and the United Kingdom; the Australia, New Zealand, United States (ANZUS) Alliance; and the Central Treaty Organization involving the U.S., the United Kingdom, Turkey, Iran, Iraq, and Pakistan. The U.S. established alliances and/

or military assistance programs bilaterally with many countries around China, including Thailand, South Vietnam, and the Philippines. In 1954, it also signed a Mutual Defense Treaty with Chiang Kai-shek's ROC government in Taipei.

To isolate the PRC diplomatically, the U.S. and most of its allies withheld recognition from it and treated the ROC in Taiwan as the legitimate government of all China. The key exceptions were Britain, which recognized China in 1950 because it needed diplomatic ties with Beijing in order to manage its colony in Hong Kong, and France, which switched diplomatic recognition from the ROC to the PRC in 1964 as part of its pursuit of an independent foreign policy under Charles de Gaulle.[4] With Western support, the ROC continued to occupy the China seat in the UN. U.S. secretary of state John Foster Dulles said that he expected the Communist government in China to fall and that Washington should encourage this demise through "peaceful evolution." Mao took such comments seriously.[5]

Twice the U.S. publicly threatened the use of nuclear weapons against China. During the 1952 presidential campaign and in early 1953, President Dwight D. Eisenhower said he would use tactical nuclear weapons if necessary to end the war in Korea. Washington again threatened to use nuclear weapons in 1954 to end the first Taiwan Strait crisis. In 1957, the U.S. deployed Matador surface-to-surface tactical nuclear missiles in Taiwan.

China's mutual defense pact with Moscow anticipated such threats. It called for the Soviet Union to provide "military and other assistance" to China should it be attacked by Japan "or any state allied with her." Because Japan was under American occupation, lacking foreign policy or defense autonomy, there could be no mistaking that the U.S. was the ultimate target of the pledge.

Third, the Soviet alliance helped China economically. The new regime had to repair an economy devastated by years of invasion and civil war. But its ambitions were larger. It aimed to modernize the backward, predominantly agrarian economy, to build the industrial basis for a powerful military, and to provide the people with a prosperous socialist way of life—all at high speed. The Chinese Communists believed that Stalin had shown the way to carry out just such a process of forced development: he had used coercion and state planning to squeeze capital out of a backward peasantry, to mobilize a vast labor force, and to direct investment into national needs.

In this way, he had created a world-class heavy industrial sector in the space of a generation, catapulting the Soviet Union to the status of a world power with advanced weaponry, including nuclear weapons.

To the Chinese Communists—and to many non-Communist intellectuals in China and the West in the 1940s and 1950s—the Soviet experience seemed to prove that socialist planning, not capitalism, was the royal road to escape from backwardness.[6] Just as in Russia, the Communist leaders in China believed that a big agricultural surplus was being wasted in luxury consumption by landlords and rich peasants, which the state could seize by collectivizing agriculture. At the same time, the reorganization of inefficient small-scale agricultural production would promote a surge in output. Mao therefore moved to collectivize agriculture, and he set up Soviet-style economic-planning agencies and industrial ministries to invest the anticipated surplus in new industries.

Meanwhile, the West had imposed an economic embargo as part of the policy of containment and isolation.[7] Even though the Soviet Union could afford only limited help because of the damage done to its own economy in World War II, it provided key loans and technical assistance. During Mao's 1950 visit to Moscow to arrange for the Mutual Defense Treaty, Stalin agreed to China's request for a five-year $300 million loan. The loan would be instrumental in building fifty key industrial and infrastructural projects devoted to the recovery and modernization of Chinese heavy industry, defense industry, and energy production. Later agreements brought the total number of Soviet-aided projects to 156 and the total value of Soviet loans to $430 million. Although by today's standards the amount of the loans may appear ungenerous—and the Soviets did not supply any grants-in-aid—these loans were crucial to the success of China's First Five-Year Plan (1953–1957), which laid the basis for the country's industrial economy. Equally important, the Soviets sent some ten thousand planners and technicians to help set up the Chinese bureaucracy and design the projects.[8]

The fourth reason for the PRC's decision to ally with the Soviet Union was the need to be on good terms with a potentially threatening neighbor. Russia had a long history of involving itself in Chinese affairs and a leader, Josef Stalin, known for his ruthlessness. In the 1920s, Moscow had assisted the Nationalist revolution while also guiding the formation of the rival CCP. In the late 1930s, the USSR was a major outside supplier for

Nationalist China in the war against Japan, sending weapons, military supplies, and "volunteer" pilots to China. At the same time, Stalin meddled frequently in CCP affairs, sending instructions, at times supporting Mao's rivals, and maintaining a "Bolshevik faction" in the CCP to report on and pressure Mao. At the end of World War II, when the Nationalist government seemed likely to survive, Stalin gave only weak help to the CCP in its struggle with the KMT.[9]

But once the Communists came to power, Stalin sought maximum influence in Beijing. Secret protocols to the Mutual Defense Treaty granted Moscow the right to transport troops over a railway it had formerly controlled on Chinese territory and to ship military equipment to a Chinese port it had formerly controlled, Lüshun, without having to notify Chinese authorities. The protocols also prohibited China from allowing any non-Soviet foreign business activity in Xinjiang and the three northeastern provinces. Stalin encouraged Mao to enter the Korean War but delayed in fulfilling his promise to provide Soviet planes and pilots until he was confident the U.S. would not retaliate against the USSR. He sent weapons and equipment to Chinese forces in Korea but required China to pay for nearly everything it received. Throughout these events, Mao remained anxious to demonstrate his loyalty to Stalin. He even invited the master to send an ideological expert to review his selected writings for any lapses before their publication, an inspection they fortunately passed.[10]

The armistice in Korea ushered in a short period of optimism for PRC leaders. China had bloodied the Americans, many of the regime's domestic enemies had been cowed or killed, and the industrial economy was growing at a rate of 18 percent a year. On balance, the Soviet alliance seemed to have been a good decision.

THE SINO–SOVIET SPLIT, 1958–1960

Yet by the end of the 1950s, Mao broke with Moscow. He did so because each of the four motives that had caused him to align with the Soviet Union turned in the opposite direction.

First, Mao began to see the Soviet relationship as a threat rather than a benefit to internal security. Stalin died in 1953. In 1956, his successor,

Nikita Khrushchev, gave a secret speech to the Twentieth Soviet Party Congress exposing Stalin's crimes and denouncing his cult of personality. Khrushchev's apostasy indirectly called into question the legitimacy of Mao's policies because the latter were modeled in so many respects on Stalin's. And his speech undermined Mao's authority because Mao was just in the process of establishing his own cult of personality as a way of consolidating his control of the CCP and the party's control of China. Khrushchev had not told even his own comrades, much less foreign Communist leaders, what he was going to say. His failure to consult Beijing led Mao to conclude that Khrushchev would not take the interests of his Chinese colleagues into account in his future decisions. Also, with the influx of Soviet advisers to China and the frequent visits by top Chinese to Moscow, Mao feared the buildup of a pro-Soviet faction within the CCP and the government. In 1954, he purged two high-ranking colleagues, Gao Gang and Rao Shushi, accusing them of being Soviet agents. In 1959, he purged Marshal Peng Dehuai for speaking in opposition to the Great Leap Forward and for being too close to Moscow.

Second, toward the mid-1950s, Soviet priorities on relations toward the U.S. began to diverge from China's. Khrushchev introduced the doctrines of "peaceful coexistence" between the socialist and capitalist worlds and "peaceful transition" from capitalism to socialism. He hoped that by slowing the arms race and forswearing violent revolution, he could buy time for the socialist camp to settle its internal differences, stabilize its regimes and borders, and catch up with the West in economic and military strength. This objective became even more urgent following upheavals in the satellite states of Poland and Hungary in 1956. Washington responded favorably to Moscow's interest in détente but kept up the pressure on China in hopes of driving a "wedge" between the two allies.[11]

In 1957, after the Soviets launched a space satellite ahead of the U.S., Mao proclaimed that the "east wind prevails over the west wind," meaning that the Communist bloc was now stronger than the Western bloc and should be able to roll back U.S. global influence. At conferences of the international socialist camp, China urged the Soviet Union to behave more forcefully.[12] Yet in 1959, to Mao's displeasure, Khrushchev visited the U.S. presidential retreat at Camp David, seeking to reduce tensions with President Eisenhower. Soviet policy on the interlinked issues of nuclear cooperation and Taiwan further estranged the two capitals. In 1957, Moscow had promised to assist China in developing nuclear weapons by providing a sample bomb and missiles as well as technical information.[13] The idea was that possession of these weapons would enable China to resist American nuclear blackmail, thus reducing the need for direct Soviet involvement in any future Sino–American crises. But within a year Moscow began to worry that sharing nuclear technology with China would cripple its negotiations with the U.S. on a limited test ban treaty, so it started to drag its heels in fulfilling its promises. In 1958, Mao launched the second Taiwan Strait crisis by ordering artillery barrages against two offshore islands held by the ROC without first informing Moscow, even though Khrushchev had just been visiting Beijing. Moscow verbally supported China's claim to Taiwan but feared that Chinese "adventurism" might drag the Soviet Union into war with the U.S. Khrushchev kept silent on the Taiwan crisis until it was over and soon formally canceled the nuclear agreement. When Khrushchev and President John F. Kennedy signed the Limited Nuclear Test Ban Treaty in 1963, China charged that the two superpowers were colluding to deny nonnuclear states the means to defend their national sovereignty. Also at this time, Khrushchev withheld support in China's brewing border conflict with India, with which Moscow was developing a cooperative military and diplomatic relationship. When the border dispute led to the Sino–Indian war in 1962, Moscow verbally sided with India, the first time a Communist state had broken ranks with an ally in a war.

Third, the Chinese developed misgivings about the Soviet economic model. Despite agricultural collectivization, by the mid-1950s the proceeds from forced grain sales and the grain tax fell short of what the leaders had expected. They were also displeased with the bottlenecks in transport, energy, and construction materials that emerged as a consequence of rapid industrialization and with the inability of the Soviet-style planning apparatus to overcome these bottlenecks. Mao pushed the formation of a new kind of more regimented and larger rural collective ("people's communes") that he thought would spur production and improve the government's ability to get control over rural output. And he pushed factory managers to produce beyond plan quotas by any means possible, even if doing so caused "imbalances" that upset the planners. As an additional benefit, Mao's new development strategy did away with the influence of the managers and technicians with pro-Soviet sentiments. The Soviet advisers cautioned against Mao's experiments, partially out of self-interest because the communes made it look as if China was "entering communism" before the Soviet elder brother. But he forged ahead, launching the Great Leap Forward, a breakthrough development push that through a set of mistakes eventually caused an estimated 45 million deaths from hunger.[14]

Fourth, Mao perceived Khrushchev's policies as more directly threatening to Chinese security than Stalin's. In 1958, Khrushchev proposed to build long-range radio facilities on Chinese soil to enable Moscow to communicate with its Pacific Fleet. Moscow later suggested basing what it called a "joint" flotilla of nuclear-powered submarines in China, even though China had no submarines. Such arrangements were not unusual in the context of a military alliance, but Mao interpreted them as proposals to establish Soviet bases on Chinese territory. Meeting with Soviet ambassador Pavel Yudin, he railed, "Yesterday you made me so enraged that I could not sleep at all last night. . . . [We] will not satisfy you at all, not even give you a tiny [piece of our] finger."[15] When Khrushchev visited Beijing later that year, Mao accused him of encroaching on Chinese sovereignty and seeking to "take away all our coastal areas." He warned the Soviet leader, "We have already driven away the British, Japanese, and other foreigners who stayed on our soil for a long time. Comrade Khrushchev, I'll repeat it for the last time. We will never again allow anyone to use our land to achieve their own purposes."[16]

For all these reasons, Mao feuded with Khrushchev both in private meetings and in a variety of coded public statements and communiqués. In 1960, the Sino–Soviet split went public. Without warning, Khrushchev withdrew the Soviet advisers from China. Chinese media published denunciations of what they called "modern revisionists," clearly referring to Khrushchev. Starting in 1963, Mao issued a long series of polemics that excoriated Moscow's supposed betrayal of socialism, assailed the Soviet Union's credentials as the leader of the socialist bloc, and mocked Khrushchev's standing as a Marxist–Leninist. He positioned himself as the senior interpreter of Marxism–Leninism in the socialist camp and the defender of orthodoxy against Stalin's revisionist successors. The Chinese labeled the Soviet Union's attempt to dominate its alliance partners as "hegemonism" and devised the insulting concept of "social imperialism" to describe Moscow's efforts to gain influence in other countries. Mao's critique of the Soviet model became the ideological basis for the Cultural Revolution, which attacked a "capitalist class within the party" and promoted "uninterrupted revolution." The split made China the enemy of both superpowers at once.

DUAL ADVERSARIES AND
MORTAL THREATS, 1960–1971

Although China was able to stand up to Washington and Moscow at the same time, it did so at a price. While U.S. threats continued, Soviet threats grew. A new leader, Leonid Brezhnev, took power from Khrushchev in a coup in 1964. He mounted a massive military buildup to deter China from acting against Soviet interests.

In Soviet eyes, a hostile China presented a many-faceted threat. First, China disputed Moscow's leadership throughout the socialist camp. Beijing kept close ties with fractious satellites Romania and Albania. Beijing made it hard for the Soviets to ship aid and equipment through China by rail to assist North Vietnam's war effort against South Vietnam and the U.S. North Korea was able to play Beijing against Moscow to drive up the price of its allegiance. In the Angolan civil war, Beijing provided military assistance to Jonas Savimbi's anti-Soviet/pro-U.S. National Union for the Total Independence of Angola, despite the fact that the Soviet-supported Popular Movement for the Liberation of Angola was the sole Marxist–Leninist faction there. In Rhodesia (later Zimbabwe), China supported the Zimbabwe African National Union against the Soviet-supported Zimbabwe African People's Union. In South-West Africa (later Namibia), China supported the South-West African National Union, whereas the USSR supported the South-West African People's Organization. The Chinese also competed with the Soviets for influence in Tanzania, Zambia, Zaire, Ethiopia, and Mozambique. In Latin America, Mao broke relations with Soviet-dependent Cuba, competed with the USSR for influence among local Communist parties, and sided with Latin American governments in diplomatic positions against both the Soviet Union and the U.S. Everywhere China was active, it complicated Moscow's main struggle, which was against the U.S.

Second, Soviet security planners saw Russia's expansive, thinly populated Soviet Far Eastern region as an exposed target for Chinese encroachment. A pretext for attack existed so long as China disputed long stretches of the existing borders, denouncing as unfair the "unequal treaties" under which imperial China had ceded hundreds of thousands of square miles of territory to Russia. Third, China's defection made it more expensive for the Soviets to balance the U.S. military position in Asia. Moscow spent enormous sums building its Pacific Fleet based in Vladivostok into its largest fleet, designed to put pressure on the U.S. and its ally Japan, without the benefit of access to Chinese ports. Fourth, in 1964 China joined the club of nuclear states with a successful test explosion, having continued its nuclear weapons program on its own after the withdrawal of Soviet support. Moscow feared that these new arms would increase the Chinese willingness to confront the Soviet Union. Fifth and most nightmarish—although at the time seeming unlikely—was the thought of Beijing's cooperating in any way with Washington.

Brezhnev increased the forces deployed in the Soviet Far East and Siberia from about twelve divisions in the early 1960s to more than fifty in the mid-1980s, mostly positioned directly on the Chinese border, some in the Mongolian People's Republic next to China. The number of Soviet combat aircraft in the theater rose from about two hundred to some twelve hundred between the early 1960s and the mid-1970s. In addition, approximately fifty older SS-4 medium-range ballistic missiles and SS-5 intermediate-range ballistic missiles in the region were replaced by more than double the number of newer SS-11 variable-range ballistic missiles during the same period.[17]

The Soviet forces possessed several options. On the high end, they could launch a nuclear strike or a general ground invasion. More plausible scenarios were a limited nuclear strike on China's nuclear weapons base in Xinjiang and selected industrial sites[18] or a limited ground attack into industrial northeastern China employing tactical nuclear weapons, which were favored in Soviet military doctrine. China's military had no defense against such threats except a "people's war" (chapter 11).

Chinese anxiety concerning Soviet intentions reached a peak after Soviet-led Warsaw Pact armies invaded Czechoslovakia in August 1968 to terminate the Prague Spring—an attempt to liberalize communism. Enunciating what came to be known as the "Brezhnev Doctrine," the Soviet leader asserted Moscow's right to intervene in any socialist state by force of arms to defend socialism against counterrevolution. Counterrevolution was exactly what Russian polemics for years had been accusing the Chinese of conducting.

Although poised, the Soviet forces did not strike China on a large scale. There were frequent border clashes in many locations. In Xinjiang, the Soviets encouraged ethnic unrest and probed the possibility of carving a breakaway buffer state out of Chinese territory, as they had attempted to do in the 1940s. A sizable battle broke out on the eastern part of the contested border in March 1969. The most widely accepted explanation is that Beijing decided to occupy a Soviet-claimed island in the Ussuri River (the Damansky in Russian, the Zhenbao in Chinese) to signal its resolve in the face of Soviet provocations.[19] Soviet troops ousted the Chinese, inflicting eight hundred casualties; attacked Chinese troops elsewhere along the border, including in Xinjiang; and threatened nuclear attack. The Chinese blinked by inviting Soviet premier Alexei Kosygin to talks in Beijing to defuse the crisis.

Soviet deployments on the border were complemented by the diplomatic and military encirclement of China, undertaken as part of Moscow's drive to increase its global influence. The Soviet Pacific Fleet grew to more than eighty principal surface combatants, including two aircraft carriers. It also included 120 submarines, 32 of them nuclear-powered ballistic missile submarines.[20] It established a strong presence in the Sea of Okhotsk, the Sea of Japan, the South China Sea, the Strait of Malacca, and the Indian Ocean. To China's east, Moscow increased military aid to win North Korea's loyalty. To the south, Moscow tightened its relationship with North Vietnam, using military assistance to bring Hanoi to its side in the Sino–Soviet conflict. It also signed a Treaty of Peace, Friendship, and Cooperation with India in 1971. Moscow's open military pipeline to New Delhi fueled the modernization of the Indian armed forces, reducing China's advantage along the contested border and sharpening Chinese anxieties about the security of Tibet, whose exiled ruler, the Dalai Lama, had taken refuge on Indian soil in 1959 (chapter 6). Later that year the Soviet-armed Indian army assisted the breakaway rebellion of Pakistan's eastern province, which established the new nation of Bangladesh, thus weakening one of China's few allies.

Meanwhile, the Americans remained firm in their policies of recognizing the ROC as the government of China and isolating the PRC. During

1963 negotiations with Moscow over the Limited Test Ban Treaty, Kennedy tried to interest Khrushchev in allowing U.S. military action to prevent the nearly-completed development of the Chinese nuclear weapon, but Khrushchev did not agree.[21] In 1964, in anticipation of the Chinese nuclear bomb test, U.S. policymakers under Lyndon Johnson again considered bombing the Chinese test site. According to U.S. government documents declassified in 1998, CIA support to Tibetan exiles continued until 1972. The escalation of the U.S. military presence in Indochina posed an additional threat, with the possibility that the Americans would bomb or attack North Vietnam's so-called sanctuaries in China.

China had no outside support. Beijing's search for sympathizers took on an insurgent quality. Under the slogan "We have friends all over the world," the PRC engaged in a mixture of people-to-people diplomacy, state visits for leaders of international Maoist splinter groups, and relations with odd-lot Third World dictators. The CCP's International Liaison Department served as a second foreign ministry, managing relations with non-Soviet-aligned Communist parties in the Third World. Overall, China's foreign policy in these years had an air of boastful self-confidence that others read as expansionist and aggressive, but that in reality masked weakness and isolation.

RAPPROCHEMENT AND THE STRATEGIC TRIANGLE, 1972–1982

In 1969, Mao ordered four retired marshals to analyze the changing global situation. Their report concluded that the Soviet Union now posed a greater threat than the U.S.: Moscow was bent on war with China. Although the senior military men seem to have told Mao what he wanted to hear, their ostensibly independent study helped justify his decision to authorize contacts with the U.S. Officials in the Kennedy and Johnson administrations had been thinking for some time about how to harvest the benefits of the Sino–Soviet split but had been unable to justify a thaw with China while the U.S. was escalating the war in Vietnam to fight the spread of communism.[22] Now, however, under President Richard M. Nixon, the U.S. was looking for a way out of Vietnam. Moreover, Washington evaluated the Soviet military threat as increasingly serious under Brezhnev. After several years of mutual signaling, testing, and secret talks, Nixon made his dramatic visit to China in February 1972, declaring, "This was the week that changed the world."

Nixon's meetings with Mao and Zhou initiated the period of what Western strategists called the "strategic triangle." The triangle was remarkable in two ways. First, it allowed a country that was poor, isolated, and unable to project military power beyond its borders—China—to become the third most important strategic actor in the world, playing a larger role than England, France, Germany, India, Japan, or any state other than the two superpowers. Only China had the strategic location and diplomatic flexibility to make itself consequential as a swing player. Second, this weakest of the three countries reaped the most benefits from tripolar diplomacy because it was the asset in play in the three-way game.[23] These benefits fell into three categories.

First, the triangle made China safe for the first time from both U.S. and Soviet attack. A series of developments eliminated any U.S. military threat to China. The transformation of China in American public opinion from a Red menace to a fascinating quasi-ally made it politically possible for Nixon to negotiate a face-saving withdrawal from the war in Vietnam. Beijing gave an assist by pressing Hanoi to accept the terms of the 1973 Paris Peace Accords, which temporarily stopped the fighting. Regarding Taiwan, Nixon assured Mao that the U.S. would no longer promote independence or consider using the island as a base to attack China. The main U.S. military ally in Asia, Japan, moved quickly to establish diplomatic relations with China.

The Soviets responded at first by intensifying their military buildup around China. In 1978, a unified Vietnam entered a formal alliance with the Soviet Union and then invaded Cambodia, extending Moscow's influence throughout Indochina. Soviet access to bases at Cam Ranh Bay and Danang enhanced Moscow's ability to project naval and air power into the Indian Ocean and the South China Sea. China mocked Hanoi's role as Moscow's junior partner, referring to Vietnam as a "small hegemonist." China attempted to push back by aiding the Khmer Rouge. Then in 1979 Soviet forces invaded Afghanistan, a country sharing a short border with China and a long border with China's ally Pakistan.

But China's new tie with the U.S. became an effective deterrent to Soviet attack on China itself. The U.S. pullout from Vietnam freed resources to build up American and western European military assets that increased pressure on the Soviet Union. According to Secretary of State Henry Kissinger's memoirs, when Brezhnev probed in 1973 to see how the U.S. would react to a Soviet attack on China, Kissinger replied that Washington would view such an attack as damaging to American interests.[24] When China attacked Soviet ally Vietnam in 1979, the U.S. again sent messages to Moscow to deter any Soviet military action against China.[25]

Second, the opening to the U.S. allowed China to move from diplomatic isolation into the diplomatic mainstream. As soon as Nixon's plan to visit China was announced, the UN General Assembly voted to take the China seat in the UN away from the ROC and give it to the PRC. Over the next few years, country after country switched diplomatic recognition from Taipei to Beijing. The PRC replaced the ROC in a host of intergovernmental organizations ranging from the WHO to the Asian Development Bank, leaving Taiwan to scramble for other ways to participate in global affairs (chapter 9).

China could now begin to counterencircle Russia, seeking good relations with Soviet neighbors stretching from Japan through Iran to eastern and western Europe. China tacitly backed the U.S.–Japan security alliance while siding with Japan in its territorial dispute with Moscow over the Kuril Islands. China courted Germany's Franz Josef Strauss, who warned about the danger of Soviet expansionism, and found fault with East Germany, one of Moscow's staunchest allies. Beijing cheered efforts to strengthen the North Atlantic Treaty Organization (NATO), casting Europe's pacifist Left as dupes influenced by the Kremlin's propaganda. Seeking to exploit dissatisfaction with Moscow after the invasion of Czechoslovakia, China mended relations with Yugoslavia, whose leader, Marshal Josip Broz Tito, it had earlier reviled in the crudest terms.

Third, rapprochement opened the way for a breakout from economic isolation. China's improved security situation allowed Premier Zhou Enlai to announce that military modernization was the last of four modernization priorities after industry, agriculture, and science and technology, and the end of hostility with the West meant that Western markets and capital were no longer off limits. Zhou's vice premier Deng Xiaoping guided the first small steps in the economic opening to the West, thus establishing a precedent and some initial expertise for what became the full-scale embrace of globalization after Mao's death.

Although the strategic triangle improved China's external security, it did so at the expense of internal security. Mao's chosen successor, Lin Biao, appears to have disagreed with the opening to the U.S.; he ended up dead after an obscure power struggle that the regime described as a coup attempt against Mao. Mao's wife and three other senior officials— a group later known as the Gang of Four—mounted crippling political attacks on Zhou Enlai and Deng Xiaoping in the last years of Mao's life. Many ordinary Chinese were puzzled by even the limited information they were given about Nixon's visit and the fall of Lin Biao. These events were inconsistent with the myth of Mao's revolutionary infallibility. They triggered the beginning of a popular loss of faith in Maoism, a change that eventually made it not only possible but necessary for Mao's successors to abandon his ideas of self-reliance, class struggle, and uninterrupted revolution and to do whatever it took to bring China into the modern world. A limited opening to the West for purposes of strategic power balancing thus created the conditions for far-reaching reforms that led to the abandonment of everything Mao stood for.

NORMALIZATION WITH MOSCOW, 1982–1989

As the loser in the strategic triangle, the Soviet Union naturally sought to rebalance it. The Soviet leaders saw Mao as a mentally unbalanced "ultra-left revisionist" and believed that his death would bring China back to the path of sanity. When Mao died in 1976, Brezhnev announced that Moscow would like to improve relations with Beijing, but the post-Mao leadership was in flux and gave no response. Shortly after Ronald Reagan took office in the U.S. and began a military buildup that increased pressure on the already overextended Soviet Union, Brezhnev reached out to China again in a 1982 speech in the Central Asian city of Tashkent, offering to hold talks on a basis of mutual respect to seek normalization of relationships between the two Communist parties. (State-to-state relations had not been formally broken.)

China took advantage of this opening to pressure the new U.S. administration to distance itself further from Taiwan. It announced what it called "an independent foreign policy of peace," signaling a move toward equidistance between Washington and Moscow, which helped persuade the U.S. to sign the 1982 Shanghai Communiqué, pledging a gradual reduction of arms sales to Taiwan in quantity and no increase in quality (chapter 4).

Toward Moscow, China responded cautiously. Deng demanded that the Soviet Union overcome what he called "three obstacles" before the two parties could normalize relations: the occupation of Afghanistan, troop deployments along the Sino–Soviet border and in Mongolia, and support for Vietnam's occupation of Cambodia. Each of these demands had a strategic rationale in terms of Chinese security, but at the same time each involved an important Soviet security commitment that appeared difficult to negotiate. By setting the bar so high, Beijing showed that it did not trust the Soviet Union and at the same time reassured Washington that it was in no hurry to come to terms with Moscow. Yet shifts in Soviet global strategy under Brezhnev's successor Mikhail Gorbachev, who came to power in 1985, produced progress on the three obstacles sooner than anyone expected.

Soviet troops had invaded Afghanistan in 1979 to prevent the collapse of Moscow's client regime there. Afghanistan's strategic significance to China derived less from its short shared border with Xinjiang Province than from its long borders with Pakistan and Iran, two states China valued as bulwarks against Soviet expansion. China believed that Moscow's move into Afghanistan was part of the historic Russian push toward the South, foreshadowing increased pressure on Islamabad and Tehran to acquiesce in the expansion of Soviet influence. China also wanted to demonstrate its reliability as an ally to Pakistan and maintain solidarity with Washington at a time when the U.S. was pressing Moscow to withdraw SS-20 nuclear missiles from the border with China. Moscow had a great deal at stake in Afghanistan, yet it found itself losing the war there — in part because of U.S. and Chinese military aid to the Afghan resistance — and it made the hard decision to withdraw by 1989. The Afghanistan obstacle to Sino–Soviet normalization was thus eliminated.

Soviet troop deployments along the Sino–Soviet border and in Mongolia came under reconsideration as part of the "new thinking" that Gorbachev introduced into Soviet foreign policy to rectify what he viewed as the over-extension of Soviet military commitments. In July 1986, he announced a plan to reduce troop levels in Soviet Asia. The following year he withdrew a division of troops from Mongolia and began to remove SS-20 intermediate-range missiles from the Sino–Soviet border in accordance with a new treaty with the U.S. on the reduction of intermediate-range nuclear forces. In 1988, he further reduced the Soviet military presence along the border, and Beijing reciprocated with troop reductions of its own. The two countries also made progress on settling previously intractable border issues. By 1987, Moscow and Beijing had reached a preliminary agreement on the eastern part of the border. A number of border crossings reopened, and cross-border barter trade increased rapidly. In these ways, the second obstacle was surmounted.

Soviet support for Vietnam's occupation of Cambodia turned out to be the most difficult of the three problems. Hanoi's easy victory in January 1979 over China's Cambodian client Pol Pot infuriated the Chinese. They were then disappointed a month later when the PLA's limited incursion into northern Vietnam did not force Vietnam to yield to China's demands. Moscow's economic support and security guarantee enabled Vietnam to hang on in Cambodia over the next decade: hence, China's insistence that Moscow squeeze the Vietnamese. Yet Vietnam was a sinkhole for Soviet aid, and Gorbachev was trying to liquidate his predecessors' bad overseas investments. Moreover, the Soviets wanted to improve relations with China in order to reduce defense expenditures. The Soviets opened direct negotiations with China over the war in Cambodia and leaned on Vietnam to withdraw. Hanoi was forced to comply. Beijing's perseverance thus helped to remove the last obstacle to Sino–Soviet normalization.

The Sino–Soviet rapprochement culminated with a summit between Gorbachev and Deng in Beijing in May 1989. The leaders pledged to settle all future disputes peacefully. Unfortunately for Deng, the summit coincided with the student pro-democracy movement in Beijing and other cities that led to the crackdown on June 4 known as the "Tiananmen incident." The Chinese leaders were embarrassed to lose control of their own capital just as Gorbachev was visiting, but their regime survived. Tiananmen turned out to be the first in a series of upheavals throughout the Communist world that culminated in the fall of communism in Eastern Europe in 1989 and the dissolution of the Soviet Union in 1991.

INSTITUTIONALIZING COOPERATION AFTER 1991

The collapse of the Soviet Union transformed China's strategic environment again and not entirely for the better. The strategic triangle gave way to a unipolar world in which a triumphal America acted more assertively than ever. Among other measures that affected Chinese interests directly or indirectly, the U.S. invaded Iraq in 1991; intervened in the breakup of Yugoslavia; expanded the NATO alliance to former Soviet bloc countries in the eastern part of Europe and the Baltics; advanced cooperative ties with Mongolia, Vietnam, and India; intensified military coordination with Japan; placed sanctions on Chinese friends North Korea and Iran; and sent aircraft carriers to deter Chinese military action against what Beijing perceived as increasing separatist policies in Taiwan. As for the once-menacing Soviet Union, it was replaced by a dangerously weak Russia that could no longer balance the U.S. and that Chinese strategists feared might behave erratically as well as by five fragile new Central Asian states, three of them directly on China's borders. We discuss China's relations with the Central Asian states in chapter 6.

China might have taken advantage of Russia's weakness as the U.S. did. It instead sought to institutionalize cooperation on the basis of mutual interest so that Russia would be in the habit of cooperating with China when it recovered its strength in the future. Even in its weakened condition, Russia remained a significant power because of its vast territory, strategic location, natural resources, and advanced technology, including nuclear and space technology. Chinese policymakers believed these assets would bring about a resurgence of Russian power sooner or later. By building a relationship that served Russian as well as Chinese interests, Beijing hoped to create a lasting framework based on mutual attentiveness to one another's security interests.

Beijing promptly gave recognition to all the post-Soviet successor states, despite the fact that the Chinese leaders considered as tragically mistaken the policies of Gorbachev and his successor, Boris Yeltsin, that had led to the emergence of these states.[26] They set aside their personal disdain for the undisciplined Yeltsin and ignored his unwelcome promotion of democracy in Russia in order to hold a series of seven summits with him during his eight years in office. In the March 1996 "Beijing Declaration," the two sides announced a "strategic partnership." Starting under Yeltsin's successor Vladimir Putin in 2000, Sino–Russian summits became annual events. In July 2001, Jiang Zemin and Putin signed a Treaty of Good-Neighborliness and Friendly Cooperation. Although not a mutual defense pact like the two countries' 1950 accord, the treaty pledged cooperation in many fields of bilateral activity and laid down a common stance against American unilateralism, conveying the point with euphemisms such as "maintenance of global strategic balance" and "strict observation of universally acknowledged principles and norms of international laws." China supported Russia in opposing NATO expansion and in rejecting Western condemnation of Russian human rights abuses in Chechnya.

Instead of trying to replace Russia as the dominant outside power in Central Asia, China hosted in 1996 the first of a series of annual summits that included Russia and the three Central Asian states contiguous to China—Kazakhstan, Kyrgyzstan, and Tajikistan. The five addressed China's primary security concern in the region by agreeing to oppose what they called the "three evils of terrorism, separatism, and extremism" (the last referring to Islamic fundamentalism). This agreement assured Beijing that the neighboring states would not allow the region to be used as a base for Uyghur resistance to Chinese rule in Xinjiang. The states signed a series of agreements to demilitarize their borders by pulling troops back one hundred kilometers from the boundaries with China. They agreed not to target each other with missiles, to increase transparency in defense matters, and to give advance notice of military exercises. They set up military-to-military exchanges as well as bilateral and multilateral military exercises, including some antiterrorism exercises. In 2001, the five states, joined by Uzbekistan, formed the SCO. This framework assured China that it would not be excluded from Central Asia as Russian power recovered.

In the UN, China and Russia—sometimes along with France—cooperated to check the American impulse to intervene in trouble spots around the world. In 1999, they blocked Security Council approval for a military intervention in Kosovo, which therefore had to be carried out as a NATO instead of a UN operation. Both worked for an early lifting of UN sanctions on Iraq. They made it impossible to get a Security Council authorization for an invasion of Iraq in 2002, which then went ahead as what the U.S. called a "coalition of the willing." The two blocked harsh sanctions on Sudan, Iran, and North Korea. These diplomatic efforts substantially delayed, limited, or in some cases prevented actions the U.S. wanted to take.

Beijing and Moscow settled their long-running border disputes. Talks had begun in 1986 and achieved a major breakthrough in 1989 but were not completed until 2004. The negotiations and demarcations involved mutual concessions of land on both sides, some of which upset nationalists in the Russian Far East.

Trade soared in two areas: arms and oil. As China upgraded its military equipment in a big way starting in the 1990s, it needed to import high-end weaponry that it could not yet manufacture itself. Russia was the only country with the necessary level of technology that did not participate in the G7's post-Tiananmen arms embargo against China. (As of 2012, the ban on high-technology arms sales to China by G7 countries was still in place.) Russia emerged as China's main arms supplier, and China as Russia's main arms buyer, based on transactions involving advanced fighter planes, submarines, and destroyers. Between 1990 and 2007, Russia sold approximately \$15.8 billion in arms to China.[27] As Chinese defense industries became more advanced, however, Russian arms sales to China declined.

A second natural complementarity existed in the area of oil. At the same time that China shifted in the early 1990s from oil self-sufficiency to being a net oil importer, Russia's oil and gas exports grew to become the world's largest. China naturally turned to Russia for supplies. Oil imports from Russia climbed to 20 million tons in 2010. Yet Russia continued to rank behind Saudi Arabia, Angola, and Iran as an energy supplier to China for a mixture of reasons, among them price disputes, the unreliability of Russian supply, Japanese competition for Russian supplies, and lagging construction of a pipeline to supply natural gas.[28]

There are other complementarities between the two economies: China can offer consumer goods and labor, and Russia can offer heavy industrial goods and raw materials. But trade and investment have been inhibited by poor transport, the sparseness of the population in the Russian Far East, the weakness of the Russian consumer economy, and the limitations of Russian and Chinese financial institutions. As a result, cross-border trade has remained largely local, and except for pipelines there has been no large-scale investment from either side in the other. The two governments tried to make up for the weakness of natural ties with government-to-government barter trade. In 2009, China–Russian two-way trade amounted to $38.8 billion. Trade was one sided, with Russia having a $13.6 billion deficit with China. Whereas China was Russia's top trading partner, Russia ranked only ninth in China's list of trade partners.

Growing numbers of Chinese found work in the Russian Far East. Fewer than 7 million people inhabit the Russian Far East compared with more than 100 million in the three contiguous Chinese provinces. Because of the population imbalance, local Russian authorities fear a Chinese influx that might be tantamount to colonization. However, these concerns are overblown. As of 2003, there were only about two hundred thousand Chinese residents and a similar number of short-term Chinese workers and students in the Russian Far East.

Cooperation between the two countries remained robust as the Russian economy recovered and Russia became more assertive internationally under Vladimir Putin's leadership, first as president and then from 2008 on as premier, with his former subordinate Dmitry Medvedev serving as president. But the relationship has its limits. Two such huge states with a long common border and many neighbors in common inevitably remain sensitive to the possible damage each can wreak on the other's security. Such suspicions are validated by history and reinforced by differences in political systems and culture. The two countries continuously jockey for influence in Central Asia, the Korean Peninsula, and elsewhere. Except for arms sales and coproduction of weaponry, military cooperation is limited. Energy sales are fraught with controversies and disappointment on both sides. The economic and cultural interactions between the two societies remain too thin to create a sense of easy comfort with one another.

For both China and Russia, each in its own way, the relationship with the U.S. in the post–Cold War period has been more important than the relationship with each other. For Russia, the U.S. relationship is crucial to its quest to be recognized as a major voice in Europe and in global policy. For China, the U.S. is the most important outside power because of its pervasive influence over China's strategic environment and economy. China benefited from the collapse of the Soviet Union by the removal of what for forty years had been its main threat, but it was also presented with a new challenge in the form of American preeminence. With the end of the Cold War, the U.S. replaced Russia as the primary focus of Chinese foreign policymaking.

4

DECIPHERING THE U.S. THREAT

Throughout the Cold War, there was a robust American threat to China that derived from Washington's Cold War strategy to weaken the Soviet bloc. The U.S. had decided at the end of the Chinese civil war that it did not care about China for itself; instead, Washington shaped a policy toward Beijing based on its status as an ally of Moscow and strove to split the two apart. Once the split came about, the U.S. moved to capitalize on it, using relations with China to put pressure on the Soviet Union.

For China as well, the U.S. was a secondary threat, in light of the Soviet Union's geographical proximity and its apparently rising power until near the end of the Cold War. Twisting and turning to find a way to deal with the Soviet Union, as we saw in the last chapter, China shifted from bandwagoning to isolation and dual deterrence, to balancing on the side of the U.S., to equidistance around 1982 as the Soviet threat receded and U.S. assertiveness increased. Then history did China a strategic favor by bringing about the disintegration of the Soviet bloc and the collapse of the Soviet Union. China used the postcollapse phase to institutionalize cooperative relations with Russia and the Central Asian successor states.

These developments left the U.S. for the first time as the principal potential threat to China. From its position of enhanced relative power, the U.S. was now able to set the limits within which China had to operate, placing greater or lesser pressure on Beijing and creating greater or lesser challenges to Chinese security. In this sense, Chinese policy remained—as it was in the Cold War period—chiefly reactive to the terms set by another power and has begun only recently and in limited ways to try proactively to shape the global security environment and international regimes to serve its interests the way the U.S. has long done.

Beginning with the Nixon visit to China in 1972, a succession of American leaders have assured China of their good will. Each American administration has stated in one form or another that China's prosperity and stability are in the interest of the U.S. And in actual policies as well, the U.S. has done more than any other power to contribute to China's modernization. It has drawn China into the global economy, provided markets, capital, and technology, trained Chinese experts in international law, provided military security for Chinese exports and imports as they moved in growing volumes across the world's oceans, prevented the remilitarization of Japan, maintained the peace in Korea, and avoided a war with China over Taiwan.

Yet what strikes Chinese policymakers as most significant is the fact that the American military remains deployed all around China's periphery even though the Soviet threat to the U.S. has disappeared. The U.S. has a wide network of defense alliances and other military relationships with China's neighbors (chapters 5 and 6). Washington continues to frustrate Beijing's efforts to gain control over Taiwan (chapter 8). The U.S. pressures China over its economic policies and maintains a host of official and unofficial programs that seek to influence Chinese civil society and politics.

What are Washington's real intentions? With the U.S. as China's primary security threat, the understanding of American motives is the primary determinant of Chinese decisions about how to evaluate the threat posed by domestic dissent; how to make foreign economic policy; how to deal with Japan, Korea, Taiwan, Vietnam, India, and other states; how to arm and train the Chinese military; what strategy to take on energy security; and many other issues. The question is not as simple to answer as it was during the Cold War because, we suggest, Washington's intentions are ambivalent—wishing Beijing both well and ill.

MIRROR DEBATES

The Chinese effort to understand America's China strategy in some ways mirrors the U.S. effort to understand China's America strategy. Just as Americans wonder whether China's rise is good for U.S. interests or represents a looming threat, so Chinese policymakers puzzle over whether the U.S. intends to use its power to help or hurt China.[1] But there are some important differences in the two situations. The American debate is public, whereas the Chinese debate is largely held behind closed doors, so it is easier to know what the Americans are saying and doing. But in another sense the American debate is the more inscrutable of the two. Although the Chinese elite's long-term strategic intentions are secret, they probably do exist. In the pluralist American system, long-term strategic intentions may not actually exist in a stable sense because power is so divided, and the top leadership changes at least every eight years. Even so, a long-term U.S. strategy seems to have emerged out of a series of American actions toward China. So it is not a hopeless exercise—indeed, it is necessary—for the Chinese to try to analyze American capabilities and intentions.

Three reinforcing perspectives shape Beijing's understanding of U.S. policy. First, Chinese analysts draw on a set of ideas that are part of Chinese strategic culture, which include "preconceived stereotypes of the strategic disposition of [China and other countries] derived from a selective interpretation of history, traditions and self-image."[2] They see their own country as heir to an "oriental" strategic tradition that dates back thousands of years and that is pacific, defensive minded, and nonexpansionist. They consider China's approach to interstate relations ethically fair and reasonable, and they attribute the existence of this unusual approach to the fact that China is a continental power that was historically agrarian and sedentary. In contrast, they see Western strategic culture as militaristic, offensive minded, and expansionist, growing out of the experience of maritime powers that are mobile and mercantilist. The two images define each other by contrast.[3]

In light of these ideas, Chinese analysts are prone to interpret American actions almost anywhere in the world as secretly directed against China. For example, few Chinese have ever accepted the American claim that

the bombing of the Chinese embassy in Belgrade in 1999 was the acciden-
tal result of faulty CIA maps. They respect the CIA too much to accept
such claims and believe that by giving such an obviously weak excuse,
the Americans seek to reinforce the message of the bombing itself, which
was that the U.S. will punish any challenger with brutal force. Likewise,
Chinese analysts interpret American protestations about human rights and
democracy as a screen for cynical power plays.[4]

These preconceptions are reinforced by a second, more recent Chinese tradition, Marxism. It posits that the relations of imperialist powers
with the rest of the world are economically exploitative. An imperialist
power extends its military force around the world and politically manip-
ulates foreign governments to perpetuate its economic advantage. Even
though China runs trade surpluses with the U.S. and accumulates foreign
exchange, its analysts believe the U.S. is getting the better of the relationship by using cheap Chinese labor and credit to live beyond its real means.
As China increasingly moves out into the world to protect its economic
security by competing with the U.S. for resources and markets (chapter 10),
it sees signs of American resistance.[5]

Third, American theories of international relations have become popular among younger Chinese policy analysts, many of whom took advanced
degrees in the U.S. The most influential body of international relations
theory in China is an approach called offensive realism. It reinforces the
two older views by arguing that a country will try to control its security
environment to the full extent that its capabilities permit.[6] According to
this theory, the U.S. cannot be satisfied with the existence of an independent China. It naturally tries to promote a "color revolution" (the popular
overthrow of an authoritarian system) that will replace the CCP with a
regime that is weaker and more pro-American. Many in Beijing see evidence of this intent in the long American record of anticommunism, in
Washington's regular calls for greater democracy and more respect for
human rights, and in its stubborn support for what China sees as separatist
movements in Taiwan, Tibet, and Xinjiang.

China's U.S. specialists understand that the American system is politically and ideologically pluralistic, but all three Chinese analytic traditions
converge on the view that a great power such as the U.S. must ultimately
have a strategy toward China. When confusing and contradictory signals
emanate from the American political system, as they often do, Chinese

analysts deploy an idea that is similar to one that Americans often use about China: the idea of deviousness. The U.S. may be hiding its strategic intentions behind soothing words; it may be justifying its actions as a search for peace, human rights, and a level playing field; it may be putting forward apparently pro-China persons to manage its dealings with China; it may even be giving China some real help if only out of a search for short-term gain. But its words and actions are "two-faced."[7] Washington's ruses reveal rather than hide its true intention to remain the unchallenged global hegemon and its determination not to allow China to grow strong enough to challenge American power.

A small group of analysts argues that Chinese and American interests are not totally at odds. The two countries are sufficiently remote from one another that their core security interests do not inevitably clash. They can gain mutual benefit from trade and from policies that pursue such common interests as keeping Japan from embarking on an autonomous security policy. Therefore, Beijing can usefully engage Washington even though it has to keep struggling to free itself from the constraints imposed by the U.S. There is a larger body of dissenters on the other side of the spectrum who hold harsher rather than softer views of American policy and have more confrontational ideas about how China should respond. They believe that China must stand up to the U.S. militarily and that it can win a conflict, should one occur, by leapfrogging U.S. military technology and mobilizing its own superior morale. These views are widespread in the Chinese military and security agencies, but they are usually kept out of sight to avoid frightening both China's rivals and its friends.[8]

AMERICAN CAPABILITIES

To peer more deeply into the logic of American China strategy, Chinese analysts—like analysts everywhere—look at both capabilities and intentions. American military, economic, ideological, and diplomatic capabilities are relatively easy to discover, and from the Chinese point of view they are potentially devastating.

First, American military forces are globally deployed and technologically advanced, with massive concentrations of firepower all around the

Chinese rim. The U.S. military is divided into six regional "combatant commands," of which the largest in geographic scope and manpower[9] is the U.S. Pacific Command (PACOM), whose area of responsibility includes China. (There are also four functional commands.) PACOM has its headquarters in Honolulu and has forces stationed throughout Asia and the Pacific. More than 230 of the 800 U.S. overseas military installations are located in Japan and South Korea, and there are major air and naval bases on the island of Guam, 2,000 miles from China.[10] Besides China, PACOM's area of responsibility includes Taiwan, the South China Sea, Southeast Asia, Australia, New Zealand, and most of the Pacific and Indian oceans. As of 2010, PACOM's assets included about 325,000 military personnel from the army, navy, air force, and Marine Corps; some 180 ships, 1,500 navy and marine aircraft, and 400 air force aircraft.[11] Among PACOM's components are the Third Fleet and Seventh Fleet and, most of the time, five of the eleven U.S. aircraft carrier strike groups. At the western borders of China and India, PACOM gives way to the U.S. Central Command (CENTCOM). CENTCOM is responsible for the area from Pakistan and Central Asia west to Egypt. Before September 11, 2001, CENTCOM had no forces stationed directly on China's borders except for its training and supply missions in Pakistan, but after that date CENTCOM placed tens of thousands of troops in Afghanistan and gained access to an air base in Kyrgyzstan. As one Chinese analyst put it, "The United States has taken . . . steps to build . . . [a] strategic ring of encirclement in China's neighboring regions; . . . significantly strengthened its network of military bases in the Asia-Pacific region and its alliance relationship[s] with China's neighboring countries; further strengthened the U.S. Pacific Fleet and established forward military bases in Central Asia which is contiguous to China's Western region, in the name of counterterrorism."[12]

The operational capabilities of American forces in the Asia-Pacific are magnified by five bilateral defense treaties (with Australia, New Zealand, Japan, Korea, and the Philippines); a close defense cooperation with Australia, New Zealand, the Philippines, Thailand, and Singapore; and a host of cooperative arrangements with other countries in the region. U.S. forces have access to port facilities and airfields throughout the region for refueling, resupply, and repair. Australian, Japanese, and South Korean forces are trained to operate in conjunction with U.S. forces. Despite assurances that Washington will wind down weapons sales to Taiwan, the U.S. continues to equip and train the Taiwan armed forces. To backstop its capabilities in the region, the U.S. possesses some 5,200 strategic nuclear warheads deployed in an invulnerable "triad" of land-based missiles, submarine-based missiles, and aircraft-borne bombs.[13]

Chinese analysts became fully aware of the technological level of U.S. military capabilities only when the U.S. put them on global display during the televised Persian Gulf War of 1990–1991. In the two decades preceding that war, the American military had quietly carried out a program of modernization, the Revolution in Military Affairs. By the early 1990s, the U.S. possessed a global network of space satellites that provided real-time intelligence on the state of any battlefield in the world. The operations of all U.S. service arms were integrated through computer-networked communications that allowed so-called joint operations of air, naval, and land forces. Smart bombs and drone aircraft provided accurate targeting with low risk of injury to American troops. Advanced "logistic lift" allowed the transport of the required quantities of troops, weapons, and supplies to distant battlefields in short time frames.

Since 1991, the Chinese have tried to keep informed about continuing advances in American military capabilities. This attempt was undoubtedly one reason behind the agreement Beijing made with Washington in 1997 to permit U.S. naval vessels to make regular port visits to Hong Kong after the retrocession of the colony from British to Chinese sovereignty. For their part, American officers are happy to display U.S. capabilities selectively to Chinese officers during military-to-military exchanges in order to impress Chinese officers with the destructive power they would face if a conflict broke out and to send the message that the U.S. constantly adjusts its capabilities in order to keep a step ahead of any rival's military modernization.

To Chinese analysts, the message is clear. China for now has no forces stationed outside its borders in Asia except for a small antipiracy patrol in the Gulf of Aden and hundreds of personnel in UN peacekeeping operations. It has limited access to port facilities outside its borders for naval and air operations and no military alliances save for the 1961 treaty still technically in effect with North Korea. Its military capabilities, in short, are located within its own borders and around its coasts. As it builds up these capabilities (chapter 11), it sees the U.S. respond by reinforcing its own position around China's periphery. Any U.S.–China conventional conflict that might occur would have to take place around—and possibly within—China because there are no Chinese forces anywhere else.

Second, Chinese security analysts observe an extensive American capability to damage Chinese economic interests. Even though China has diversified its export markets and sources of investment and technology, the U.S. is still its single most important market (unless one counts the EU as whole) and one of its major sources of foreign direct investment and advanced technology. Since the 1980s, the U.S. has used its economic power more to help than to harm China, contributing in many ways to China's growth, but it has occasionally sent the signal that it can turn this help into a weapon if it wants to. For example, after the 1989 Tiananmen crackdown, Washington imposed economic (as well as diplomatic) sanctions on China. The sanctions included restrictions on advanced technology transfers, and the U.S. has not only continued to enforce these restrictions but has pressured its European allies to maintain them as well. At that time, Congress also debated whether to punish China by cancelling the low tariff rates enjoyed by Chinese imports—so-called most-favored-nation tariff treatment. Again in the 2000s, American legislators discussed whether to sanction China for what they called currency manipulation—that is, Beijing's refusal to allow a more rapid increase than it wanted in the exchange rate of the Chinese currency, the renminbi. Even though the post-Tiananmen sanctions were mild and the trade sanctions that Congress discussed were not imposed, to Chinese analysts these political events were reminders of how vulnerable China would be to U.S. actions if Washington decided to punish China economically. In addition, crucial raw materials reach China across sea lanes whose security is controlled by the U.S. Navy (chapter 7). Even though the U.S. has never threatened to do so, Chinese analysts believe that in a crisis the U.S. might cut off China's supplies.

Even without the intent to punish, the U.S. economy is so huge that it can hurt China by scrambling for its own interests. For example, Chinese strategists do not believe that strategic commodities such as oil and ores are distributed through an open global market to which every country has equal access. Instead, they believe that these commodities are largely controlled by enterprises based in the U.S. and its allied countries through ownership stakes, long-term contracts, and political influence and that price relationships and shortages are often solved in ways that help the West and hurt others. To deal with this unfavorable situation, China has been purchasing part ownership of oil fields as well as iron, copper, and other mines wherever it can around the world. In response, Western media and politicians have expressed anxiety about these moves, revealing Americans' reluctance, in Beijing's view, to allow others to play the game the same way that they have played it. In 2005, U.S. politicians halted the acquisition of the Unocal energy company by the China National Offshore Oil Corporation, and in 2009 political resistance in Australia blocked a Chinese state-owned corporation's acquisition of a stake in mining giant Rio Tinto. To Chinese analysts, these acts confirmed that their suspicions are correct: If the market were truly open, why would Chinese ownership be an issue?

Finally, the U.S. economy is so big that it can hurt China simply by mismanaging itself. For example, the U.S. dollar has become the main currency that countries use to trade with one another and the main currency that most countries use to accumulate foreign exchange. The makeup of China's foreign exchange reserves is not publicly known, but they probably include about 70 percent of dollar-denominated assets. Even if China would like to hold fewer dollar assets, it is hard to do so when the dollar accounts for nearly half of international bank deposits and debt securities, 60 percent of global foreign exchange reserves, and 80 percent of all foreign exchange transactions.[14] The dollar's ubiquity gives the U.S. the ability to damage Chinese interests simply by trying to solve its own economic problems by printing dollars and borrowing. When the U.S. does these things, it drives down the value of both China's exports and its foreign exchange reserves.

China is not as vulnerable to economic pressure as some countries because it is a large continental economy with vast natural resources, diversified overseas markets, and an increasingly robust domestic market. Nevertheless, the U.S. possesses a substantial capability to damage China's prosperity. So far it has not used this capability with that intention in mind. But if it did, China's ability to retaliate would be limited. Its supplies to the U.S. consist mostly of consumer products that are not strategically significant, and it cannot dump American dollars without damaging its own ability to conduct foreign trade and the value of its foreign exchange holdings.[15]

Third, Chinese analysts see the U.S. as possessing potent ideological weapons and the willingness to use them. "Democracy" and "human rights" are ideas that are accepted everywhere, and the U.S. has gained an outsized ability to define what these ideas mean. This acceptance is not, according to Chinese officials, because American ideas are better. Instead, the U.S. took advantage of its position as the dominant power after World War II to write its ideas into the Universal Declaration of Human Rights and other human rights instruments and to install what China sees as "Western-style" democracies in Japan and eventually in Korea, Taiwan, and other countries around the world. Chinese officials argue that today the U.S. is only using the ideas of democracy and human rights to cover up class exploitation at home and neocolonialism abroad. Ideological power supports military and economic power. With these ideas, the U.S. delegitimizes and destabilizes regimes that espouse alternative ideas such as socialism and Asian-style developmental authoritarianism.

In the Chinese analysis, the U.S. government—abetted by foundations and NGOs that claim to be private but that in actuality work in parallel with national policy—keeps rivals on the defensive by carrying out "democracy promotion" and promoting "color revolutions." The Ford Foundation and Asia Foundation support pro-reform activists in China. The National Endowment for Democracy supports dissidents. Freedom House rates China as "unfree." Voice of America and Radio Free Asia broadcast news and opinions that the Chinese media try to suppress. The U.S. offers political asylum to those who have opposed the Chinese regime and provide refuge and support for Tibetan and Uyghur activists. American missionaries in China promote unauthorized forms of Christian belief, the so-called house churches. U.S.-based NGOs subject Chinese practices to a wide range of criticism and seek to embarrass the government before its own people. American universities expose Chinese students to Western ideas. To be sure, foundation support has benefited China by contributing to regime priorities, and the training of Chinese students has helped China learn valuable technology. Yet none of these benefits came for free. No other country besides the U.S. has fielded such a robust set of tools to challenge other regimes' ideological control of their own societies.

Finally, Chinese analysts believe that the U.S. uses its dominant diplomatic position in the world to reinforce its other capabilities. The U.S. military presence outside its borders is put into legal form by treaties and agreements that other nations have signed under U.S. pressure as well as by UN Security Council resolutions that the U.S. has extracted by arm twisting. The U.S. uses arms control to prevent other countries from challenging its dominance and manages the arms control regime in such a way that attempts by North Korea, Iran, and other countries to shield themselves from U.S. pressure by acquiring nuclear weapons get classified as violations of international law. The U.S. dominates the World Bank, the IMF, the WTO, and other rule-making bodies of the international economy in such a way as to benefit itself. It has by and large dominated the international human rights regime, although it refuses to subject itself to some of the key treaties (chapter 12).[16] The U.S. arrogates to itself the right to label some governments "rogue" regimes, such as those in Burma, Sudan, and Iran, and to force other countries to join in imposing sanctions on them. Although its diplomatic power has been weakening, the U.S. can still use the international system to benefit itself and, often enough, to make life more complicated for China.

To all three schools of Chinese analysts that we described earlier—the culturalist, the Marxist, and the realist schools—it is only logical to assume that a country as powerful as the U.S. will use its power resources to preserve its privileges and will treat efforts by other countries to protect their interests as threats to its own security. The implications for all three are pessimistic: as China rises, the U.S. can be expected to resist.

LESSONS OF HISTORY: NEGOTIATIONS OVER TAIWAN

Beyond capabilities, Chinese analysts look at the history of U.S.–China relations to sharpen their understanding of U.S. intentions and practices. The lessons of history reinforce the logic of capabilities: in Beijing's view, the U.S. has treated China harshly in pursuing its power interests. From 1950 to 1972, the U.S. tried to "contain and isolate" China (chapter 3). Among other actions, it prevailed upon its allies to withhold diplomatic recognition from the PRC, organized a trade embargo against China, built up the Japanese military, intervened in Korea, supported the rival regime in Taiwan, supported Tibetan guerillas fighting PRC control, and threatened to use nuclear weapons. U.S. China policy changed after 1972, but only to serve Washington's needs—to counter the Soviet Union and to gain the economic advantage of doing business in China after China adopted an open-door policy. Even then, the U.S. continued to hedge against China's rise by maintaining Taiwan as a strategic distraction, further building up Japanese military strength, continuously modernizing its naval and other forces in Asia, and pressuring China on human rights.

More specifically, the Chinese have taken lessons about American China policy from several sets of negotiations with Washington. These negotiations included intermittent ambassadorial talks during the 1950s and 1960s,[17] negotiations over arms control in the 1980s and 1990s,[18] and negotiations over climate change in the 2000s. Two sets of negotiations made especially strong impressions on the Chinese: those over Taiwan in the 1970s and 1980s and those over the WTO in the 1990s. We examine the WTO negotiations more fully in chapter 10, but, in summary, the Chinese believe that the Americans dragged out the negotiations, drove an unduly hard bargain, and ratcheted up their demands in bad faith at the last moment when Premier Zhu Rongji came to Washington in 1999 to offer what China thought would be final concessions. After initially agreeing to Zhu's offer, President Bill Clinton cited congressional dissatisfaction with the deal as a reason for demanding still more concessions. The lessons of this experience for Beijing were that the U.S. never relents even on minor details, that negotiating with the U.S. is politicized and chaotic because no one is fully in charge, and that the U.S. drives the hardest possible bargain to maximize its own benefits rather than seeking a fair deal that serves both sides.

Even more decisive for Chinese understandings of U.S. policy were the three rounds of negotiations that took place over Taiwan in 1971–1972, 1978–1979, and 1982. These negotiations are worth studying in detail because they created the "communiqué framework" that governs American Taiwan policy to this day.[19] The PRC has always labeled Taiwan as its highest-priority issue in its relations with Washington. The issue has existential importance for China because control of Taiwan is essential to Chinese security (chapter 8). To Chinese policymakers, the crux of the "Taiwan problem" has never been Taiwan's separation from the mainland as such, but the U.S. role in perpetuating that separation. Had the U.S. not intervened in the Chinese civil war to protect the losing KMT side, Chinese policymakers believe that Taiwan would long since have been taken over by the PRC. Instead, with the outbreak of the Korean War in 1950, President Harry S. Truman directed the U.S. Navy to interpose itself in the

Taiwan Strait; the U.S. maintained diplomatic recognition of the ROC as the government of all China instead of shifting recognition to the PRC; and Washington hedged its bets on the relationship of Taiwan to China by stating that "the determination of the future status of Formosa [i.e., Taiwan] must await the restoration of the security in the Pacific, a peace settlement with Japan, or consideration by the United Nations," a legalism that allowed the possibility of Taiwan independence to remain on the table. In 1954, Washington signed a defense treaty with Taipei and started supplying military aid, which further consolidated the island's independence from the mainland. These events formed the background for U.S.–China negotiations over Washington's Taiwan policy.

When U.S.–China rapprochement began, PRC policymakers assumed that Washington would give up its support for Taipei in exchange for the benefits of normal state-to-state relations with Beijing. Indeed, at each stage of the negotiations the Americans seemed willing to disengage. Yet decades later the U.S. remains involved in Taiwan and is, in Beijing's view, still the chief obstacle to the realization of the PRC's reunification policy. How did this happen?

When Richard Nixon went to China in 1972, he told the Chinese that he was willing to sacrifice Taiwan because it would no longer be strategically important to the U.S. once the U.S. and China started cooperating. But he told Mao and Zhou that it was politically impossible to sever ties with Taipei at the same time that he opened ties with Beijing. He promised to break diplomatic and military relations with the ROC in his second term. After hard bargaining, the Chinese side accepted this two-step solution. In the 1972 Shanghai Communiqué, they restated their absolutist position—"[T]he liberation of Taiwan is China's internal affair in which no other country has the right to interfere; and all U.S. forces and military installations must be withdrawn from Taiwan"—but they also allowed the U.S. to make a parallel declaration within the same document. The crucial language in the communiqué reads as follows.

The United States acknowledges that all Chinese on either side of the Taiwan Strait maintain there is but one China and that Taiwan is a part of China. The United States Government does not challenge that position. It reaffirms its interest in a peaceful settlement of the Taiwan question by the Chinese themselves. With this prospect in mind, it affirms the ultimate objective of the withdrawal of all U.S. forces and military installations from Taiwan. In the meantime, it will progressively reduce its forces and military installations on Taiwan as the tension in the area diminishes.

In this way, the Chinese obtained what they read as a definitive acknowledgment of Chinese sovereignty over Taiwan and a commitment to end U.S. military support for the ROC government.

Yet U.S. negotiators later maintained that they had not "recognized" (*chengren*) Chinese sovereignty over Taiwan but merely "acknowledged" (*renshi*) the Chinese *belief* in this sovereignty. As for Washington's pledge to break relations with Taipei, it was an oral side promise, not a written commitment, and it turned out to be hard to achieve. Although the U.S. undertook to reduce its military presence in Taiwan, it made this reduction contingent on the reduction of the Chinese military threat, a threat that Chinese negotiators had always insisted was a sovereign right that they could not give away. The U.S. even paradoxically managed to tighten its commitment to Taiwan while loosening it: it asserted a never-before-stated "interest" in the *manner* in which the Taiwan question would be settled (i.e., peacefully), an interest that it would later use to justify continuing to support Taiwan militarily and in some ways diplomatically even after it broke formal diplomatic relations with the ROC. In sum, after the 1972 communiqué Washington remained on exactly the same footing with the ROC as before, all its promises to Beijing in the future, whereas China had given ground by allowing the U.S. position to be stated and even to be strengthened in a joint communiqué on Chinese soil. In retrospect, Chinese analysts came to believe that the Americans had taken advantage of Mao Zedong and Zhou Enlai, using a legalistic manipulation of the letter of an agreement to trap the Chinese, who naively put faith in the spirit of the agreement.

As events played out, Nixon was unable during his second term to normalize relations with Beijing because of Watergate. His successor, Gerald Ford, was also too weak politically to fulfill Nixon's promise. The Chinese learned a second lesson—surprising to them at the time—about the weakness of leaders in democratic systems and the consequent unreliability of their promises.

When the next president, Jimmy Carter, wanted to normalize relations with China in order to increase pressure on the Soviet Union, the Chinese insisted that the flaws in the 1972 arrangement be repaired. After tense negotiations, as part of the deal to establish diplomatic relations with Beijing on January 1, 1979, Washington agreed to break diplomatic relations with Taipei, give the legally required one-year notice of termination of the Mutual Defense Treaty, "recognize" the PRC government as "the sole legal government of China," and say again that it "acknowledges the Chinese position that there is but one China and Taiwan is part of China."[20] The U.S. insisted, however, on including a sentence in the joint normalization communiqué that said, "Within this context, the people of the United States will maintain cultural, commercial, and other unofficial relations with the people of Taiwan." Moreover, despite Chinese objections, the U.S. issued a unilateral statement that said that "the United States continues to have an interest in the peaceful resolution of the Taiwan issue and expects that the Taiwan issue will be settled peacefully by the Chinese themselves." The Chinese responded with their own unilateral statement saying, "[A]s for the way of bringing Taiwan back to the embrace of the motherland, it is entirely China's internal affair." But this could only contradict, not undo, Carter's reaffirmation of the American interest in a peaceful resolution first asserted by Nixon. As to U.S. military assistance to Taiwan, China demanded that Washington give an exact date for its termination, but the American negotiators refused. The normalization deal thus brought the Chinese some steps forward but reinforced the lesson that Washington would not let go of any advantage unless the other side had an absolute upper hand in the negotiations.

What happened next was a yet another painful lesson for the Chinese side. On April 15, 1979, the U.S. Congress carried out a partial rebellion against the deal Carter had struck—careful though it was—by adopting the Taiwan Relations Act (TRA). The TRA restated the U.S. "interest" in peaceful methods of "determining the future of Taiwan" (as if, Chinese commentators protested, there was something about the future of Taiwan that still needed to be determined). The act expressed Congress's intent to "maintain the capacity of the United States to resist any resort to force or other forms of coercion that would jeopardize the security . . . of the people on Taiwan." It committed the U.S. to provide defense "articles and services" sufficient to enable Taiwan to defend itself, "based solely {on] . . . the needs of Taiwan"—meaning that future administrations were forbidden to bargain with Beijing over U.S. arms sales to Taiwan. It established a quasi-governmental framework that enabled Washington to maintain what were in effect state-to-state relations with Taipei[21] and said that the U.S. would continue to treat Taiwan in every way except in protocol terms as if Taiwan were a state under international and domestic law.

In short, from Beijing's perspective, the TRA took back much of what Nixon and Carter had yielded. In place of the old U.S. policy that recognized the ROC as the government of all China—and hence at least acknowledged the unity of China—the TRA now recognized an entity called Taiwan that the U.S. would treat as if it were separate from China and that enjoyed all the substantive attributes of statehood in its dealings with the U.S. except for formal diplomatic recognition. In place of progressive abandonment of the American military commitment to Taiwan, the TRA entrenched the U.S. in the position of guaranteeing protection as long as Taiwan needed it. Indeed, American officials have used the TRA over the years since its enactment to justify a range of public and private diplomatic interventions, arms sales, military contingency planning, and even shows of force to defend Taiwan from PRC threats. When Chinese diplomats complained about the TRA's inconsistency with Nixon's and Carter's promises, they were told that in the American constitutional system the Congress could do what it wanted. Beijing had already learned that the power of the presidency was unstable. Now it discovered that the U.S. could use the principle of separation of powers to claim the right in effect to renege on its agreements.

In 1982, Beijing saw another chance to correct the errors of its previous negotiations with the U.S. As a presidential candidate, Ronald Reagan had signaled his intention to upgrade relations with Taiwan, but when he became president, he found that he needed Chinese cooperation against the Soviet Union. In return for such cooperation Beijing insisted on concessions on the issue of American arms sales to Taiwan. After intense negotiations, the two sides issued a second Shanghai Communiqué on August 17, 1982. The key passage read:

> Having in mind the foregoing statements of both sides [that is, that China is seeking peaceful resolution of the Taiwan issue while the U.S. has no intention of infringing Chinese sovereignty], the U.S. Government states that it does not seek to carry out a long-term policy of arms sales to Taiwan, that its arms sales to Taiwan will not exceed, either in qualitative or in quantitative terms, the level of those supplied in recent years since

the establishment of diplomatic relations between the United States and China, and that it intends to reduce gradually its sales of arms to Taiwan, leading over a period of time to a final resolution.

China had now forced the U.S. to make its 1972 commitment to reduce arms sales to Taiwan more specific. But once the agreement was in place, the Americans proceeded to use legalistic reasoning to empty it of all meaning. They set the benchmark year at 1979, when arms sales had been at their highest; calculated annual reductions at a small marginal rate, adjusted for inflation so that they were actually increases; claimed that the more advanced weapons systems that it sold Taiwan were the qualitative equivalents of older systems rather than advances on them; and allowed commercial firms to cooperate with Taipei's armaments industry under the rubric of technology transfer rather than arms sales. By the time George W. Bush approved a large package of advanced arms to be sold to Taiwan in April 2001, it was clear that the 1982 communiqué was a dead letter. Meanwhile, as America indefinitely prolonged its involvement with Taiwan, changes took place there that put unification farther out of Beijing's reach (chapter 9).

Reviewing this history, Chinese strategists ask themselves why the Americans are so stubbornly committed to Taiwan. Although Americans often answer this question by citing the imperative to defend a loyal, democratic ally from subjugation by a dictatorship, most Chinese see strategic motives at the root of American behavior. They believe that keeping the Taiwan problem going helps the U.S. tie China down. As one group of mainland military strategists framed it, "[S]ince the end of the Cold War, Taiwan has become an increasingly important chess piece used by the United States to keep China in check."[22] The lessons of this experience thus confirm Chinese expectations from theory. The U.S. will use all its instruments of power to hold back the rise of a rival.

THE POLITICIZATION OF CHINA POLICY

Congressional intervention in U.S.–China relations in the case of the TRA was not an aberration. It was part of a trend of congressional assertiveness in foreign policy that had started several years earlier and that has continued to complicate the American relationship with China. During the Cold War, the principle of foreign policy bipartisanship decreed that "politics stops at the water's edge." With the exception of the sterile debate in the early 1950s over "who lost China," China policy enjoyed the support of both the Republican and Democratic parties until 1979 because of the broad consensus at first on the need to oppose communism and later on the contribution that U.S.–China cooperation made to the containment of the Soviet Union. Maoist totalitarianism created one of the most brutal governments in history, yet Americans rejoiced at the warm reception that Chairman Mao offered Richard Nixon. Deng Xiaoping's regime, although an improvement over Mao's, remained a repressive government, but Americans focused on positive trends in Chinese politics and economics, believing that the Chinese were moving toward American values.

But congressional deference on issues of foreign policy had been eroding in the late 1960s and early 1970s under the impact of the Vietnam War and Watergate, both of which undermined trust in the president's word. The 1973 War Powers Resolution, limiting the president's ability to deploy troops into hostile situations, was an early sign of the new mood. The battle over the TRA was another benchmark in Congress's assertion of foreign policy power. The June 1989 Tiananmen incident, followed by the end of the Cold War, transformed American attitudes toward China. What had been perceived as a liberalizing Chinese regime was now seen as an atavistic Communist dictatorship oppressing the Chinese people. The collapse of the Soviet Union eliminated the strategic imperative to cooperate with Beijing. Closer U.S.–China economic ties generated frictions in various affected sectors of society. China policy became one of the most divisive issues in American foreign policy.

In these circumstances, interest-group politics assumed an increased importance in U.S. China policy, working its effect in part through Congress. China's political system elicits opposition from human rights organizations (chapter 12); its population control policies anger the right-to-life movement; its repression of unofficial "house churches" is condemned by American religious communities; its inexpensive consumer goods exports trigger demands for protection from organized labor; its reliance on coal and megadams for energy worries environmental groups; its arms and technology exports offend arms control activists; its rule in Tibet arouses protests from Tibetan expatriates and their American supporters; the film, software, and pharmaceutical industries demand protection of their copyrights in the Chinese market. Indeed, starting in the 1980s, China seemed to attract the attention of more American interest groups than any other country. The media and think tanks devoted increasing attention to China, usually following the principle that only bad news is worth reporting. Starting in the late 1990s, public discussion focused on the idea of a "China threat," an idea that, in Chinese eyes, not only denies the legitimacy of Chinese aspirations but seems to voice a threat itself to Chinese interests.[23]

Members of Congress have pressured the White House or voted for legislation to promote policies toward China that meet the demands of vocal constituencies. In recent years, the spectrum of congressional critics of the U.S. China policy has run from the progressive wing of the Democratic Party to the Republican Right and has covered the gamut of issues from human rights and Tibet to trade barriers and currency manipulation, from Taiwan to intellectual property rights, from climate change and the environment to the Chinese military threat. The more important China becomes, the more necessary it seems to be for each member of Congress to take a strong position on one or another issue relating to China. Some members specialize in issues they feel strongly about personally—often religious freedom, Tibet, or human rights. Others respond to issues important to their constituents for reasons of economic interest or ethnic identity—currency, trade, Taiwan. And others select issues related to the policy specializations they have carved out in Congress, such as trade or defense. Small groups of citizens encourage attention to the issues they care about by "bundling" campaign contributions, which the campaign finance law otherwise limits to $2,500 per individual donor and $5,000 per group.

Most congressional debate on China is only that—debate—but Congress occasionally takes action, sometimes in unexpected ways that can have a real impact on Chinese interests. Passage of the TRA in 1979 is a prime example. From 1990 to 1994, Congress debated every year whether to cancel China's most-favored-nation trade status, which would have raised tariffs on Chinese imports into the U.S.[24] Although it never did so, the possibility that it might do so caused China to make concessions on human rights issues every year during that period. In 1995, a "sense of Congress" resolution forced the administration to grant a visa to Taiwan president Lee Teng-hui in contravention of previous State Department commitments to

Beijing, an event that led to the 1995–1996 Taiwan Strait crisis (chapter 9). In 1997, Congress forced the State Department to appoint an ambassadorial-level "special coordinator" for Tibetan issues, a step that China protested as infringing on its internal affairs. In 1999, as noted earlier, congressional opposition forced President Bill Clinton to raise the price he demanded for U.S. approval of Chinese admission to the WTO. Congress often only barked, but sometimes it bit.

Of course, there are also many advocates in Congress, the think tanks, the media, and academia who support positions favorable to China on the basis that cooperation is important for American farmers, exporters, banks, and Wall Street or that strategic cooperation over issues such as Korea or climate change is more important than disputes over rights or religion. Those voices may be more powerful in the long run than the voices critical of China, but they tend to speak more quietly and work more often behind the scenes.[25] To Chinese analysts trying to make sense of the cacophony of views expressed in the American policy community, the signals are mixed and often alarming.[26]

SUGAR-COATED THREATS

In trying to ascertain American intentions, Chinese analysts also look closely at authoritative policy statements by senior figures from the executive branch. Coming from a political system where the executive dominates, Chinese analysts consider these statements the most reliable guides to American strategy. They find that such statements often combine two themes: seeking to reassure Beijing that Washington's intentions are benign, but at the same time reassuring the American public that Washington will make sure that China's rise does not threaten American interests. This combination of themes produces what Chinese analysts perceive as sugar-coated threats.

For example, in 2005 Deputy Secretary of State Robert B. Zoellick delivered a major China policy statement on behalf of the George W. Bush administration. He told his American audience that China's rise was not a threat because China "does not seek to spread radical, anti-American ideologies," "does not see itself in a death struggle with capitalism," and "does not believe that its future depends on overturning the fundamental order of the international system." On that basis, he said, the two sides could have "a cooperative relationship." But cooperation would depend on certain conditions. "China's . . . national interest would be much better served by working with us to shape the future international system"—rather than, implicitly, by working against Washington. China should take measures to calm what he called a "cauldron of anxiety" in the U.S. about its rise. It should "explain its defense spending, intentions, doctrine, and military exercises"; reduce its trade surplus with the U.S.; and cooperate with Washington on North Korea and Iran. Above all, Zoellick advised, China should give up "closed politics." In the American view, he said, "China needs a peaceful political transition to make its government responsible and accountable to its people." In conclusion, he said that the U.S. welcomed China in the role of a "responsible stakeholder" in world affairs and that the U.S. and its allies would meanwhile "hedge relations with China" to see how China would act.[27]

Chinese analysts were fascinated because in China a speech like Zoellick's would be carefully vetted through an interagency process and reflect the considered opinion of the whole government. They fanned out to ask their U.S. contacts what was meant by the Americanisms *stakeholder* and *hedge*. They concluded that Zoellick was telling Beijing that it must cooperate with Washington or else and that in the meanwhile the U.S. would continue to try to change China's form of government.

Other authoritative statements in the Bush administration sounded similar themes. The 2006 *Quadrennial Defense Review*—a document issued every four years by the U.S. Defense Department—said, "U.S. policy seeks to encourage China to choose a path of peaceful economic growth and political liberalization, rather than military threat and intimidation. . . . The United States . . . will attempt to dissuade any military competitor from developing disruptive or other capabilities that could enable regional hegemony or hostile action against the United States or other friendly countries, and it will seek to deter aggression or coercion. Should deterrence fail, the United States would deny a hostile power its strategic and operational objectives."[28] The 2006 edition of *The National Security Strategy of the United States of America* said, "China's leaders must realize, however, that they cannot stay on [a] peaceful path while holding on to old ways of thinking and acting that exacerbate concerns throughout the region and the world. . . . Only by allowing the Chinese people to enjoy these basic freedoms and universal rights can China honor its own constitution and international commitments and reach its full potential. Our strategy seeks to encourage China to make the right strategic choices for its people, while we hedge against other possibilities."[29]

The same ideas were repeated—albeit in gentler language—by the Barack Obama administration.[30] The first major policy speech on China under that administration, given by Deputy Secretary of State James B. Steinberg in September 2009, introduced the idea of "strategic reassurance." Steinberg defined the principle in the following way: "Just as we and our allies must make clear that we are prepared to welcome China's 'arrival' . . . as a prosperous and successful power, China must reassure the rest of the world that its development and growing global role will not come at the expense of security and well-being of others." China would need to "reassure others that this buildup does not present a threat . . . , [to] increase its military transparency in order to reassure all the countries in the rest of Asia and globally about its intentions, . . . [and to show that it] respects the rule of law and universal norms."[31] The Obama administration's first *National Security Strategy*, issued in 2010, said: "We will monitor China's military modernization program and prepare accordingly to ensure that U.S. interests and allies, regionally and globally, are not negatively affected. More broadly, we will encourage China to make choices that contribute to peace, security, and prosperity as its influence rises."[32] The first *Quadrennial Defense Review* of the Obama years, issued in 2010, said, "[L]ack of transparency and the nature of China's military development and decision-making processes raise legitimate questions about its future conduct and intentions within Asia and beyond. Our relationship with China must therefore be multidimensional and undergirded by a process of enhancing confidence and reducing mistrust in a manner that reinforces mutual interests."[33] To Chinese analysts, these statements were consistent in substance and conveyed the message that Washington wanted cooperation on its own terms and would seek to deter China from developing a military capability adequate to defend its own security interests.

Rendering U.S. policy even more dangerous and inflexible in Chinese eyes is its ideological character. Policymakers in a democracy use ideology—clear, simple themes that make sense out of complex actions—to unify influential political actors, mobilize public support, and coordinate the bureaucracy.[34] Chinese leaders do the same but less extensively because the Chinese public pays less attention to foreign policy than Americans do, and there are fewer actors with independent influence. Chinese leaders are usually able to deal with foreign policy issues on a pragmatic basis behind closed doors but feel that American officials often fail to recipro-cate: according to one Chinese analyst, "The United States needs ideology to distinguish friend from foe."[35] The public ideology of U.S. diplomacy appears to the Chinese as evangelical—both literally in that the U.S. pro-motes what it considers Judeo-Christian values and figuratively in that the U.S. promotes its values with a religious-like fervor. Understanding U.S. policy as ideological helps Chinese elites make sense of decisions that oth-erwise do not seem coherent to Beijing, such as the U.S. interventions in Somalia in 1992–1994 and Serbia in 1999, Washington's prolonged anti-Castro policy toward Havana, and its frequent criticism of other govern-ments for human rights violations.

Indeed, in the eyes of many in Beijing, since the end of the Cold War the U.S. has revealed itself to be not a conservative power intent on resist-ing structural change in the international system, but a revisionist power that is taking new initiatives to reshape the global environment in its favor. These initiatives include NATO expansion; interventions in Panama, Haiti, Bosnia, and Kosovo; two Persian Gulf wars; the Afghanistan War; the extension of U.S. military power into Central Asia; and the effort to deny North Korea's and Iran's rights (as the Chinese see it) to self-defense. In the economic realm, the U.S. has tried to expand its advantages by pushing for free trade, running down the value of the dollar while other countries are forced to use it as a reserve currency, and trying to make developing coun-tries bear an unfair share of the cost of mitigating global climate change. The U.S. has shown its aggressive designs by pushing its version of human rights and democracy in other countries and by promoting color revolu-tions in Georgia, Ukraine, and Kyrgyzstan. According to one rising star in the CCP, "[The Americans'] real purpose is not to protect so-called human rights but to use this pretext to influence and limit China's healthy eco-nomic growth and to prevent China's wealth and power from threatening [their] world hegemony."[36] There is, Chinese analysts conclude, a pattern of aggressiveness to the American use of power.[37]

This Chinese suspicion of the U.S. confronts the huge anomaly that the U.S. has done so much to promote China's rise. For Chinese analysts, however, history provides an answer to this puzzle. The U.S. contained China for as long as it could. When the Soviet Union's rising strength made it necessary, the U.S. was forced to engage with China in order to reinforce its hand against Moscow. Once the U.S. started to engage with China, it came to believe that engagement would make China into a democracy and would win back for the U.S. the strategic base on the mainland of Asia that Washington had lost in 1949. Moreover, after China started down the path of reform and opening, the U.S. began to earn huge economic benefits from its investments in China, the supply of cheap Chinese goods, and the Chinese willingness to support the U.S. trade and fiscal deficits by buying U.S. Treasury bonds. In the Chinese view none of this was done out of idealism or generosity. Meanwhile, until the late 1990s, American strategists underestimated China's potential. Now, Chinese analysts believe, the U.S. perceives China as a threat but no longer has any realistic way to prevent it from continuing to develop. In this sense, the U.S. strategy of engagement failed, whereas Deng Xiaoping's strategy of "hiding our light and nurturing our strength" worked (chapter 1). Now that it is faced with a China that has risen too far to be stopped, the U.S. can do no more than it is doing: demand cooperation on American terms, threaten China, hedge militarily, and continue to try to change the regime.

SLIVERS OF HOPE

These depressing views have not prevented China from cooperating with the U.S. in many areas of common interest. It has had no choice but to do so. According to Hu Jintao, "Neither side gains if relations deteriorate." Former PRC vice president Zeng Qinghong said, "Avoiding conflict is a long-term task for both sides." According to Premier Wen Jiabao, "What determines the direction of development of U.S.–China relations is the two countries' basic interests. . . . [C]ommon interests are greater than the divisions between the two countries."[38]

Such thinking reflects the realistic, instrumental thinking that guides Chinese foreign policy, in which common interests trump ideological differences. Beijing believes that the more the U.S. needs China for its own economic prosperity and to solve issues such as North Koreannclearization, proliferation of nuclear weapons to Iran, and global climate change, the more likely Washington is to choose cooperation over conflict. As Zeng Qinghong put it in the 1990s, "[G. H. W.] Bush and Clinton are both clear—to form bad relations with China is against their long-term basic national interest. Therefore, the United States will not develop bad relations with China in the long term, and U.S.–China relations cannot evolve into [something similar to] the former U.S.–Soviet relations."

For China, as for the U.S., however, the logic of security has no horizon. The stronger—and in a certain sense the more secure—a country is, the more security it needs. Each major power prefers to dominate the other rather than to compromise. Beijing analysts expect the U.S. to remain the global hegemon for several more decades, despite the best efforts of Russia, China, and others to restrain it and despite what they perceive as the initial signs of U.S. decline. For now, as one leading Americanist put it, "The superpower is more super, and the many great powers less great."[39] Survey research among Chinese elites shows that most do not think the hegemonic power of the U.S. will disappear quickly.[40]

Chinese policymakers thus assume that each power is likely to continue to build up its capability to constrain the other, aiming to be free of dependence on the other for its own security. But that is a distant goal for either side, unless the other side withdraws from the race. Instead, the two are growing increasingly interdependent economically, and as China's military power grows, the two sides—although not equal—will have the increasing ability to cause each other substantial harm (chapter 11). In this mutual vulnerability lies the best hope for now for cooperation. It is fear of each other that keeps the imperative to cooperate alive in the face of mutual suspicion.

5

THE NORTHEAST ASIA REGIONAL SYSTEM

Japan and the Two Koreas

If the Soviet Union and the U.S. have served as the PRC's chief security threats throughout its history, the third greatest threat has consistently come from Japan. Japan is by many measures a more powerful country than any of China's other immediate neighbors. Its population, at 130 million, ranks tenth in the world. Its GDP was the second largest after that of the U.S. until 2010 and still stands third in the world after China's. Moreover, China's GDP has overtaken Japan's not because of superior productivity but because of its larger population. Japan continues to outpace China as an innovator, investor, financial power, and exporter of high-tech manufactures and cultural products.

Japan is also a formidable military power. It has the sixth-largest defense budget in the world, and because it spends the smallest percentage of GDP on defense of any major power, it would have plenty of room to increase military spending if it decided to do so. It supports a military establishment (known as the Self-Defense Forces [SDF]) that is trim in manpower at 237,000 personnel but rich in high-tech weaponry and skills at sea, in the air, and in space.[1] The SDF is backed by world-class electronics, nuclear technology, and heavy industrial sectors. It operates in coordination with the U.S., which stations 36,000 troops on Japanese soil. This redoubtable power is located in intimate proximity to China, only about 500 miles across the East China Sea from Shanghai and within 1,200 miles of most of

China's population. These distances can be traversed in a day by a modern combat ship, in half an hour by a fighter plane, and in a matter of minutes by a missile.

Yet no other neighbor—not even Russia—offers equally large prospects to China of mutual benefit because of the near-perfect complementarity of Japan's high-tech, resource-needy economy with China's hunger for capital and technology and its ability to supply resources and labor. The puzzle of China–Japan relations is why the conflicts have been so difficult to resolve and the benefits so hard to achieve.[2] The answer lies in geopolitics: the undesired intimacy of two large countries in a small space. Areas crucial to Japan's security include Korea, Taiwan, and the East China Sea, all of which are also vital to China's security. The two countries are so close together that their security needs compete, generating a classic security dilemma where each side's moves to increase its own security threaten the security of the other side.[3] Advances in technology and intensified economic interactions have made distances in the region even less significant than they were in the past. Any effort to reconcile Chinese and Japanese interests is further complicated by the turbulent dynamics of a regional system that includes the two Koreas, Taiwan, Russia, and the U.S.

SCORPIONS IN A BOTTLE: THE CHINA–JAPAN SECURITY DILEMMA

Japan's geostrategic position makes it the most insecure of any major modern power. Its four long, narrow, densely populated main islands stretch for about 1,400 miles alongside the Asian mainland, lying only 200 miles from Russia, 155 miles from the Korean Peninsula, and, as noted, 500 miles from China. These distances were sufficient under premodern conditions to protect Japan and the Asian mainland from each other except once, when the Mongols briefly attacked Japan in the thirteenth century. But as soon as the two countries built modern steam-driven battle fleets in the late nineteenth century, their security perimeters began to overlap. They clashed in a battle for regional predominance in 1894–1895, which Japan won. As part of the settlement, Japan gained Taiwan as a colony, laying the basis for the separation of Taiwan from China that continues today. Ten years later Japan fought with the new Russian navy and army over preeminence in northeastern China and Korea. Japan's victory in that war laid the basis for its colonization of Korea in 1910 and its invasion of Manchuria, large parts of China, and most of Southeast Asia over the next few decades. Yet this position proved unsustainable, and Japan's defeat in World War II reconfirmed the home islands' ultimate vulnerability.

A second vulnerability, created by modernization, is economic. Under premodern conditions, the islands were self-sufficient. As the country started to industrialize in the Meiji period (1868–1912), it came to depend on outside sources for raw materials and energy resources unavailable at home. By the 1930s, Japan already imported 90 percent of its iron and 84 percent of its oil (today the numbers stand near 100 percent). These dependencies made the country mortally susceptible to any disruption of its access to sea lanes along the China coast and through Southeast Asia — the same shipping routes on which China has also come to rely since the 1980s for its imports and exports. Japan's lifelines are also open to strangulation at a number of straits closer to home, including the Tsushima Strait near Korea, the Tsugaru Strait between the Japanese main islands of Honshū and Hokkaidō, and the La Pérouse or Soya Strait near Russia.

A third area of Japanese vulnerability has been generated by the increasing importance of maritime and undersea resources in modern times, the resulting new salience of maritime territorial boundaries, and the expansion of competing territorial claims at sea under recent international law. Modern fishing fleets are able to go farther from shore and feed larger populations than traditional fleets. New drilling technology made it possible to exploit oil and gas reserves beneath the seabed. At the same time, the 1982 UN Convention on the Law of the Sea (UNCLOS) — to which both China and Japan acceded in 1996 — expanded the size of the maritime zones over which states could claim various kinds of jurisdiction (full sovereignty over a 12-nautical-mile territorial sea, limited sovereignty over a 24-nautical-mile contiguous zone, economic rights in a 200-nautical-mile EEZ, and so on). These developments led to nearby states' lodging overlapping claims to rights that were of growing economic as well as strategic value. Although the UNCLOS contains provisions to settle competing claims, they are too complex to produce unambiguous answers. China claims island groups that Japan holds — notably the Senkaku Islands (in Chinese, the Diaoyutai Islands), which are located at the lower end of the

Ryukyu island chain approximately 120 nautical miles to the northeast of Taiwan—and disputes Japanese claims to certain seabed resources, notably the Shirakaba (in Chinese, Chunxiao) gas field in the East China Sea, where the Japanese accuse the Chinese of siphoning off gas from their side via wells on the Chinese side.[4] Japan also has territorial disputes with Korea over the Dokdo (or Takeshima) Islets in the Sea of Japan and with Russia over the four southernmost islands of the Kuril island chain, which were seized by the Soviets after World War II and are known as the "Northern Territories" in Japan. Russia has not relinquished the Kuril Islands because they have a strategic position in controlling the Sea of Okhotsk, substantial natural resources, and Russian populations.

Adding to Japanese concern about the rise of Chinese power are the two countries' competing interests in Taiwan and Korea. Although Japan does not openly oppose the unification of Taiwan with China, it has an interest in postponing that outcome. Taiwan's separation from China serves Japan's interests because of the island's strategic position near the main shipping lanes, because China's preoccupation with Taiwan ties up military assets that might otherwise be used to threaten Japan, and because of Japan's large economic interests in Taiwan. For years, Japan served as the main base for the Taiwan independence movement, with the unofficial support of some powerful Japanese, until most of the activists returned home to participate in domestic politics after Taiwan's democratization. Japan lines up with its ally the U.S. in insisting on "peaceful resolution of the Taiwan issue," has promised to provide facilities to support the U.S. defense of Taiwan in case of armed mainland attack, backs Taiwan's participation in international organizations, and allows official contacts at a relatively high level. Beijing sees these actions as obstacles to the success of its Taiwan policy.

And the two countries' interests clash over Korea. China is interested in the stability of the North Korean regime and supports it as a client, whereas Japan is threatened by Pyongyang's nuclear weapons and missile-delivery systems. Part of the Japanese response has been to develop a ballistic missile defense system in cooperation with the U.S., which in turn reduces the deterrence value of Chinese missiles and makes China less secure.

Japan in modern times has tried two different grand strategies to assure its security.[5] Neither has produced satisfactory results for Japan, and both have threatened China. The first, before World War II, was to build an empire on the model of European empires of the time in order to assure military control of a wide security perimeter and access to raw materials and markets. After annexing Taiwan as a colony in 1895, Japan developed the island into a supplier of cotton, sugar, and rice. It added Korea to its colonial resource base in 1910. From there, Japanese troops and administrators moved into northeast China (called Manchuria at the time) to create the client state Manchukuo (1932–1945). Starting in 1937, Japan seized control of large parts of China and most of Southeast Asia, building the Greater East Asia Co-Prosperity Sphere. Imperial Japan overreached, however, and the strategy ended in defeat, having imposed tragic costs on China and the other victim nations as well as on Japan itself.

Japan's second grand strategy, pursued after World War II, was to depend on U.S. protection in exchange for serving as the main base for American power in Asia. (A third option, neutrality, was advocated by the former Japan Socialist Party but never tried.) The U.S. occupied Japan at the end of the war and imposed the so-called Peace Constitution, which says in Article 9, "[T]he Japanese people forever renounce war as a sovereign right of the nation and the threat or use of force as means of settling international disputes."[6] With the start of the Cold War, however, the U.S. shifted course and began to rearm Japan. Japan accepted a subordinate security position in the U.S. alliance system under a policy that came to be called the Yoshida Doctrine, which said that the country should take advantage of American military protection in order to place its priority on economic development. The two countries signed a Mutual Security Assistance Pact in 1952, which was replaced in 1960 by a Treaty of Mutual Cooperation and Security. Under this arrangement, the protection of Japan's territorial integrity—and eventually also of its strategic straits and sea lanes—became a joint endeavor. The U.S. extends its threat of nuclear retaliation to deter any nuclear attack on Japan, bases troops in Japan, and patrols the sea lanes that are crucial to Japan. The countries cooperate in developing military technology, and they constantly renegotiate the operational division of labor between their forces as the regional security environment evolves.[7]

Some scholars say that culture—the lessons of Hiroshima and Nagasaki, the revulsion against war, the commitment to Article 9—explains Japan's postwar preference for this second security strategy because it has allowed Japan to adopt a pacifist posture behind the shield of a U.S. defense guarantee.[8] Indeed, there are intense pacifist feelings in some sectors of Japanese society. For example, the 1960 decision to renew the alliance with the U.S. aroused large protest demonstrations. But geostrategic reasons ultimately best explain Tokyo's choice. The failure of the imperial strategy proved that Japan could not assure its security on its own. This was even more so under Cold War conditions, when the chief threat was the Soviet Union, with its nuclear arms, its vast Pacific Fleet, and its alliances with China (for a time) and North Korea. If Japan did not wish to be dominated by Russia, it had to put its hope for protection in the other superpower. Not only was partnering with a superpower the only practical choice, but it also held down defense costs and allowed more of the nation's energies to be devoted to economic growth.

The U.S. partnership did, however, require Japan to invest significantly in its own defense, and over time Washington pushed Tokyo further to increase its military capabilities in order to reduce the American defense burden. In 1969, Richard Nixon articulated the Nixon Doctrine, under which America's allies should provide for their own defense with U.S. help and under the U.S. nuclear umbrella. As time went by, Japan accepted a wider range of defense duties. In 1981, Tokyo agreed to take responsibility for defending the sea lanes to a distance of 1,000 nautical miles from the main islands, far enough to encompass the Senkaku Islands and reach to the edge of Taiwan. In 1983, Prime Minister Yasuhiro Nakasone stated that Japan would develop the capability to bottle up the Soviet fleet in the Sea of Okhotsk by controlling the three nearby straits. In 1988, Prime Minister Noboru Takeshita yielded to U.S. demands that Japan pay a larger share of the costs of basing U.S. troops in Japan. In the 1990s, after U.S. criticism of Japan for not contributing more to the Gulf War effort, the Diet (Japanese Parliament) adopted a bill allowing Japanese troops to participate in UN-mandated peacekeeping operations overseas. The 1997 version of the *Guidelines for U.S.–Japan Defense Cooperation*—an implementing document for the Treaty of Mutual Cooperation and Security—included a new provision for "cooperation in situations in areas surrounding Japan," which implicitly called for Japanese involvement if the U.S. found itself engaged in conflicts over Korea or Taiwan. In 2004, Japan dispatched SDF forces to Iraq as part of U.S.-led coalition forces, even though only for police work and sea supply, marking the first time since World War II that Japanese military personnel had entered areas where combat operations were taking place. In 2007, the Japan Defense Agency was upgraded to cabinet level and renamed the Ministry of Defense. Japan made major financial contributions to the U.S.-led war effort in Afghanistan. Each of these policy shifts was accompanied by increases in defense expenditures and capabilities.

Chinese policymakers and some foreign analysts labeled these trends "remilitarization."[9] Beijing took note when, after the Soviet threat to Japan disappeared, China itself began to be cited as a reason for building up the Japanese military. In 1995, Japan punished China for conducting nuclear weapons tests by temporarily suspending its official development assistance (ODA). Japan's 1997 defense white paper expressed concern about China's ballistic missile arsenal and its expanding maritime capabilities. Around that time, Tokyo began building a missile defense system in cooperation with Washington. Although Japan cited the North Korean threat as the reason, the system also threatened to reduce the value of China's nuclear deterrent. In 2004, for the first time, Tokyo's *National Defense Program Guidelines* explicitly named China as a potential threat. In 2005, a committee of top U.S. and Japanese security officials adopted a communiqué that listed peaceful resolution of the Taiwan issue as a "common strategic objective" for Japan and the U.S. One result of Tokyo's growing concern with Beijing's naval developments was the decision in 2005 to more than triple the annual equipment budget of Japan's coast guard, which is officially a civilian organization rather than part of the military, but more heavily armed than most country's coast guards.[10] Japan's 2008 defense white paper complained about China's lack of military transparency. In 2009, Japan put what it called a "helicopter-carrying destroyer" into service, which China saw as tantamount to an aircraft carrier and a significant increase in Japan's power-projection capability. In 2010, Japan publicly pressured China to cease expanding its nuclear arsenal and published the new *National Defense Program Guidelines*, which called for a shift of forces away from the northern front facing Russia to the southwestern front facing the maritime boundaries disputed with China. In Chinese eyes, this series of steps and others reflected not only Japan's deep suspicion of China, but also its participation in the ongoing American plan to hedge against the rise of China by maintaining a military balance in Asia unfavorable to China.

For Japan, the problem with the U.S. alliance has been—as Mao discovered in dealing with Khrushchev—that the interests of security partners are seldom identical. The U.S. at various times has failed to defend interests Japan regards as important (for example, by giving low priority in negotiations with North Korea to the issue of Japanese citizens abducted by Pyongyang), has insisted on Japan's performing missions that most Japanese do not wish Japan to perform (pressing Japan, for example, to contribute money and manpower to the war in Iraq), has ignored Japanese interests when pursuing interests of its own (for example, when Richard Nixon "shocked" Japan by making his historic breakthrough with China without informing Tokyo in advance or when President Bill Clinton made a nine-day visit to China in 1998 without a stopover in Tokyo), and has pressured Japanese officials into tolerating actions in secret that they had publicly vowed not to permit (for example, by bringing nuclear weapons into Japanese ports on navy ships in violation of a public Japanese government policy that forbade this very act). Moreover, the American commitment has seemed politically shaky, especially when the U.S. seemed poised to reduce its commitment to Asia (such as after the Vietnam War) or when Americans were angry about the trade deficit with Japan in the 1980s and 1990s.

These problems have fostered discussion in Japan of a potential new security strategy, widely referred to as the "normal country" strategy. Advocates argue that Japan should revise Article 9 of the Peace Constitution so as to regain the right to use force held by any other state. Beyond this specific point, the normal country policy is ill defined. Some say Japan should continue to cooperate with the U.S. but act more independently, not seeking military dominance in any part of the world, but engaging in more military activity than it has in the past. Others seem to want Japan to move to an equidistant position between the U.S. and China. A third group points vaguely toward a more assertive, nationalistic posture. It is hard to know how such a policy would work, but if put into effect it would only intensify Beijing's perception of a Japanese threat. From China's point of view, Japan's alliance with the U.S. therefore remains the least bad of many bad options. At least it has reduced Japan's incentive to go nuclear, a function sometimes impolitely called "keeping the cork in the bottle."[11]

The ideal security solution for countries situated as Japan and China are with respect to one another would theoretically be the construction of what scholars call a "security community."[12] A security community is a group of nations, such as the members of the EU, who see their security interests as consistent rather than conflicting so that threats from each other are no longer included in national security planning. But the conditions that made such an outcome possible for Europe are lacking in the case of China and Japan. They included the presence of a common threat (the USSR) that was greater than the threat posed by one another; a common security guarantor, the U.S.; technological developments that devalued the control of disputed pieces of territory for economic or security purposes; levels of prosperity combined with levels of military technology that made war more costly than any potential benefit it could bring; mutual military "burnout"; and deep agreement on core cultural values—including a common interpretation of what happened between the member nations in the past—and intense people-to-people and economic ties. There is no prospect that this demanding suite of preconditions will be realized in the China–Japan relationship any time soon.

Tokyo has nonetheless done what it can to create a community of interests with China.[13] It broke formal ties with the ROC and normalized diplomatic relations with China in 1972; signed a Treaty of Peace and Friendship with China in 1978; offered a series of apologies for World War II atrocities in China; and since 2000 has hosted more than seventy thousand tertiary-level students from China each year. Japan was the first country to end the sanctions imposed on China by the G7 countries after Tiananmen. It endorsed and pushed for China's admission into the WTO. It channeled nearly $21 billion worth of ODA to China in the three decades from 1979 to 2009, making China the largest recipient of Japanese ODA and Japan the biggest aid donor to China. The two countries have signed numerous agreements for cultural, scientific, and technological exchanges, and since 1997 Japan has intermittently promoted the idea of an "East Asia community" that would intensify cooperation in economics, health, environment, and other fields among Japan, China, South Korea, and the ten ASEAN countries.

Most important, thanks to the complementarity of their economies, the two countries have built trade and investment ties that rank among each country's largest overseas economic relationships. Japan has been one of China's top trading partners since the early 1970s, and China one of Japan's top trading partners since the 1990s. China imports medium- and high-tech goods, machinery and equipment, cars, and metals from Japan and sells clothing, footwear, information technology products, foodstuffs, oil, and coal to Japan. And Japanese firms have been among the largest sources of foreign direct investment in China.

Yet the two countries remain politically far apart. Their economic relations have been filled with contention as well as cooperation. Each has many other important economic partners, so neither is economically dependent on the other.[14] Japan is not as open to Chinese immigrants and students as are the U.S. and Europe, and there are fewer people-to-people ties. Each country's public attitudes toward the other are negative. Instead of a security community taking shape, there is the perception in Beijing and Tokyo that each other's security priorities are fundamentally opposed.

CHINA CONDITIONS JAPAN

Because China cannot eliminate the threat that it perceives from Japan, its goals in the relationship have been more defensive than proactive (in contrast, for example, to Beijing's strategy toward Russia after the Cold War, described in chapter 3). China seeks to minimize Japanese support for Taiwan's separation from the mainland, to hold the line on territorial claims, and, above all, to discourage Japan from moving further toward the more assertive security posture that China pessimistically sees as the likely trend given Tokyo's current policy trends and American pressure.

To pursue these goals, China has used a "conditioning" strategy: it rewards politicians and interest groups in Japan's factionalized political scene who show sensitivity to Chinese interests and punishes those who do not. Positive incentives include trade and investment deals for cooperative companies, smiling diplomacy with favorably inclined party leaders and prime ministers, and exchange and cooperation agreements. Negative incentives include trade and investment hindrances for unfriendly companies, assertive naval and air patrolling, popular demonstrations in Chinese cities against Japan, and, whenever Japanese policy seems headed in the wrong direction, loud criticisms of those policies and of the Japanese wartime atrocities that they allegedly resemble. This reward-and-punish approach sometimes produces an impression of inconsistency, but it is better understood as a way of using relatively weak and imprecise influences to try to steer the direction taken by a large neighbor that is itself cross-pressured by strong domestic and international forces. In conditioning Japan, the Chinese government draws on nationalistic public sentiments that are real but modulates the timing, duration, and intensity of their expression and what issues they include. Chinese leaders have tried to leverage Japanese feelings of guilt and claim the moral high ground as the victim in order to extract economic and political concessions. Conflicts over history and memory serve as signals rather than drivers of policy.[15]

Thus, in the 1950s and 1960s, even though Japan officially participated in the U.S. trade embargo against China, China concluded a variety of private trade agreements with friendly Japanese companies and politicians, using frameworks known as "friendship trade" and "memorandum trade." In 1969, when the U.S. put pressure on Japan to extend its defense posture under the Nixon Doctrine, China denounced Prime Minister Eisaku Satō as a militarist and tightened the conditions for Japanese companies that it would be willing to trade with. In 1972, when Japan gave China diplomatic recognition, China responded with an era of good feeling. Beijing awarded a huge steel mill project at Baoshan near Shanghai to Nippon Steel in 1977 in part because the company's chairman was a longstanding friend of China.[16] In 1978, Deng Xiaoping visited Japan, followed by a visit in 1983 by CCP general secretary Hu Yaobang. Deng and Hu sought Japanese aid and investment to power their new program of reform and opening. Speaking of the Senkaku Islands dispute, Deng said it was not urgent and could be left to future generations.

In the 1980s, however, when Japanese leaders intensified defense cooperation with the U.S., China responded with negative signals. On the fortieth anniversary of Japan's 1945 defeat, China mounted exhibitions, events, performances, and ceremonies throughout the country that focused on Japanese war crimes during the invasion of China. China protested when Prime Minister Nakasone visited Tokyo's Yasukuni Shrine, which honors the spirits of Japanese war dead, including World War II war criminals. Nakasone's visit helped trigger anti-Japan student demonstrations, which the Chinese government allowed to continue on and off for several weeks. For the next few years, China complained about one issue after another: the way Japanese textbooks described World War II atrocities, a meeting held in Tokyo to commemorate Chiang Kai-shek, a Japanese court's award of a contested dormitory building to ROC instead of PRC authorities, and the cutting of scenes of the Nanjing massacre from the version of the film *The Last Emperor* distributed in Japan. Economic frictions happened to intensify at the same time as the fast development of the Chinese economy generated a trade imbalance with Japan and led to China's cancellation of a number of orders and contracts.

Beijing again softened its rhetoric in the early 1990s to reward Tokyo for taking the lead in relaxing post-Tiananmen sanctions. Prime Minister Toshiki Kaifu visited China in 1991, the emperor was welcomed in 1992, Jiang Zemin visited Japan in 1993, and Prime Minister Morihiro Hosokawa visited China in 1994. Both the emperor and Hosokawa showed sensitivity to Chinese concerns by apologizing for Japanese aggression. Therefore, when a private Japanese nationalist group placed a marine signal station on one of the Senkaku Islands to emphasize Japanese sovereignty, China responded in a low-key manner.

China turned up the loudspeaker again in the mid-1990s in response to more assertive trends in Japanese policy. In a trade dispute over agricultural products, China responded to Japanese protective duties with heavy tariffs on a wide range of goods, forcing Japan to back down. After Japan declared an EEZ around the Senkaku Islands in 1996, Beijing protested and allowed a private patriotic group based on Chinese soil to conduct three small-scale attempts to land on the islands (during which one protester, a man from Hong Kong, drowned). PLA ships, submarines, and aircraft stepped up their patrolling near and sometimes within Japanese-controlled waters and airspace. On a 1998 summit visit to Tokyo, Jiang Zemin said that previous Japanese apologies were insufficient and demanded unsuccessfully that more explicit language be put in writing. Both countries made preparations to drill gas wells in the disputed area of the East China Sea, and each protested the other's activities.

In 2001, a new Japanese prime minister came to office espousing policies that alarmed Beijing. Jun'ichirō Koizumi promoted enhanced defense cooperation with the U.S., ballistic missile defense, an expansion of the SDF's role and its dispatch to Iraq, and the upgrading of the SDF to ministry status. During the election campaign, Koizumi had vowed to visit the Yasukuni Shrine regularly while in office. China—along with South Korea—protested and imposed a freeze on relations. In 2005, the CCP Propaganda Department conducted a massive campaign to mark the sixtieth anniversary of the victory over Japan. Fresh student demonstrations broke out, targeting the Yasukuni visits, Japanese textbooks' treatment of the Nanjing massacre, and Japan's candidacy for a permanent seat on the

UN Security Council (UN secretary-general Kofi Annan had recently proposed Security Council reform). Koizumi's successors seemed to have gotten the message: none visited Yasukuni while in office. China rewarded this stance with exchanges of high-level visits in both directions.

China's conditioning policy toward Japan carries risks. At home, nationalist passions can turn into a xenophobia that might be hard to control. For example, in 2004 the Japanese national team in the Asian Cup soccer tournament was the target of abuse when it played matches in the central city of Chongqing. The defeat of the Chinese national team by the Japanese team in the championship game in Beijing provoked extreme hostility from Chinese fans. Any appearance of not standing up to Japan may cause this anger to turn against the Chinese government. In Japan, Chinese harping on historical issues (along with Korean and Filipino attacks on similar issues) risk fostering a more nationalistic response rather than deeper apologies. Although Japan's relationship with the U.S. makes Beijing uncomfortable, a weakening or collapse of the alliance might lead Japan to arm itself even faster than it has done under U.S. prodding. For this reason, China has not called for an end to the alliance since the Sino–Soviet split. As realists, Chinese leaders have little hope for smooth relations with Japan in the foreseeable future. The most they can do is keep trying to get Japanese policymakers' attention so that Japanese actions do not make the two countries' security dilemma even worse than it is.

THE KOREA PROBLEM

Even closer to China than Japan lies a spur of land between the two large neighbors whose existence only intensifies the security threat that each offers to the other. The Korean Peninsula is often described as "a dagger aimed at the heart" of both China and Japan because of its potential to be used as a channel for an attack on either of them by the other or by a third power such as Russia or the U.S. Korea is also of strategic importance for any power seeking to contain Russia (with which Korea shares a short border), as it was for the U.S. during the Cold War. This location has made the Korean Peninsula one of those unfortunate territories on which outside powers pursue their rivalries by spilling local people's blood. The history of Korea is one of invasions by both China and Japan, colonial occupation by Japan in the early twentieth century, warfare in the early 1950s, and division since 1945 in a constant state of crisis.

Korea would be considered a large country by any standard except that of its three immediate neighbors, and in any other neighborhood it would exert considerable influence. The two Koreas' combined population totals 71 million, ranking eighteenth in the world just behind Turkey. The peninsula covers an area of 84,500 square miles, making it nearly two-thirds the size of Japan and six times as large as Taiwan. The South Korean economy at about $833 billion in 2009 was the world's fourth largest, approximately one-sixth the size of China's (the North Korean economy is too small to change the country's rank if it were added in). The total manpower of the two Koreas' armed forces—approximately 1.8 million personnel—is second in the world only to China's. South Korea's army is well equipped and well trained. North Korea's conventional forces are antiquated, but the country commands an arsenal of ballistic missiles and has perhaps half-a-dozen nuclear devices that are close to being usable as weapons. If integrated, they would constitute a formidable force.

Korea is historically one country, and its people have a shared culture and identity. All Koreans' abiding goal is to establish independence from great-power meddling and provide for their own security without depending on foreign patrons. Until the peninsula is unified, Korea's strength is wasted through division and competition, and disunity provides an ongoing excuse for foreign nations to remain involved. Tragically for the Koreans, however, although no outside power openly opposes unification, none actively supports it. No outside power can hope to dominate a unified peninsula the way China and Japan did at different times before 1945 because the others would oppose it. Nor can any of the surrounding powers be sure that a unified Korea would not ally with its enemies. For each of the great powers, therefore, the safest course is to allow the peninsula to remain divided as long as possible so that no other power dominates. In this way, North Korea will continue to provide China with a buffer against the U.S. and Japan, and South Korea will continue to provide Japan and the U.S. with a buffer against China, as it did against Russia in the Cold War era.

Even without outside interference, unification would not be easy to achieve because of the enormous differences between the political and social systems of North Korea and South Korea. Only one regime and one way of life can survive the process. Hence, the impulse for unification has generated not rapprochement but competition between the two Koreas ever since they emerged after the end of World War II. The opening gambit of the Democratic People's Republic of Korea (DPRK) in the North in 1950 was to attempt the military conquest of the Republic of Korea (ROK) in the South. When this failed, Pyongyang maintained a high level of military threat along the armistice line that ran in the vicinity of the Thirty-Eighth Parallel, sent teams of agents to try to destabilize the Seoul regime, and in the 1980s engaged in acts of international terrorism aimed at South Korean officials. For military supplies and economic support, Pyongyang relied on the patronage of its two large Communist neighbors. The onset of the Sino–Soviet dispute in 1960 enhanced the value of Pyongyang for both Moscow and Beijing, creating a "small strategic triangle" that North Korean dictator Kim Il-sung (1912–1994) skillfully played to enhance the flow of benefits to his regime.

South Korea's strategy went through a number of stages. After an interlude of weak democratic government, Seoul began to focus on economic growth under the stewardship of military strongman Park Chung-hee (r. 1961–1979). South Korea leveraged its growing economic power to develop a more independent diplomacy, at first in Asia and then in the 1980s also in other parts of the world. By that time, the two Koreas had achieved rough parity diplomatically, economically, and politically. They had enjoyed comparable rates of growth, with Pyongyang holding an edge over Seoul in some areas. Both Koreas dramatically increased the number of states with which they had full diplomatic relations from slightly more than a dozen in 1960 to seventy-five for the DPRK and ninety-three for the ROK in 1978. Unlike the PRC and the ROC, the two Koreas allowed other countries to maintain diplomatic relations with both of them at once on the ground that both were legitimate states pending unification. The major patrons of each Korea, however, denied diplomatic recognition to either other's client.

The 1980s brought a shift in the balance of advantage. South Korea's globalization-linked economy grew at annual rates of around 8 percent, whereas North Korea's isolated economy stagnated. South Korea went through a transition to democracy in 1987 that enhanced its international prestige, whereas the North carried out a protracted dynastic succession in the context of a bizarre cult of personality as Kim Il-sung's eldest son, Kim Jong-il, gradually consolidated his personal power from the mid-1980s until his father died in 1994. As South Korea grew, Pyongyang's diplomatic allies in the socialist bloc flocked to establish economic and diplomatic ties with Seoul, at first under the cover of the 1988 Seoul Olympics (a process dubbed "sports diplomacy") and then with full diplomatic recognition as the socialist bloc dissolved. This process culminated in the normalization of relations with Seoul by Pyongyang's major patrons, the Soviet Union in 1990 and China in 1992. With the collapse of the Soviet Union, Russian economic aid to the DPRK ended, and Chinese aid was reduced. Starting in the early 1990s, the country encountered serious economic difficulties, and North Koreans began to suffer famine.

As Pyongyang's patrons set their erstwhile client adrift, the two Koreas entered into direct talks, each side trying to improve its position in the new circumstances. Direct contacts had taken place three times previously: in 1972–1973 in response to the strategic shock both Koreas suffered from Sino–American rapprochement, in 1979–1980 after the assassination of South Korean president Park Chung-hee, and in 1984–1986 after severe floods in North Korea. Officials in 1991 signed the Agreement on Reconciliation, Nonaggression, and Exchanges and Cooperation; in 1992 the Joint Declaration on the Denuclearization of the Korean Peninsula; and later the same year a nonaggression protocol. In 1993, however, Pyongyang broke off talks with Seoul, believing that the nuclear crisis that emerged that year created an opportunity to force Washington into direct talks.

THE KOREAN NUCLEAR CRISES

The series of Korean nuclear crises that began in 1993 had their roots in programs to develop nuclear weapons and ballistic missiles that Pyongyang started in the 1960s. These programs aimed to benefit the regime in several ways. They were status symbols that helped hold the loyalty of the elite, military officers in particular. They were commercial ventures that brought millions of dollars into Pyongyang's coffers through sales of missiles and nuclear technology to countries such as Iran and Syria, virtually Pyongyang's only source of foreign exchange except for the counterfeiting of U.S. dollars. And weapons of mass destruction were a deterrent against what Pyongyang believed was an American strategy to undermine or possibly even attack the regime.[17]

In the early 1990s, North Korean leaders discovered another use for these programs. When the U.S. began to put pressure on the DPRK to end the programs, Pyongyang saw the opportunity to use them as leverage to force the U.S., Japan, and South Korea into negotiations for diplomatic recognition, security guarantees, and economic aid. Under Soviet pressure, the DPRK had signed the Nuclear Nonproliferation Treaty (NPT) in 1985, stating that its nuclear program was for peaceful uses only. In 1989, however, a classified U.S. assessment that Pyongyang was developing nuclear weapons was leaked to the media. Claiming to disprove the media report, North Korea allowed International Atomic Energy Agency (IAEA) inspectors entry to its Yongbyon nuclear facility in 1992. The inspectors raised serious questions about the amount of plutonium North Korea might have produced and discerned major discrepancies in Pyongyang's official accounting of its fissile materials. Under increasing U.S. pressure, in March 1993 Pyongyang threatened to withdraw from the NPT and in May tested its Nodong-1 missile by firing it into the sea between itself and Japan. Then, in May 1994, North Korea began the removal of the Yongbyon reactor's fuel rods unsupervised by IAEA inspectors, which meant there was no way to know if any plutonium in the rods was being extracted and used to make nuclear weapons. One month later Pyongyang announced that it would withdraw from the IAEA and expel that organization's inspectors. As tensions mounted, the Clinton administration began serious consideration of military action to destroy North Korea's nuclear capability.

This sequence of events came to be called the first North Korean nuclear crisis. It was only the intervention by former President Jimmy Carter that resolved the standoff. He flew to Pyongyang and initiated a dialogue with the elderly Kim Il-sung in June 1994, persuading Kim to allow the IAEA inspectors to remain . This dialogue led to direct negotiations between Washington and Pyongyang that resulted in the Agreed Framework, signed by the two governments in October 1994 (the elder Kim had died in July and been succeeded by his son Kim Jong-il). The framework established the Korean Peninsula Energy Development Organization (KEDO) to build two proliferation-resistant light water nuclear reactors in North Korea for nuclear energy and, until the first of the two reactors was completed, to supply five hundred thousand tons of heavy fuel oil annually to help North Korea meet its energy needs. The U.S., Japan, and South Korea were the initial members of KEDO; some other countries joined later. Pyongyang in exchange promised to dismantle its Yongbyon reactors, to remain a signatory to the NPT, and to permit international monitoring.

Building on this success in enhancing the status of his regime and stabilizing the economy, Kim Jong-il reached out to each of the other major powers around the peninsula as well as to South Korea to extract benefits for his regime. In May 2000, he made the first of a series of visits to China to obtain commitments for economic aid and diplomatic support. In the following month, he held a summit in Pyongyang with President Kim Dae-jung of South Korea, who pursued a diplomatic thaw with the North that he called the "sunshine policy." Kim Dae-jung and his successor, Roh Moo-hyun, hoped to facilitate a "soft landing" for the North by providing relief aid, investment, and diplomatic engagement. In 2001, Kim Jong-il met with Russian president Vladimir Putin in Moscow and he visited Russia again in 2004. Perhaps the most remarkable diplomatic initiative took place between North Korea and Japan. Japanese prime minister Koizumi visited Pyongyang twice (in 2002 and 2004) in an attempt to normalize relations. The effort failed because of the North's unwillingness to give a full accounting of the fate of Japanese citizens who had been abducted by Pyongyang in the late 1970s and early 1980s to serve in the North as language tutors and in other capacities. Although Koizumi did return to Tokyo with a handful of surviving abductees and their offspring, the initiative felt short of resolving the issue and did not result in normalization.

Despite all this activity, Pyongyang was unable to achieve a breakthrough with Washington. North Korea was of two minds about normalizing relations with the U.S. On the one hand, this step would create a less threatening security environment for Pyongyang; on the other, it would eliminate the great adversary that provided the rationale for Kim Jong-il's "military-first" policy and his repressive rule. Nonetheless, in keeping with its commitments under the Agreed Framework, Pyongyang started taking apart the Yongbyon facility. But KEDO's construction of the two reactors and its supply of fuel oil lagged, in part because of funding disagreements among the organization's member states. Perhaps to get the West's attention, in 1998 Pyongyang conducted a test of its Taepodong-I missile, sending the projectile over Japan to land in the Pacific Ocean. Western intelligence agencies reported that Pyongyang was also selling missiles to Pakistan, Iran, and countries in the Middle East. The U.S. again considered military options but decided to try to engage Pyongyang instead. U.S.

secretary of state Madeleine Albright visited North Korea to discuss plans for a possible summit visit by President Clinton.

But the Clinton administration left office before this summit could take place. The George W. Bush administration, which took office in January 2001, decided to take a tougher line. In his second State of the Union address, the new president labeled Pyongyang part of an "axis of evil." Shortly thereafter the U.S. charged that a Pyongyang diplomat had acknowledged to a U.S. diplomat the existence of a second, previously unknown, nuclear weapons program based on highly enriched uranium rather than plutonium.[18] Charging that this program was a violation of the spirit—although not the letter—of the Agreed Framework, KEDO suspended fuel oil shipments. In retaliation, Pyongyang withdrew from the NPT, expelled the IAEA inspectors, and resumed its Yongbyon program; KEDO in turn suspended the light water reactors program. The U.S. now demanded "complete, verifiable, irreversible dismantlement" of the North's nuclear program—in effect, unilateral disarmament—as the precondition for resuming talks. This sequence of events is known as the second Korean nuclear crisis.

CHINA STEPS IN

These developments alarmed China. On the one hand, Pyongyang was within its rights under international law in everything it had done save for its initial violation of the NPT. It had not broken any of its promises to the U.S. For example, it had never promised not to have a highly enriched uranium program—the Americans had neglected to ask for such a guarantee. Pyongyang's basic negotiating objective was reasonable in Beijing's eyes: an assurance that the U.S. would not attack it. The regime had shown its ability to survive and to wrest deference and aid from its more powerful neighbors. And the North Korean regime's survival was in China's interest insofar as the likely alternatives were a messy collapse, the loss of a valuable buffer state, and a flow of refugees from North Korea into adjacent Jilin and Liaoning provinces.

On the other hand, Beijing considered Kim Jong-il its most difficult neighbor. He extorted food and oil from China by the threat of regime collapse. He ignored Chinese advice for economic reform to feed his people and for political liberalization to allow North Korea to begin to modernize. He created tension between Beijing and Washington by motivating American policymakers to pressure China to rein him in. His missile firings near Japan spurred Japan's remilitarization, its creation of a theater missile defense system, and its tightening of defense ties with the U.S. It was North Korea's 1993 missile test and 1996 preparations for another test (later aborted) that precipitated the inclusion of new language in the 1997 *U.S.–Japan Defense Guidelines* about defense cooperation in "situations in areas surrounding Japan," language that Beijing believed also applied to Taiwan.

Perhaps most distressing, Beijing judged that Kim Jong-il's brinkmanship created a real risk of war, with its attendant risks of possible nuclear contamination affecting nearby Chinese populations, a South Korean takeover of the North, and the ultimate presence of American troops on China's border. The U.S. had just demonstrated its willingness to use force by invading Afghanistan and Iraq. Beijing was worried that Washington would take on Pyongyang next.[19] Because the U.S. refused to engage in bilateral negotiations with Pyongyang, the Chinese devised the idea of multilateral talks, which eventually came to involve all the stakeholders—both Koreas, the U.S., China, Japan, and Russia. The Six-Party Talks began in 2003. Beijing conceived them as a fig leaf for negotiations between Washington and Pyongyang, mediated by the Chinese, with the other parties being perceived as little more than observers.

Beijing served as host and facilitator but also pursued some goals of is own that were different from Washington's. China worried about instability and war on its borders and thus favored a gradual and cautious approach to minimize tensions, whereas the U.S. was concerned that North Korea would use its missiles to threaten Japan and would sell nuclear and missile technology to rogue regimes or terrorists and thus wanted quick changes in Pyongyang's policies. Washington wanted China to force North Korea to yield, but the Chinese believed that Washington's hard line made a solution impossible. Beijing lobbied both sides to soften their positions but asked for more changes in Washington's position than in Pyongyang's.

Beijing signaled Pyongyang that the North should not expect China to come to its rescue in a military conflict of its own making. It did not, however, cancel the 1961 Treaty of Friendship and Cooperation and Mutual

Assistance. China appeared to find that piece of paper still useful in a number of ways. First, it gave China the right to counsel Pyongyang against rash action and diminished the incentive for North Korea to lash out in panic. Second, it helped to deter an attack on Pyongyang by other states. Finally, the treaty would provide a justification if China ever felt that it needed to intervene militarily on Korean soil.

China's hosting and tortuous mediation efforts produced some results. In September 2005, the Joint Statement of the Fourth Round of the Six-Party Talks announced that the six parties agreed to the goal of verifiable denuclearization of the Korean Peninsula (so stated to include a commitment by South Korea not to go nuclear and by the U.S. not to station nuclear weapons on the peninsula). But immediately following this round of talks, the U.S. Treasury Department—apparently working without coordination with the State Department—accused a financial institution located in Macao that held substantial North Korean assets, Banco Delta Asia, of money laundering for Pyongyang. To avoid U.S. sanctions, the monetary authority of Macao froze the bank's accounts and thus Pyongyang's money. North Korea responded by canceling talks, firing seven test missiles in July 2006, and detonating an underground nuclear test three months later. Beijing issued its first public condemnation of Pyongyang in the form of votes in favor of two UN Security Council resolutions that condemned North Korean actions and imposed symbolic sanctions. They were the first of a series of Security Council votes that China was to cast against North Korea in subsequent years.

After further mediation efforts by China, in 2007 the U.S. removed Banco Delta Asia from its watch list, Macao's financial regulators freed up the North Korean assets, and North Korea again agreed to shut down its Yongbyon reactor, to allow the return of IAEA inspectors, and to make full disclosure of past activities (which in principle would have included the alleged highly enriched uranium program). The U.S. and its allies renewed their commitment to provide two light water reactors and fuel oil.

In short order however, the implementation of the agreement unraveled as Pyongyang and Washington accused each other of not making good on their respective promises. North Korea further raised tensions with a new series of missile and nuclear tests in 2009, followed in 2010 by the torpedoing of a South Korean navy ship, the *Cheonan*; the revelation of a sophisticated new uranium-enrichment facility; and the shelling of a

South Korean–held island in waters disputed between the two sides. These events constituted the third Korean nuclear crisis.

BEIJING'S KOREA STRATEGY

Although this unsettled state of affairs was a major headache for Beijing, it had some upsides for China. The long-running crisis tied down the Americans in a complex diplomatic venture, and the Six-Party Talks gave China the prestige of a diplomatic convener and responsible member of the international community. Korea required constant attention by the U.S. military and threatened to complicate American and Japanese actions if a war were to occur over Taiwan. Washington was less free to challenge Beijing on other issues because it relied on China as its bridge to the rulers in Pyongyang. The crisis created tensions between the U.S. and its allies in Japan and South Korea—the former because during the talks the Americans placed low priority on the issue of the Japanese abductees and the latter because the hard line pursued by the Bush administration overlooked the importance for South Korea of avoiding war or a collapse of the North Korean regime. (The Obama administration, by contrast, coordinated its positions closely with Seoul.) The talks increased South Korean trust in Beijing because China's stress on gradualism and stability mirrored South Korean concerns. Above all, the extended crisis served to prop up the Pyongyang regime by fostering an atmosphere of heightened tension within North Korea, cementing the loyalty of the North Korean military to the ruling group, and sustaining the flow of economic aid and diplomatic attention from the other parties. As the talks dragged on, the only outcome that would have constituted failure from China's point of view would have been their collapse. Process was success.

In the longer term, Beijing hoped to emerge from a period of unpredictable change on the Korean Peninsula as its most influential outside power.[20] One part of the strategy never seemed to gain traction: persuading Pyongyang to undertake Chinese-style reforms in order to generate the economic resources to survive. In pursuit of this goal, Chinese leaders treated Kim Jong-il with flattering deference and offered him numerous chances to tour Chinese reform projects to see how profit-making entrepreneurship could be combined with political control. Beijing refused to give up on Pyongyang—China increased its infusion of trade, investment, and aid. At least one-third of Beijing's total foreign economic assistance budget reportedly went to Pyongyang. Chinese businesses invested in North Korean mining, food processing, and the service sector.[21] But given his government's repressive political controls and insulated society, Kim seems to have judged that any significant opening would be tantamount to regime suicide. The North Korean leadership held tightly to its failing totalitarian system, and the populace continued to live on the edge of starvation. Beginning in 2008, Kim Jong-il showed signs of ill health, and upon his death in 2011 power passed to his youngest son, Kim Jung-un. Beijing supported the new leader verbally and with stepped-up economic aid, for the time being at least consolidating its position of special influence in Pyongyang.

China worked simultaneously to strengthen relations with South Korea, counting on the gravitational pull of its economy to bring South Korea closer, to build trust, and eventually perhaps to reassure the Koreans that they would not need American troops on their soil to feel secure. South Korea's economy complemented China's, with its technically adept, export-oriented manufacturing skills and its needs for natural resources and cheap labor. South Korea was especially attractive as an economic partner because of its unique ability to serve industry by industry as a lower-cost competitor to Japan. South Korean entrepreneurs were comfortable in China, and their head offices were a short airline flight across the Yellow Sea from the provinces of Shandong and Liaoning. Following the opening of trade offices in Beijing and Seoul in 1991 and the normalization of relations in 1992, trade and investment boomed. To facilitate rapid development of ties, the government in Beijing allowed provincial and even municipal authorities to deal directly with South Korean enterprises. In 2004, China replaced the U.S. as South Korea's largest trading partner, and South Korea became China's fourth-biggest trade partner. Also in 2004, South Korea became the third-largest contributor of foreign direct investment to China.

Chinese policymakers are not adamantly opposed to an eventual unified Korea under the dominance of the South, but they seem to have decided that they will do everything they can to postpone or even prevent a collapse of the North Korean regime. Beijing fears that regime change in the North Korean buffer would be dangerously destabilizing. If and when a unified peninsula comes into being, China can be expected to seek an end to the U.S. military presence or at least a smaller U.S. footprint and to encourage Korea to anchor its future security strategy in cooperation with China. But this hope confronts obstacles. The growing operations of China's navy in the seas on either side of the peninsula may make a unified Korea feel that its security is threatened. For example, in 2010 Beijing vigorously protested planned U.S.–South Korea naval exercises inside the 200-mile EEZ it claims in the Yellow Sea, even though the area also falls within South Korea's EEZ. There is no open territorial dispute, but parts of the China–Korea land boundary remain undefined.[22] Some South Korean strategists are worried by revisionist analyses published by Chinese historians that argue that the ancient kingdom of Koguryo (37 B.C.E.–668 C.E.) was a Chinese dynasty rather than the forerunner of modern Korea, signaling, some think, a possible future Chinese claim to Korean territory. The 2-million-strong Korean ethnic minority that is concentrated in part in China's Yanbian Korean Autonomous Prefecture near the border is the single largest diaspora of Koreans in the world and retains a close linguistic and cultural affinity with the homeland, so China's treatment of this minority may become an issue with a unified and more ambitious Korea.

Economic ties are a strong basis for a good relationship—although they are never without their own potentials for conflict—but China will need to deal wisely with a host of other issues to keep a postunification Korea from selecting the more obvious path of continuing to balance against its large, close neighbor with security ties to more distant powers such as the U.S., Japan, and even Russia. In the meantime, Beijing is satisfied to maintain the fragile balance of a divided Korea.

UP AGAINST THE FIRST ISLAND CHAIN

The Northeast Asia regional system, which includes Taiwan because of its historical ties and geographical connection to the security of Japan, forms an arc of territory only a few hundred miles from China's coast, extending for 2,000 miles from the northern tip of the Japanese main islands to the southern tip of Taiwan. Taking account of the smaller Japanese-administered islands that stretch between Japan and Taiwan, this chain of islands hems China tightly in. Chinese strategists view this arc of territory as the northern section of what they call the first island chain, which continues into Southeast Asia along the coasts of the Philippines, Brunei, and Malaysia (chapter 11). As seen by Chinese defense analysts, this chain forms a base for potential hostile action by rivals and a barrier to the China navy's expansion from the near seas to the high seas. The three components of the northern section of the chain—Korea, Japan, and Taiwan—are close U.S. allies. Although the strategic goal of weaning them from their alliances with the U.S. is aided by China's economic rise, the rise also paradoxically creates the incentive for these states to stay close to the U.S. as a counterbalance to China. If China's strategic imperative is to seek regional preeminence, the path to that goal is strewn with obstacles.

6

CHINA'S OTHER NEIGHBORS

The Asia-Pacific

The challenges to China around its periphery do not end in Northeast Asia. That region—from northern Japan to southern Taiwan—runs past only one-seventh of China's circumference. Five more regional systems complete the circuit. Because these other regional systems are farther from the Chinese heartland than the Northeast Asian system, they pose less fundamental threats to Chinese security. Yet each neighboring system is important in its own way for China's territorial integrity, prosperity, and regime survival.

Continuing south and west from Taiwan is the region of maritime Southeast Asia, consisting of six countries that surround the South China Sea on three sides: the Philippines, Malaysia, Brunei, Indonesia, Singapore, and Vietnam. These states contend with one another and with China for access to the sea's fishery and energy resources and for the ability to protect the vital shipping lanes that pass through it. Beyond Southeast Asia to the south and east is Oceania, a region that includes Australia, New Zealand, Papua New Guinea, Fiji, and twelve microstates.[1] This region requires China's attention because of its economic, diplomatic, and military assets.

Farther west along China's southern border lies continental Southeast Asia. Three of its states—Vietnam, Laos, and Burma—share 2,400 miles of land boundaries with China's Yunnan Province, the Guangxi Zhuang

Autonomous Region, and the Tibet Autonomous Region. Continental Southeast Asia also includes Cambodia and Thailand. These five countries lie close to some of China's most difficult-to-control mountain and jungle terrain and some of its densest concentrations of national minority peoples. China can potentially use them as buffer states and land bridges to protect itself and influence others, but they also have the ability to influence China's stability and prosperity through refugee movements, trade, smuggling, disease transmission, and cultural influences. Together, the ten states of maritime and continental Southeast Asia have formed the ASEAN, an organization whose existence challenges China's ability to deal with the member states one on one.

Still farther west, China's borders run for 7,700 miles along the edge of South Asia, a turbulent region that includes direct neighbors India, Bhutan, Nepal, and Pakistan as well as indirect neighbors Bangladesh, Sri Lanka, and the Maldive Islands. South Asia abuts China's sensitive region of Tibet, contains two nuclear powers (India and Pakistan), and commands access to the Indian Ocean and the Arabian Sea, through which flows most of the oil consumed by the industrial states of East Asia.

As China's borders turn north and then curve back to the east, they link China to Central Asia, which consists of the adjacent states of Afghanistan, Tajikistan, Kyrgyzstan, and Kazakhstan; their neighbors Turkmenistan and Uzbekistan; and—occupying a geographic niche of its own to China's north—Mongolia. The states of Central Asia are important for the stability of Xinjiang, for their energy resources, and in military terms as either potential buffers or sources of threat for China.

During the Cold War, China shaped its policy toward each of its neighboring regions to support its policies toward superpowers: it was "a regional power without a regional policy."[2] Most of its neighbors were aligned for most of the time with either the U.S. or the Soviet Union, which put China regularly at odds with these states and created a legacy of mistrust. When the Cold War ended, Beijing adopted the rhetoric of "good-neighbor diplomacy." It sought to reassure its neighbors that its rise would not threaten their interests in order to dissuade them from coordinating with one another or linking up with outside powers to resist China's economic expansion and naval buildup. China settled boundary disputes with many neighbors and opened negotiations with others. It tried to engage nearby countries in guarantees of mutual noninterference and respect for territorial integrity, including promises not to try to destabilize China's minority regions. Beijing doubled the frequency of senior leader visits to its neighbors. Visits to other regions also rose, but those to the Asia-Pacific constituted more than 43 percent of the total.[3] China created economic links that gave its neighbors a positive stake in its growth, and it worked in various ways to diminish U.S. power around its periphery. At the same time, however, it yielded none of its core strategic goals and sometimes pushed them assertively.

Even though China's influence has grown around its periphery, it has not become the dominant power in any of its neighboring regions. In each of the regions, it confronts a strong Japanese economic presence. In Central Asia, Russia remains the major outside power. Most important, in all five regions Chinese influence is countered by a vigorous, multidimensional U.S. presence, just as it is in Northeast Asia. Indeed, China's rise has reinforced America's interest in Asia and the local countries' willingness to welcome American power.[4]

MARITIME SOUTHEAST ASIA: CHINA'S STAKE IN THE SOUTH CHINA SEA

Once an unexplored backwater, the South China Sea has become one of the most important bodies of water in the world in economic and strategic terms. About one-half of the world's maritime trade measured by merchant fleet tonnage passes through it each year, making its sea lanes among the most heavily traveled in the world. Their disruption by pirates or warring powers would affect the economic security of all the surrounding countries and that of Taiwan, Korea, and Japan as well as their protector, the U.S. With modern fishing technology, the sea yields more than 10 million tons of fish per year, and the technology now exists to begin to exploit the potentially vast and still unmeasured reserves of oil and gas that lie under its seabed. Seen in terms of China's military interests, the land formations surrounding the South China Sea complete the chain of obstacles that block Chinese naval power from easy expansion onto the high seas. The first island chain discussed in chapter 5 continues from the south of Taiwan around the east and south of the South China Sea and comprises

Philippines, Brunei, and Borneo. From there, Indonesia, Singapore, peninsular Malaysia, Thailand, and Vietnam form further barriers to the projection of Chinese maritime power.

Starting in the 1970s, the countries surrounding the South China Sea gained the naval capability to map the region and stake their claims as well as the commercial capability to exploit them. The Chinese, Vietnamese, and Malaysian navies advanced gradually through the region surveying the waters, locating hundreds of small islands, reefs, and other land formations, and installing observation platforms, meteorological stations, and small harbors. (The Philippine and Brunei navies were not equipped to compete with the others.) Fisheries fleets moved farther from shore, and surrounding countries began to lease offshore oil and gas fields to international companies.

All the surrounding countries laid claims to various territorial rights to portions of the South China Sea and clusters of its islands. As noted in chapter 5, international law gives every country around an international body of water some rights. These rights range from the right to exclude other countries' ships except for "innocent passage" (usually within 12 nautical miles of the relevant land body) to the right to exclusive economic exploitation (usually within 200 nautical miles). The legal principles give outsize importance to small islands, reefs, and atolls because their owners can claim special rights in large areas of sea around them. There are many different bases for plausible claims to islands, including first discovery, historical possession, and geographical connection to the home country's continental shelf. Where countries are close together around a body of water, as is the case with the nations surrounding the South China Sea, it is not unusual for their claims to overlap—as they also do between China and Japan over the Senkakus (chapter 5).

The South China Sea contains four main clusters of outcroppings widely scattered across its surface. The Paracel Islands (in Chinese, Xisha Qundao), located in the northern part of the South China Sea about equidistant from Vietnam and China, consist of more than thirty small islands and other land formations scattered across some 6,000 square miles of water. The Spratly Islands (Nansha Qundao), located farther south some 300 miles from the coast of Vietnam and 700 miles from China's Hainan Island, consist of more than one hundred small bits of land spread over about 160,000 square miles of water. The Pratas Islands (Dongsha Qundao), in the northeast part of the South China Sea not far from Hong Kong, consist of three islands. The Macclesfield Bank (Zhongsha Qundao) is a group of rocks close to the Philippines. (The sea also contains a number of other land features in addition to these islands.) Taken as a whole, these formations include only about 10 square miles of land surface above the water. Few are habitable without outside supplies of food and water. But if countries use them as the basis for claiming their 200-nautical-mile EEZs, then they potentially provide title to large, valuable expanses of the South China Sea.

China claims all of these outcroppings.[5] Its claims overlap in various ways with those of Vietnam (whose claims include the entirety of the Paracel and Spratly islands and are the largest after China's) and those of Malaysia, the Philippines, and Brunei.[6] If China were to make good on all its claims and enforce a 200-mile EEZ around them, it would own the whole South China Sea except for small zones just off the coasts of the surrounding states. Indeed, such a claim to the entire sea was illustrated by a famous map originally published by the Nationalist government in 1947 and republished by the PRC in 1992, called the "nine-dotted line map" because it showed Chinese claims in a sweeping arc of nine long dashes around the sea's perimeter. In 1993, China also published a map seeming to show a claim to the Natuna Islands in the far south of the South China Sea, which are held by Indonesia, but this claim has not been clarified or repeated.

Starting in the 1970s, China pushed steadily forward to consolidate its position with a mix of military, diplomatic, and economic tools, while trying not to frighten its rivals into a united front against it.[7] In 1974, Chinese naval forces clashed with the forces of the Republic of Vietnam (South Vietnam) in the Paracel Islands. The larger PLA Navy flotilla bested the four-vessel Vietnamese force, and China seized the Paracels' western group, taking control of the entire archipelago. In 1988, PLA Navy forces fought with forces of the Socialist Republic of Vietnam in the Spratly Islands. The main battle, which took place at Johnson Reef, was won by the Chinese, and they went on to occupy six nearby reefs claimed by Vietnam and the Philippines. In 1992, China granted a concession to the Crestone Energy Corporation for work in the southwestern corner of the South China Sea, adjacent to the Spratlys. In 1995, the Philippines discovered that the Chinese navy had moved onto the Mischief Reef, a formation in the Spratly group close to the Philippines, and had built a permanent structure there, which was manned with Chinese sailors who drove Filipino fishermen away. In 1997, a state-owned Chinese energy company drilled for gas in contested waters off the coast of Vietnam. Punctuating these events were a series of clashes between vessels of China's maritime security forces and fishing boats from various countries that they encountered in waters that China claimed.

Beijing reinforced its claims in 1988 by upgrading Hainan to provincial status and assigning each of the islets, reefs, and atolls that it claimed in the South China Sea a place in Hainan's administrative hierarchy. In 1992, the NPC Standing Committee adopted the Law of the People's Republic of China on Territorial Waters and Contiguous Territories, which asserted China's claims to the South China Sea in broadly inclusive language.

These actions exacerbated longstanding suspicions of China around the region. For the states of Southeast Asia, China's legacy was as a fomenter of revolution. Under Mao, China had supported Communist insurgencies verbally and sometimes materially in the Philippines, Indonesia, Singapore, Malaysia, Thailand, and Burma. Beijing cut its ties with these insurgencies starting in the late 1970s. In many cases, the insurgencies were heavily ethnic Chinese in composition. Even though the PRC had ceased to claim the sizable ethnic Chinese populations in these countries as citizens starting in 1954 (chapter 1), it still referred to them as Overseas Chinese and gave them the right to return to China to study and settle. As recently as 1979, China had fought with Vietnam in part over the treatment of the ethnic Chinese there. The 1995–1996 Taiwan Strait crisis (chapter 9) created new fears among Southeast Asian nations that China was becoming assertive and threatening.[8] This historically rooted perception of China as a threat was reinforced by Beijing's steps to exercise sovereignty claims in the South China Sea.

Beijing recognized that it had an image problem and sought to address it. In 1997, Foreign Minister Qian Qichen chose the annual meeting of the ASEAN Regional Forum held in Malaysia as the venue for the first high-level exposition of China's "new security concept" (chapter 1) . The concept echoed the Five Principles of Peaceful Coexistence, which Zhou Enlai had presented at the 1955 nonaligned summit in Bandung.[9] China's response to the 1997–1998 Asian financial crisis also helped soften its image: Beijing played a stabilizing role by not devaluing its currency and by offering low-interest loans to countries in the region. In 2002, Beijing signed the Declaration on the Conduct of Parties in the South China Sea, which had been drafted by ASEAN in part at the instigation of Vietnam, China's main competitor for South China Sea real estate. The parties pledged peacefully to resolve sovereignty disputes, but the declaration contained no specific provisions to resolve them. In 2004–2005, the China National Offshore Oil Corporation joined with the Philippine and Vietnamese national oil companies in a Joint Marine Seismic Undertaking to explore portions of the South China Sea seabed for energy resources. But this cooperative effort eventually unraveled. In 2011, as a result of U.S. prodding, China agreed to pursue confidence-building measures with ASEAN states in the South China Sea.

In none of these actions, however, did Beijing concede any territorial claims. It avoided legalistic debates under which it would have had to specify the detailed historical and legal bases of its claims. Instead, it pushed forward to consolidate its physical presence. Incidents continued in which vessels from various Chinese maritime agencies fired on fishing boats and harassed naval vessels of other Southeast Asian countries, while Beijing warned oil companies against exploring for oil in concessions granted by Vietnam. In the early 2000s, Chinese air and naval forces began to challenge U.S. air and sea craft on surveillance and monitoring missions just outside China's 12-mile territorial limit. The U.S. considered these missions legitimate in international waters and airspace, but China viewed them as provocative. In 2001, a Chinese fighter plane shadowing an American EP-3 surveillance aircraft about 70 miles off the Chinese coast collided with it, causing the damaged American plane to land in Hainan and triggering a diplomatic standoff that lasted several weeks while the Chinese fighter pilot, who died, was lionized in the official press. In another incident in 2009, Chinese maritime forces surrounded the USNS *Impeccable* when it was operating in waters about 75 miles south of Hainan, making navigation dangerous. China's apparent goal was to push back the scope and range of U.S. military activities in the South China Sea. In 2010, Chinese leaders told American officials that the South China Sea was a "core interest," although the claim was not publicly articulated. Southeast Asian neighbors viewed such actions as part of a broader pattern of Chinese assertiveness that was being shown at the same time in the Senkakus (chapter 5) and in China's overall naval buildup (chapter 11).

Although China is expanding its naval presence, there is no near-term prospect that it can achieve its maximum goal of controlling all the island groups and their EEZs. Other navies in the region challenge China occasionally, but look to the U.S. Navy for support as the PLA Navy upgrades itself beyond what ASEAN members can collectively or individually match.[10]

OCEANIA

Of the six regional systems around China, Oceania has been the least important to it. The area is relatively remote, contains no major powers, and—with the exception of Australia, New Zealand, Papua New Guinea, and Fiji—consists of tiny states spread over a vast ocean. This region, which encompasses the entire South Pacific and includes the three sub-regions of Micronesia, Polynesia, and Melanesia, was controlled in the nineteenth century by European powers (especially the United Kingdom, France, Holland, and Germany). During the twentieth century, the U.S. administered various trust territories in Micronesia and, along with France, dominated Polynesia, and Melanesia fell under the watchful eyes of Australia and New Zealand. The region was beyond Beijing's influence for more than four decades.

In the 1990s, China began to engage Oceania, driven by three motives. First, the diplomatic rivalry between Beijing and Taipei intensified (chapter 9). Small states mattered because their maintenance of formal diplomatic relations with the ROC challenged the PRC's claim to be the sole legitimate government of all China. Beijing and Taipei became embroiled in the domestic politics of the microstates as island politicians sought to extract funds or aid projects in exchange for maintaining or switching diplomatic ties. In 2002, Nauru severed ties with Taipei to establish relations with Beijing, reportedly for tens of millions of dollars in aid and debt relief. Three years later a different administration on the island moved to reestablish diplomatic relations with the ROC in exchange for Taipei's paying off the national airline's multi-million-dollar debt. In 2006, the cross-strait rivalry helped trigger a political crisis in the Solomon Islands. The proximate cause of the violence was the island Parliament's selection of an unpopular figure as prime minister in what was widely considered a rigged vote bought with Taiwanese money. As of 2012, ten states—Australia, New Zealand, the Cook Islands, the Federated States of Micronesia, Fiji, Niue, Papua New Guinea, Samoa, Tonga, and Vanuatu—maintained diplomatic relations with Beijing, and six states—the Solomon Islands, Kiribati, the Marshall Islands, Nauru, Palau, and Tuvalu—maintained diplomatic ties to Taipei.

Second, greater attentiveness to Oceania was driven by China's growing hunger for natural resources. Oceania is home to an estimated two-thirds of the global tuna population. Many of the small island states in the South Pacific do not possess their own fishing fleets and sell the rights to fish in their EEZs to outsiders such as China. By 2005, China had become Papua New Guinea's top trading partner and the largest market for its lumber.[11] A Chinese corporation owns stock in the vast Australian iron-mining conglomerate Rio Tinto and in mid-2009 made an unsuccessful bid to buy a larger stake. Other key commodities sourced from the region include coal, liquefied natural gas, wool, and nickel.

Since 1988, China has been represented at the Pacific Islands Forum (before 1999 the South Pacific Forum). China donated $3 million to the forum secretariat in 2000 to fund (among other projects) a trade office in Beijing. In April 2006, Premier Wen Jiabao visited Fiji to attend the inaugural China–Pacific Island Countries Economic Development Cooperation Ministerial Conference, the first time that a Chinese head of government visited a South Pacific island nation. By 2007, China reportedly had more diplomats posted in the region than any other country.

China's economic involvement has been a mixed blessing for the region's small states. It has become the third-largest aid donor to the region (behind the U.S. and Australia)[12] at a time when U.S. interest has waned. The aid has helped cash-strapped local governments with a number of projects, including equipping government ministries with computers (in Papua New Guinea), building a fishing fleet and investing in a seafood-processing plant (in the Cook Islands), constructing a sports complex (in Kiribati), building a law school (in Fiji), and constructing a parliament building (in Vanuatu). However, some of this aid has been for frivolous projects, and most has been dispensed with little transparency. As in Africa,

Chinese trade and investment have often resulted in what local people regard as the plundering of natural resources. Locals also resent the influx of PRC citizens, both legal and illegal, often viewing them as carpetbaggers who take jobs from citizens and compete with local businesses. In a number of cases, this view has prompted xenophobic backlashes. The most serious case was an anti-Chinese riot in the Solomon Islands that forced the Chinese embassy in Papua New Guinea to organize an airborne evacuation of several hundred citizens from Honiara in 2006.[13]

Third, Beijing's interests in Oceania include a geopolitical dimension. As China works toward projecting its maritime power into the Pacific Ocean (chapter 11), it seeks to wean Australia and New Zealand from their habit of close cooperation with the U.S. Navy.[14] Senior Chinese leaders made seven visits to Australia and six visits to New Zealand in the period 1992–2006. The warm welcome afforded Hu Jintao when he visited Australia in 2003 formed a sharp contrast with the cool reception given to U.S. president George W. Bush a few days earlier. In 2007, an unabashedly pro-American Australian prime minister was succeeded by Kevin Rudd, a former diplomat who spoke fluent Chinese and chose Beijing as the destination for his first official overseas trip. But underlying tensions resurfaced before long—over Chinese efforts to buy stakes in Australian natural resources companies, over the Chinese conviction of four executives of the Australian mining corporation Rio Tinto for bribe taking and commercial espionage, and over Chinese efforts to get Australian organizers to withdraw an invitation from Uyghur activist Rebiya Kadeer to attend a film festival in Melbourne. Such difficulties underscore the challenges Beijing faces in maintaining a positive image in Australia and the rest of Oceania. By 2011, relations between Canberra and Washington had been revitalized: President Obama received a warm welcome to Australia, and bilateral defense cooperation was expanded (see chapter 11).

CONTINENTAL SOUTHEAST ASIA

China's relations with Vietnam, Laos, Cambodia, Thailand, and Burma present a mix of security threats and opportunities as challenging as those that most countries face with their most difficult neighbors. First, sections of the international borders in these hilly, jungle regions remain contested. Second, ethnic groups straddle the borders, presenting problems of refugee movements, crime, drugs, smuggling, and public health. Third, as with other buffer states around China such as Korea and Kazakhstan, these neighboring pieces of territory can be used as much by other states to threaten China as by China to project power farther toward major rivals, depending on who has the most influence. Fourth, political instability in fragile states such as Burma can create disorder and potentially draw enemy powers closer to China's borders. Fifth, these neighbors are potential economic partners, competitors, and sometimes both. And sixth, each can line up with or against China in the halls of international diplomacy on issues ranging from the status of Taiwan to international climate and trade negotiations to the multilateral politics of Asian regionalism (discussed in the next section). Although none of these states presents the kind of existential threat that Russia did in the past or that Japan might in the future or the risk of major war as Korea and Taiwan do, they all are important to China's security in many ways.

Vietnam, like Korea, is a large country that appears small only by juxtaposition to its much larger neighbor; also like Korea, it was divided after World War II as a result of its location between the two Cold War camps. North and South Vietnam fought a long civil war, with U.S., Soviet, and Chinese involvement, before coming under unified Communist control in 1975. Vietnam today is a country of 90 million people, with a large, competent military of about half a million that defeated the U.S. in the Vietnam War and withstood a Chinese attack in 1979. It has a stable authoritarian political system and a rapidly developing economy that is increasingly oriented to the West.

The main foreign policy challenge for Vietnam has always been to maintain its autonomy from China.[15] It has used two strategies: to dominate its neighbors Laos and Cambodia and to align with powers farther away. China has tried to frustrate both of these goals so that Vietnam does not become strong enough to threaten Chinese interests.

During the Cold War, China saw Vietnam as a battleground against U.S. containment. It gave substantial economic and military aid to North Vietnam in its battle against the U.S.-supported South Vietnamese regime. The Vietnamese leaders believed that China's goal in doing so was to see the war continue as long as possible rather than to have it end soon with

Hanoi's victory. Nevertheless, China's support was useful. The fact that Vietnam was next to China prevented the U.S. from invading North Vietnam to cut off supplies and manpower for the Communist movement in the south. And it was Beijing's opening to the U.S. in 1972 that gave Richard Nixon the political cover to pull out of Vietnam, which served Hanoi's interests.

Once Vietnam was unified in 1975, however, Beijing turned from help to hindrance as it tried to prevent Hanoi from aligning with Moscow. China's attempts to pressure Hanoi led to an open split.[16] In 1978, Vietnam and the Soviet Union signed a Treaty of Friendship and Cooperation, and the Soviet navy gained access to the former U.S. naval bases in South Vietnam, enhancing Moscow's ability to project naval power in the South China Sea and the Indian Ocean. That same year, Vietnam invaded Cambodia, ousting the Chinese-supported Khmer Rouge regime there and installing a government friendly to itself. In return, in 1979 Chinese troops invaded Vietnam. Chinese leader Deng Xiaoping said the war was "to teach Vietnam a lesson"—partly about border issues and the mistreatment of ethnic Chinese, but chiefly about Hanoi's temerity, bolstered by Soviet support, in challenging Chinese strategic interests by invading a neighboring state.[17] For the next ten years, China aided the Khmer Rouge resistance in Cambodia, tying down Vietnamese troops in a long conflict. As we saw in chapter 3, Beijing declared the Vietnamese occupation of Cambodia to be one of the "three obstacles" to normalization of Sino–Soviet relations. It was also during this period that tensions intensified over competing Chinese and Vietnamese claims in the South China Sea.

The fall of the Soviet Union handed China the gift of a Vietnam that was not aligned with a major rival. China seized the opportunity to initiate the same policy of reassurance that characterized its post–Cold War relationships around most of its periphery. Vietnam was willing to play along. A series of high-level meetings culminated in a 1991 summit of premiers and party secretaries in Beijing, at which the two sides declared the normalization of relations at the state and party levels. Rail links were restored in 1996. In 1999, the two countries signed an Agreement on Friendship, Good Neighborliness, and Longstanding Stability and settled their land-border issues in principle, although it took another nine years to complete the demarcation. China became Vietnam's second-largest trading partner and a major investor.

But Vietnam remained distrustful and tried to balance against Chinese influence by intensifying relations with the U.S. Washington's normalization of relations with Cambodia in 1993 and with Vietnam in 1995 signaled the reengagement of the U.S. in the mainland of Southeast Asia following a two-decade hiatus. After extending "normal trade relations" (favorable tariff treatment) to Vietnam in 2001 and facilitating its accession to the WTO in 2007, the U.S. became Vietnam's largest export market, largest source of foreign direct investment, and one of the largest donors of development aid. Washington and Hanoi also pursued a low-profile program of military-to-military contacts.

In addition, Vietnam reached out to ASEAN. It joined the regional grouping in 1995 and used the ASEAN and U.S. connections to try to get China to negotiate South China Sea issues multilaterally. The multilateral approach was in both Hanoi's and the other Southeast Asian claimants' interest because all have claims against China, but few have claims against each other. As noted earlier, in 2002 ASEAN persuaded China to sign a nonbinding agreement in which signatories pledged not to use force to settle disputes in the South China Sea. The strategy of drawing on U.S. support scored a success in 2010 when the U.S. announced that it had a "national interest" in freedom of navigation in the South China Sea and offered to mediate territorial disputes there.

In Cambodia, China abandoned its support for the Khmer Rouge once Vietnam withdrew, took part in a postconflict multinational peace settlement, and contributed a contingent of troops to the postconflict peacekeeping operation. It supported the new Cambodian government (headed by former Vietnamese puppet Hun Sen) with arms supplies, trade, and diplomatic support. Cambodia developed close economic relations with China, and as an authoritarian regime it lined up with China on the position that Western countries should not intervene over human rights issues. In this way, Cambodia was neutralized as a strategic battleground and no longer formed part of a threat to Chinese interests.

In Laos, China settled its border issues and normalized relations in 1989. Although Vietnam remains the most influential outside power there, that relationship no longer poses a threat to China, which has become Laos's main trading partner and source of investment.

The situation in Burma during its nearly five decades of military rule concerned Beijing for the opposite reasons from the situation in Vietnam.

The military regime that ruled from 1962 to 2011 was weak and oppressive. Much of the country was occupied by armed ethnic groups at odds with the central government, the people were poor, and the mountainous border regions were virtually uncontrolled. This disorder made Burma a fertile source of cross-border "nonconventional security" issues for China (and for Burma's neighbors to the east and west, Thailand and Bangladesh), including drug smuggling, human trafficking, and criminal syndicates. In 2009, domestic upheaval spilled over into China with a cross-border exodus of refugees belonging to the Kokang ethnic group, who are of Chinese extraction. The nominally civilian regime that succeeded the military in 2011 tried to address some of these problems in new ways, but with uncertain success.

On the positive side, Burma is for China a rich source of natural gas, lumber (including highly prized teak, which is cut illegally), jade, pearls, and precious stones as well as a growing market for Chinese consumer goods such as garments, tobacco, beer, vehicles, and machinery. Chinese immigrants have flocked into northern and central Burma from Yunnan and other provinces to do business, many taking Burmese citizenship. Northern cities such as Mandalay show a heavy Chinese influence in construction and commerce. The Burmese trade is important to the prosperity of flourishing border towns in Yunnan.

Even more important is Burma's strategic utility to China. Its primary foreign policy orientation since independence in 1948 has been to avoid foreign intervention or control. Under U Nu (r. 1948–1958 and 1960–1962) and Ne Win (r. 1962–1988) during the Cold War, the country pursued a policy first of neutrality and then of isolation and nondevelopment. In that period, China brought pressure to bear chiefly by supporting the Burmese Communist Party. Beijing withdrew that support in the 1980s, and the Burmese Communist Party broke up in 1989. China then supported the Burmese regime on the condition that it not align itself with any of China's rivals. The international pariah status of the military junta that ruled until 2011 left the country with limited options. As a result, Burma moved closer into Beijing's embrace economically and militarily.

Owing to Burma's diplomatic near isolation because of the regime's human rights abuses, the ruling generals tightened ties with China as their chief source of aid, arms, and diplomatic protection. In exchange, China received strategic access to the Bay of Bengal and the Andaman Sea off

Burma's west coast facing India. China's development assistance went to improve the country's road system, thus providing both commercial and potential military access for landlocked southwestern China to Burmese ports. China supported the building of a navigable waterway down the Irrawaddy River, which would have both commercial and possibly military applications. From the Irrawaddy, which goes to Rangoon, a road branches off to the port of Kyaukphyu on the Bay of Bengal, again for commercial but also possible military use. China is helping to build gas and oil pipelines that will run from Burma's west coast into Yunnan Province, thus providing a source of energy for China's Southwest that is more direct and less vulnerable than shipment through the South China Sea. China has also reportedly constructed at least one intelligence-monitoring installation on Burmese-owned islands in the Andaman Sea.

Neighboring countries viewed these moves as a part of a long-term Chinese strategy to build a chain of naval installations encircling India and, viewed in conjunction with Chinese moves in the South China Sea, to gain greater control over the sea lanes that stretch from the Middle East to Japan and the rest of East Asia on both sides of the Strait of Malacca. To weaken Burma's dependency on China, the regional ASEAN grouping admitted the country to membership in 1997, and in 2009 the U.S. began to explore the possibilities of engagement with the regime. A new, nominally civilian regime installed in 2011 initiated reforms that enabled it to position itself more equidistantly between China, India, and the West. China retained privileged access, but it was not clear for how long.

China's concerns in Thailand are mainly an offshoot of its concerns in Vietnam and Burma. In the late Cold War, Thailand joined the U.S. and China in supporting Cambodian groups resisting the Vietnamese occupation of Cambodia and was the frontline state supplying arms to the Khmer Rouge. China pledged to help Thailand in case of a Vietnamese invasion and established a military hotline in 1985 for this purpose. China sold the Thai army guns, tanks, armored personnel carriers, and anti-aircraft guns at "friendship" prices. The close ties with China formed by Thai military and commercial elites in the course of the struggle over Cambodia subsequently continued to serve both sides' interests. With the rapid expansion of Chinese foreign trade since the 1990s, China has become Thailand's second-largest trading partner after Japan. But prospects for further development of relations are limited by fact that the two countries no longer share important strategic priorities, and their economies are more compet-ing than complementary.

ASIAN REGIONALISM: CHINA AND ASEAN

Asia exited the Cold War without an overarching "security architecture," in the sense of inclusive multilateral institutions with broad security man-dates, like NATO and the Warsaw Pact in Europe. A congeries of small and medium powers, Southeast Asia had no dominating internal actor, no polarizing strategic rivalry, no focal crisis point that might have sparked the creation of such structures. The U.S. organized its Asian allies during the Cold War in a "hub-and-spoke" system centered on itself, consisting of a mix of bilateral ties (defense relationships with Japan, Korea, the Phil-ippines, South Vietnam, and the ROC) and small-scale multilateral alli-ances (SEATO and the ANZUS Alliance).[18]

What has come to be called "Asian regionalism" made its modest start in 1967 with the formation of the ASEAN by Indonesia, Malaysia, Sin-gapore, the Philippines, and Thailand. The group was founded to com-pensate for the region's fragmentation. Southeast Asia's islands, jungles, and mountains had long been home to a multitude of ethnic groups. The entire region except for Thailand had been carved up into colonies by the European powers from the seventeenth to the twentieth centuries, who then encouraged the in-migration of Indian and Chinese workers and trad-ers. The independent states that were created after World War II inherited disputed borders, ethnic and ideological insurgencies, and fragile national identities.[19] In 1963, Indonesia declared a state of confrontation (*konfron-tasi*) with the newly formed neighboring state of Malaysia. Three nearby states sought to ease the crisis by bringing the two enemies into an organi-zation for building consensus.

After being little more than a talking shop for a quarter-century, ASEAN expanded in the 1990s as the politics of the region grew more fluid after the Cold War and the member countries became wealthier thanks to glo-balization. It added five new members, for a total of ten, thus covering the entire region except for Timor-Leste (a tiny new country that became independent from Indonesia in 2002). The organization negotiated the lowering of intraregional tariff barriers, anticipating the creation of an ASEAN Free Trade Area, and struck trade agreements with major partners outside the region. To socialize outside powers to local concerns and perspectives, ASEAN began to hold meetings with "dialogue partners," including China, India, Japan, the U.S., the EU, Australia, and New Zealand. It created annual meetings, such as ASEAN+3 (China, Japan, and Korea); Asia–Europe Meeting (ASEAN+3 plus Europe); ASEAN Regional Forum (ASEAN members, ten dialogue partners, and various observers); and East Asia Summit (ten ASEAN members, nine outside powers, and some observers). Such forums helped the region's ten relatively weak states get their concerns onto the agendas of outside powers. ASEAN internally developed regional programs in areas such as health, culture, education, and environment. In 2008, the heads of state adopted the ASEAN Charter, which committed the member states to tighten cooperation, hold biannual summits, and resolve any crisis through consultation and consensus.[20]

Although some other international organizations exist or have been proposed in Asia—in particular the Australian-sponsored Asia-Pacific Economic Cooperation—ASEAN remains the primary focus of regional action. Southeast Asian diplomats present the "ASEAN Way" as a crystallization of the wisdom of Asian culture. Culture aside, it represents a sensible strategy for a collection of smaller powers to show a united front to bigger powers and induce them to engage with the local states in a process of consultation and consensus building.

ASEAN's expansion in some ways facilitated and in some ways frustrated China's regional grand strategy of reassurance. Beijing was initially wary, believing that it could get more out of one-on-one negotiations with each ASEAN state than it was likely to get from dealing with the ten ASEAN states together. But it came to appreciate that cooperating with ASEAN was a good way to reduce suspicion of China's rise, to gain support against U.S. human rights pressure, to undermine the ASEAN states' quiet economic and diplomatic cooperation with Taiwan, and to legitimize China's voice in addressing a range of regionwide conventional and unconventional security issues, including the security of the sea lanes, piracy, environmental pollution, natural disasters, and the problem of Burma.[21] China started participating in the ASEAN Regional Forum in 1994; helped cofound the ASEAN+3 in 1997; and in 2002 signed four agreements with ASEAN, including the Declaration on the Conduct of Parties in the South

China Sea. In 2005, China acceded to the ASEAN Treaty of Amity and Cooperation, thereby gaining the right to participate in the annual East Asia Summit.

China also reassured Southeast Asian states of its benign intentions by peacefully resolving certain border disputes. Beijing concluded border agreements with Vietnam and Laos during the 1990s and 2000s. The Sino–Vietnam land border was fully demarcated by 2008, as was the maritime border in the northern sector of the Gulf of Tonkin, although the southern portion, which includes the Paracel and Spratly islands, remains to be resolved.[22] Senior Chinese military figures and PLA delegations began to make regular friendly visits to the ASEAN states. China conducted bilateral military exercises with Thailand in July 2007 and July 2008 and a multilateral maritime exercise in Singaporean waters in May 2007.

China's open policies toward foreign direct investment starting in the 1980s (chapter 10) enabled Southeast Asian manufacturers to move labor-intensive stages of their manufacturing operations to China, while continuing to produce higher-value-added components at home. As China lowered tariffs on imports from Southeast Asia first in the run-up to and then in the implementation phase of the China–ASEAN Free Trade Agreement, which came into force in 2010, it increasingly imported both raw materials and components for manufactured goods from around the region and exported computer chips, apparel, and electronic consumer products, among other goods. A global supply-chain system of manufacture emerged that tied all the advanced Asian economies to China in a win–win pattern of cooperation.[23] The China market became an engine of growth for Asian economies, helping them surmount the impact of the global financial crisis that started in the U.S. in 2008. Many of the Southeast Asian entrepreneurs in these supply chains who were ethnically Chinese reduced their loyalty to the regime on Taiwan as their cooperation with mainland China grew.

As always, however, close economic ties also produced areas of friction. China's appetite for lumber, jade, and other minerals damaged the environment in Burma, and Chinese merchants outcompeted local businessmen in the northern part of that country. In Vietnam, public outrage erupted in 2008 over a Chinese corporation's efforts to mine bauxite. Chinese development assistance in places such as Cambodia, Laos, Burma, Indonesia, and the Philippines often went to build infrastructure projects that benefited Chinese logistical access to the region. The fact that these projects were funded with loans tied to the use of Chinese suppliers and construction companies often generated resentment similar to that generated by the same kinds of Chinese policies in Africa (chapter 7).

Perhaps no China-related issue has captured the concern of the continental Southeast Asian states more than the management of river systems. The headwaters of some half a dozen major rivers in the region, including the Irrawaddy and the Mekong, lie in China. As the Chinese build numerous dams for hydropower and water management, they exert a serious downstream impact, threatening agriculture and fisheries especially in Cambodia and Vietnam.[24] In 1995, the governments of Vietnam, Laos, Cambodia, and Thailand formed the Mekong River Commission and recruited China and Burma as "dialogue partners" to try to attract China's attention to the downstream impacts of its activities. Popular resistance caused Burma's new civilian government to cancel a large Chinese-financed dam project on the upper reaches of the Irrawaddy in 2011.

An aspect of Southeast Asia's ethnic complexity that has presented a special problem for Chinese diplomacy is the residence throughout the region of tens of millions of people of Chinese descent—the Overseas Chinese (*huaqiao*). They are often involved in business and include some of the region's leading entrepreneurs. In some countries, such as Thailand, they are culturally assimilated; in most of the region, however, they retain a distinct identity and are sometimes suspected by other ethnic groups of loyalty to China. Indeed, Chinese-supported Communist insurgencies in Southeast Asia were often based in the ethnic Chinese community; during the Mao years, China offered free education to any ethnic Chinese who came home, no matter from where; and when China opened up economic ties with the region, the leading role in developing these ties was often played by ethnic Chinese. China also tried to protect its brethren when it could. When Indonesians rioted against ethnic Chinese in 1965, China rescued some victims by ship, citing humanitarian motives. When Vietnam oppressed ethnic Chinese living along the Chinese border and in urban areas in 1978–1979, China cited it as one of the reasons for the invasion of Vietnam. And when ethnic Chinese fled repression in northern Burma in 2009, China received them in refugee camps in Yunnan. At the same time, however, it tried to avoid conflict with regional states over the citizenship of the *huaqiao*. In 1954, as noted earlier, it adopted a nationality law that forbade dual citizenship, and Zhou Enlai declared that Chinese living permanently abroad should take local nationality. The position was reinforced in the 1980 nationality law.

Many of the countries in the region were aligned with the U.S. during the Cold War in its effort to resist Communist expansion and had given diplomatic recognition to Taiwan. With Singapore's switch of relations to the PRC in 1990, however, China gained the full sweep of formal diplomatic ties in the region. But it needs to work hard to maintain full diplomatic support against Taiwan. The Southeast Asian countries share the American interest in a "peaceful resolution" of the Taiwan issue, although they never say so. They recognize PRC sovereignty over Taiwan, but they would regard a PRC attack on Taiwan as a sign of China's having both intentions and capabilities threatening to their own security. Taiwan has a strong economic and informal diplomatic presence in most Southeast Asian countries.

Although its influence is growing, China is far from being able to fully reassure, much less to dominate, Southeast Asia. The U.S., Japan, and the EU are as important trading partners as China for the region and are more welcome because they present no strategic threat. In the military realm, U.S. forces, spearheaded by the Seventh Fleet under the Pacific Command, are the main counterweight to the PLA. Even with the growth of the Chinese navy and missile forces and China's advantage of proximity, the American forces remain superior in technology and performance. And the U.S. enjoys the local states' open welcome and often tacit cooperation because its presence provides the collective good of regional security, reduces the need for arms races among the local powers, and, above all, counterbalances the influence of a China whose long-term intentions none of the local states fully trusts. Thus, Singapore provides maintenance and repair services to U.S. Navy ships; Indonesia has accepted U.S. military training; the Philippines cooperates with U.S. special forces in combating domestic terrorism; Thailand has long had close ties with the U.S. military, including regular exercises; and Vietnam and, most recently, Malaysia now participate in military exercises with U.S. forces.

Any Chinese attempt to lobby against the ASEAN states' deep strategic interest in the U.S. presence would alarm them, thus undercutting Beijing's assurance strategy. A true rise to dominance for China in this region would require the voluntary reduction of the U.S. presence. There are no visible signs that an American disengagement from Asia is in the cards, however. On the contrary, the Obama administration declared in 2012 that U.S. diplomatic and military engagement in Asia would increase even as the U.S. reduced its military expenditures elsewhere.

SOUTH ASIA

Along with China, India is the other great rising power of Asia—a demographic giant whose population is set to overtake China's around 2030, a rising economy standing at number ten in the world, a continental power with security interests ranging from East Africa and the Middle East to Central Asia to Southeast Asia, and a nuclear-armed military power with an advanced navy and air force.

China and India are not direct competitors, at least not yet. China's main security concerns face away from India toward its east and south, whereas many, although not all, of India's main security concerns involve regions far from China to its own south and west. The two countries' conflicts for the time being are relatively specific, focusing on the band of territory stretched along the Himalayan mountain range that runs between the two countries, from Pakistan in the west to Burma in the east.[25] As China's navy grows, the Indian Ocean may emerge as a new area of strategic rivalry.

The primary area of rivalry is Tibet, an expansive region controlled by China that abuts almost all of the 1,600-mile northern border of India and its client states Nepal and Bhutan. Tibet is a natural buffer either for the Chinese heartland against India or for the Indian heartland against China. With their Buddhist culture and Sanskrit-based writing system, the Tibetans traditionally identified more with India than with China, and India under the British enjoyed greater political influence in Tibet than China. Since the Chinese army took control of Tibet in 1951, India has accepted that Tibet is part of the PRC.

But India has done what it can at low cost to weaken Chinese control. When the Dalai Lama fled Tibet in 1959 after a failed uprising against Chinese rule, India allowed him to set up a government in exile in the hill town of Dharamsala. Tens of thousands of other Tibetan exiles have also been welcomed in India. From that base, the Dalai Lama has conducted an international campaign to press China to grant Tibet greater autonomy (chapter 8). The Chinese claim that unrest inside Tibet is instigated by the Dalai Lama and supported by outside forces. And China is aware of the existence of a nine-thousand-strong paramilitary frontier force in the Indian military composed largely of ethnic Tibetans, which is trained and equipped to fight in the Himalayan environment.

To weaken Indian support for the Tibetan exile movement is thus a prime goal of Chinese diplomacy. In the course of the diplomatic thaw between China and India starting in 1988, China repeatedly prevailed upon New Delhi to acknowledge that Tibet is part of China and to promise not to "allow Tibetans to engage in anti-China political activities in India." But the Indian government claimed that most Tibetan activities in India were not in fact "anti-China," thereby allowing the Dalai Lama and his associates to maintain their exile government and travel freely to mount international pressure on China. Indian statements continued to emphasize that Tibet should be "autonomous" within the PRC, using the same term the Chinese government uses but implying a higher degree of autonomy than the Chinese government grants. India has never acknowledged the Chinese claim that Tibet was historically "always" part of China, which would imply that Chinese rule is irrevocable.

China's efforts to secure its borders and improve control over ethnic Tibetans are also driving recent efforts to get closer to Nepal. Beijing is pressing Kathmandu to crack down on political activities by Tibetans living in Nepal, and to tighten its borders with China because thousands of Tibetans have used the porous border to make visits to India, including pilgrimages to see the Dalai Lama. In exchange, China offers various kinds of aid, improved transportation links, and the lure of greater trade and economic investment.

A second area of Sino–Indian conflict concerns three sparsely populated but strategically important parcels of land along the edge of the Tibetan plateau. To the west lies the 14,000-square-mile area Aksai Chin, administered by China but claimed by India. It is strategically important for China because a road through it connects western Xinjiang Province with western Tibet and for India because it lies to the east of the disputed territory of Kashmir, which is claimed in its entirety by both India and Pakistan and is currently divided between the two of them. To the southeast of Aksai Chin, China and India disagree over the ownership of a 770-square-mile area occupied mostly by India that contains a series of mountain passes from

Tibet into India on the western edge of Nepal. On the eastern sector of the Tibet–India border, China claims 35,000 square miles of the territory of the Indian state Arunachal Pradesh, which is important to both sides both because of its strategic location and because it contains a sizable population of ethnic Tibetans. The 1962 Sino–Indian war was fought over control of these territories but did not produce any lasting change in control. A thaw between the two countries after Mao's death led to the beginning of boundary talks, which have continued on and off without resolving the issues.

The third area of competition centers on Pakistan, which is India's prime security threat and the only country besides North Korea with which China has maintained a consistently friendly relationship since the 1950s. Pakistan has served China as a counterweight to India, a bridge to the Islamic world, and a trusted friend in diplomacy—helping, for example, to facilitate Kissinger's secret visit to Beijing in 1971. China's relationship with Pakistan became closer after the Sino–Soviet split because India was aligned with the USSR, and it was further promoted by the 1962 Sino–Indian border war and the conclusion of a 1963 Sino–Pakistani border agreement. Following India's 1974 nuclear test, China began covertly assisting Pakistan in its nuclear weapons program.[26] This program came to fruition with Islamabad's test explosion of five nuclear devices in 1998, thus maintaining strategic pressure on New Delhi at little cost to Beijing. China shifted its position on Kashmir in the late 1970s, from explicitly supporting Pakistan's position in favor of a referendum that would be expected to give control of the territory to Pakistan to calling for peaceful resolution through negotiations. But Indian leaders worry that this neutral-sounding proposal fortifies Islamabad's position that the Indian claim to the territory is not legitimate.

During the long, slow Sino–Indian thaw that began in the 1980s, China maintained its ties to Pakistan. At least through the 1990s, if not later, China continued to supply nuclear and missile technology even while cutting off supplies to most other clients.[27] In the 2000s, the two countries undertook joint production of an advanced combat aircraft, the JF-17 Thunder, and signed a Treaty of Friendship, Cooperation, and Good-Neighborly Relations in 2005.

In the 1960s and 1970s, China built the Karakoram Highway, which linked Xinjiang with northern Pakistan. This highway delivered a double blow to Indian interests by supporting Pakistani control of its sector of Kashmir and strengthening China's position in Aksai Chin. In coming years, assuming the highway is upgraded and properly maintained, it will form part of a strategic transport route between Chinese territory and the Pakistani port of Gwadar on the Arabian Sea, whose expansion is being financed by China. This route can be used to bring Middle Eastern oil and other commodities into northwest China and potentially to support Chinese naval operations in the Arabian Sea.

Despite the longevity of the China–Pakistan relationship, from the Chinese point of view it serves limited purposes. Besides counterbalancing India and opening a land route to the Arabian Sea, Pakistan may cooperate in suppressing the Uyghur independence movement. This was one of the reasons Beijing invited Islamabad to participate in the SCO as an observer. Pakistan has refused asylum to Uyghur activists and handed them over to Chinese authorities, and it conducts biannual counterterrorism exercises with China focused on how to protect Xinjiang from infiltration from Pakistani soil. But as Islamabad has gradually lost control over the training of Islamic fundamentalists and terrorists on its own territory, new frictions have arisen with Beijing over what China views as a growing Uyghur threat emanating from Pakistan.[28]

Finally, China and India conduct an uneven rivalry for influence in Burma, whose seacoast occupies a strategic position along the Bay of Bengal opposite India's east coast and its strategically important Andaman and Nicobar islands. Burma has historical ties to India because both were part of the British Indian Empire. It is a valuable source of natural resources for the Indian economy. But India gained the distrust of the Burmese military regime by supporting the pro-democracy movement in 1988 and has only slowly restored ties, whereas China gained influence as the regime's main arms supplier and diplomatic supporter.

China, for now, has the upper hand in all four areas of rivalry with India, except for India's occupation of Arunachal Pradesh. As a consequence, Indian policymakers are more worried about China than vice versa. The China threat was one of the reasons New Delhi gave for declaring itself a nuclear weapons state in 1998, although neither country has a realistic reason or strategy for using nuclear weapons against the other. India views with alarm the Chinese role in developing seaports in its neighboring states of Pakistan, Burma, Sri Lanka (the port of Hambantota) and, potentially, Bangladesh (Chittagong). Although the ports are being developed for commercial use, Indians worry that they might eventually serve as bases for the

Chinese navy as it expands into the Indian Ocean and beyond. They note that China seems to be lacing together what some Americans have dubbed a "string of pearls"—a skein of naval bases in friendly countries stretching from the South China Sea to the east coast of Africa.[29]

For China, the main worry about India is its intensifying cooperation with the U.S. India aligned itself with the Soviet Union during the period when Moscow was Beijing's prime enemy. Once the U.S. emerged as China's chief security concern, India lined up again against China. Even though the U.S. disapproved of India's 1998 nuclear tests, Bill Clinton paid a state visit to India in 2000, becoming the first sitting U.S. president to do so in forty years. In 2004, George W. Bush abandoned sanctions the U.S. had put in place to protest the nuclear tests and signed an agreement to cooperate on peaceful uses of atomic energy. In 2010, Barack Obama endorsed India's long-expressed desire to become a permanent member of the UN Security Council. Combined with Washington's deeper engagement in Pakistan after September 11, 2001, its invasion of Afghanistan, and its establishment of military bases in Central Asia, these developments appeared to Beijing to be part of a strategy to encircle China.

To reduce tensions with India and consolidate what is currently a balance of power relatively favorable to China, Beijing has tried to build on elements of potential partnership. Beijing and New Delhi exchanged a series of summit visits starting in 1988 and pursued border talks that prevented major military clashes, although they did not produce progress on the issues. During the early 2000s, bilateral trade boomed, growing from less than $3 billion in 2000 to almost $52 billion in 2008. China consistently runs a significant surplus because India's exports are mostly raw material and iron ore, while its imports are value-added manufactures and machinery. The first direct commercial air link between Beijing, Shanghai, and New Delhi was established in 2002. Four years later the two countries agreed to increase the number of direct flights from seven to forty-two per week. In 2003, Beijing and New Delhi agreed to reopen the Nathu-La Pass, one in a series of road and rail projects to improve cross-border transportation. In addition, the two countries appear to be developing a Sino–Indian "land bridge" through Burma, a twenty-first century version of the Burma Road.[30]

As both countries rise in commercial and diplomatic influence and their navies grow, their antagonism may intensify around the rim of the Indian Ocean. Beijing believes that New Delhi has overambitious "great-power dreams."[31] Looking toward that possibility, China has used development aid, arms sales, and commercial relations to develop friendly relations with all the other states in the South Asian regional system—not only Pakistan, but also Bangladesh, Bhutan, the Maldives, Nepal, and Sri Lanka. All these countries fear domination by India and are open to relations with the only outside power that has an interest in helping them fend off New Delhi's embrace. None except Pakistan is likely to challenge India directly, but China is laying the groundwork for a soft encirclement of its South Asian rival.

CENTRAL ASIA: FORGING COMITY

In the wide sweep of Chinese history, the regional system that has posed the greatest challenge for successive rulers has been Central Asia. Twice, in the thirteenth and seventeenth centuries, China was occupied by armies from the north but survived as a political and cultural entity by sinicizing the occupiers. The western frontier, separated from the heartland not just by great distance but also by wide deserts and rugged mountain ranges, seemed less threatening than the North, serving as an undeveloped frontier and a trade route—the Silk Road—to Europe and the Middle East. During the period of the Sino–Soviet split in the 1960s and 1970s, however, China's northern and western frontiers were tense and militarized. But the thaw of the late 1980s witnessed troop reductions on both sides of the border and the Red Army's withdrawal from Afghanistan, culminating in the Gorbachev–Deng Xiaoping summit in 1989 (chapter 3).

The collapse of the Soviet Union two years later presented China with new challenges along its Central Asian frontiers. Former Soviet satellite Mongolia became a democracy and started to lean toward the West; five fragile independent states—Kazakhstan, Kyrgyzstan, Tajikistan, Turkmenistan, and Uzbekistan—emerged west of Xinjiang, the first three of them bordering on it directly; and Islamic fundamentalists stood poised to take power in the aftermath of the Soviet withdrawal from Afghanistan. This post–Cold War threat was something novel: not one overly strong neighbor bent on military invasion, but several overly weak neighbors that might incubate cross-border ethnic movements that would destabilize Xinjiang (chapter 8). Besides preventing such destabilization, China sought to make sure that the Soviet Union's successor regimes inherited and continued Moscow's policies of peacefully settling border disputes with China and demilitarizing their borders. Further, China needed to persuade Moscow to accept the legitimacy of an influential role for Beijing in this formerly off-limits region. And over the longer term, it hoped to benefit from the region's energy and other resources. In all, Chinese strategy in the region sought to extend influence in a way that would contribute to stability, that could be accepted by all the local regimes, and that would not be perceived by Russia as threatening.

Beijing moved deliberately in pursuit of these goals. As we have seen in chapter 3, Chinese leaders swallowed their distaste for Gorbachev's successor Boris Yeltsin and worked to institutionalize cooperation with Russia diplomatically and economically. Beijing extended immediate recognition to each of the Soviet successor states and continued negotiations to demilitarize their borders with Xinjiang. And China hosted a series of five-power summits starting in 1996 that engaged Kazakhstan, Kyrgyzstan, and Tajikistan along with Russia in discussion of China's priority of opposing what Beijing labeled the "three evils" of terrorism, separatism, and extremism (in plain language, Islamic fundamentalism that might threaten Xinjiang). These moves created the basis to establish in 2001 a formal entente, the SCO, which included the original Shanghai Five plus Uzbekistan.[32] In 2003, the SCO's members established a secretariat in Beijing and selected a Chinese diplomat to serve as the secretary-general.

The SCO has paid dividends for China. First, it has focused the attention of Central Asian states on preventing threats to Chinese control of Xinjiang, a policy that is also in their interests because these weak states are also subject to threats from ethnic minorities and Islamist movements. The member states concluded a series of agreements on intelligence sharing, denial of asylum, and guaranteed extradition of one another's wanted individuals.[33] An antiterrorism information-sharing center, the Regional Anti-Terrorism Structure, established in 2002, provides a mechanism for building blacklists and sharing intelligence. This mechanism is especially useful because the greatest concentration of Uyghurs beyond China's borders is in Central Asia, and the vast majority—an estimated four hundred thousand—resides in Kazakhstan.[34] In October 2002, several hundred Chinese and Kyrgyz soldiers conducted a bilateral counterterrorism exercise in

Kyrgyzstan under the gaze of observers from other SCO member states. It was China's first joint exercise with another country on foreign soil. The following year, China conducted its first multinational military exercise on Chinese territory. More than a thousand Chinese and Kyrgyz troops participated under the watchful eyes of China's minister of national defense as well as Russian, Kazakh, and Tajik observers. Bilateral Sino–Russian and multilateral SCO military exercises also occurred in 2005 and 2007, supposedly directed against terrorists. Such exercises build trust and facilitate communication among regional militaries, while sending an intimidating signal to activists who might be inclined to challenge existing regimes.

Second, the SCO has softened Russian resistance to Chinese influence in Central Asia. Russia still views itself as the main power in the region. It has long-standing political and economic ties there, supports the ruble as the currency used for intraregional trade, tries to protect ethnic Russian populations left over from the Soviet era, and maintains military bases in Tajikistan, Kyrgyzstan, and Kazakhstan. It established its own umbrella organizations that cover Central Asia—the Commonwealth of Independent States and the Collective Security Treaty Organization, both of which include the same four Central Asian states as the SCO, along with several other states. Yet Moscow finds the SCO useful because it provides a cooperative rather than competitive framework for the extension of Chinese influence to the region. Moreover, the SCO contributes to regional stability by helping the member states collaborate to stay in power. Each benefits from the legitimacy extended by the others and from cooperation against domestic opponents and foreign critics.

Third, SCO serves as a gatekeeper for access by other states that have a strategic interest in the region. Since its formation, the SCO has added four "observer states" (India, Pakistan, Iran, and Mongolia), two "dialogue partners" (Belarus and Sri Lanka), and three "guests" (Afghanistan, the Commonwealth of Independent States, and ASEAN). Conspicuous absentees from the SCO are the fifth Central Asian Soviet successor state, Turkmenistan, which is farthest away from China and shows little interest in any regional mechanisms, whether Russian or Chinese led, and the U.S., which put out feelers about establishing an affiliation but received a cool response. Instead, at their 2005 summit, the six countries—more under Uzbek and Russian than Chinese urging—issued a statement urging the U.S.-led coalition forces to "determine a deadline" for their withdrawal from bases in SCO member countries being used to support the war in Afghanistan. At the same time, Uzbekistan forced the U.S. to close its airfield at Karshi–Khanabad. Kyrgyzstan allowed the U.S. to keep its airbase at Manas open in return for greater compensation. From Beijing's point of view, such actions were not intended to undercut the U.S. effort in Afghanistan but to discourage a permanent U.S. military presence at China's back door.[35]

China sees great economic potential in Central Asia and its surging economy is better positioned than Russia's to exploit these opportunities. Particularly important are the region's energy resources, which have the advantage of not needing to be shipped over the exposed maritime transport lanes through the South China Sea. China has worked hard to compete with U.S. interests for oilfield development rights, pipelines, and oil supplies. Progress has been slow owing in part to poor transportation links and underdeveloped infrastructure. In 1997, the China National Petroleum Corporation and the governments of China and Kazakhstan agreed to build an oil pipeline, but construction did not begin until September 2004, and the pipeline did not begin delivering crude oil from central Kazakhstan to western China until May 2006. In December 2009, a pipeline began pumping natural gas from Turkmenistan to Xinjiang through more than a thousand miles of rugged terrain across Uzbekistan and Kazakhstan. Besides cooperation regarding oil and gas, China has promoted the rapid growth of trade ties throughout the region, making it one of the highest-ranking trade partners of most of the Central Asian republics. At the 2003 SCO heads-of-government meeting in Beijing, Premier Wen Jiabao suggested the establishment of a free-trade agreement among the members to speed the development of these ties.

Afghanistan looms larger in Beijing's security agenda than the sixty-mile length of the two countries' border would suggest. Beijing views the country as a hotbed of Islamic radicalism, which it fears can spread in Central Asia and spill over into Xinjiang. In 2000, the Chinese ambassador to Pakistan met with Taliban leader Mullah Omar, reportedly in an unsuccessful attempt to forge an agreement under which the Taliban would undertake not to support Uyghur militants in Xinjiang in exchange for Chinese support for Afghanistan in the UN. The U.S. intervention in 2001 made China uneasy, yet China wishes the U.S. success in its battle against terrorism. China moved into Afghanistan as soon as conditions permitted to begin to develop copper, iron, oil, and other mineral resources there.

Mongolia moved out of Moscow's orbit in the early 1990s. Unlike a number of the former Soviet republics, it no longer allows the stationing of Russian troops. Nor is there a significant ethnic Russian population. Mongolia has sought to develop closer relations with the U.S. In 2005, George W. Bush became the first U.S. president to visit the country. Ulan Bator and Washington have a significant but modest security relationship, which has included participation by small Mongolian units in coalition forces in Iraq and Afghanistan. The existence of an independent Mongolia exerts an appeal on the approximately 4 million ethnic Mongols living in China, many of them in the adjacent Inner Mongolian Autonomous Region. There is no territorial dispute between China and Mongolia, a border agreement having been reached in 1964. China's concerns here are twofold: to ensure that Ulan Bator's improved relationship with Washington remains limited and that pan-Mongolian nationalism is kept in check. China's chief power asset is economic: like China's other smaller neighbors, Mongolia finds its prosperity increasingly tied to the booming Chinese economy, and it depends on transport routes through China for access to the rest of the world.

China's management of its relations with Central Asian neighbors has largely proved successful. Its influence seems likely to grow, gradually rivaling and perhaps even surpassing that of Russia. U.S. involvement is likely to remain limited, but significant for as long as Washington views Afghanistan as a U.S. national security priority.

LOCAL POWER OF GLOBAL SIGNIFICANCE

Despite China's dramatic rise, it remains a regional power rather than a true global power, as we argue in chapter 7. Its insatiable quest for natural resources, although global in scope, is heavily concentrated in the Asia-Pacific. The rise of Chinese military power will be felt in this region first and most. But the preceding chapter and this one have shown that China looms larger in its own region than do other regional powers both in Asia and beyond, such as Japan, Russia, Brazil, or South Africa. And local eminence in Asia means more for global influence than does local eminence in South America or Africa: the Asia-Pacific macroregion defined by China's presence at its core contains 40 percent of the world's population, 31 percent of its GDP, and more than three-quarters of the Eurasian landmass, which is the central strategic zone of world politics. Local power in this neighborhood is of global significance.

Beijing's growing strength and its preoccupation with its immediate periphery have combined to produce a Chinese soft version of the Monroe Doctrine: not a claim to deny access to other powers, but the ambition to achieve a strong voice on all regional issues. At a minimum, Beijing aspires to a buffer zone of stable neighbors, free of great-power dominance and deferential to Chinese interests.

Yet this quest faces obstacles. If China's rise has produced growing deference from its neighbors, it has also created growing frictions. Everywhere around its periphery on land and at sea, China faces the powerful presence of the U.S. The more China rises, the more most of China's neighbors welcome this presence as a counterbalance.

The Second Ring and Third Ring will absorb most of the energy of China's foreign relations for the foreseeable future. A host of challenges will continue to preoccupy Beijing: territorial disputes on land and at sea, access to resources, security of sea transport, spillover ethnic groups and other nonconventional security issues, and the competition with the U.S., Japan, Russia, India, and other actors for influence over neighboring states. This extensive agenda of interests and concerns will preclude China's playing a much greater role in the regions beyond Asia for some time to come. As long as Asia absorbs so much of Beijing's energy and resources, China's policy aims in the rest of the world will remain focused on a limited set of economic and diplomatic priorities.

7

CHINA IN THE FOURTH RING

As the world's second-largest economy and the major regional power in Asia, China has taken a place at the center of world politics. It is a global actor, with a voice on every world issue. But China is not yet what the Soviet Union once was and the United States is today, a true global power—that is, a country with comprehensive strategic interests and influence in every corner of the world. In Europe, the Middle East, Africa, Latin America, and Canada, China's interests and influence are limited to two spheres, economic and diplomatic.

We have labeled these widely disparate regions the Fourth Ring because they lie beyond China's immediate neighborhood. As long as local regimes in the Fourth Ring accommodate Chinese economic and diplomatic interests, China has no stake in their ideological character, domestic politics, military posture, or strategic alignments. The one strategic interest China has in the Fourth Ring is stability, because war or regime change threaten to disrupt its economic access and diplomatic ties. But Beijing does not need to care what kind of stability prevails—democratic or authoritarian, military or civilian, theocratic or secular, tribal or class based—so long as it is not an arrangement that excludes China. Nor can China afford to care about such issues, because China does not have the resources that would be required to promote a specific ideology in the Fourth Ring, support client regimes, or build a significant military presence.

China's emergence as an actor in the Fourth Ring has been recent and dramatic. Under Mao Zedong, Beijing's ties outside of Asia were limited to a few governments and political parties that had put themselves at odds with Moscow and often with Washington as well. In Eastern Europe, the PRC maintained relations with two of the three countries that had broken from the Soviet bloc, Albania and Romania (but not with Yugoslavia, whose regime was too liberal for Mao's taste). In the Middle East, China both recognized the Palestine Liberation Organization and cultivated ties with Iran in the late years of Shah Reza Pahlevi's regime in an effort to increase its influence in a region dominated for decades by the two superpowers. In Angola, Rhodesia, South-West Africa, and elsewhere in Africa, China aided governments and insurgencies that were anti-Soviet, even if they were right wing (chapter 3). China supported a variety of small pro-China Communist parties worldwide, including one in the U.S. In Western Europe, the PRC got diplomatic recognition from the four Nordic states and two major American allies—Britain in 1950 because it needed a channel to Beijing in order to manage Hong Kong and France in 1964 because it wanted to make a point of its foreign policy independence.

China's role in the Fourth Ring increased after 1971, when the PRC took the China seat in the UN. Along with its Security Council seat, Beijing acquired diplomatic recognition from most governments, but it was still a minor presence outside Asia. Only after the PRC entered the WTO in 2001 and began to reach across the globe for commodities and markets did it acquire extensive interests and influence beyond its own neighborhood.

China's policy agenda in the Fourth Ring today focuses on three economic issues and three diplomatic issues. In the economic category, first, Beijing is engaged in a quest for secure sources of petroleum to help satisfy its growing need for energy. Second, more generally, it seeks access to other commodities and to markets and investments around the world. Third, Beijing is engaged in arms sales, chiefly for profit rather than for strategic reasons. On the diplomatic front, fourth, China seeks cooperative relations with as many regimes as possible in order to protect economic access. Fifth, Chinese diplomats work country by country to maintain China's policy of diplomatically isolating Taiwan and the Dalai Lama. Sixth, China seeks support from Fourth Ring governments for its position in a range of multilateral negotiations over international norms and regimes.

To shift from this specialized agenda to a more comprehensive role as a global power would require more than incremental change. The Fourth Ring is too large, too far away, too politically complex, and still too much dominated by the traditional colonial and neocolonial powers to come easily under the sway of a remote Asian power, even one as large and dynamic as China.

THE QUEST FOR PETROLEUM SECURITY

China's growth as a manufacturing hub for exports and its citizens' rising living standards caused a huge increase in its energy use starting in the 1990s and with it a growing reliance on imported oil.[1]

Fortunately from its own security standpoint, most of China's energy—71 percent in 2008—comes from domestically produced coal, which is used to produce electricity. This makes China the world's largest coal consumer. Coal has environmental disadvantages because it is dirty to mine, transport, and burn, but it has a security advantage because China does not have to import much of it. (Some is imported, more when prices are low and less when they are high.) China also produces energy domestically from nuclear power, hydropower, and wind power. But oil provides a large and growing proportion of its energy. Oil is irreplaceable under current technology because no other source can be used on a large scale for road transport. It is also a key input in many of China's most important industrial products, including petrochemicals, fertilizers, and plastics. China became a net oil importer in 1993 and by 2007 imported almost half its oil, making it the world's second-largest oil importer after the United States. According to various estimates, China will import 70–80 percent of its petroleum by 2030, becoming the world's largest consumer of imported oil. The major sources of Chinese oil imports have been Saudi Arabia, Angola, Iran, Oman, Russia, Sudan, Iraq, Kazakhstan, Kuwait, Brazil, and Libya, with their rank varying year by year. Oil comes to China from many other countries as well.

Dependence on imported oil leaves China, like other oil-importing countries, vulnerable both to price fluctuations and to interruptions in supply. China's situation is not as bad as that of Japan, Germany, South Korea,

India, and many other countries that import even higher proportions of their energy resources. Nevertheless, an oil disruption would severely damage China's economy, political stability, and military preparedness. Chinese strategists believe that oil supplies might be disrupted for several reasons, including instability in oil-producing states, terrorism, piracy, and war. In such contingencies, they worry that Western governments and Western-dominated international oil companies might use their ownership of much of the world's oil reserves and their cozy relations with major suppliers such as Saudi Arabia and Mexico to give priority to Western consumers. Or if China–U.S relations were to deteriorate, Washington might squeeze China's oil supplies to hold back the country's economic growth.

To reduce this vulnerability, China has adopted a multipronged approach that is similar to that of other petroleum importers. Policymakers have pushed for more efficient use of petroleum (for example, by raising mileage standards for cars and gradually raising the price of gas). They have tried to increase the use of other energy sources, such as natural gas, nuclear power, hydropower, solar power, and wind power. China has defended its claims to what it believes are large oil and gas reserves in the East China and South China seas (chapter 6). Starting in 2000, it created a strategic petroleum reserve, aiming for the capacity to store a ninety-day supply of oil by 2020. A strategic petroleum reserve helps a government control the domestic price of oil by filling the tanks when oil is cheaper and emptying them when prices surge, and it provides a cushion to deal with interruptions in supply. China has helped to construct oil and gas pipelines in Central Asia that provide access to supplies of hydrocarbons that would not be accessible otherwise. If proposed pipeline projects in Pakistan and Burma come to fruition, they would provide land routes to move oil from the Middle East and Africa into the Chinese interior along pathways that would be less exposed to disruption than seaborne supplies in certain wartime scenarios. But pipelines are expensive and time consuming to build. In 2006, China established the Energy CLSG in the CCP center to coordinate energy policy (chapter 2).

As part of the push for energy security, Beijing decided in the late 1990s that its state-owned oil companies should "go out" to get oil. It would not be enough just to buy oil on international markets: the oil companies should also seek ownership stakes in foreign oil reserves (referred to as "equity oil" in distinction to "commodity oil"). The three major Chinese national oil companies are the China National Petroleum Corporation (known as PetroChina on foreign stock exchanges), the China Petroleum and Chemical Corporation (Sinopec), and the China National Offshore Oil Corporation. Propelled by generous credit from Chinese state banks, these latecomers to the international oil game moved into countries where political conflict with the West or difficult natural conditions left resources open for acquisition, and they made some sizable investments in oil operations. Some analysts criticized this policy, saying that China overpaid for equity stakes and should have relied on the international oil market, which is open to all. But Chinese policymakers saw the West treating oil as a strategic asset and believed that they should do the same. For example, Beijing was impressed by the visceral U.S. political reaction that derailed the attempted purchase of an American oil company, Unocal, by the China National Offshore Oil Corporation in 2005. Besides, China had a great deal of foreign exchange that it needed to invest. And equity oil investments served the Chinese oil companies' business interests because oil production was profitable, and stakes in foreign oil reserves bulked up the companies' asset values. As of 2010, about 20 percent of the Chinese national oil companies' production came from fields outside China.

China's equity oil investments are located in nearly fifty countries, some in Asia, but most in the Fourth Ring. For the most part, these investments are modest in comparison to the large stakes held by the local national oil companies and the international majors. They entail no more than the usual political complications that attend large business deals in most emerging markets.

In two cases, however, China became more than usually politically entangled. It was no coincidence that the Chinese companies, as latecomers, made some of their largest investments in countries whose political environments were among the world's most forbidding. They were able to do so because other outsiders were cautious about investing in these countries or had pulled out.

One such country was Sudan. A vast, underdeveloped country, Sudan contains hundreds of ethnic groups and tribes that often engage in armed conflict. Its two largest civil wars were those between the Arab North and the Christian South and between the Arab-dominated central government and the non-Arab (black African) tribes of the Darfur region. The North–South war went through two phases, the second of which ended in a peace agreement in 2005 that led, in turn, to the creation of the independent Republic of South Sudan in 2011. The Darfur conflict broke out in 2003 and went through several phases of intense conflict, which many observers labeled a genocide. To press the Khartoum government to end its attacks in Darfur, the U.S. and Europe imposed sanctions, the UN imposed an arms embargo, the African Union proposed reconciliation and offered a peacekeeping force, and in 2008 the International Criminal Court indicted Sudanese president Omar al-Bashir for genocide and crimes against humanity. The conflict also spilled over into neighboring Chad, whose government was hostile to the government of Sudan.

It was in this environment that China had by 2006 invested an estimated $10 billion in Sudanese oil fields, mostly in the South, pipelines between South and North, and refineries and port facilities in the North. Sudan became one of China's half-dozen or so top oil suppliers overall and by far the largest source of oil that China's national oil companies produced in Africa. This status made China Sudan's largest trading partner and investor, so China could hardly avoid entanglement in the country's internal and external conflicts.

China's interest, however, was not in the outcome of these battles, but in maintaining relationships with all contending parties so as to protect its economic assets and diplomatic relationships. Beijing needed good relations with the national government in Khartoum because Sudan's pipelines, refineries, and port facilities were in the North; with the southern authorities because most of its oilfields were located there or along the North–South border; with the Darfurian rebels to the extent possible because they had the capability to attack certain Chinese installations; with Chad because China also had oil investments in that country; with other concerned African states because of its ties with each of them; and with the West. These multiple needs resulted in a complex policy, which Beijing improvised in response to shifting pressures from different actors. On the one hand, Beijing treated the regime in Khartoum with all the respect it gave to any national government. It sold arms until the UN imposed its arms embargo (and some say, even after that) and showered President al-Bashir with state visits, high-level protocol treatment, and aid projects. This largesse continued even after al-Bashir's indictment by the International Criminal Court. China was not bound to honor the indictment because it was not a signatory of the treaty that established the court.

On the other hand, China bent its principle of noninterference by supporting the 2005 North–South peace agreement, contributing police and troops to the UN peacekeeping operation in the South, and lobbying the Khartoum government for peaceful settlement of the conflict in Darfur. Hu Jintao pressed Sudanese president al-Bashir on the Darfur issue face to face during al-Bashir's visit to Beijing in 2006 and during Hu's return visit to Khartoum in 2007, and the Chinese government made a point of announcing publicly that he had done so. In 2007, Beijing appointed an ambassador with the special mission of promoting peaceful resolution of the issue. China allocated several million dollars of humanitarian assistance for the region. Also in 2007, it voted in the Security Council to support the African Union's policy of sending a joint UN–African Union peacekeeping mission to Darfur, on condition of Khartoum's acceptance of the mission. Beijing allocated a contingent of engineers to the mission and pressed Khartoum to agree to its deployment. These moves were in part a response to pressure from international human rights groups who linked the Darfur genocide to the upcoming 2008 Beijing Olympics. But the timing and nuance of Beijing's actions revealed its primary emphasis on avoiding damage to its investments.

The second country where large hydrocarbon investments imposed a complex political calculus was Iran.[2] Here the issue was not internal strife (although there was plenty of that), but the international crisis caused by Iran's attempt to enrich uranium for nuclear weapons. As the West intensified pressure on Iran to stop its program in the early 2000s, Western oil companies began to pull out as contractors (although they continued to buy Iranian oil on the market), but at the same time Chinese companies moved in to help the Iranian national oil company explore and exploit Iranian oil and gas fields. With the election of Mahmoud Ahmadinejad as president in 2005 Iran's confrontation with the West sharpened. The UN Security Council imposed a series of sanctions, which China supported. At the same time, driven by its growing energy needs, China increased its investments. Iran became China's third-largest oil supplier.

On the one hand, Beijing did not support Iran's development of nuclear weapons. Like the U.S., France, Russia, and several other countries, China had previously given assistance to Iran's nuclear energy program. This assistance was provided ostensibly for peaceful purposes, but it also reflected Beijing's tolerant attitude in the 1980s and early 1990s toward nuclear proliferation. Once China joined the nonproliferation regime (chapter 10), however, and acquired a large stake in oil supplies from Iran and its neighbors, it worried that a nuclear Iran would destabilize the region. It urged Iran to cooperate with the IAEA and not to pursue weapons-grade uranium enrichment.

But Beijing did not give the same priority to stopping the Iranian nuclear program as the Western powers. For one thing, the Chinese did not believe the program was as far advanced as Western policymakers claimed. Beijing even considered the possibility that the West exaggerated the crisis in order to contain Iran and, as a side benefit, to complicate China's search for energy. Second, China believed that confrontational sanctions would only make the Tehran regime feel more insecure and thus strengthen rather than weaken its determination to resist the West. (Beijing perceived this same flaw in Western sanctions policies toward North Korea and Burma.) Third, as a promoter of nuclear energy, China did not want to see sanctions framed in such a way as to erode the principle that all states have the right to develop nuclear energy for peaceful purposes (chapter 10). Fourth, China wanted to maintain good relations with Tehran so that Iran would continue the hands-off policy toward Xinjiang that it had pursued since the early 1990s. To encourage this attitude, China invited Iran in 2004 to become an observer member of the SCO. Fifth, China wanted to protect its sizable export market in Iran, which included consumer goods and military equipment. Finally, the protracted struggle between Iran and the West helped tie down American forces that might otherwise have been deployed closer to China. So long as Tehran was not on the very brink of developing a nuclear weapon, therefore, China was content to let the crisis simmer.

Coordinating closely with Russia in order to avoid diplomatic isolation, Beijing used its position at the UN Security Council to allow but to delay and weaken sanctions against Iran. It never used its veto on the issue, both because it wanted to maintain good relations with the U.S. and other Western powers and, more fundamentally, because it did want Iran to stop developing nuclear weapons.

In Sudan, Iran, and elsewhere, China's search for energy security did more to align its interests, however imperfectly, with those of other industrial economies than to set them apart. Its investments contributed to supply and price stability on world markets by producing oil from sources that Western companies were not using. When crises broke out in particular oil-producing countries, China wanted them resolved with minimal disruption of supply as much as the West did. In Libya, for example—an important oil supplier to China and many Western countries—once the Qaddafi regime was faced with a widespread uprising in 2011, China shared the European and American interest in a quick resolution to the crisis even though it was reluctant to see the fall of a government with which it had good relations. Beijing therefore used an abstention to allow the UN Security Council to authorize the use of force, ostensibly to prevent attacks on civilians, but in effect to hasten Muammar Qaddafi's exit from power. The cases of Sudan, Iran, and Libya all illustrate a broad convergence of China's interests with those of the West, along with the desire to project an independent policy stand, disagreements about what policies would work, and Beijing's relative paucity of means to influence the situation on the ground on its own. The Western powers still took the lead in these cases. China was able to benefit from Western interventions without entirely endorsing them.

COMMODITIES, MARKETS, AND INVESTMENTS

In the 2000s, Chinese policymakers became engaged in protecting the supply of other commodities from the Fourth Ring besides oil and in gaining access to markets for exports, services, and investments. China's economic boom in the 1980s and 1990s had been Pacific centered, depending on the import of semifinished products from the rest of Asia and their assembly and export to the U.S. But as the economy surged in the twenty-first century, China acquired important economic interests in the Fourth Ring. It has become a major importer of a wide range of minerals and agricultural products, besides oil, that supply both its export industries and its growing domestic consumer market. Some of its most important mineral imports are copper, iron, manganese, lead, chromium, silver, and zinc, and among its most important agricultural imports are soybeans, cotton, and wood. At the same time, Chinese exporters developed new markets in the Fourth Ring for their manufactured products. And cash-rich Chinese enterprises and government agencies looked for places to invest where they might earn better returns than from U.S. government Treasury bills.

By buying, selling, and investing, China emerged as a major—in some cases, the major—economic partner of several countries in the Fourth Ring. To consolidate these ties, China has followed a path well worn by other outside powers, involving a mix of diplomatic flattery, development aid, political relations with elites, and—to an unknowable degree—corruption. China has not, however, acquired a strategic stake in particular regimes or regimes of a particular type. It stands ready to transfer its friendship to whomever emerges in power.

In Africa, China's major economic partners are Angola, Sudan, Chad, Libya, the Congo, Nigeria, Equatorial Guinea, Gabon, and Cameroon. All supply oil. In addition, many are major suppliers of copper, iron ore, other minerals, and cotton. China has made some spectacular investments, such as in copper and cobalt mines in the Democratic Republic of Congo. In return, Africa is a growing market for Chinese electrical appliances, light-industry products, and mechanical and electrical products. Perhaps a million Chinese have moved privately to Africa in recent years to set up small businesses.[3] China has become the continent's largest trading partner, followed by the U.S. and France.

Compared to other outside powers in Africa, China has both advantages and disadvantages. It has no colonial history there; it offers development aid and business contracts without political or moral strings attached; and local leaders are comfortable with the Chinese way of doing business. But this comparative advantage is more marked in the more corrupt and less stable countries, precisely the countries in which business relationships are riskiest and most difficult to manage and where Chinese staff and workers are least safe. In more stable countries in Africa, elites maintain closer ties with former colonial powers, and it is harder for Chinese enterprises to compete. China has worked to develop closer cultural ties with the continent, welcoming several thousand African students to China each year and opening twenty-five Confucius Institutes in Africa by 2010. But English and French remain the main foreign languages spoken throughout the continent; few Africans immigrate permanently to China; and many Africans see the Chinese as a new neocolonial power, no less exploitative than the Europeans and Americans who preceded them. China has no military presence on the continent that can help it support its clients in the way France and the U.S. have sometimes done.

In Latin America, China's role is built chiefly around trade, which has grown rapidly but still accounts for only about 5 percent of the region's foreign trade. The continent's largest economy, Brazil, is China's most important trading partner there. It is an important source of iron ore and agricultural products such as soy beans, grains, and meat, a large market for Chinese goods, and a partner in high-tech pursuits, including aeronautics and space satellite launches. The two have pioneered the use of currency swaps—settling certain trade deals in Chinese renminbi and Brazilian real in order to reduce the need to deal in U.S. dollars. Chile and Peru are among China's major suppliers of iron ore and copper. To broaden economic ties, Beijing signed free-trade agreements with these two countries in 2005 and 2009, respectively. In its trade with Argentina, China imports soybeans, meat, and other farm products and exports manufactured goods. In Venezuela, it invested and loaned tens of billions of dollars to oil exploration, oil production, and transportation projects, which helped to buttress the efforts of the Hugo Chávez regime to establish economic independence from the U.S. Even trade with Cuba has grown dramatically, reversing the traditional hostility rooted in Cuba's support for Moscow in the Sino–Soviet dispute. By 2007, China was Cuba's second-largest trading partner.

Latin American countries have welcomed China's economic presence as a counterweight to traditional U.S. dominance, but there have also been frictions. As in Africa, concern has been raised that China is developing a neocolonial relationship with Latin America based on imports of raw materials and exports of manufactured products. After suffering a trade deficit with China, Argentina undertook investigations of alleged Chinese dumping of manufactured goods (selling at below-cost prices to drive local competitors out of business). In Mexico and Central America, competition from manufacturers in China has hurt industries that exported to the U.S. The U.S. remained the dominant outside power in the region, with stronger economic, political, and cultural ties than any other country and an exclusive military presence.

In the Middle East, China paid for its oil imports by selling a variety of goods and services, among them manufactured products and military supplies (discussed in the next section). China also undertook large construction projects in the Persian Gulf states, supplying technicians, workers, equipment, and supplies. Because of the importance of oil supplies, China runs an aggregate trade deficit with the region. Beijing maintains good relations with all Middle Eastern countries, including Israel and the Palestinian Authority, but China has no military presence there and can be considered a strategic partner of only one of these countries, Iran.

The EU in 2004 surpassed the U.S. to become China's largest trading partner. Europe sells advanced manufactured goods such as automobiles and aircraft to China, and China in return sells computers, mobile phones, digital cameras, and textiles. The Eurozone financial crisis of 2011 brought China more heavily into the market for European government bonds, earning goodwill for Beijing for purchasing the bonds of governments in trouble, such as Greece, Portugal, Spain, and Italy, even though these purchases fell well short of the bailout some Europeans hoped for. Growing economic relations have generated some issues. Some Europeans charge China with predatory economic behavior that enables it to corner European markets and acquire European enterprises at low cost. Such views led the EU to resist Chinese pressure to grant it full "market economy status" (which carries fuller privileges of economic access) sooner than 2016, when it was scheduled to achieve such status automatically under its WTO accession agreement. The Chinese have offered to buy sophisticated military equipment from European suppliers, but the U.S. has pressured the EU to maintain an embargo on high-end weapons that was imposed after the Tiananmen crisis in 1989.

China has no vital interest in the security issues that most engage Europe—the stability of East and Central Europe, the problem of how to assimilate growing populations of Muslims, dealing with refugees and illegal migrants from North Africa, and preventing terrorism. Europeans are anxious about Chinese inroads into their traditional zone of influence in Africa but have done nothing to counter it. Europe has no defense commitments in Asia. Without armed forces in each other's region, Europe and China present each other with neither a military threat nor a possibility of significant military cooperation.

The primary political issue between the two sides concerns human rights. European leaders and EU diplomats keep the issue alive in relations with China as part of their values-based security strategy. But as China's economic importance grows, the Europeans have pursued the human rights issue less consistently (chapter 12).

ARMS SALES

A subset of China's commercial relations in the Fourth Ring consists of arms sales. When China joined the world economy in the 1980s, military-owned arms enterprises looked for markets overseas to supplement their incomes. This approach broke an earlier pattern under which Chinese arms transfers were limited to a few partners and had strategic rather than commercial motivations. At different times in the late twentieth century, China aided North Korea, Pakistan, and Iran with the development of nuclear weapons and missile technologies (and in the case of Iran, chemical weapons capabilities), in each case seeking to buttress a key ally and complicate rival powers' defense calculations (chapter 11). But by the late 1990s, China had joined international arms control and nonproliferation regimes and had—so far as is publicly known—eliminated its transfer of weapons of mass destruction.

China remained, however, active in the commercial arms market, selling all interested buyers weapons and technology not proscribed by the arms control regime. Some of these sales drew U.S. opposition even though they were legal under the treaties China had signed; the U.S. argued that the sales had a destabilizing effect on local military balances. For example, in the 1980s, China's sale of shore-to-ship Silkworm missiles to Iran created a new threat for U.S. warships sailing in the Persian Gulf, and the sale of CSS-2 missiles to Saudi Arabia, M-9 and M-11 missiles to Syria, and a nuclear reactor to Algeria posed threats to U.S. allies and the risk of fueling local arms races. After strenuous negotiations, the U.S. prevailed on China to stop these sales.

These agreements left China by the mid-1990s with a market in small arms, light weapons, aircraft, armored vehicles, artillery, small ships, and the like. It briefly became the world's fourth-largest exporter of conventional weapons. Most of its major customers, except for Pakistan and Burma, were in the Fourth Ring; they included Iran, Iraq, Egypt, Sudan, and Zimbabwe. Demand for Chinese weapons declined in the late 1980s and early 1990s. The reasons varied but included the end of the Iran–Iraq War in 1988—a war in which China had sold large quantities of arms to both sides—higher demand for more advanced U.S. technology following the spectacular performance of U.S. forces in the first Persian Gulf War in 1990–1991, and greater availability of Russian arms on the world market following the collapse of the Soviet Union. Today, China is among the top half-dozen or so arms-exporting countries (the rank varies from year to year) but stands well below the U.S. and Russia—consistently the two major arms-exporting powers—in the quantity and technological level of the weapons it sells, and usually lags Germany, France, and the United Kingdom as well.

Arms sales relationships are in part political because they support friendships with local regimes, as in Pakistan, Burma, and Zimbabwe. But in no case have China's arms sales been used to nurture a deeper defense relationship in the way U.S. arms sales often are. Chinese arms sales of the recent past were not made on a concessionary basis. They came without training. China made no effort to encourage other states to use weapons and equipment compatible with those of its own armed forces because it does not anticipate operating side by side on the battlefield with forces from other countries.

FRIENDSHIP DIPLOMACY

After economic interests, the second category of Chinese interests in the Fourth Ring is diplomatic. China seeks friendly relations with as many of the world's governments as possible in order to contribute to three specific goals: to maintain access to Fourth Ring economic resources, to gain other states' cooperation in the diplomatic isolation of Taiwan and the Dalai Lama, and to win support for Chinese negotiating positions in a range of multilateral forums. Absent from China's Fourth Ring agenda are the kinds of interlocking political, territorial, and security issues that shape its relations with key Second and Third Ring neighbors such as Japan, Vietnam, Burma, Pakistan, and the SCO states. In the Fourth Ring, Zhou Enlai's principles of peaceful coexistence fully apply, especially noninter-ference in internal affairs, equality, and mutual benefit. The strategy is transactional: China provides material and symbolic support and diplomatic backing, and it expects to receive economic access and diplomatic cooperation in return.

To create goodwill, foreign leaders invited to the Middle Kingdom are given royal treatment no matter what the size or significance of the country from which they hail, and they always return to their countries with scholarships, loans, development projects, and trade agreements. In return, Chinese leaders travel tirelessly to promote their country's image as a loyal member of the developing world, bringing gifts wherever they go. In 2006, the Chinese president, premier, and foreign minister visited a total of seventeen countries in Africa. According to a South African analyst, this activity was "unprecedented." He continued: "I can't think of any other head of state, including [South African president] Thabo Mbeki, who has visited as many African countries as that."[4] With especially important regional powers such as Egypt, South Africa, Mexico, and Brazil, Beijing has declared the creation of "strategic partnerships." The West shuns certain governments as rogue states; China treats them with the same pomp and circumstance it treats other states.

China has become an active joiner in multilateral forums and institutions throughout the Fourth Ring. Among other roles, it is an observer member in the Organization of American States, a donor member of the Inter-American Development Bank, and a member of the Asia–Europe Meeting. Beijing has organized its own multilateral dialogue mechanisms, including the China–Latin America Forum, the China–South American Common Market Dialogue, the China–Andean Community, the Sino–Arab Cooperation Forum, the Forum on China–Africa Cooperation, and the China–Caribbean Economic and Trade Cooperation Forum. Their carefully choreographed meetings flatter and impress foreign officials. For example, the 2006 Beijing Summit of the Forum on China–Africa Cooperation hosted some seventeen hundred delegates from forty-eight African countries amid warm hospitality and luxurious accommodations. Each such organization showcases Chinese aid, trade, and investment amid a rhetoric of mutual respect and cooperation.

In the Mao period, China was a small aid donor to a short list of Asian and African countries, most famously helping Tanzania and Zambia build a railway to link the two countries' interiors to the sea. In the first decades of the post-Mao years, China was an aid recipient, receiving support especially from Japan, the UN Development Program, and the World Bank. Starting in the 2000s, aid flowed back out, focusing on those countries in Southeast Asia where China sought to calm suspicion of its rise and to increase economic interdependence (chapter 6), in South Asia where it sought access to port facilities (chapter 6), and in Africa and Latin America where it sought diplomatic support and natural resources.

Although Chinese aid in the Fourth Ring remains far less than what is offered by the U.S., European countries, Japan, and the World Bank, its funds are given without political conditions, often for stadiums, office buildings, roads, bridges, and other projects that enhance local regimes' prestige. Regime type is not a factor. Chinese aid has helped democracies such as Brazil and Chile; partly democratic regimes such as Mozambique, Nigeria, and Colombia; and dictatorships such as Angola, Gabon, and Equatorial Guinea.[5] The common feature of China's main aid recipients outside Asia is their importance as suppliers of oil or other commodities. Chinese aid has often been criticized because it comes in the form of loans that have to be repaid, because the loans are tied to the use of Chinese companies and workers, and because aid goes either to prestige projects or to infrastructure that benefits Chinese resource extraction. Nonetheless, such projects give impetus to the image of China as a global power and a generous friend.[6]

Also a resource for friendship diplomacy is China's position as a permanent member of the UN Security Council. Although seldom wielding a veto, China has been able to serve the interests of Fourth Ring states by delaying or softening sanctions resolutions. It did so not only in the cases of Sudan and Iran, but also at different times in the cases of Iraq, Libya, and Serbia. Beijing made rare use of its veto power in 2008 to protect the regime of Robert Mugabe in Zimbabwe against an arms embargo and other sanctions.[7] China also gained gratitude by supporting the elections of controversial countries such as Iran and Venezuela to seats as nonpermanent members of the Security Council.

China earned diplomatic goodwill by participating in UN-sponsored peacekeeping operations. These multinational forces are deployed under UN Security Council authorization, normally with the host government's approval, to help create or support the conditions for peace after an episode of internal conflict. Although the first such mission dates to 1953, the use of peacekeeping expanded greatly after the Cold War. China became heavily involved in the 2000s and by 2011 had deployed more than seventeen thousand peacekeepers on nineteen missions, including those in Kosovo, Lebanon, Darfur, South Sudan, Congo, Côte d'Ivoire, Liberia, Western Sahara, and Haiti. Besides providing learning opportunities for Chinese military and police personnel, these deployments created channels of cooperation with both government and opposition forces in the host countries and with other countries that contributed forces to the mission, often from the same region.[8]

China's soldiers have contributed further to friendship diplomacy since the 1990s by conducting exchanges with other militaries. As of 2008, China had military attachés posted in 109 countries, and 98 countries posted defense attachés in Beijing. In recent years, the PLA has sent hundreds of soldiers to study abroad while hosting thousands of foreign officers in China. It has also held a biannual international seminar on security, the Xiangshan Forum, in Beijing since 2006 as well as several iterations of an international symposium on Sun Zi's *Art of War*. It has participated in a range of bilateral and multilateral military exercises with the armed forces of a variety of countries, including Australia, France, India, New Zealand, Pakistan, South Africa, Thailand, the United Kingdom, the U.S., Russia, and the other SCO members. It has hosted foreign soldiers in military education institutions and conducted military-to-military exchanges with armed forces from a wide range of countries. Since 2008, Beijing has deployed three-ship flotillas to the Gulf of Aden to help protect ships transiting the Suez Canal.

CONSTRICTING THE INTERNATIONAL SPACE OF TAIWAN AND THE DALAI LAMA

The second purpose of Chinese friendship diplomacy, besides opening the door for economic relations, was to help maintain China's diplomatic isolation of Taiwan and the Dalai Lama (chapters 8 and 9). Beginning in the 1980s, the Dalai Lama pursued a strategy of seeking support for Tibet's autonomy in the international arena; Beijing countered this strategy by discouraging friendly countries from offering the Dalai Lama visas or high-level meetings. For the most part, this diplomatic battle unfolded in the U.S. and Europe, where the Dalai Lama commanded wide public respect. In 2008, China pulled out of an EU–China summit meeting when the occupant of the EU's rotating presidency, French president Nicolas Sarkozy, held a meeting with the Dalai Lama. In 2011, Beijing successfully pressured the South African government to refuse a visa to the Dalai Lama to join a meeting hosted by fellow Nobel Peace Prize winner Desmond Tutu.

As for Taiwan, after South Korea switched diplomatic recognition from the ROC to the PRC in 1992, the primary battleground for Beijing's strategy of isolating Taiwan diplomatically shifted from Asia to the Fourth Ring. At that point, some thirty countries still recognized the ROC. On the one hand, Beijing was able to win some of them to its side, including such relatively important ones as South Africa, Malawi, and Costa Rica. On the other hand, from time to time a country that recognized the PRC switched relations back to the ROC, often after receiving a big aid and trade package from Taipei as well as—it was later revealed—in some cases under-the-table private payments. These countries included Niger, Liberia, Lesotho, Chad, Grenada, Saint Lucia, and Macedonia. In a see-saw battle, Beijing would then mount expensive efforts to win these countries back to its side. In 2007, for example, to help recover recognition from Grenada and consolidate relations with neighboring states, China built cricket stadiums in Grenada, Jamaica, and Antigua with imported Chinese laborers at no cost to the governments concerned, so they could host that year's Cricket World Cup.[9]

Foreign ministries outside Asia were often confused about the protocol technicalities and "name games" that characterized the struggle over Taiwan's international status. The ROC maintained trade or other representative offices in many countries that formally recognized the PRC, staffed by diplomats who worked to get the highest possible protocol treatment in order to emphasize Taiwan's international standing. PRC diplomats had to intercede with governments to make sure that ROC representatives did not receive the kind of treatment that would be accorded to a delegate from an independent state. At the UN, the PRC mission had to brief Fourth Ring diplomats on the logic of its opposition to a proposal that some of the ROC's diplomatic partners put forward annually starting in the 1990s to study some form of UN participation for Taipei. At the WHO, PRC diplomats had to lobby with other members against an American proposal for Taiwan's admission as a member, until 2009 when Beijing acceded to observer status for Taiwan.

The PRC did allow Taiwan to enjoy membership under various special names in more than two dozen intergovernmental organizations (chapter

9). However, Chinese diplomats had to remind representatives of other member states about the distinction between Taipei's being represented in the organization in some nonstate capacity (varying for each organization), which Beijing allowed, and its being a state, which Beijing forbade. In all these efforts, good relations with the home government were essential to achieve cooperation.

If China relied mostly on positive incentives to win cooperation for its Taiwan policy in the Fourth Ring, it could also be tough on occasion. In 1995, it used its position on the UN Security Council to reduce the size of the UN peacekeeping mission in Haiti because the Haitians had invited Taiwan's vice president to attend the inauguration of their new president. (China later took a more positive attitude and sent police and judicial experts to participate in the Haiti mission.) In 1997, the PRC vetoed a Security Council resolution to deploy military observers to monitor a cease-fire in Guatemala because Guatemala maintained diplomatic relations with the ROC. (It allowed the resolution to pass on a second vote after Guatemala agreed to stop supporting Taiwan's bid for participation in the UN.) In 1999, China vetoed an extension of the UN Preventive Deployment Force in Macedonia because of that country's switch of diplomatic recognition from Beijing to Taipei.[10]

A tacit truce settled over this diplomatic battleground during the cross-strait rapprochement that started with Ma Ying-jeou's accession to the ROC presidency in 2008 (chapter 9). Around that time, Paraguay was reportedly prepared to switch recognition to the PRC, but Beijing postponed seizing the prize. President Ma pledged that his administration would not practice "checkbook diplomacy." But the issue of Taiwan's status has not disappeared, and Chinese diplomats continue to guard against any erosion of China's position against Taiwanese statehood.

INTERNATIONAL NORMS AND REGIMES

Finally, China uses friendship with Fourth Ring governments to cultivate support for its positions in the many systems of international norms and institutions that govern interactions among states in the age of globalization (see also chapter 10). These regimes cover almost every field of international interaction—trade and finance, navigation, dispute resolution, arms control, migration, human rights, climate change, and so on, as well as a host of specialized yet important subjects such as fishery rights, species diversity, and intellectual property rights. The regimes evolve constantly in the course of interactions among the member states. Some of these interactions take place through dispute-resolution tribunals such as the International Court of Justice and the WTO Dispute Resolution Mechanism; some are bilateral negotiations; some take the form of tests of strength. But with increasing frequency, major international norms are developed in multilateral contexts involving large numbers of countries, where decisions are made by consensus. China's friendly relations with smaller powers helps it to build coalitions in these negotiations.

Starting in the 1970s and accelerating during the 1990s and 2000s, the UN convened a series of world conferences and summits that had great influence on evolving international norms. Among the most noteworthy were the 1992 Earth Summit, the 1993 World Conference on Human Rights, the 1994 International Conference on Population and Development, the 1995 World Summit for Social Development, the 1995 Beijing Women's Conference, the 1996 Habitat Conference, the 2002 World Summit on Sustainable Development, the 2003 World Summit on the Information Society, the 2000 Millennium Summit, and the 2005 World Summit. The meetings' outcome documents not only codified broad aspirations for the world community but also set down specific policy guidelines and norms in areas as consequential as peaceful settlement of disputes, humanitarian intervention, migration, refugees, transnational crime, the world trading system, disarmament, the environment, poverty and development, reproductive health and women's rights, children's rights and welfare, public health, human rights, democracy, Internet freedom, and the structure and functions of the UN itself. Even though these documents were not legally binding in the way that treaties are, they were important as benchmarks by which states' behavior would be judged by other states, global media, and global civil society. They also set the floor from which future international negotiations would proceed, which might in turn lead to legally binding outcomes such as treaties or UN Security Council resolutions. And most of the meetings led to follow-up conferences that kept up the pressure on member governments. For all these reasons, these conferences were important.

The meetings generated feverish lobbying both among states and on the part of civil society organizations, whose representatives attended by the thousands. The smaller states often had less settled positions than the larger states either because they had less at stake or because they lacked the staff to gain expertise on the issues. Working with Fourth Ring friends helped Beijing's diplomats influence the outcome documents in many areas. For example, they tried to restrict the conditions under which a government's failure to exercise its "responsibility to protect" its people might lead to an international intervention; established the principle that all states should be subjected to the same human rights review, not just selected states (nonselectivity); and fought for each government's right to regulate its own domestic Internet.

China also lobbied for its friends' support in more technical negotiations. For example, in the WTO, where it sought the earliest possible recognition of its "market economy status," it was able to gain such recognition on an accelerated basis from Argentina, Brazil, Chile, Peru, Venezuela, and other friendly states. Also in the WTO, China formed a common front with countries in Africa and Latin America to oppose richer countries' use of agricultural subsidies to protect their farmers against competition from third-world farmers. In the IMF, China and some other developing countries opposed a strengthening of the organization's mandate to criticize governments' exchange-rate policies. In climate change negotiations, China (along with India) led the developing countries in pushing the principle that advanced industrial economies should compensate the rest of the world for the costs of cutting greenhouse gas emissions. In the UN-linked Conference on Disarmament, China pushed for the establishment of nuclear-weapon-free zones, argued that major nuclear powers should disarm before smaller nuclear powers, and pushed to ban the deployment of weapons in outer space.[11] In the UN Human Rights Council, China played a leading role in developing the mechanism of Universal Periodic Review, which treats all states in the same way instead of singling out human rights violators for special attention (chapter 12).

Success in multilateral negotiations builds on the common interests China shares with many other countries as a developing country, a non-Western culture, a nondemocracy, a country without an imperial past, and a country opposed to intervention in other states' internal affairs. It is facilitated by the transactional character of Chinese diplomacy, which opens doors and makes it easier to bridge differences. China's growing presence in the Fourth Ring has given it new resources to influence the future evolution of international regimes.

LIMITED ASPIRATIONS, LIMITED MEANS

The arrival of a new economic and diplomatic power in the Fourth Ring provides a counterweight to these regions' traditional domination by the U.S., Great Britain, and France. But China has not displaced Western influence. Even as the Chinese presence grows, the other major powers have sustained and sometimes increased their stakes.

China's role in the Fourth Ring in some ways resembles that of Japan, which also has major investments and trading relationships throughout the world, gives development aid, and pursues cooperative diplomatic relations, but takes little interest in issues of regime type, ideology, development model, ethnic relations, interstate rivalries, or great-power alignments. To be sure, China's trade and investment in the Fourth Ring are outpacing Japan's as the Chinese economy grows. But its interests there, like Japan's, remain segmental. For China to become a strategic actor in the Fourth Ring will require more than an expansion of its economic presence. It will require China to cultivate ideological and cultural influence, build military bases, sign defense treaties, and find ways to project significant military power thousand of miles from its own shores. Because such actions are expensive, China is unlikely to undertake them without good reasons. Such reasons will emerge only if it cannot achieve its limited aspirations for Fourth Ring economic resources and diplomatic support by the use of economic and diplomatic means.

PART III

HOLDING TOGETHER

Territorial Integrity and Foreign Policy

8

PROBLEMS OF STATENESS

Tibet, Xinjiang, Hong Kong, and Taiwan

Even as China's global influence increases, it is bedeviled to an unusual degree for a major power by what political scientists call "problems of stateness." In Tibet and Xinjiang—vast inland territories in the west and northwest that account for almost one-third of the PRC's area—non-Han ethnic groups have long resisted Beijing's control. In Hong Kong and Taiwan, smaller but strategic territories off the southern coast, the residents belong to the Han ethnic group but have separate political systems and in Taiwan's case, for many residents, a separate national identity. In contrast to the other security problems in the First Ring, resistance to Beijing's rule in these four territories presents a threat not only to the regime (because loss of these lands might trigger popular opposition to the leaders who let it happen), but also to the state itself, as defined by its current boundaries and its multiethnic conception of citizenship.

Not all of China's territory has been nonnegotiable. Over the years, Beijing has yielded 1.3 million square miles of claims to North Korea, Laos, Burma, Pakistan, Tajikistan, Kyrgyzstan, Kazakhstan, Russia, and other states in order to settle territorial disputes.[1] But Tibet, Xinjiang, Hong Kong, and Taiwan are different. Each is populated by citizens whom the Chinese government and the states with whom it has diplomatic relations define as Chinese citizens, even if some of them do not accept that identity. No other country either claims these territories or says they should be independent. The territories are economically valuable. And from a strategic point of view, they all are crucial to China's security. Any one of them that escaped Chinese control might serve as a base for an outside power to threaten China. They are the key pieces of a geographically deep, politically unstable hinterland that Beijing must control in order to assure the security of the Han heartland. Resistance to Chinese rule in these four territories is the legacy of two kinds of imperialism, one committed by China and one against it. First, the entity now known as China is the product of centuries of demographic and political expansion that reached something close to its current shape in the latter part of the last dynasty, the Qing, at the turn of the nineteenth century. As in other traditional empires, this process brought many different ethnic groups under various more or less direct forms of rule. In 1912, China changed from an empire to a nation-state, although a weak one. Its first president, Sun Yat-sen, declared the Republic of China to be a multiethnic state that included a main population group, which he labeled the "Han," and four main ethnic minorities, which he identified as the Tibetans, the Mongols, the Manchus, and the Hui (the latter an inclusive term for Chinese Muslims that is today used more narrowly for a specific subgroup of Muslims). Mao Zedong's regime retained Sun's concept of a multiethnic state but expanded the list of recognized national minorities to fifty-five. Among those that were added were the Uyghurs of Xinjiang.

In this modern concept of citizenship, Chinese are considered to have diverse ethnic identities along with an overarching loyalty to the state. The leaders borrowed from theories of race and nation that were then prevalent in the West—in Mao's case, particularly from Stalin—to argue that ethnic identities are backward, often connected with religious superstitions, and will be dissolved by modernization, leaving civic identity victorious.

Over time, this theory has succeeded to some extent with many of China's minorities—those that are assimilated, isolated, or small. The country's largest officially designated minority are the Zhuang—actually a congeries of previously existing cultural groups—who live mostly in the Guangxi Zhuang Autonomous Region bordering on Vietnam and the Tonkin Gulf. They are linguistically and often culturally assimilated and generally accept Chinese civic identity.[2] The Koreans in the Northeast, the Dai in Yunnan Province near Thailand, and some other groups appear to resent Chinese rule but are too small to present any threat to it. Ethnic minority citizens who have moved to the cities are often assimilated and content with Chinese rule.

There is greater dissatisfaction with Chinese rule in the Inner Mongolian Autonomous Region, a grassland region along the northern border that used to be inhabited mainly by Mongols. Starting in the 1950s, an influx of Han settlers reduced the Mongol proportion of the population to what is now less than 20 percent. During the Cultural Revolution in the 1960s, the regime violently suppressed expressions of local identity. In the reform era, modernization has damaged the environment and undermined the Mongolians' traditional way of life, leading to occasional outbreaks of protest. Chinese Mongols might expect some support from fellow ethnics across the border in Mongolia, a country that has been independent since 1924 and democratic since 1990, but fear of China's military and economic power has kept the Mongolian government from challenging Beijing. Mongolia is one of the world's poorest countries and used to depend economically on the Soviet Union. Now it trades heavily with China and sends much of the rest of its foreign trade through the port of Tianjin. As a result, it sees little benefit in encouraging discontent across the border. Chinese rule in the Inner Mongolian Autonomous Region is thus secure.[3]

The situation is different in Tibet and Xinjiang. There, ethnic relations have grown worse instead of better in recent decades. Indeed, the more money Beijing has poured into these regions in the post-Mao period to develop their economies, the greater the scale of local resistance, because local people see Han-sponsored modernization as an attack on their culture, whose benefits go not to them, but to Han people who are flooding into their regions from the outside.

China's problems of stateness also derive from imperialism in a second way: the regions of doubtful loyalty were among those occupied or influenced by foreign powers during the age of imperialism. In the nineteenth century, the British created a colony in Hong Kong and expanded it. Britain also moved from its base in India to secure dominance in Tibet and help Lhasa establish autonomy from Beijing. Russia intermittently occupied parts of Xinjiang and supported an independence movement there. It helped outer Mongolia declare independence from China. The Japanese took over Taiwan as a colony, and after they lost World War II, the U.S. intervened to protect Taiwan from a mainland Chinese takeover. Even though in time the PRC reestablished control over these areas—with the exceptions of outer Mongolia, which remains an independent state, and Taiwan, which remains separate from China without having declared independence—the memory of separation continues to shape the identities of the people living in these places. Taiwan, Tibet, and Xinjiang have diasporas that cultivate distinct identities and draw support from foreign societies. (Hong Kong does not.) In different ways, foreign governments have guaranteed Hong Kong's semiautonomous status and prevented China from taking control of Taiwan. Some foreigners see many problems in these regions that Beijing would like to define as purely domestic as involving issues of principle, such as self-determination and human rights. Even though the age of imperialism is over, it is easy for Chinese leaders to believe that the problems they face in exerting control in these territories are sustained at least in part by foreign interests who want to constrain China's rise.

Perhaps no other major state faces as much external involvement with its internal territorial issues. In Russia, for example, minority populations constitute 20 percent of the population, compared to only about 8 percent for China, but Russian minorities are concentrated in only about 30 percent of the national territory, compared to the spread of minorities over about two-thirds of China's land area. Most of the Russian autonomous republics lack the strategic locations and the extensive foreign economic ties and cross-border coethnic populations that might motivate foreign interest. Only in the Caucasus—in Chechnya and nearby regions—do Russia's internal minorities attract significant foreign attention.

For China, establishing and maintaining control of its strategic hinterland therefore remains a major task. Domestic strategies of exerting control must go hand in hand with diplomatic strategies to cut off support for those who resist. The diplomatic effort required to manage the international aspects of these problems subtracts from the power China has available to use on other issues. Whether China likes it or not, its internal problems of stateness are also issues of external relations.

THE THREAT IN TIBET

China's security interest in Tibet is obvious from any map. At stake is not just the 471,700-square-mile Tibet Autonomous Region (TAR), but the entire Tibetan-populated area Cholka-Sum, which extends beyond the TAR to large parts of the four adjoining provinces of Qinghai, Gansu, Sichuan, and Yunnan. This region, from which Beijing carved out the TAR, is about twice the size of the TAR, covers about one-quarter of the territory of the PRC, and reaches to within 800 miles of Beijing. Most of it consists of high plateau and mountains at elevations higher than nine thousand feet, thinly populated and difficult to garrison and supply.

If China were to lose control of Tibet, its security would be greatly diminished. It would lose most of its border with India as well as borders with Nepal, Bhutan, and part of Burma; its ability to influence these countries would diminish, whereas India and other rival powers would gain a new opportunity to constrain or threaten China. Water resources for the parched Chinese heartland might be compromised because the Yangtze, Yellow, and many other rivers flow out of the Tibetan plateau. China would lose access to Tibet's hydroelectric potential as well as to gold, copper, and other mineral resources it has recently started to develop there.[4] China's resolution in opposing separatist movements in Xinjiang and Taiwan would come into question. And the loss of national territory might spark a nationalist reaction among the Han.

Tibet was originally not a single political unit, but a collection of chiefdoms and principalities that shared a commitment to lamaist (or Yellow Sect) Buddhism, with Chinese dynasties exercising greater or lesser influence over different parts at different times. In the seventeenth century, Tibet came together as a theocracy under the Dalai Lama, who emerged as the highest in a hierarchy of lamas, and who recognized a special relationship with the emperor of China. In 1904, the British invaded and established a direct relationship with the Tibetan government, offsetting Chinese military and political power. Tibet functioned as a de facto autonomous state from 1913 to 1951, although its independent sovereignty was not internationally recognized. This complex history gave rise to the opposing legal claims that figure in Beijing's arguments with Tibet independence advocates today. Both views are founded on historical fact: on the one hand, Tibet has long been subordinate to China; on the other, it long operated independently from Chinese rule.[5]

In 1950, the army of the newly established PRC entered Tibet, and in 1951 the Dalai Lama's delegates in Beijing signed an agreement that Tibet belonged to China while enjoying autonomy within China. This seventeen-point agreement (Agreement of the Central People's Government and the Local Government of Tibet on Measures for the Peaceful Liberation of Tibet) committed Beijing to allow religious freedom, recognized the role of the Dalai Lama, promised that the central authorities would not alter the existing local political system, and gave Beijing control of the territory's external relations. But the Chinese sent to govern Tibet undermined the positions of Tibetan Buddhism and local elites, sparking resistance in various places. In 1959, protests broke out in Lhasa, which the PLA put down. The Dalai Lama fled to northern India and established a government in exile in Dharamsala. From this base, he built up international pressure on China to give Tibetans political and religious freedom.

To control Tibet, China over the years has employed a combination of methods. It has maintained a large military garrison and in 1959, 1989, and 2008 used its armed forces to put down unrest. During the Cultural Revolution, Chinese authorities closed the monasteries and destroyed many of them. Under Deng Xiaoping, Beijing allowed the practice of Tibetan Buddhism to resume but controlled the monasteries' personnel, finances, and teaching and forbade monks from displaying pictures of the Dalai Lama. As part of Deng's economic reforms, China tried to win over the Tibetans by developing transport, tourism, construction, mining, and other industries.

Yet resistance to Chinese rule did not weaken; indeed, it seemed to strengthen. Most Tibetans consider reverence of the Dalai Lama central to their faith. Although living standards had improved, many local people claimed they were being pushed to the economic margins and overwhelmed by Han immigration as Chinese traders and workers flooded the territory, dominating the modern sectors of the economy. They feared that the Chinese intended to solve the Tibet problem by eliminating their culture. Everyday forms of resistance continued, and protests and disturbances erupted periodically, notably in 1989 and 2008, with the latter constituting the largest and most widespread unrest on the Tibetan Plateau since 1959. A wave of self-immolations by Tibetans, mostly monks and nuns living in the Tibetan areas outside the TAR, began in 2011 in protest of Chinese rule.

In the 1980s, the Dalai Lama rejected the advice of some of his followers to authorize the use of violence to struggle for independence and decided instead to pursue a strategy of internationalization of the Tibet problem. On the one hand, he abandoned the goal of full Tibetan statehood in the international system and offered to accept an "association with China" under which Tibet would maintain no military forces and would accept Chinese control of its foreign affairs.[6] On the other, he began to travel around the world to generate foreign pressure on Beijing to negotiate with him. He visited heads of state, spoke to parliaments, and gave speeches. His government in exile established offices in Washington, D.C., Geneva, Taipei, and other cities. He became a global celebrity, won the Nobel Peace Prize in 1989, and made the fate of Tibet a major issue between the PRC and the Western democracies.

But Beijing saw more risk than gain in negotiating. First, the scope of the autonomy that the Dalai Lama sought was far beyond what China was willing to grant. To be sure, Beijing already classified Tibet as an autonomous region, but this meant little more than allowing ethnic Tibetans to occupy some government posts, to use the local language in some educational settings and some media, and to practice their religion within official restrictions, as well as granting minority women more generous reproductive rights than Han women. By contrast, the Dalai Lama defined autonomy in a way that would have excluded real Chinese influence. In a speech to the European Parliament in Strasbourg in 1988,[7] he described China's relationship to Tibet as an "invasion" and "neocolonialism" and said, "Every Tibetan hopes and prays for the full restoration of our nation's independence." He argued that Tibet should enjoy democratic self-government with "the rights to decide on all affairs relating to Tibet and the Tibetans"; full freedom to exercise Tibetan religion (which because of the wide-ranging authority of lamas in Tibetan Buddhism would convey great policy authority on religious leaders); conversion of Tibet into a zone of peace via "a regional peace conference" in which neighboring states would serve as guarantors; the right for the Tibetan government to maintain relations with other countries in fields such as commerce, culture, religion, and tourism; and a halt to Han immigration. And the Dalai Lama asked for these concessions across "the whole of Tibet," meaning not only the TAR but also the Tibetan areas of neighboring provinces. Such arrangements would mean the departure of Chinese troops, religious officials, and government administrators as well as of Han workers from the whole Tibetan plateau. In effect, Tibet would revert to where it was before 1951, with a nominal special position for Beijing akin to what diplomats used to call "suzerainty," but not full sovereignty. This was far more autonomy than the PRC's framework for minority autonomy ever contemplated. The Dalai Lama's negotiating position remained in place until 2008, when his envoys presented Beijing with a "Memorandum on Genuine Autonomy for the Tibetan People."[8] This document abandoned the language that Beijing found most objectionable but not the core idea of a scope of autonomy far greater than Chinese policymakers were willing to consider.

Second, the Dalai Lama's mobilization of foreign influence over the years made Beijing mistrust his intentions. Instead of working within the provisions of the 1951 agreement, he had fled to a rival power, India. From 1956 to 1972, the Tibetan resistance movement accepted training and other assistance from the CIA and the governments of India, Nepal, and (to a minor extent) Taiwan. Between 1979 and 1985, Beijing allowed the Dalai Lama to send four fact-finding delegations and two political delegations to China to see the situation in Tibet and discuss a way for the Dalai Lama to return to an honorific position in China, although he would not be allowed to live in Tibet.[9] From 2003 to 2006, Chinese authorities conducted eight more rounds of talks with the Dalai Lama's representatives. But the Dalai Lama continued to refuse China's terms, which fell far short of meeting his goals, and kept up his international campaign to force Beijing to negotiate over a wider form of Tibetan autonomy. Instead of recognizing Tibet's status as "an inseparable part of China," as Beijing demanded, the Dalai Lama argued to foreign audiences that the Chinese presence violated Tibetans' political, religious, cultural, and environmental rights. In 1989, both the Nobel Peace Prize Committee and the Dalai Lama in his acceptance speech referred to Tibet as an occupied country. UN human rights bodies criticized China for its Tibet policies. In 1993, President Bill Clinton tried to condition U.S.–China trade relations on progress in "protecting Tibet's distinctive religious and cultural heritage."[10] Chinese leaders perceived these and numerous other events as a signal that outside actors were willing to cooperate with the Dalai Lama to use Tibet as a tool to place pressure on Beijing.

Third, Beijing apparently feared that the Dalai Lama was so popular that his return to Tibet could lead to a runaway mass movement that he could not control among the more than 5 million ethnic Tibetans. (That was why Beijing's offer to let him return included the proviso that he could not live in Tibet.) Alternatively, if China's forces were removed, more radical independence advocates might take power in the Tibetan community and raise even greater demands. In the worst case, such events might lead to a loss of Chinese control.

Beijing's strategy in Tibet has therefore been to wait out the Dalai Lama, who in 2012 was seventy-seven years old and in uncertain health.[11] By tradition, the ability mystically to recognize the Dalai Lama's reincarnation, who is his successor, belongs to the second most important leader in Tibetan Buddhism, the Panchen Lama. Likewise, a reincarnated Panchen Lama is identified by the Dalai Lama. After the tenth Panchen Lama died in 1989, the Dalai Lama identified a young boy from a family loyal to him as the eleventh Panchen Lama. The Chinese authorities responded by taking the boy into custody. His whereabouts remain unknown. Beijing named another child as Panchen Lama and has supervised his education in the expectation that he will follow Beijing's preferences when the time comes to recognize a new Dalai Lama. In 2007, the CCP strengthened its grip on the succession by decreeing that no incarnation of any lama would be valid in future without government approval. The Dalai Lama developed the beginnings of a counterstrategy. In 2011, he yielded his duties as political leader of the Tibetan community in exile to an elected prime minister and spoke about the possibility of being reincarnated in a location outside Tibet.

Meanwhile, Beijing continues to promote the region's economic development—for example, by opening the 1,200-mile Qinghai–Tibet railway in 2006—and the Han in-migration that goes with it, creating an apparently irreversible demographic and economic transformation that Tibetan advocates call "cultural genocide." A series of government-run "patriotic education campaigns" have required monks and nuns to thank the motherland (meaning China) for the gift of modernization and to denounce the Dalai Lama for "splittism." In 2008, when young monks and citizens mounted street demonstrations that turned violent, Beijing blamed the Dalai Lama for instigating the riots from abroad. The TAR party secretary, a Han, declared (without using the usual honorific "Lama"), "The Dalai is a wolf in a monk's robe, a monster with a human face and a beast's heart; we are in a sharp battle of blood and fire with the Dalai clique, a life and death battle between us and the enemy."[12]

Beijing has not had much success in discrediting the Dalai Lama personally either in Tibet or abroad, but it has leveraged its role as a rising power to convince other governments to give him less support. At the start of the Sino–Indian thaw in 1988, Delhi made its clearest statement up to that time recognizing Chinese sovereignty over Tibet. As the Sino–Indian thaw advanced, in 2003 New Delhi undertook not to "allow Tibetans to engage in anti-China political activities in India."[13] The Indian government implemented this promise by, for example, restricting Tibetan demonstrations against the 2008 Beijing Olympics and the 2009 Lhasa crackdown. In the U.S., presidents and other administration officials began to meet the Dalai Lama "privately" rather than publicly. In 2008, Britain switched from recognizing Chinese suzerainty in Tibet to recognizing Chinese sovereignty. A year later France announced its opposition to "any form of Tibet independence." For each of these countries—and others—smooth relations with Beijing had become more important than showing support for the Tibetan cause.

Thanks to his personal prestige and a broad-based international movement dedicated to his cause, the Dalai Lama has been able to create inconvenience for PRC diplomacy in the U.S., Europe, and elsewhere, but he has not been able to make Beijing negotiate. Although the situation in Tibet continues to cause trouble for Beijing, the latter sees little reason to change its strategy. From the Chinese government's point of view, no alternative holds more promise of eventual success.

GRASPING XINJIANG

The strategic importance of Xinjiang for China is similar to that of Tibet. The Xinjiang Uyghur Autonomous Region is China's largest provincial-level unit. It covers about one-sixth of the country's territory; shares borders with Mongolia, Russia, Kazakhstan, Kyrgyzstan, Tajikistan, Afghanistan, Pakistan, and India; and can be used as a base either by China to influence neighbors or by outside powers to threaten China. Like Tibet, Xinjiang has economic value for its oil and gas resources and as a pass-through for energy resources from Kazakhstan. It is also the site of China's nuclear weapons and missile testing.[14]

The region has been possessed or claimed by different forces through history. Over the centuries, Xinjiang's deserts and mountains were crisscrossed by merchants, migrants, and armies, who sometimes allied themselves with the rulers in power in Beijing and sometimes broke free. The few Chinese who went there before the nineteenth century encountered diverse Islamic populations, with mostly Turkic or Persian languages and cultures, who saw the Chinese as infidels. The region was fully incorporated into the Chinese administrative system only in 1884, when it was made a province and given the name "Xinjiang," or New Frontier. But Chinese control was still fragile. In the nineteenth and twentieth centuries, China and Russia competed for influence, and when the Chinese presence was weakest in 1944, local people declared the short-lived Eastern Turkestan Republic, supported by Moscow, which lasted until the newly established PRC reasserted control in 1949.[15]

To consolidate its control, China used the same methods as elsewhere around its periphery: colonization, trade, cultural assimilation, administrative integration, and international isolation, backed when necessary by the use of police and military force. As early as the mid–eighteenth century, the Qing government established Han-populated state farms near Urumqi. Han traders came in force during the nineteenth century. After 1949, the PRC brought the region under state planning and directed its trade entirely to the domestic Chinese economy, closing off the trade and migration that had been common across the region's ill-defined and ill-maintained borders. In 1954, Beijing established the quasi-military Xinjiang Production and Construction Corps to settle demobilized soldiers and other Han migrants in farms, mines, and enterprises. More Han came with the establishment of prison labor camps, whose inmates were kept in the province when released from custody. During the Cultural Revolution in the 1960s, hundreds of thousands of middle school graduates from the cities, especially Shanghai, were "sent down" to Xinjiang, mostly to live on the production and construction farms. In 2007, Han officially constituted approximately 8.2 million of the region's approximately 20 million people, with the real number probably higher; the Uyghurs, the largest of several recognized minority groups, stood at 9.6 million.

For decades before 1980, development was slow because of the region's ruggedness and distance from the rest of China as well as its exposure to the then-hostile Soviet Union. But under Deng Xiaoping's reforms in the 1980s, the coastal development policy discussed in chapter 10 created a need for Xinjiang's coal, oil, and gas reserves, which make it one of China's largest fossil fuel producers. In the 1990s, China started building pipelines to bring far western oil to interior markets. In 2001, Beijing announced a "develop the West" policy aimed at more fully exploiting Xinjiang's resources. The central government invested billions of dollars to build infrastructure and created policy incentives to bring in Chinese and foreign businesses.

Beijing expected Chinese civic identity to grow stronger as local populations became more prosperous, educated, and modern. Indeed, some Uyghurs did well. Yet, as in Tibet, Beijing encountered what it viewed as a paradoxical response from local populations: resistance to Chinese civic identity. During much of the Mao period, the Uyghurs as well as the smaller local minorities of Kazakhs, Kyrgyz, and others had been pressured to abandon Islam, learn Chinese, and give up their traditional customs.[16] The Chinese garrison suppressed occasional revolts. The largest occurred in 1962. After it was crushed, tens of thousands of Kazakhs and Uyghurs fled to the Soviet side of the border. After Mao's passing, religious practice was allowed again, but only under close supervision. Uyghur and other local languages were phased out as languages of instruction and increasingly taught only as second languages, if at all.[17] Uyghurs had to learn Chinese to get ahead in business or government. Many Uyghurs remained poor, whereas newly arrived Han prospered. Class differences thus reinforced ethnic antagonism.

As in Tibet, many Uyghurs believed that their land was being inundated by Han migrants and overtaken by an unwelcome, externally imposed way of life.[18] With the breakup of the Soviet Union in 1991, Uyghur communities in the three neighboring Central Asian states of Kazakhstan, Kyrgyzstan, and Uzbekistan saw cultural and religious revivals, creating a new sense of hope and entitlement among Uyghurs in Xinjiang. For some Uyghurs—because of Chinese government information control, it is impossible to know how many—the alienation went so far as to support the idea of an independent "East Turkestan."

Demonstrations, riots, and occasional assassinations and terror bombings occurred with increasing frequency from the 1980s to 2001. The government claimed that the perpetrators' goal was to separate Xinjiang from China, that Uyghur separatists were terrorists, and that Uyghur separatism was linked to al-Qaeda. All these claims were controversial because most Uyghurs are either secular or practice a moderate form of Sunni Islam, the resistance does not seem to be organized, and the community has not coalesced around specific demands. Many incidents reported by Chinese authorities as part of a terrorist, separatist movement seem to have had diverse and sometimes personal causes and often to have resulted in low casualties.[19] In any case, the authorities mounted a series of "strike hard" campaigns that resulted in widespread arrests, imprisonments, and executions. After 2001, the provincial authorities intensified repression, and the frequency of open resistance decreased, but by all signs the Uyghur community was as resentful as ever of Chinese rule.[20] In July 2009, Xinjiang witnessed the most serious unrest in China since 1989 with an official death toll of 197.

China tried to cut off what it claimed was support for separatism and terrorism from Uyghur diasporic communities overseas. It received strong cooperation from the potentially most threatening neighbors, those right across the border. During the Sino–Soviet dispute, the USSR had supported resistance to Chinese rule, in part through a clandestine "Eastern Turkestan People's Party" based in Kazakhstan.[21] But with the end of the dispute, the breakup of the Soviet Union, and the formation of the SCO in 2001 (chapter 3), the neighboring governments declared their opposition to what China called the "three evils" of terrorism, separatism, and religious extremism and agreed to extradition of one another's terror suspects (chapter 6). Kazakhstan, Kyrgyzstan, and Tajikistan placed new restrictions on the activities of Uyghur exile organizations. Pakistan, which became an SCO observer, arrested and extradited some Uyghurs wanted by China, although some Uyghurs continued to attend Pakistani madrassas. Countries farther away cooperated less fully. Turkey reduced support for Uyghur activists after a state visit by Chinese president Jiang Zemin in 2000 but continued from time to time to protest against Chinese repression in Xinjiang. Germany allowed the formation of the World Uyghur Congress in 2004, rejecting Chinese charges that it is a terrorist organization.

U.S. policy has been ambivalent. In 2002, a U.S. Presidential Executive Order designated an obscure Uyghur organization, the East Turkestan Islamic Movement, as a terrorist organization but refused Chinese demands to add other Uyghur organizations to the list. (In fact, most exile Uyghur organizations forswear violence.[22]) U.S. forces in Afghanistan picked up about two dozen Uyghurs and interned them at Guantanamo but refused to extradite them to China. Washington granted political asylum to a leading

Uyghur activist, Rebiya Kadeer, even though China called her a separatist and blamed her for instigating riots in Urumqi, and the independent but congressionally funded National Endowment for Democracy gave funding to organizations that she headed. The U.S. government–funded Radio Free Asia makes Uyghur-language broadcasts to Xinjiang, reporting information that is censored in China; the Chinese government normally jams the broadcasts.

The international Uyghur movement remains far weaker than the international movement in support of Tibet. Although China portrays Rebiya Kadeer, like the Dalai Lama, as a powerful outside instigator of troubles within, in fact her influence is less extensive than his, even among her own ethnic group, not to mention among foreign governments and publics, and the Uyghur community remains internally divided. Despite rising international criticism of Chinese human rights violations in Xinjiang, no outside government supports the idea of an independent Uyghur state. The exile community's main achievement has been to keep Uyghur identity alive.

HONG KONG: SMALL BUT IMPORTANT

In contrast to China's Inner Asian regions, Hong Kong and nearby Macao are tiny territories populated mostly by Han. For the most part, their residents comfortably inhabit dual identities as citizens of both the PRC and distinctive local systems. They are economically and culturally tied to the mainland yet enjoy institutions and ways of life rooted in their histories as colonies of Britain and Portugal, respectively. The two territories were successfully reintegrated into the PRC as Special Administrative Regions— Hong Kong in 1997 and Macao in 1999. But in the process of regaining control, Beijing embraced treaty obligations and broader political commitments to allow more freedoms in the returned colonies than it allows elsewhere. Loss of control could lead to a challenge to the regime's ability to rule on the mainland. That possibility is not imminent, but it is real, particularly in Hong Kong, thanks to the legacies of the takeover: independent local institutions that have the capability to challenge Beijing; local dissatisfaction that flares up from time to time; and treaty-based rights for foreign countries to protest if China should violate the special rights of the

Hong Kong people. A further constraint is the possibility that a mishandled crisis in Beijing's relations with Hong Kong will alienate the public in Taiwan.

Hong Kong Island and the small peninsula of Kowloon were ceded to Britain as colonies in two nineteenth-century treaties. The other 90 percent of the Hong Kong Special Administrative Region consists of the New Territories, an area that Britain leased in 1898 for a period of ninety-nine years. Neither Hong Kong nor the nearby enclave of Macao was ever considered viable as an independent state. Perhaps for this reason, Beijing for years gave little urgency to their recovery. Even though Britain legally held Hong Kong Island and Kowloon in perpetuity, it would have made no sense to keep them without the New Territories, whose lease was due to run out in 1997. So in 1982 the British raised the possibility of extending the lease. Deng Xiaoping, however, insisted on the return of sovereignty to China.

Beijing had economic and political interests in a smooth transition. Hong Kong was a regional financial center and entrepôt, with a GDP at the time worth 20 percent of the mainland's. Hong Kong capitalists were the largest foreign investors in China, employing an estimated 3 million mainlanders in factories whose products were trucked to Hong Kong's state-of-the-art container terminals for transshipment to U.S. and other markets. Multinational corporations used the territory as their base for mainland business activities. (Hong Kong has continued to be economically crucial: as of 2009, for example, it was China's third-largest trading partner after the U.S. and Japan and was still China's top source of foreign direct investment inflows.) The spread of mainland corruption to Hong Kong or disruption of Hong Kong's sophisticated financial, communications, transportation, and legal infrastructures or political instability there might have driven the lucrative foreign presence to another regional center, such as Singapore, Tokyo, or even Taipei, and undercut efforts to liberalize the economy at home.

For all these reasons, Deng offered the formula of "one country, two systems," which was formalized in the Sino–British Joint Declaration of 1984. Beijing promised that Hong Kong would "enjoy a high degree of autonomy" for at least fifty years after retrocession in 1997. It would be governed by Hong Kong people and preserve its social and economic systems unchanged. A Basic Law, or miniconstitution, adopted by China's national legislature in 1990, provided for the former colony's further evolution toward fully democratic direct election of the chief executive and legislature at an unspecified time in the future. Meanwhile, it set up complex electoral arrangements that guaranteed Beijing's control over the choice of chief executive and a majority of the legislature. A separate, similar Chinese agreement with Portugal provided for the return of Macao.

Between the agreement and the return of Hong Kong to Chinese control in 1997, events in Hong Kong began to create challenges for Beijing. The Chinese understood the Joint Declaration to imply that they would inherit the executive-led structure that the British had found so workable in governing Hong Kong as a colony for 150 years. Because Beijing would appoint the chief executive, it could expect to dominate the local government as easily as London had done. Beijing also expected the Hong Kong people to be as pragmatic and apolitical as they had always been. But the 1989 Tiananmen incident unexpectedly sparked the development of a democratic movement in Hong Kong, which in turn motivated Britain to move Hong Kong as far toward democracy before retrocession as it could within the constraints of the Joint Declaration and Basic Law.

To serve as the territory's last governor, the British government replaced a Foreign Office diplomat with a populist politician, Chris Patten, who proposed to empower all Hong Kong citizens older than eighteen with a direct vote for Legislative Council representatives and to create a Legislative Council majority of directly elected members. To Beijing, Patten's reforms seemed a Trojan horse, designed to transfer to China a turbulent Hong Kong vulnerable to Western influence. In Beijing's view, to tolerate dissent or disorder would have given encouragement to the democracy movement at home and to separatists in Tibet, Xinjiang, and Taiwan. China chose to respond toughly, denouncing the reforms as they were carried out and then rolling them back by decree as soon as it took over the territory.

With the support of the local business community, China maintained the indirect election system that gave it the ultimate say over the choice of chief executive and the makeup of the Legislative Council majority and put off the promise of direct elections to the indefinite future. With nothing happening in electoral politics, Hong Kong citizens gradually returned to their pre-reform attitude of realistic apathy, and the democratic movement shriveled. At several crucial points, the NPC in Beijing exercised its constitutional prerogative to interpret the Basic Law, doing so in such a way as to prevent unwelcome assertions of Hong Kong's autonomy. Although they valued their free way of life, Hong Kong people have also been proud of China's prosperity and growing international stature and have increasingly accepted PRC rule.

Hong Kong still has the potential to challenge China politically. In 2002–2003, the local pro-democracy movement blocked an attempt by the chief executive to adopt an antisubversion law that Beijing wanted to have passed (referred to as "Article 23 legislation" because its adoption was mandated by that article of the Basic Law). Human rights groups maintain offices in Hong Kong; members of the banned Falungong spiritual movement conduct demonstrations there; the local Catholic Church maintains its official ties to the Vatican; and some of the local media publish sharp criticisms and sensitive leaks from China. Substantial groups of citizens come out every year on the anniversary of the June 4, 1989, killings in Beijing to memorialize this incident that Beijing prefers to forget. One wing of the pro-democracy movement uses street politics and new media to build pressure for faster progress toward democracy. Because elections have to be held for the Legislative Council every four years and for chief executive every five years, the question keeps coming up of when and how Beijing will make good on its commitment under the Basic Law to allow these elections to be direct and democratic.

Should a political crisis occur, China's behavior in Hong Kong will fall under a brighter international spotlight than even in other parts of the country—in part because many foreign businesspeople live there, in part because under the Basic Law, Hong Kong is covered separately from the rest of China by certain human rights treaties that the United Kingdom had signed before sovereignty was returned to China, and in part because China's promises to Hong Kong in the Joint Declaration are considered a treaty commitment to Britain under international law. Also, after retrocession, London gave some Hong Kong residents semirestricted British passports, and all others the right of visa-free entry to Britain, so political, economic, or administrative mismanagement of Hong Kong might lead to an exodus of Hong Kong residents to Britain and produce a political crisis. The Americans, too, asserted a special interest in Hong Kong's political welfare in 1992 by adopting the McConnell bill (the U.S.–Hong Kong Policy Act), in which Congress asserted that the U.S. has an interest in Hong Kong's economic autonomy, political stability, and human rights.

Beijing's bruising conflicts with the last colonial governor and the Hong Kong democratic movement demonstrated China's vulnerability in a world where economic interests and the power of ideas have become as important as military power. China could have taken Hong Kong long before it did just by turning off the water. It chose to negotiate a peaceful transfer because its interests in the territory were so heavily intertwined with foreign interests. It dealt carefully with challenges because a crackdown would have damaged relations with Britain and other powers. That gamble has paid off so far, thanks to China's rise and Beijing's skillful behind-the-scenes management of Hong Kong politics.[23]

CHINA'S TAIWAN PROBLEM

Of all the issues of territorial integrity, Taiwan carries the highest risk of failure for Beijing. It is the only part of the self-defined Chinese state that the PRC does not control and, because of its physical separation from the mainland, the only part that might be viable as an independent political entity without Beijing's acquiescence. Moreover, in contrast to Xinjiang, Tibet, and Hong Kong, Taiwan is more than just a problem of territorial integrity: it is the site of a rival Chinese government,[24] the ROC, which has ruled its own territory and functioned as an autonomous international actor since the establishment of the PRC in 1949. Even though Taiwan is accepted in principle by all states as part of Chinese territory,[25] the U.S. has committed itself—as it never did with regard to Tibet, Xinjiang, or Hong Kong—to use force if necessary to guarantee "peaceful resolution" of the issue of its relation to China, and a handful of countries continues to recognize the ROC as officially the government of all China. It is not surprising, then, that the Taiwan problem has been an obsessive focus of much of Chinese diplomacy, as we have seen in previous chapters, and that it has absorbed much of China's military modernization effort, as we will show in chapter 11. We consider Taiwan's foreign policy in chapter 9. Here we discuss the problem from the mainland's point of view.

Beijing views control of Taiwan as crucial for defense of the mainland against external enemies. A little more than a hundred miles from the Chinese coast, the island is equipped with major air bases and ports. It sits astride China's southeastern coastal shipping channels and overlooks the navigation routes from Europe and the Middle East to China, Korea, and Japan. Across from a coastal part of China that is difficult to defend and increasingly prosperous, Taiwan is always in a position to threaten the mainland, especially if it were to offer military, intelligence, or propaganda facilities to a great power. U.S. general Douglas MacArthur called Taiwan an "unsinkable aircraft carrier and submarine tender."[26] For years after 1949, the island was used as a base from which to land amphibious KMT attack teams on the Chinese coast, to spy on China, to broadcast anti-Communist propaganda into China, and to support the American role in the Korean and Vietnam wars. Just as the U.S. is determined to prevent a rival's military access to Cuba, Chinese leaders are determined to prevent Taiwan from once again becoming a rival power's strategic asset.

Taiwan presents not only a potential military threat to the mainland, but a possible political threat. The government in Taiwan has avoided direct political provocations, such as a Taiwan-based seaborne radio station that pro-democracy Chinese wanted to establish to broadcast programs into the mainland, and has given only limited support to mainland Chinese dissidents. The larger subversive potential comes from Taiwan's simply being what it is—a modern Chinese society that is economically prosperous and politically democratic. Furthermore, if China were to allow self-determination for one of its major territories on the grounds that its people see themselves as culturally distinct, it would set a precedent for other territories where populations feel estranged to claim the right to break away.

The Taiwan–China relationship differs from some other cases of divided nations in modern history, such as Germany and Korea. These countries were divided by the superpowers after World War II, but the division was considered temporary. Pending reunification, each of the two divided governments recognized the separate statehood of the other. No domestic force or foreign power challenged the ultimate goal of reunification. Taiwan's case is different in two ways: first, the two sides of the strait do not recognize each other's statehood, even on a temporary basis, each claiming to be the legitimate government of all China; second, a substantial political force in Taiwan wants to make it an independent state.

As elsewhere around the Chinese periphery, the sense of separateness is grounded in history. The island was sparsely populated by people of Malay stock (aborigines) until Han Chinese started arriving from southeastern

China in the seventeenth century. China did not lay claim to the island of Taiwan until 1683 and did not make it a province until 1885. In 1895, China ceded Taiwan to Japan as a colony, and the residents were taught to speak Japanese and to think of themselves as subjects of the Japanese emperor. During World War II, the Allied leaders pledged the return of Taiwan to China in both the Cairo Declaration of 1943 and the Potsdam Proclamation of 1945. At the end of the war, the Chinese government took over Taiwan and reaffirmed that it was a Chinese province. Driven out of mainland China by Chinese Communists in 1949, the ROC government retreated to this last province. It refused to recognize the legitimacy of the authorities in Beijing, calling them "Communist bandits," and expressed its determination to "recover the mainland." Beijing denied the legitimacy of the government in Taipei, calling it the "Chiang Kai-shek clique." The PRC prepared to invade Taiwan in 1950 to finish off the rival regime, but the U.S. intervened after the outbreak of the Korean War and remained involved afterward to prevent military conflict sparked by either side (chapter 3).

For decades, the ROC and PRC governments made common cause in insisting that Taiwan was a part of China. Until 1971, the ROC occupied the China seat in the UN and was recognized as the government of China by most countries. In 1971, the UN General Assembly voted to give the China seat to the PRC, and most governments subsequently switched their diplomatic recognition to Beijing. Both governments refused to accept recognition from any government that recognized the other.

The U.S., however, resisted pressure from both the mainland and Taiwan to express agreement with their common position on Taiwan's status. After the Chinese Communists took control of the mainland, and the Korean War was under way, the U.S. backed away from its positions at Cairo and Potsdam. It arranged for Japan, in the San Francisco Peace Treaty of 1951, to renounce its claims to Taiwan without saying to whom it ceded them. Over both PRC and ROC objections, the U.S. took the position that "sovereignty over Taiwan and the Pescadores [nearby smaller islands in the Taiwan Strait controlled by Taiwan] is an unsettled question subject to future international resolution."[27] When the question came up again during the process of U.S.–China rapprochement, the U.S. still refused fully to accept the Chinese position. In both the 1972 Shanghai Communiqué and the 1978 normalization communiqué, Washington "acknowledged" the Chinese claim to Taiwan without either endorsing or challenging it. Moreover, on both occasions the U.S. asserted an interest in the peaceful resolution of the Taiwan issue, in effect claiming a right to intervene in what the Chinese considered a domestic political issue (chapter 4).

Meanwhile, in 1954 the U.S. had signed a Mutual Defense Treaty with the ROC. Without that American defense commitment, Taiwan would likely have been integrated into the PRC long ago. This is why Beijing considers the heart of what it calls the "Taiwan problem" not to be Taiwan's separation from the mainland, but the American role in perpetuating it. Many Chinese believe that the U.S. wants to separate Taiwan from China either permanently or, failing that, for as long as possible. Although separation is not the U.S. policy's expressed intent, so far it has been the policy's effect. The American commitment to the security of Taiwan has roots in both grand strategy and domestic politics (chapter 4). It has been maintained by Republican and Democratic administrations and supported by Congress for half a century and so is not likely to change.

China's concerns about Taiwan separatism are not baseless. Most of the current population are descendants of immigrants from southeastern China who had a special local dialect and culture when they came over and whose sense of separateness in later generations was intensified by fifty years of Japanese rule. From colonial times onward, there has been an active Taiwan independence movement. When Taiwan returned to Chinese control in 1945, the demoralized KMT army that came over from the mainland repaid the initial welcome of Taiwan's residents with repression and corruption. The mainlander ROC regime imposed martial law until the late 1980s. It outlawed the use of the Taiwanese dialect in media and education and forbade independent media and political parties.

Prosperity and generational change gradually eased conflicts between the mainlanders and the Taiwanese. The KMT began a process of "Taiwanization" in the 1970s on by recruiting and promoting Taiwanese party members and government officials. In 1986, President Chiang Ching-kuo initiated a democratic reform, which ten years later led to the first direct election of a president in Chinese history, Chiang's successor as head of the KMT, Lee Teng-hui, himself a Taiwanese.

These developments ameliorated social tensions on the island, but they did not create enthusiasm for unification with mainland China. On the contrary, the more economic and cultural contacts occurred across the Taiwan Strait from the late 1980s on, the more Taiwan residents, both native Taiwanese and those of mainlander origin, valued Taiwan's autonomy. They felt like strangers when they visited the mainland and were repelled by the backwardness and corruption that persisted there. The majority of Taiwan residents opposed any form of reunification under which the mainland authorities would exercise real power over them.

During the 1950s, PRC Taiwan policy focused on weakening Washington's commitment to Taiwan. In 1954 and 1958, Beijing tried to deter American cooperation with Taiwan by creating military tension in the Taiwan Strait, but these efforts were counterproductive, instead strengthening the U.S. commitment to Taiwan (chapter 3). Only in the process of developing security cooperation with the U.S. in the 1970s did China succeed in creating some distance between the U.S. and Taiwan and begin the process of isolating Taiwan internationally. Other countries began to desert the ROC in 1971 as soon as Henry Kissinger's secret visit to the PRC became public and the PRC gained the China seat in the UN.

The American transfer of recognition to the PRC in 1979 marked another victory for PRC strategy. The U.S. promised to withdraw military support from Taiwan, although linking this withdrawal to the expectation of peaceful resolution of the Taiwan issue. The residual American defense commitment, as expressed in the TRA of that year, was vaguer and had less legal standing than the Mutual Defense Treaty that was canceled. Derecognition struck a blow to the prestige of the KMT government, which was also being tested by the rise of a large, pro-democracy Taiwanese middle class. The end of the year saw the worst episode of violent political repression in Taiwan since the 1940s, when police beat and arrested demonstrators in Kaohsiung. Eight were given long jail terms. Their cases became a rallying cry for further growth of the opposition movement and intensified international criticism of Taiwan's human rights violations.

But the game was not yet won. Twenty-two governments still recognized the ROC as the government of China, and it enjoyed quasi-diplomatic relations with the U.S. and others. The U.S. continued to take steps to deter the forceful imposition of PRC rule. Although Taiwan still considered itself in principle part of China, it was not yet governed by Beijing.

AN OFFER TOO GOOD TO REFUSE

With the U.S. willing to accept reunification as long as it was peaceful, the time seemed ripe for Beijing to turn its attention to the leaders in Taipei and construct an offer at once too threatening and too appealing to refuse. Beijing's policy targeted the mainlander KMT leaders still governing Taiwan, especially President Chiang Ching-kuo. With the withdrawal of American diplomatic recognition, the leaders' claim to be the legitimate government of all China had lost credibility. At home, they faced a rising middle class and a pro-democracy movement (the so-called *dangwai* or nonparty movement) that demanded an end to authoritarian rule. Beijing crafted a new, four-pronged policy that sought to make reunification attractive while cutting off other options.

First, in a series of communications Beijing said that if Taiwan's ruling party accepted mainland control, the mainland would license its leaders as local rulers, offering an escape from the twin dilemmas of isolation abroad and political challenges at home. On January 1, 1979, the date of establishment of U.S. diplomatic relations with Beijing, China's national legislature issued the "Letter to Taiwan Compatriots." It called for an end to the state of enmity between the two sides and quick, peaceful reunification; announced the end of the light, symbolic bombardment of the ROC-controlled offshore islands of Quemoy and Matsu that had been taking place since 1958; and called for "three contacts and four exchanges" (commercial, postal, and aviation contacts as well as cultural, art, sports, and science and technology exchanges). In 1981, PRC head of state Ye Jianying supplemented this proposal with the Nine Points, offering Taiwan a "high degree of autonomy" (a phrase later incorporated into the Sino–British agreement on Hong Kong). The 1982 PRC Constitution included a new provision for the establishment of Special Administrative Regions (also later used for Hong Kong), of which Taiwan could become one. In 1983, Deng Xiaoping stated that Taiwan's high degree of autonomy would include the right to maintain its own defense forces and that the mainland would not send military or civilian officials there. Finally, in 1984, when Deng articulated the theory of "one country, two systems" as the principle for reincorporating Hong Kong into China, he added that the principle would also apply to Taiwan.

All this established a bottom-line offer: reunification would be a party-to-party deal between the two organizations that had fought the Chinese civil war in the 1940s, the CCP and the KMT. Beijing would take good care of KMT elites (for example, Chiang Ching-kuo could be appointed a vice president of the PRC, and his father's body would be moved to his native county on the mainland for reinterment). Although the ROC would disappear as an entity in the international system, the KMT would continue to rule as it wished within Taiwan. China would not use Taiwan's air and naval bases for power projection but would satisfy itself with exercising a veto over the island's ties with outsiders, thus fulfilling its basic security need to prevent Taiwan from being used by others for hostile purposes.

Second, China narrowed Taipei's alternatives through a strategy of diplomatic isolation. Under the "one-China principle" accepted at the time by both Beijing and Taipei, any country that recognized the PRC had to break diplomatic ties with Taiwan. On the eve of Sino–U.S. rapprochement, sixty-six countries recognized the ROC and fifty-one recognized the PRC. Within months after Nixon's visit to China, the balance shifted to forty-two for the ROC versus eighty-six for the PRC. The break in relations with the U.S. accelerated Taiwan's loss of diplomatic standing, so that on January 1, 1979, it was recognized by only twenty-two countries. In the 1990s, Taiwan lost the most important among its remaining diplomatic partners as China's global influence grew. After some ups and downs, as of 2010 Taiwan had formal diplomatic relations with twenty-three states, all minor: the Holy See in Europe, six island nations in the Pacific (Kiribati, the Marshall Islands, Nauru, Palau, the Solomon Islands, and Tuvalu), four states in West Africa (Burkina Faso, Gambia, San Tome and Principe, and Swaziland), and twelve countries in Central and South America and the Caribbean (Belize, El Salvador, Guatemala, Honduras, Nicaragua, Panama, Paraguay, Haiti, Dominican Republic, St. Christopher and Nevis, St. Lucia, and St. Vincent and the Grenadines). In international organizations as well, Beijing was vigilant against any rise in the ROC's diplomatic status, insisting, for example, that Taiwan could not join the WTO until after the PRC had done so and then only as a "customs territory," and blocking Taiwan's participation in the WHO, until finally in 2009 allowing it to attend only as an observer.

Third, China reached out to the business community around Chiang to offer positive incentives for trading and investing on the mainland. Beijing promulgated a series of regulations and preferential policies for "Taiwan compatriots" to travel, invest, own houses, live, and do business in China. They were given investment and trade preferences, tax shelters, and special travel documents. By the early 2000s, China was Taiwan's number one investment venue, absorbing more than half of Taiwan's foreign direct investment, most of which was directed at creating manufacturing plants for exports to the West of products formerly produced in Taiwan. China was also Taiwan's number one trading partner, with 28.9 percent of Taiwan's foreign trade. China allowed Taiwan to maintain a large trade surplus, which became crucial to the island's prosperity as its trade-dependent economy faced several global downturns in the 1990s and 2000s. An estimated one million Taiwan businesspeople, students, and family members took up residence in China.

The Taiwan government tried to slow the pace of economic integration without much success. It imposed financial caps, technical limits, and licensing requirements on investments in China and various barriers to trade, while promoting trade and investment in other parts of the world such as Vietnam. But the logic of comparative advantage was too strong. Taiwan was in the process of pricing itself out of its export markets with the rising cost of labor, but it still had outstanding technological capabilities, management expertise, manufacturing and packaging skills, and international marketing channels. China had a cost-efficient labor force in a policy environment that encouraged manufacturing for export. The two sides shared a language and a business culture. The two economies flowed together like water running downhill. As a political consequence, estrangement from China diminished among Taiwanese who worked or visited there or whose livelihoods depended on the growing relationship. Support for moderate cross-strait policies grew among the Taiwan electorate.

Fourth, "smiling diplomacy," as some called it, was supplemented with a tough side. The threat of force had always been part of China's Taiwan policy. In the 1950s, Beijing refused American demands to forswear the use of force, insisting that the right to use military power within one's own territory was an inalienable attribute of sovereignty. When Taiwan's opposition party adopted a platform calling for independence in 1991, President Yang Shangkun stated that "those who play with fire will perish by fire."

At first, Beijing lacked a realistic capability to overcome the daunting problems of projecting military power across the Taiwan Strait in the face of probable American opposition. This status began to change in the 1990s. First, the defense budget ended a long period of stagnation and began to increase. Second, American victory in the 1990–1991 Gulf War impressed the Chinese leadership with the necessity of participating in the Revolution in Military Affairs or else accept a permanent position of military inferiority. Third, as detailed in chapter 9, the policies of Taiwan's then president, Lee Teng-hui, seemed to be evolving in a pro-independence direction, causing China to begin a military buildup with several components: a missile capability aimed at coercing Taiwan; a combination of aircraft, amphibious, and joint-operations capabilities aimed at making it possible to cross the strait in force; and submarine, antisatellite, and other forces that could be used to prevent American access to the Taiwan theater by blinding American surveillance from space and fighting off American aircraft carrier strike groups at sea (for China's possible military strategies toward Taiwan, see chapter 11).

To underscore the seriousness of the military option, in 2005 the NPC passed the Antisecession Law, which stated in Article 8, "In the event that the 'Taiwan independence' secessionist forces should act under any name or by any means to cause the fact of Taiwan's secession from China, or that major incidents entailing Taiwan's secession from China should occur, or that possibilities for a peaceful reunification should be completely exhausted, the state shall employ nonpeaceful means and other necessary measures to protect China's sovereignty and territorial integrity." By putting China's commitment to use force under certain conditions in the form of a statute, China signaled that its determination to defend its interests was just as strong as the commitment to defend Taiwan that the American Congress had expressed in the TRA.

Meanwhile, political infighting, economic troubles, and tensions with the U.S. prevented Taiwan from upgrading its own military equipment, training, and strategic doctrine. By the early 2000s, the once-even military balance across the Taiwan Strait had shifted in favor of the PRC. China could not stand as a military equal with the U.S., but it had established the ability to make the Americans think twice before risking lives in a crisis to defend an ally that seemed unwilling to pay the price of defending itself.

PERSISTING PROBLEMS

Despite the ingenuity and expense of Beijing's efforts, its control over Tibet, Xinjiang, Hong Kong, and Taiwan remains incomplete and in varying ways internationally contested. None of these territories has a realistic chance of breaking away, but each in its own way represents a continuing challenge for China's foreign policy agenda.

The most complex of the four issues in foreign policy terms is Taiwan because it continues to reside beyond Beijing's control. China's careful construction of an offer too good to refuse in the 1980s did not work. Chiang Ching-kuo decided to spurn Beijing's offer to allow him stay in power as the mainland's proconsul on the island and instead took the risky decision to strengthen his regime's position through democratic reform at home. Over the course of a decade starting in 1986, he and his successor, Lee Teng-hui, lifted martial law, released political prisoners, ended controls on speech and the press, allowed the formation of opposition parties, and conducted full-scale elections for the National Assembly, the Legislative Yuan, the presidency, and all local offices. By restructuring its legitimacy on a democratic footing, the government created the domestic base to withstand the mainland diplomatic offensive and international isolation. In the newly democratic Taiwan, it was even made legal to advocate independence from China, and some politicians did.

The emergence within Taiwan of new political obstacles to unification was supplemented by a reverse course in America's Taiwan policy. Growing U.S.–China discord in the 1990s increased sympathy in Washington for Taiwan's defense and diplomatic needs. In 1992, President George H. W. Bush all but openly breached the 1982 U.S.–China arms reduction communiqué by agreeing to sell 150 F-16 fighter planes to Taiwan. In 1994, the Clinton administration modestly upgraded the protocol status of Taiwan officials in the U.S. Finally, under congressional pressure in 1995, the White House authorized a visit by President Lee Teng-hui to his alma mater, Cornell University, to receive an honorary degree, thus according him a higher level of protocol treatment than the U.S. had granted to any president of Taiwan since the break in formal relations.

These developments complicated Beijing's task, above all by introducing a new actor into the picture, the Taiwan electorate, which possessed an effective veto over any outcome. Once democratization had started, no leader of Taiwan could reach any agreement with Beijing that the electorate did not support, but the Taiwan electorate did not want unification. Even as it was putting the last pieces of its four-pronged Taiwan policy in place, Beijing had to rethink it. The next chapter describes the new internal developments in Taiwan and Beijing's response to them.

9

TAIWAN'S DEMOCRATIC TRANSITION AND CHINA'S RESPONSE

Chiang Ching-kuo's decision to launch a transition to democracy in Taiwan changed the game for Beijing as well as for the self-appointed guarantor of "peaceful resolution" of the Taiwan issue, the U.S. Now that the democratic electorate in Taiwan had a voice in determining its own future, Beijing and Washington had to figure out what the Taiwan voters wanted and how to influence them. China did not change its goal, to exercise sovereignty over Taiwan, or the four prongs of its strategy—the offer of special autonomy within the PRC, diplomatic isolation, economic integration, and military threat. But a success that had seemed near at hand now faded into the indefinite future as Beijing scrambled to respond to changes in Taiwan's cross-strait policies that were rooted in the evolution of its domestic politics.

CHIANG'S CHOICE

Before Taiwan's democratic transition, Taipei and Beijing officially agreed on the legal status of Taiwan. Both held that Taiwan was part of China: that Taiwan's separation from the mainland was a feature of an unfinished civil war between two political parties contending for control of China; and that the end of the civil war would bring about the divided country's reunification. In the 1972 Shanghai Communiqué, the U.S. said it did not challenge that view (chapter 4). When the U.S. switched official diplomatic relations from the ROC to the PRC in 1979, China pressed its advantage with an offer based on these premises—a party-to-party deal that would give KMT elites an honorific place in the Chinese political system and leave them in control of local government in Taiwan but without international statehood.

But Taiwan's president, Chiang Ching-kuo, replied, "No negotiations, no compromise, no contacts." Instead, at a moment when he seemed to have no options, he found another way out. He had prepared the ground to some extent over the previous decade by promoting Taiwanese cadres in the KMT (a process called "Taiwanization"), allowing elections for a limited number of so-called supplemental seats in the Legislative Yuan (the national legislature), building up the ruling party's local electoral machines, going down to the grass roots to create a populist personal image, and tolerating limited activity by a pro-democracy movement called the *dangwai* (or "outside the party"). But no one expected his decision in 1986 to allow the *dangwai* to violate existing law by forming a new political party, the Democratic Progressive Party (DPP). People were surprised again by his 1987 decision to lift martial law, which had been in place since 1949.

Scholars have speculated about Chiang's motives. Among them surely were his awareness of his impending death from diabetes, his lack of a plausible successor within his family or immediate circle, the growing challenge to the regime presented by the pro-democracy movement, and his government's international isolation after the U.S. switch of recognition to Beijing.[1] Under these conditions, there were two ways the regime that he headed might have survived beyond his death. One—accepting the patronage of Beijing—would have left in charge a hardliner faction that had diminishing local support, with all the prospects of turmoil this situation would have implied. The other—relegitimating the regime as the democratic representative of the people it ruled so that it could preserve its separate existence as long as it needed to in order to strike the best bargain with Beijing—was the option he chose. The latter choice ran the risk of eventually separating Taiwan from China, which would have been an historical crime in the eyes of a Chinese patriot such as Chiang, but it gave the 23 million people of Taiwan a chance to bargain over their fate with a regime in Beijing that Chiang deeply distrusted.

Early in 1988, Chiang died. He was succeeded as president by a Taiwanese whom he had selected as vice president, Lee Teng-hui. Serving as president until 2000, Lee completed Taiwan's transformation into a full democracy. Elections took place in fast succession: the first full election for the Legislative Yuan in 1992 and new elections every three years thereafter; the first direct presidential election in 1996 and every four years thereafter; and elections for mayors, county magistrates, local legislatures, and other offices almost yearly from the late 1980s on. Lee's government allowed the Taiwanese dialect to be used in schools and in the media. It conducted an inquiry into a government massacre of civilians that had taken place on February 28, 1947, during the KMT takeover of the island, issued an official apology, and created a memorial to the victims. Universities began to study and teach the previously forbidden subject of Taiwan history. Music, literature, architecture, cuisine—all reflected a resurgent pride in Taiwan's unique historical accomplishments and often a sense of tragedy at the people's suffering during the colonial and authoritarian periods.

WHAT DO TAIWAN VOTERS WANT?

Taiwan's voters had no shortage of policy issues to debate, such as the environment, the economy, and social welfare policy. But the main electoral issue was the island's relation to the mainland. On this issue, politicians pressed the voters to consider the conflicting imperatives of identity and pragmatism.

The identity issue was rooted in the ethnic history of Taiwan. Aside from some five hundred thousand aborigines, about 85 percent of the island's population consider themselves Taiwanese because they are descended from Han Chinese who came from the mainland before 1945, most of them speaking Minnan (southern Fujian) or Hakka dialects (the Hakka, or Guest People, are a distinct cultural group within the Han category, who are centered in various locations in southeastern China as well as in Taiwan). The other 15 percent of the population consider themselves to be mainlanders (*waishengren*—people from provinces outside of Taiwan) because they are descended from officials, soldiers, businessmen, and others who came from the mainland with the KMT regime starting in 1945. From 1945 to the late 1980s, the authoritarian KMT regime enforced a Chinese identity on the entire population, outlawing the use of the Taiwanese dialect in education and the media, teaching loyalty to the ROC as the government of all China, and governing Taiwan not as a nation, but as a province.

The DPP positioned itself on the side of Taiwanese pride with emotional rhetoric, symbols, and music. As the political system democratized, the KMT too increasingly emphasized the local roots of most of its politicians and its commitment to "Taiwan first." Beijing contributed unwittingly to the rise of Taiwan identity by denouncing it and by threatening to use force if the voters elected pro-independence officials. In public-opinion polls, the number of respondents who said they "thought of themselves as Chinese" declined from 54 percent in 1989 to 4.2 percent in 2008. Those who thought of themselves as Taiwanese went from 18 percent to 50.8 percent, and those who thought of themselves as "both" went from 28 percent to 40.8 percent.[2]

Cross-cutting the question of identity was the question of policy preference: Did the voters want unification with the mainland, independence, or preservation of the status quo? As Taiwan identity increased, so did the desire for independence. From 1991 to 2003, those who wanted independence provided that "Taiwan can maintain a peaceful relation with the PRC government" increased from 42.1 percent to a high of 75.8 percent in 1996 and then fell back to 63.2 percent in 2005. Those who would like unification—provided that "China and Taiwan have the same social, economic, and political conditions"—declined from a high of 76.3 percent in 1991 to a low of 46.6 percent in 2005.

But Taiwan voters knew that the cost-free assumptions of these hypothetical questions were contrary to reality. Thus, when the Taiwanese were asked in polls dating from 1996 to 2008 whether they favored immediate unification, only 1–5 percent of respondents said "yes." Likewise, voters knew that if Taiwan declared independence, it would not be able to maintain a peaceful relationship with the PRC. So only 3–14 percent said they would like independence no matter what. Robust majorities favored one or another version of the status quo, including "status quo now, decision later," "status quo indefinitely," "status quo now, independence later," and "status quo now, unification later." Although it is hard to know exactly what respondents had in mind when they said they favored the status quo, at a minimum it included avoidance of armed conflict with the mainland. The electoral environment thus constrained political leaders while also leaving space for creativity. The government had to assert Taiwanese identity in some way—which ruled out accepting unification on the terms Beijing had offered—but it had at the same time to maintain peace across the Taiwan Strait and allow the growing benefits of economic interactions across the strait. Within these constraints, political leaders could pursue their agendas for cross-strait relations.

LEE TENG-HUI AND THE "TWO-STATE THEORY"

Under these fluid political conditions, Chiang Ching-kuo's successor, Lee Teng-hui, created a revolution not only in Taiwan's domestic political system, but also in Taiwan's international stance. He came to office as the head of an authoritarian one-party system and as custodian of his predecessor's position that Taiwan was a part of China. He left office with Taiwan a full democracy, claiming an equal status with the PRC as one of two states in what he called "a special state-to-state relationship."[3]

Lee was a surprising revolutionary.[4] Chiang Ching-kuo had selected him as vice president in 1984 because he was the archetype of a loyal technocrat. To be sure, he had briefly flirted with Marxism in the 1940s, but he had become a faithful KMT member and a Presbyterian after that. With a Ph.D. in agricultural economics from Cornell University, he spent his early career in the agricultural policy bureaucracy in Taiwan, then rose to a series of appointed administrative posts, including mayor of Taipei and governor of Taiwan. When he succeeded Chiang as president in January 1988, both the old mainlander elite in Taiwan and the leaders in Beijing expected him to uphold the orthodoxy that Taiwan was a part of China. It emerged, however, that Lee was a superb tactician, able to bide his time and keep his counsel. His presidency revealed what—at least in Beijing's later view—must always have been his aspiration: to establish during his term in office the bases for Taiwan's eventual claim to permanent political separation from the mainland: first, to make that claim politically legitimate by grounding it in the will of the people expressed through an institutionalized democratic system of government; and, second, to make it internationally legal by gaining acknowledgment of Taiwan's existence as a sovereign entity distinct from the PRC. Lee was willing to conceive of some pro forma framework linking the island and the mainland, but not to meet Beijing's goal of full political unification. His strategy to fend off China's pressure was to drag out the process of cross-strait rapprochement and at the same time to engineer domestic political reform and pursue diplomatic initiatives to shore up Taiwan's international standing.

Lee's cross-strait strategy had three components, which he phased in over time. The first consisted of what observers labeled "pragmatic," "substantive," or "flexible" diplomacy. This component sought to buttress the ROC's deteriorating position in the international system by modifying the traditional stance that the ROC must be recognized as the sole Chinese government, instead moving closer to the German and Korean models, which allowed foreign governments to recognize two states pending unification. Lee argued that the ROC was a distinct system or "political entity" within a vaguely defined broader China, having historically continuous sovereignty since its founding on the mainland in 1912, currently maintaining effective control over a certain piece of territory, and hence possessing the attributes of legitimate statehood. This argument was no more than what Chiang Ching-kuo had said years earlier, when the U.S. broke relations with the ROC.[5] What was new was that Lee now acknowledged as a corollary that the Beijing government was a parallel entity: no longer an insurgency (what the KMT used to call "Communist bandits"), but a legitimate state governing another part of China. The larger China entity had therefore become "one country with two governments."

Taipei fought hard on this basis for diplomatic ties with small countries by using its well-funded International Economic Cooperation and Development Fund, prompting Beijing to accuse Taipei of "dollar diplomacy." These efforts produced short-lived gains. Taipei's roster of diplomatic recognitions rose from a low of twenty-one in 1988 to a high of thirty-one in 1995, then fell again. Taipei also made known that it would accept recognition as the ROC from countries that recognized the PRC without, as in the past, requiring them to break relations with Beijing. But because Beijing would not accept dual recognition, the few third-country attempts to grant it never survived.

In countries where Taiwan could not get full diplomatic recognition, it increased its subdiplomatic representation by opening offices that did consular, trade-promotion, and diplomatic business and that even enjoyed diplomatic status without being called embassies and consulates. The model for this approach was the system of representative offices established between Japan and Taiwan after Japan switched diplomatic recognition to the PRC in 1972. The U.S. followed this model with the switch of recognition in 1979, establishing formal diplomatic ties with Beijing while establishing ostensibly nongovernmental relations with Taipei. The U.S. established the American Institute in Taiwan, staffed by foreign service officers on leave from the State Department, to handle relations with Taipei, and Taiwan established the Coordination Council for North American Affairs (later renamed the Taipei Economic and Cultural Office) in the U.S. Taiwan followed the same model elsewhere in the world. With the end of the Cold War, Taipei's delegates were welcomed in the capitals of most trade- and aid-hungry post-Communist states and even in the capital of Communist Vietnam. As of the early 2000s, Taiwan had about a hundred quasi-diplomatic offices around the world under various names.

Taiwan also cultivated membership in as many intergovernmental organizations as possible, including the WTO, the Asian Development Bank, the Asian and Pacific Economic Cooperation forum, the Permanent Court of Arbitration, the World Customs Organization, the Western and Central Pacific Fisheries Commission, the International Seed Testing Association, the Interim Scientific Committee for Tuna and Tuna-Like Species in the North Pacific Ocean, and others. On a case-by-case basis, Beijing dropped its opposition to Taiwanese participation in such organizations, in some instances because it was trying to gain entry itself (as in the WTO), in other instances in hopes of enticing Taiwan into increased contact. To find a rubric acceptable to both Taipei and Beijing under which Taiwan could participate as a governmental entity but not a state, the two sides played the "name game." Taiwan joined the WTO as the "customs territory of Taiwan, Kinmen, Penghu, and Matsu" (Kinmen [Quemoy], Penghu, and Matsu are island groups administered as part of Taiwan) and the Commission for the Conservation of Southern Bluefin Tuna as the "Fishing Entity of Taiwan." But the most common name was "Chinese Taipei," which had been brokered by the International Olympic Committee in 1981 to facilitate Taiwan's return to participation in the Olympics after the PRC had taken the

China seat in the international Olympic movement. This "Olympic formula" came to be used to describe Taiwan's delegations to many international forums because its ambiguity made it acceptable to both sides. Beijing translated it into Chinese as the equivalent of "Taipei Belonging to China" (Zhongguo Taibei), and Taiwan translated it as "Taipei That Is Culturally Chinese" (Zhonghua Taibei) — differing by only one syllable.

Taiwan also pursued membership in as many international NGOs as possible. It performed especially well in the international Little League movement, winning numerous championships. It gave high priority to its membership in the Olympic movement as a powerful symbol of nationhood. These measures stabilized Taiwan's international position and, virtually unnoticed at the time, laid the initial conceptual foundation for the later claim of statehood.

Lee phased in the second aspect of his strategy starting in the early 1990s. He created a thaw in relations with the mainland by putting forward proposals that policymakers in Beijing interpreted as conciliatory, then used the relaxation in relations to move Taipei further toward equality with Beijing as one government negotiating with another government. In 1991, he revoked the "state of Communist rebellion" that Chiang Kai-shek had declared decades earlier. In doing so, Lee formally acknowledged the PRC as a "political entity that controls the mainland area" and described the ROC as "a sovereign state on Taiwan." On their face simple statements of fact, these formulas differed critically from Taipei's traditional claim to be the sole legitimate government of all China. They vacated the ROC's claim to sovereignty over the mainland and thus logically suggested the existence of a separate state on a territory limited to Taiwan (plus a few smaller islands held by the ROC).

In March 1991, Taipei issued the Guidelines for National Unification. The guidelines envisioned unification in an affirmative manner and posited that it would take place in three phases, which seemed to be a step in the direction of meeting Beijing's demands, but the document described these phases as so protracted and as placing such high reciprocal conditions on Beijing that the reunification process would stretch into an endless future. In the first phase, Taiwan would continue people-to-people contacts. In return, the mainland was to cease threatening the use of military force, denying Taiwan's existence as a political entity, and restricting Taiwan's activities in the international arena; at the same time, it was to carry out economic reform and democratization to make itself a more acceptable partner for unification. Had the mainland met these conditions, it would have given up all its bargaining leverage over Taiwan. The guidelines put off to the second and third phases the establishment of government-to-government contacts and final consultations toward unification.

Meanwhile, Lee pursued direct talks with Beijing. First, he built trust by conducting secret talks through intermediaries in Hong Kong. Meanwhile, in 1990 Taipei established a nominally private but government-funded organization, the Straits Exchange Foundation (SEF), to conduct talks with Beijing. Policy guidance for the SEF was provided by a new government body, the Mainland Affairs Council. Because the SEF was private, it was able to negotiate as an equal partner with a parallel, ostensibly private, organization on the Chinese side, the Association for Relations Across the Taiwan Strait (ARATS), headed by retired Shanghai mayor Wang Daohan. The two sides cleared an obstacle to talks in 1992 by agreeing to the principle of "one China with separate interpretations" (*yige Zhongguo gezi biaoshu*). This formula, later dubbed the "1992 consensus," satisfied Beijing's "one-China principle" while committing Taipei to nothing in particular. The two sides' delegates met in Singapore in 1993 and signed agreements on technical matters such as how each side could authenticate wills, deeds, and marriage certificates for the other side and how to deal with each other's lost registered mail. These agreements facilitated interaction by citizens across the strait and pointed the way toward solving other issues, such as how to handle fishing disputes, stowaways, and hijackers.

But the two sides had difficulty agreeing on ground rules for their third meeting. Meanwhile, Lee derided China's "one country, two systems" offer as inadequate, pointing out that Taiwan was not a colony like Hong Kong. He proclaimed the superiority of Taiwan's economic and political models to the PRC's and talked about his personal preference for Japanese language and culture, which he had learned as a student during the colonial era. He promoted Taiwanese identity through changes in educational policy and by memorializing the KMT repression of Taiwanese citizens on February 28, 1947. He abolished the provincial level of government in Taiwan, so that the island was now governed directly from the national level as if it were a nation-state. Democratizing reforms increased the degree to which Taiwan looked more like a self-standing state. Institutions brought over in 1949 from the mainland were overhauled: the National Assembly was abolished, and the Legislative Yuan and presidency were directly elected by the voters of Taiwan alone, without mainland representation.

Beijing had thought at first that Lee was jockeying for more autonomy within an eventual unified China but now began to perceive a drive toward independent statehood. In 1993, China issued a warning to Lee Teng-hui in the form of a white paper titled *The Taiwan Question and Reunification of China*.

> It should be pointed out that notwithstanding a certain measure of easing up by the Taiwan authorities, their current policy *vis-á-vis* the mainland still seriously impedes the development of relations across the strait as well as the reunification of the country. They talk about the necessity of a reunified China, but their deeds are always a far cry from the principle of one China. They try to prolong Taiwan's separation from the mainland and refuse to hold talks on peaceful reunification. . . . The Chinese Government is closely following the course of events and will never condone any maneuver for "Taiwan independence."[6]

Beijing followed up with a statement by CCP head Jiang Zemin on Chinese New Year 1995—the so-called Jiang Eight Points—which repeated Beijing's standing offer to negotiate anything on the basis of the one-China principle but also warned of China's determination to use any means to counter what it called a "growing separatist tendency."

In response, Lee toughened his own position, and his China strategy entered its third stage. His six-point response to Jiang asserted that the one China—whose existence he continued to acknowledge, although Beijing considered such references hypocritical—contained two political entities,[7] neither subordinate to the other, which must negotiate as equals. He asked Beijing to recognize this fact, renounce the use of force, and allow the two governments to join international organizations on an equal footing. At the same time, as a result of lobbying by a firm hired by Taipei, the U.S. Congress adopted a "sense of Congress" resolution urging the U.S. administration to grant a visa to Lee to attend a reunion at his alma mater, Cornell. Lee's Cornell visit shocked Beijing, both because it violated standing U.S. policy to allow only tightly restricted transit visas to the Taiwan head of state and because Lee's speech at Cornell—delivered in his official capacity as the ROC president—was an ode to Taiwan identity.

Lee's toughness was matched by Beijing. To turn up the pressure—not only on Lee, but also on the Clinton administration—China suspended negotiations over the next stage of the SEF–ARATS talks. In July–August 1995 and again in March 1996, it also conducted missile exercises in the Taiwan Strait to demonstrate its determination to oppose Taiwan independence. The U.S. responded by dispatching two aircraft carrier strike groups to the vicinity of the Taiwan Strait.

The standoff ended without a military clash and contributed to Lee's reelection to the presidency in March 1996, but it led to the Americans' reevaluation of their policy. The Clinton administration decided it could not afford to freeze relations with Beijing in order to advance Lee's Taiwan statehood agenda. In 1998, Clinton took the opportunity of the first presidential visit to China since before the 1989 Tiananmen crisis to repeat longstanding American policy that the U.S. "doesn't support independence for Taiwan, or 'two Chinas,' or 'one Taiwan, one China,' and we don't believe that Taiwan should be a member in any organization for which statehood is a requirement." These "Three No's" helped to repair Washington–Beijing relations. Because of the way they were delivered—as a presidential statement in the rival capital—they marked a setback for Lee Teng-hui.

Lee moved into the last year of his presidential term determined to consolidate his gains as a gift to his successor, whoever that might be. In secret from his own advisers, he convened a study group headed by international law specialist Tsai Ing-wen, who would later join the opposition DPP and become its chairperson and 2012 presidential candidate. Based on their planning, in July 1999 Lee used an interview with Germany's international radio station, Deutsche Welle, to state that relations between Taiwan and the mainland were not a relationship between a legitimate government and a renegade group or between a central and a local government, but a "special state-to-state relationship." Taiwan would not declare independence, he said, because it was already independent.[8]

Lee's two-state theory drew a storm of condemnation from Beijing, which called Lee "a dog in the water" and "the scum of the nation," among other epithets. Just weeks before the election, China issued a second white paper on Taiwan that stated more clearly than ever before the three conditions under which the PRC would use force: "if a grave turn of events occurs leading to the separation of Taiwan from China in any name, or if Taiwan is invaded and occupied by foreign countries, or if the Taiwan authorities refuse, *sine die* [for an indefinite period of time], the peaceful settlement of cross-strait reunification through negotiations."[9] The third condition was new and the most threatening to Taiwan because, however vaguely, it suggested a deadline.

WEAKENING LEE'S LEGACY: CHEN SHUI-BIAN'S CHINA POLICY

Lee's successor was the leader of the DPP, Chen Shui-bian, who served two terms as president from 2000 to 2008. This was the opposition party's first chance to hold power—a chance that many of its members believed might not easily come again given the KMT's tremendous resources. Although Chen often obfuscated his goals for tactical reasons, he and his advisers sought to consolidate the juridical independence Lee Teng-hui had claimed for Taiwan and make it irreversible. But these aims were frustrated by the ambivalence of the electorate, the firmness of Beijing, and the opposition of Washington.[10] Chen left Taiwan in a weaker position than he had found it.

During his campaign for president, Chen tried to defuse KMT charges that his election would cause war with China by promising a "journey of peace" to the mainland, expressing his interest in cross-strait transport and economic links, and advocating what he called a "new middle way," which he said would avoid unification on the one side and war on the other. To support Chen, the DPP replaced its former "independence platform," which called for establishing a "Republic of Taiwan," with a softer-sounding resolution that used language already made familiar by Lee Teng-hui: that "Taiwan is a sovereign independent country" that happens to be named the Republic of China. The resolution, however, added the twist that the country could not change its status except by means of a plebiscite—a concept that was anathema to Beijing because it implied a right of self-determination.[11] Neither Beijing nor Washington had any doubt that

Chen's real agenda was to consolidate the elements of statehood that Lee Teng-hui had won for Taiwan and to expand them as far as he could, and Beijing did not bother to test the sincerity of Chen's conciliatory rhetoric.

Instead, two days before the election, Chinese premier Zhu Rongji appeared on television to wag his finger and threaten Taiwan voters "not to act on their impulse since this juncture will decide the future on both sides across the strait. I am afraid you won't have another opportunity to regret."[12] When Chen was elected anyway, China conducted military exercises designed to demonstrate its newly created capability to seize offshore islands under Taiwan's control if it chose to do so. The increase in tension alarmed the U.S. government. The Clinton administration had already invited Chen to Washington before his candidacy was official to warn him privately not to provoke Beijing. In his Inaugural Address, written with direct American involvement, Chen committed himself to "Four No's." "As long as the CCP regime has no intention to use military force against Taiwan," he said, his administration would not declare independence, change the country's name, write the doctrine of special state to state relations into the Constitution, or conduct a referendum on unification or independence.

President George W. Bush came to office in 2001 favorably disposed to Taiwan. Shortly after he occupied the presidency, he announced a large arms sales package and told a TV interviewer that the U.S. would do "whatever it takes" to help Taiwan defend itself in case of attack. But after September 11, 2001, as relations with Beijing became a priority for Washington in the new war against terror, Washington cooled on Chen. Every time Chen pushed even slightly beyond the rhetorical boundaries that Lee Teng-hui had already established, both Beijing and Washington pushed back. This process led to a sharp rebuke of Chen in 2003 when Bush appeared on television with visiting Chinese premier Wen Jiabao and stated, "[T]he comments and actions made by the leader of Taiwan indicate that he may be willing to make decisions unilaterally to change the status quo, which we oppose."

Chen needed some progress in cross-strait relations in order to show Washington and above all the Taiwan electorate that he could manage Beijing politically as well as to help his constituents profit from China's economic growth. China was interested in tightening economic bonds with the island but vigilant against Chen's attempts to use such progress to make political gains. China did make an interesting rhetorical concession shortly after Chen took power. It floated a new version of the one-China principle that replaced the standard "Taiwan is a part of China" with the new phrase "both the mainland and Taiwan belong to one China," which made the two sides' status sound more equal.

But this change in wording did not alter the bottom-line price Beijing was asking in exchange for any economic breakthrough: Taiwan would have to sign the deal in some other capacity than that of a sovereign state. No elected leader of Taiwan could pay this price. Chen was therefore able to take only unilateral steps that had little economic significance, such as opening direct postal, transportation, and trade links between the ROC's island outposts of Jinmen (Quemoy) and Mazu (Matsu) and several Chinese cities in 2001. With great labor, his administration negotiated Chinese New Year charter flights between Taiwan and the mainland in 2003 and additional charter flights for both cargo and travelers in 2006. Other than these steps, however, little progress was made at the official level on cross-strait economic ties.

Chen's main agenda was at home. His election in 2000 after a hard-fought campaign was a historic first democratic turnover of power between two parties in any part of China, but his domestic political position remained weak. The DPP, as a new party, lacked a base in the bureaucracy from which it could generate patronage to build local political machines. Its appeal was mostly identity based, but given the ambivalence of the electorate about both identity issues and risk taking in mainland relations, the DPP's vote share in Legislative Yuan elections—the best measure of its core electoral strength—never exceeded 39 percent. Chen won the 2000 election with a plurality because the KMT candidate and a breakaway candidate split the majority of the vote. He won reelection in 2004 by a margin of only one-tenth of one percent because, analysts believe, of a sympathy vote that was generated under suspicious circumstances: the KMT candidate had been in the lead until just hours before the election, when a mysterious assailant shot Chen, which put him over the election edge. The injuries turned out to be minor, and the shooter was found dead, arousing suspicions—which have never been substantiated—that the incident had been staged.

To turn such narrow victories into long-term viability for the DPP as a competitive party, Chen needed to achieve conflicting goals—to keep his base motivated and to expand his appeal to the center. This conflict led him to issue ambiguous statements about Taiwan's international status to different audiences. Thus, he told a pro-independence audience that there was "one country on each side" of the Taiwan Strait, but in his second Inaugural Address he called for "a cooperative and mutually beneficial relationship" across the strait and promised "no unilateral change to the status quo."

Chen found it useful to generate crises in which he positioned himself as a fighter for Taiwan's democracy against repression from Beijing and Washington. He suggested writing a new constitution because the existing ROC Constitution, written long ago on the mainland and now encrusted with amendments, was no longer efficient. The proposal drew condemnation from Beijing and behind-the-scenes cautions from the U.S. because writing a new constitution would break the historical legal tie of Taiwan to China. In 2004 and 2008, Chen placed referenda before the voters on such questions as whether Taiwan should strengthen its self-defense capabilities and whether Taiwan should seek to rejoin the UN and under what name. The questions were so vaguely formulated that they could not have guided policy if they had passed (which they did not because not enough voters cast ballots on them to produce valid results), but, again, they provoked opposition from Beijing and Washington on the basis that the mere conduct of referenda implied a right of self-determination.

Instead of consolidating Lee Teng-hui's foreign policy legacy, Chen's presidency left it weakened. Taiwan lost diplomatic recognition from half-a-dozen African, Central American, and Caribbean partners, bringing the number of recognitions down to twenty-three by the end of his term. Despite U.S. support, Taiwan failed to gain observer status at the WHO during his term. Its annual campaign to gain some form of representation at the UN made no progress. Its military posture also deteriorated, in part because the money to take advantage of the arms sales package offered by President Bush in 2001 remained tied up in budgetary infighting in the KMT-dominated Legislative Yuan. Relations with the U.S. were frayed as many American policymakers came to believe that Chen had placed his political interests ahead of American security interests. As Chen Shui-bian's term ended, his approval ratings reached a low point, due in part to troubles in the economy, in part to the public's exhaustion with his style of leadership, and in part to a wave of corruption scandals that enveloped many of his subordinates, his children, his wife, and—soon after he left office—Chen himself.

Meanwhile, Beijing's Taiwan policy continued to advance. In 2005, shortly after the start of Chen's second term, China's national legislature adopted the Antisecession Law (chapter 8). Beijing kept building up its missile force and conducted military exercises that demonstrated its increasing capacity to project forces cross the strait and to deny access to American forces that might seek to intervene. China reached over Chen's head to private entrepreneurs and citizens in Taiwan, intensifying economic ties and developing educational, cultural, and media exchanges. Such ties served to soften suspicion of Beijing among Taiwan voters and to tie many Taiwanese communities' prosperity to the mainland economy. Chinese leaders welcomed KMT leaders to Beijing on a party-to-party basis, sending a message about how cross-strait relations would improve if the voters put the DPP out of office. They also reached out to DPP leaders they perceived as moderate, seeking to encourage evolution within the DPP. In Washington, Chen was blamed for provoking Beijing, creating a needless risk of a war that would involve American troops, and failing to maintain Taiwan's ability to defend itself. The American commitment to defend Taiwan seemed to soften politically.

MA YING-JEOU AND THE FUTURE OF TAIWAN–CHINA RELATIONS

It was little surprise that the 2008 election resulted in a return to power of the KMT, whose candidate, Ma Ying-jeou, promised to lower tensions with Beijing and repair the relationship with Washington. Ma was a mainlander, a graduate of the New York University and Harvard law schools, a former aide to Chiang Ching-kuo, justice minister under Lee Teng-hui, and a former mayor of Taipei. He regarded Lee Teng-hui's position that the ROC was an independent sovereign state in existence since 1912 as being consistent with the ROC Constitution. But he did not press Lee's logical corollary, that the ROC could relinquish its claim to control the mainland and go on with its historically continuous existence as a sovereign state on Taiwan. Although logically Ma's position implied a continued ROC claim to sovereignty over the mainland, he left unstated his precise position on that tender question.

Instead, in his campaign against DPP candidate Frank Hsieh (also a relative moderate on cross-strait issues), Ma proposed to put theoretical disputes about Taiwan's status on hold and to subject mainland relations to a pragmatic thaw. He planned to eliminate obstacles to travel, tourism, trade, investment, and financial transactions, thus embracing the benefits of economic relations with the mainland at a time when Taiwan's economy was struggling. To calm political tensions, Ma offered to reinstate Taiwan's recognition of the 1992 consensus ("one China with separate interpretations") that Chen Shui-bian had abandoned, promised not to change the ROC Constitution, and said he would seek an agreement with the mainland to live in peace. To Washington, he promised a "surprise-free" relationship. On defense, he said he would proceed with the long-delayed arms purchases from the U.S. while pushing the military to develop an effective strategy to deter mainland attack. In all, his policy was for "Three No's": "no unification, no independence, and no use of force."

Beijing was responsive. After Ma took office, SEF and ARATS resumed meeting and signed a range of economic agreements. Beijing turned down an offer from Paraguay to switch diplomatic recognition, thus accepting Ma's proposal for a truce in the diplomatic competition between the two sides. China accepted the posting of an ROC observer delegation to the World Health Assembly (the WHO's governing body) under the label "Chinese Taipei." Direct air and sea travel and shipping began. After two years of negotiations, in 2010 the two sides signed the Economic Cooperation Framework Agreement, which led to large increases in trade, investment, and tourism across the Strait.

But Beijing remained on its guard against slippage in its legal or power positions on Taiwan. It continued to hold a stiff line against any hint of separate ROC sovereignty, insisting that Taiwan delegations attend international meetings only under the names "Taiwan, China" or "Chinese Taipei." The PRC protested vigorously when the U.S. agreed in 2011 to supply equipment upgrades to Taiwan's aging fleet of F-16 combat aircraft. It was hard to tell who benefited most from the partial thaw. The mainland tightened its grip on Taiwan's economic welfare, but in doing so it contributed to the island's viability and self-confidence. In all of the complicated negotiations, neither side made any concession on its core sovereignty claim—Taiwan's to be a sovereign government, China's to hold sovereignty over Taiwan. On the basis at least in part of this ambiguous progress in cross-strait relations, Ma Ying-jeou was elected to a second term in 2012.

Taiwan–mainland relations continue to be dominated by a dilemma of mutual vulnerability. The more the mainland tries to constrain Taiwan's options, the less safe Taiwan feels; the more Taiwan tries to increase its freedom of action, the less safe the mainland feels. A solution that serves the needs of both sides is imaginable in theory, but hard to reach in practice. Mutual trust would dissolve the security dilemma, but the dilemma makes trust hard to achieve. Even if future generations of Chinese leaders were to feel less nationalist fervor about recovering Taiwan than the cohorts of leaders who have governed the PRC so far, they would still want to control Taiwan's international relations in order to prevent the island from being used by others as a base for hostile action. Mainland economic prosperity and political reform may reduce the Taiwanese sense of estrangement, but the residents of Taiwan will still want to maintain their own political system, way of life, and foreign policy without domination from across the strait.

During Ma's first presidential term, some American policy analysts began to argue that the U.S. should end its involvement in the Taiwan issue because Taiwan no longer needs the U.S. to protect it from the PRC.[13] But a retreat from the U.S. commitment to protect Taiwan from the mainland use of force would damage American credibility as an ally in Asia so long as the PRC continues to deploy its forces for a possible attack on Taiwan. The Taiwan issue seems set to occupy a central place in Chinese foreign and security policy and in U.S.–China relations for a long time to come.

PART IV

INSTRUMENTS of POWER

10

DILEMMAS OF OPENING

Power and Vulnerability in the Global Economy

The amazing "rise of China" starting in the late 1970s was above all an economic phenomenon, which saw the country's GDP shoot up at an average annual rate of 9.6 percent starting in 1978 to reach $6 trillion in 2010. Without this surge in economic power, China would not have had the resources to make itself into a modern military power starting in the 1990s, a subject we discuss in chapter 11. Nor would it have enjoyed the prestige to begin exercising soft power in the ways that we describe in chapter 12. And of course, trade, aid, and investment were themselves direct sources of influence. Yet for China, economic growth was not a one-sided good. From a security standpoint, the boom and the strategic choices that had to be taken to make it happen also entailed great sacrifices. Growth was achieved by means of a deep engagement in the global economy that made China more vulnerable to pressures and influences from the outside world than it had ever been before.

Deng Xiaoping's policy of "reform and opening"—the revolution (or some said counterrevolution) that made rapid economic growth possible—reversed Mao Zedong's foreign economic policy of self-reliance described in chapter 3. Usually viewed as an obvious choice and an unalloyed triumph, the embrace of globalization was in fact halting, costly, and deeply ambivalent, embracing a set of dilemmas as troubling as the equal and opposite dilemmas entailed in the previous policy of autarky. In security terms, China continues decades later to benefit from and expand on Deng's gamble, but it also continues to pay its costs. By moving from autarky to interdependence, China increased not only its power over the destinies of others, but also the power of others over its own destiny.

For both Mao and Deng, to adopt a security strategy toward the outside world was at the same time to adopt an economic strategy. In this sense, "engagement" was not only a strategy utilized by the outside world to change China, but China's own strategy to find a more advantageous way of relating to the outside world. The attraction of Mao's policy had been to avoid dependence on foreign capital and markets so that China could keep full control over its own way of life and political system. Its disadvantage was that autarkic development forced the country to accumulate capital for the industrial buildup from domestic resources, which meant that money could not be devoted to improving living standards. It required suppressing people's aspirations for better lives, which required political discipline, which in turn encouraged the construction of a totalitarian political system, which in its own turn created the suffering that eventually made autarky unsustainable. Evaluated in purely economic terms, Mao's development model succeeded in constructing an industrial economy, but it did so at the cost of low efficiency and an inability to gain access to advanced technology. Another shortcoming was that autarky gave other states no stake in China's welfare, making it easier for many of China's neighbors to treat it as an enemy.

Deng's development model had the opposite benefits and costs. Global immersion gave China access to the West's technology, capital, and markets, thus speeding up economic growth, dramatically improving living standards, and allowing the regime to relax political repression. The government gained the budgetary resources it needed to start modernizing the military and the expertise it needed to join and benefit from international regimes. Countries that traded with and invested in China became attentive to China's interests. On the downside, however, the government had to compromise its control of the economy. China took on commitments to international rules on trade, finance, property rights, product safety, and other subjects. It was penetrated by foreign institutions and by market and cultural forces beyond government control that influenced its people's thoughts and behavior. China's prosperity became tied in to other countries' well-being. If autarky had created a Great Wall that protected China from outside influences at the cost of leaving it weaker than it would otherwise have been, engagement dismantled the wall and gave China new assets at the cost of exposing the country to a deluge of outside influences.

None of these issues was new. In the early nineteenth century, when the global market started its long expansion, English trading ships presented themselves at China's borders seeking to trade opium for tea. In a series of wars, foreigners forced China to open itself to trade, investment, and the missionary movement. Toward the end of the nineteenth century, Chinese leaders formed a consensus that economic backwardness was the chief cause of their military weakness. Their leading issue became how to modernize for wealth and power while preserving national independence. The Chinese debated whether to integrate with the world economy or seek self-reliance.

But that choice was constrained by the state of the world economy and China's strategic situation. A post–World War I world trade boom allowed China to develop some foreign trade, although it had little to sell and could not afford to buy much. Global protectionist trends in the 1930s forced the Chinese to think more about self-reliant development. After 1949, China was able to borrow capital and technology for a time from the Soviet Union, but Mao's decision to break with the Soviets left China in the 1960s with no alternative to autarky.

Mao reopened some minor channels to the West before he died. Meanwhile, however, much of the rest of Asia had created a development miracle based on manufacturing for Western markets. With the takeoff of globalization starting in the 1970s, international trade and investment volumes climbed to historic heights. When Deng Xiaoping came to power in late 1978, two trends therefore converged: China was ready to enter the world, and the global economy was ready to integrate China. Conditions were ripe for China to try a new model of development.

ADMITTING FOREIGN TRADE AND CAPITAL

Deng did not follow a blueprint but, as he put it, "crossed the river by feeling the stones." His initial idea was to use limited material incentives to revitalize agricultural production in the government-controlled collective farms and to stimulate management initiative in the state-owned indus-trial enterprises. As a supplement, he was willing to open the economy to limited outside technology and marketing expertise so that a few joint ven-tures could produce for export. When these first steps worked, Deng faced pressure from his advisers and foreign partners to do more. Each time he agreed to new ideas, he aroused fresh political opposition motivated by worries about the new compromises China was making, as well as fresh pressure from reformers to move another step toward reform, and he had to make new hard decisions.[1]

The economic opening to the outside world began with two domains, trade and investment. Under Mao, the central planners treated foreign trade as a residual activity, a way to get rid of the leftovers of the domestic economy and acquire those few necessities not yet produced at home.[2] China exported just a sufficient amount of agricultural products, minerals, and fuels that happened to be in surplus to cover the costs of machin-ery, equipment, and steel that had to be imported for the industrialization drive. China's foreign trade, limited almost completely to the Soviet bloc, passed its high point of $4.38 billion in 1959 and then dropped to a low of $2.66 billion in 1962 before rebounding slightly as China shipped textiles, foodstuffs, and metal ores to the Soviet Union to repay its debts for devel-opment help. In 1973, while Mao was still alive, the country made its larg-est overseas purchases since the period of Soviet aid, importing industrial plants from the U.S and Europe. By 1976, the last year of Mao's life, foreign trade had risen to $13.4 billion, with Japan and Hong Kong the leading partners.[3]

Before Mao's death, Deng, then serving as deputy premier, had advo-cated a further limited opening in trade policy. He did not break with Mao's slogan of self-reliance but reinterpreted it by saying, "By self-reliance we mean that a country should mainly rely on the strength and wisdom of its own people, control its own economic lifelines, and make full use of its resources."[4] He called for selective import of advanced foreign technolo-gies, paying for them with increased exports of arts and crafts products, industrial products, and mining products. Deng's rivals denounced his ideas as currying favor with the capitalist world, promoting old-fashioned arts and crafts in preference to modern industry, and selling off national resources and sovereignty. Their denunciations were one of the factors in Deng's fall from power in 1975.

When Deng came back to power after Mao's death, he pushed reform. Foreign trade had been monopolized by about a dozen specialized corporations under the Ministry of Foreign Trade that simply processed the paperwork for imports and exports required by the state plan. Deng's government spread the rights to buy and sell foreign commodities among what eventually became thousands of trading companies. These companies belonged to central government ministries, provincial governments, and government-owned enterprises, but they pushed their business energetically because they and their sponsoring agencies were allowed to keep a portion of the profit they earned. Under this stimulus, foreign trade almost quadrupled from 10 percent of GDP in 1978 to 38 percent of GDP in 2001, the year China entered the WTO.[5]

On the investment side, Deng moved to let in foreign capital. Mao had accepted neither foreign investments nor loans after the break with the Soviet Union. Deng saw foreign investment as a limited tool to accelerate the growth of exports by inserting capital and expertise into the export sector of the state-owned economy. As with trade, he advocated modest changes even before Mao died and was criticized by those who believed that foreign investors would harm China's sovereignty, exploit its workers, and steal its profits. After Mao's death, in 1979, China adopted the Joint Venture Law, which limited foreign ownership to less than half the value of any enterprise. Significant but relatively modest amounts of foreign direct investment flowed into China during the first dozen years of the reform period.

Under pressure from foreign investors, the government haltingly eased the limits and improved the conditions for foreign investment during the 1980s. It raised the ceiling on the size of projects, allowed foreign enterprises to purchase land-use rights for up to seventy years, eased foreign exchange restrictions for foreign-invested enterprises, and provided tax holidays on profits. In geographical terms, the government first tried to limit foreign investment to four small Special Economic Zones (of which the most famous was Shenzhen), then in 1984 extended incentives to fourteen coastal cities and the island of Hainan, in 1988 opened the entire coastal region from Liaoning in the north to Guangdong in the south to foreign investment, and in the 1990s removed virtually all remaining geographic restrictions. In sectoral terms, the original focus on foreign investment in high-tech manufacture for export was eased step by step to allow foreign investment in mining, manufacture for the domestic market, low-tech labor-intensive production for export, financial services, and infrastructure projects including freeways, power plants, and telecommunications facilities. By the mid-1990s, almost all sectors of the economy were open to foreign investment except for those related to China's traditional national industries (such as crafts and Chinese medicines), media, and national security.

Limits were removed as well on forms of investment. The joint-venture model was eased to allow all forms of foreign direct investment including wholly foreign-owned enterprises, plus portfolio investment (stocks and bonds) and commercial lending. Investment inflows rose steadily, accounting for hundreds of millions of dollars a year in the early 1980s, billions of dollars a year in the late 1980s, and tens of billions of dollars a year starting in the early 1990s. Between 1985 and 2005, Hong Kong supplied an estimated 47 percent of the total foreign direct investment (an unknown proportion of it "round-tripped" from investors on the mainland); Taiwan provided 12 percent; and the U.S., Japan, and the EU provided approximately 8 percent each.[6]

Foreign capital also entered China in the form of development loans and grants. In 1978, China broke with its tradition of being solely an aid donor (although a small one) to accept assistance from the UN Development Program. In 1980, it rejoined the IMF and the World Bank[7] and accepted aid from both, and in 1986 it joined the Asian Development Bank. By 2001, China had received a grand total of almost $40 billion in ODA from a host of multilateral organizations such as the World Bank, the UN Development Program, other UN agencies, and a variety of countries such as Japan and Canada. China continued to receive more than $1 billion of ODA per year in the 2000s.

Opening the door to foreign trade and investment required changes in the regulatory environment and support systems for foreign economic interactions. From 1979 to 2000, China adopted hundreds of laws and regulations to govern foreign economic relations. It established specialized courts and other dispute-resolution mechanisms. Visa restrictions had to be eased to cultivate the nascent tourist industry and to allow foreign businesspersons to visit easily. The flow of foreign visitors increased from 1.8 million in 1979 to 83.4 million in 2000 and kept growing after that. To accommodate them, the number of hotel rooms soared, with a massive shift from Soviet-style hotels to those meeting Western standards. Similar foreigner-friendly changes were made in banking, communications, transportation, and so on. Yet all these shifts only laid the groundwork for even more dramatic changes required at the start of the twenty-first century, when China joined the WTO.

SECURITY GAINS AND LOSSES TO THE TURN OF THE CENTURY

China's entry into the global economy turned out to have come at a good time. The long historical process of globalization took another leap forward in the mid-1980s. Between 1980 and 2007, global GDP increased by an average of 3.1 percent a year. World trade quintupled during the same period from $4 trillion to $27.5 trillion. Having entered the waters, China was carried along on the current: Chinese trade grew thirtyfold from $25.8 billion in 1984 to $762 billion in 2005. By 2004, 30.8 percent of China's industrial output was produced by factories with foreign investment. The linkage and demonstration effects of foreign trade and investment on Chinese suppliers, consumers, and competitors led to higher-quality performance across the economy. Through foreign partnerships, Chinese firms gained new technology, learned new management practices, and gained access to world markets. Even though growth was unequal, it was widespread. Every part of the country and every social class had a share. The number of Chinese below the official poverty line dropped from 250 million in 1978 to 25 million by 2005.[8]

But to gain these benefits Deng had been forced by the logic of world markets to compromise China's autonomy more than he had anticipated would be necessary. By the mid-1990s, foreign officials were monitoring Chinese tariffs, import quotas, certification requirements, factory hygiene, financial services, and retail networks. Moody's as well as Standard and Poor's passed judgment on the value of China's sovereign debt. U.S. Customs, Food and Drug Administration, and Commerce Department officials showed up to inspect Chinese factories. Foreign lawyers pointed out enforcement failures and suggested revisions in laws and regulations. China had to introduce unfamiliar institutions such as stock markets, brokerage firms, risk funds, commodities futures markets, and consulting firms. To train the staff needed to create such institutions, China had to send students and officials abroad to be trained. In 1982, China had even found it necessary to amend its Constitution to include a commitment to protect "the lawful rights and interests" of foreign investors.

The key managers of world capitalism, especially the IMF and the World Bank, inserted themselves into Chinese politics by putting their weight behind the reformists in their political struggles against the conservatives.[9] To join the Asian Development Bank, China made a concession to Western concerns by agreeing to allow Taiwan to continue as a member under the name "China, Taipei" (chapter 9). After the Tiananmen incident of June 1989, the U.S. used its dominant voting rights in the World Bank and the Asian Development Bank to block most new loans to China for several years, and Japan postponed some of its ODA loans. In 1995, Japan suspended most of its ODA grants (although not loans) to protest China's underground nuclear testing.

In a more indirect sense, each step toward prosperity made China's economic health more dependent on the health of foreign markets, especially those in the U.S., which was China's largest export market until 2007, and the EU, which subsequently became the largest market. China's prosperity was also tied to the health of the American dollar and the euro, which were the main currencies in which China, like other countries, conducted its foreign trade and kept its foreign exchange reserves.

Most risky from a security standpoint were the deep effects that the opening exerted on society and culture. Between 1978 and 2003, China dispatched more than seven hundred thousand students to study at institutions of higher education abroad, mostly to the U.S., in an effort to rapidly acquire advanced technology. Fewer than 25 percent of these students returned upon graduation, and those who did often carried ideas that undermined China's official ideology. Western-educated and oriented economists, bankers, lawyers, and traders gained a growing voice in shaping policies. Young people lost faith in old values, and, according to conservative Chinese critics, many now believed that "even the moon is brighter in the West." Christianity took off and spread among the population, including tens of millions who participated in illegal "house churches" that local officials often tolerated because it would have been too disruptive to try to close them down.

People in southern Guangdong Province began to watch Hong Kong television, drink Hong Kong soft drinks, dress in the Hong Kong style, and even circulate the Hong Kong dollar for some transactions. People in Fujian adopted many elements of Taiwan culture. People in Shanghai and Beijing adopted American and European styles and tastes. Young people in all the coastal cities went wild for South Korean music and TV shows and Japanese cartoons. Workers from poor regions in the interior migrated to the coast for manufacturing, construction, and housework jobs. State enterprises had to throw their traditional social welfare functions overboard in order to compete for foreign markets and investment. Corruption increased, and many rightly or wrongly attributed the increase to "foreign flies coming in the open window." By the mid-1980s, just a few years after the reforms started, China had exposed its economy, society, and culture more deeply to foreign influence than at any time since the era of Soviet aid in the 1950s.

These developments alarmed conservatives in the leadership. They worried that China was replacing the socialist revolution they had fought for with a consumer revolution, which they referred to as "spiritual pollution." In their eyes, the 1989 democracy movement was a devil's brew of contradictory Western impacts: on the one hand, it was sparked by public opposition to inflation and corruption associated with the open-door policy, and on the other it expressed a pro-Western democratic and individualist ethos and was cheered on and even given some material support by people in Hong Kong and the West.

Even so, Deng's open-door policy survived and was given new momentum in 1992 when he made a symbolic tour of the southern export zones to reaffirm his commitment to economic growth through globalization. This tour was Deng Xiaoping's last major political act before his death in 1997, but it had a lasting impact. The combination of Deng's authority, the death of senior conservatives who harbored doubts about his policies, and the reforms' continuing economic success put an end to policy battles over the principle of global engagement, although not over concrete decisions concerning how to implement it. The controversy over globalization continues today only at the level of intellectual debate, with thinkers on the left arguing that China has lost its way by abandoning socialist ideals and those on the liberal side arguing that China has to reform even further to solve the contradictions between its economic prosperity and its authoritarian political system.[10] Popular ambivalence about the open door is reflected in xenophobic emotions intermittently expressed on the Internet and in public demonstrations. At the policy level, however, the debate is no longer over whether to globalize, but over how to manage the process.

Not only did the open policy confront domestic opposition, but it also engendered a wide range of conflicts with foreign partners. As trade grew, irrationalities flourished at the interface between the half-reformed command economy at home and markets in the outside world.[11] Commodities and manufactures with low fixed prices under the plan could be exported for big profits, but doing so meant giving foreigners the benefit of subsidies intended for Chinese consumers. Products with high domestic prices set by the plan could fetch windfall profits for importers because they were available more cheaply abroad, but this process wasted foreign exchange and damaged domestic producers. The government tried to control surges and to patch irrationalities with ad hoc mechanisms such as import licenses, export subsidies, tariffs, tax rebates, exchange-rate manipulations, administrative controls over foreign exchange expenditures, and shifts in the percentages of profit or foreign exchange that trading firms could retain. These measures in turn embroiled China in conflicts with trading partners, who accused Beijing of protectionism and dumping (exporting products at below cost). The advanced industrial countries pushed China to accept quotas on the exports of textiles and other products and to honor foreign standards of hygiene, packaging, labeling, and the environmental friendliness of goods destined for export. Just as with disarmament and proliferation (chapter 11) and human rights (chapter 12), China found itself under pressure to comply with the preexisting norms of the international system that it was joining.

The pushback came more from the U.S. than from any other foreign partner, for three reasons. First, as the country that had taken the lead in creating institutions to foster global trade and investment since the end of World War II, the U.S. was never shy about criticizing practices that it thought were inconsistent with global norms. Second, starting in 1971, the U.S. ran a trade deficit that with a few exceptions increased year by year. While this was happening, companies producing for the U.S. market— especially those run by Hong Kong, Taiwan, and South Korean entrepreneurs—took advantage of China's friendly investment environment and low labor costs to shift manufacturing operations to China. Even when a large part of the value of a product was produced elsewhere before it was assembled in China, the entire final value was counted as an export from China. Therefore, other Asian countries' trade surpluses with the U.S. shifted to the Chinese account, and as America's aggregate trade deficit grew, it also became more concentrated on China. The U.S. deficit with China overtook that with Japan to become America's largest bilateral trade deficit in 2000 and continued to grow.[12] Third, the concentration of the deficit on a single partner produced a fat political target for constituencies in the U.S. whose interests were hurt by globalization, even if China was not the root cause of their problems. They were able to express their views through Congress and other channels available in the democratically responsive American political system.

Citing provisions of its own law—which requires a U.S. administration to sanction a foreign trading partner that fails to meet certain U.S.-legislated standards of fairness in its trading practices—the U.S. demanded far-reaching changes in China's trade regime. In 1992, China agreed to a Market Access Agreement giving the U.S. unprecedented access to Chinese markets, thereby exposing the Chinese auto, pharmaceutical, chemical, and other industries to intensified foreign competition. But China was slow to implement its promises. Among other reasons, local governments used the powers they had been granted for promoting trade to find ways to protect local industries. This protection generated continued friction with the U.S.

Washington and Beijing also engaged in a long struggle over intellectual property rights (patents and copyrights in such products as chemicals and pharmaceuticals, computer software, books, recorded music, and movies on videotape and DVD). Under Mao, intellectual products had been considered common social property that should be popularized rather than protected. In 1985, the Chinese government adopted its first patent law, but Western businesses considered it inadequate. By 1991, when the pirating of American software, music, and movies was estimated to cost U.S. copyright holders hundreds of millions of dollars a year, the U.S. gave China an ultimatum to pay fees or suffer trade sanctions. Similar ultimatums were delivered in 1994 and 1996 as the estimated losses to piracy approached $2 billion a year. In each episode of pressure, China at first threatened countersanctions but then made major concessions. In each case, the U.S. was dissatisfied and demanded more changes and better enforcement. In the course of these negotiations, Beijing agreed both to enact still more laws and regulations with U.S. advice (such as amendments to the Chinese patent law in 1992) and to allow such international standards as the Berne Convention for the Protection of Literary and Artistic Works to prevail over China's domestic legislation in cases of conflict. As the central government made concession after concession to outside demands, policy on the ground lagged behind due to local protectionism, corruption, and an inadequate legal system.[13] China's failure to fulfill its commitments generated new waves of conflict with other countries.

Part of the solution to such problems was to deepen reform. In the 1980s and 1990s, China struggled especially to carry out price reform and foreign exchange reform, both of which were slow, difficult, and controversial because of the risk of inflation and the many domestic interests affected. Price decontrol proceeded under Deng in fits and starts. Loosening of government control over foreign exchange transactions began in the mid-1980s. In 1994, the government introduced a managed floating exchange-rate system. In the 2000s, Chinese leaders tried to steer their giant economy toward higher wages, greater domestic demand, and lower export dependence and tried to move the Chinese currency in the direction of convertibility—but such changes always unfolded more slowly than foreign partners desired.

GETTING OUT BY GETTING DEEPER IN: THE WTO NEGOTIATIONS

The only path of escape from the dynamic of constant domestic criticism and international friction that beset the open-door policy was fuller engagement in the globalized economic system.[14] This in turn could be achieved only by gaining membership in the WTO. The WTO is an intergovernmental organization that sets the rules for international trade. By joining, China would bind the hands of conservative domestic opponents of globalization and put the country's tempestuous economic relations with the rest of the world on a rule-bound basis that would be relatively insulated from foreign political pressure. But WTO membership could do this only by entrenching China more deeply than ever in interdependence with its trading partners and by binding it more tightly in a complicated system of mutual commitments.

As with the other elements of Deng Xiaoping's reforms, the Chinese leaders did not conceive WTO membership in such far-reaching terms at the start. Rather, when China began its WTO bid in 1986 (when the organization was still the General Agreement on Tariffs and Trade), it intended merely to reclaim a diplomatic slot that had previously been held by the ROC and as a side benefit to gain lower tariff rates on its exports to other countries. Chinese officials at the time had little expertise in the agreement's workings, which were in any case a moving target as the organization rewrote its rules, expanded its membership, and restructured itself in 1995 as the WTO.

WTO accession negotiations are inherently demanding. They were even more so for China. The WTO is a club of what are supposed to be market economies, which agree among themselves to a set of rules governing trade, investment, and dispute resolution. States with socialist centrally planned economies or in transition from such economies to market economies have to make special concessions to offset their "nonmarket" status. An applicant for membership has to reach agreement bilaterally with each current member (there were 90 members when China first applied, 142 by the time it finished its talks) and then give the same benefits to all members ("most-favored-nation treatment"). All the concessions are made by the applicant, with each bilateral agreement providing the starting point for more demands by the next negotiating partner.

Negotiators were especially tough on China because it was the biggest nonmarket economy ever to try to join the organization. Chinese leaders were reluctant to abandon protected (and usually inefficient) state industries such as chemicals, pharmaceuticals, automobiles, and electronics to potentially devastating foreign competition without a long adjustment period. China's negotiators cited poverty and backwardness in asking permission under the concessionary program the WTO allows developing countries to prolong many of the requested reform measures. The U.S. and other Western negotiators retorted that China was too successful a world trader to be eligible for so many exemptions for so long. They feared that once China got minimal terms for entering the organization, it would feel little pressure to open its markets further. Such a big trader had to be brought into the world trading regime somehow, yet no practicable level of concessions would turn it into a true market economy in the foreseeable future.

The core issues therefore became how large a cost the rest of the world would pay to help China plunge more deeply into world markets and how rapidly China would lower its barriers to imports and foreign investments in exchange for enhanced access to WTO members' markets. The issues were politically toxic in both China and the West, and the negotiations dragged on for fifteen years. The U.S.–China agreement was finally signed in 1999; after cleaning up remaining matters with several other members, China signed an Accession Agreement in November 2001 and entered the WTO in December 2001.

The Accession Agreement was more than eight hundred pages long, with thousands of specific commitments covering virtually all aspects of the economy. Under its provisions, China undertook to make sweeping changes in its economic policies. Among these changes, it had to lower tariffs from an average of 36 percent in 1993 to 8.9 percent on industrial products and 15 percent on agricultural products in 2004 (making its economy one of the most open in the world); remove many nontariff barriers to imports, including import and export licensing and quotas; abolish export subsidies for its producers; give foreign products access to the Chinese market on the same terms as domestic products ("national treatment"); improve legal protection for intellectual property; and allow foreign-invested enterprises into hitherto banned sensitive sectors, including distribution, franchising, transport, telecom value-added services, banking and financial services, insurance, securities, legal and accounting services, construction, and education. The government had to repeal thousands of WTO-inconsistent laws and regulations and reform the courts, legal system, banking system, and relevant administrative agencies.

Merely to negotiate these commitments, not to mention to implement them, China found it necessary to create and restructure numerous government agencies and hire or train thousands of specialized bureaucrats, thus changing the DNA of its own government institutions. Moreover, to satisfy suspicious U.S. negotiators, China had to agree to a Transitional Review Mechanism under which China, alone among WTO members, was to be reviewed annually for eight years for its compliance with the Accession Agreement. In exchange for meeting its commitments to liberalize its economy, China is scheduled to receive "full market economy status" in 2016, which will immunize it from certain kinds of trade disputes. Meanwhile, however, using the WTO Dispute Resolution Mechanism, the U.S. and other trading partners have frequently sued China for dumping and have often won.

THE BEIJING CONSENSUS

But Beijing did not give everything away by joining the WTO. Instead of being forced to make a transition to a fully Western-style economy, Chinese policymakers used the accession process to help create a distinctive state-directed yet marketized and globalized economic model that was to prove more competitive than the market economies, at least for a while. No one outside the Chinese policymaking elite knows how clearly this new Chinese model was conceptualized in advance by the leaders who guided the final stages of the WTO talks (CCP general secretary Jiang Zemin and Premier Zhu Rongji). But what emerged from the changes China made to join the WTO was an economy that drew strength from global trade and investment without compromising the primary role of the domestic market in its economic growth, that benefited from but was not dominated by the surging private and foreign-invested sectors, and, above all, that used market mechanisms to promote efficiency without undermining the state's ability to rule the economy's commanding heights.

Some writers refer to the post-WTO Chinese model as the "Beijing consensus,"[15] in distinction to the "Washington consensus," which is a market-dominated approach long in vogue in Western economies and in the philosophy of the international financial institutions, which the U.S. has dominated. Other countries may not be able to fully emulate the Chinese model, given China's unique size and distinctive institutions, but leaders elsewhere who for one reason or another wanted to reject advice from Washington found inspiration in the Chinese example for the argument that there is more than one right way to manage an economy in the age of globalization.

To be sure, the post-WTO Chinese economy was in some ways a privatized market economy like those of the West. Private capitalists, including foreigners, could invest in most sectors. Private enterprises grew faster than state enterprises in the 1990s and 2000s. Prices of most goods were set by market mechanisms. Yet the state remained dominant to a far greater degree than in the West. The government continued to own all land, both rural and urban; to manage directly the energy industry, water supply, banking, and railway transportation; and to control those former state enterprises that had nominally been privatized via the party's assignment of top managers,[16] the presence of party committees, and government direction of bank credit. A thousand or so of the largest state-owned enterprises were turned into integrated "national champions" that dominated strategic sectors such as energy, telecom, heavy industry, defense industry, mining, media, banking, and transport.[17] By 2010, forty-two Chinese companies were listed in the *Fortune* Global 500, and a majority of them were more than 50 percent state owned. Direct and indirect policy levers gave the government the major voice in determining the prices of land, labor, housing, energy, and credit. Although agriculture had been privatized, the state continued to influence the prices of agricultural products through land-use controls, subsidies, and barriers to imports, among other measures.

The Chinese currency, the renminbi, was not easily convertible into foreign currencies. For trade purposes, it could be converted by anyone (on the current account), but for investments (the capital account), which are longer term and involve greater quantities of money, the currency could be exchanged only by qualified investors for certain types of investments. The exchange rate floated within a narrow band whose limits were set by the government through its buying and selling of foreign exchange, all of which it held in its own hands. The limit on free conversion of money on the capital account served as a powerful barrier to international speculation in the renminbi, which might otherwise have forced the government to allow its value to go up faster than policymakers wanted it to in light of the impact currency appreciation has on jobs and inflation. In the 1997 Asian financial crisis, when the currencies of several Asian nations collapsed in value and many countries' growth stagnated, China's nonconvertible currency remained immune from speculative pressures. China gained gratitude from its neighbors at that time for not devaluing in order to compete for export markets, yet there was no strong temptation for Beijing to do so because China's exports remained robust.

WTO membership opened the Chinese economy to foreign enterprises but did not enable a foreign takeover. Instead, aided by the economy's continental size and complexity—and, to be sure, by some cheating on WTO rules and the use of some WTO-inconsistent protectionist measures both formal and informal—domestic companies continued to dominate Chinese domestic markets by number of firms and by sales. And under a "going-out" policy initiated soon after WTO entry, the government used the reciprocal opening of other economies to prod Chinese enterprises to compete successfully in the global marketplace, helping them to do so with credit from state-owned banks.

Nor, finally, did WTO membership make China dependent on foreign trade for its growth. To be sure, China's foreign trade ratio (foreign trade as a percentage of GDP) was high for a large continental economy, around 51.9 percent in 2008. And the economy benefited from this trade to create jobs and to bring in investment, and enjoyed the demonstration effects and backward linkages that came along with foreign investment. Yet China ranked only nineteenth in foreign trade ratio in 2008, below Indonesia (54.5 percent) and not far above France (51.8 percent). Even at that rate, the China foreign trade ratio is misleadingly high because it is calculated on the basis of dollar values, which, given that the Chinese currency is undervalued, understates the denominator and exaggerates the relative size of foreign trade. The importance of foreign trade as a driver of China's economic growth is also placed in perspective if one considers that Chinese exports consist mainly of products assembled by Chinese workers from imported components for foreign brand names. Chinese policymakers in the mid-1980s dubbed this strategy "two heads outside" (*liangtou zai-wai*) because both the source of components and the market for products were outside China. In such a global supply chain, profits attributable to engineering and design, brand value, and marketing are captured by the foreign owner of the brand name; profits attributable to the manufacture of high-value components go to external manufacturers (often elsewhere in Asia); and the yield to the Chinese economy is limited to the cost of labor for assembly. According to one report, China in the mid-2000s earned only thirty-five cents of the value of a $20 doll labeled "made in China."[18]

In all, therefore, Chinese growth was less "export driven" than was the case with the so-called Asian tigers in the 1950s through the 1970s; it did not depend on running a consistent trade surplus. Indeed, on a global basis China's imports and exports were close to balanced for most of the open-door period, generating large surpluses only after 2005. The steadily growing surplus with the U.S. (and smaller surpluses with other rich countries, especially in Europe) was balanced in most years by deficits with China's sources of components, raw materials, and energy. Although exports helped economic growth, the major drivers of growth were rising productivity, efficiency, and domestic demand generated by a more affluent population. When foreign markets went into recession in 2008, China's domestic market was sufficiently large to avoid—with aid of a substantial government stimulus package—a corresponding slump in the Chinese rate of growth.

In short, China found a way to throw itself into the surging currents of globalization in a manner that not only did not hand control over its destiny to other countries or to international institutions, but in some ways even strengthened its autonomy. In domestic politics, the push to enter WTO steamrolled domestic constituencies that feared globalization: once the leaders had made up their minds to join and had signed the WTO Accession Agreement, affected ministries and regions had to adapt. Although many noncompetitive firms went out of business, their disappearance improved the economy's efficiency, and the firms that remained were stronger than before. Instead of globalization fostering domestic instability, as many observers expected, the regime drew strength from prosperity. The government used surging budgetary resources to start building a social welfare net that blunted domestic dissent. And it used its growing international respectability to cultivate the pride of its own people, which also strengthened its hold on power.

In global politics, WTO membership largely freed China from Washington's hydra-headed trade politics. Trade and investment disputes were now mostly channeled into the WTO Dispute Resolution Mechanism, a long-drawn-out process too technical to command the close attention of Congress and the media and whose decisions both Washington and Beijing accepted as binding. China sometimes won cases here (e.g., a 2002–2003 case that declared U.S. steel tariffs illegal and a 2008–2011 case that ruled against antidumping measures the U.S. had imposed against tires, pipes, and certain other Chinese products) and more often lost (e.g., a 2008 case that invalidated rules compelling Chinese car makers to obtain a certain proportion of their parts from local manufacturers). Either way, WTO rules deprived Washington of the option of threatening trade sanctions to force China to settle economic (and sometimes noneconomic) disputes on its terms. To clear the way for Chinese accession to the WTO,

Congress had been obliged to authorize "permanent normal trading relations" in 2000, which meant that tariff rates with China were no longer subject to congressional review. U.S.–China economic negotiations of course continued constantly on a range of topics, but they were less subject to political interference, in part because of China's rising economic clout, but in the main because the two nations were now mutually constrained by the WTO.

Finally, as a WTO member, China gained an influential voice in shaping future changes in the global trade regime. In the so-called Doha Round of trade talks from 2001 to 2008, China and other large developing countries clashed with the U.S. and Western Europe over measures to safeguard poor Third World farmers against possible surges in imports of agricultural commodities from rich countries. This conflict led to the collapse of this round of trade liberalization talks. Even though the WTO project of setting universal rules for world trade through multilateral negotiations was set back by this collapse—some said that the project could go no further in the foreseeable future—China continued to pursue ways to open up trade further through agreements with single partners (e.g., Chile, Australia, and Thailand) and groups of partners (e.g., ASEAN, whose free-trade agreement with China came into effect in 2010). Such agreements had little measurable impact on trade volumes, but they sent a message about multipolarity and Third World cooperation that was consistent with overall Chinese diplomatic strategy.

TRADE, AID, AND INVESTMENT: THE CONTINUATION OF POWER POLITICS BY OTHER MEANS

China's importance as a trade and investment partner altered its strategic situation in a fundamental way.[19] By 2010, China ranked as the number two trading country in the world and was an important economic partner in various ways to all the world's major powers. It was no longer conceivable that the West would unite to isolate China as it did in the era of containment. To be sure, after the Tiananmen incident of 1989, the leading industrialized countries had imposed limited trade and investment sanctions, but these sanctions had little practical impact, and most of them were quickly lifted. (The exception was an embargo on the sale of advanced arms, which the European powers wanted to lift in the 2000s, but the U.S. prevailed upon them to maintain.) They were also the last sanctions to be imposed on China, despite continuing human rights abuses and numerous economic disputes. China had become too important as a customer, supplier, and creditor to be punished by economic means. Constituencies that favored putting pressure on China—the human rights and labor movements, manufacturers crushed by Chinese competition, victims of copyright and patent infringement—found themselves politically checkmated by constituencies having a positive economic stake in relations with China—the financial industry, importers, firms with factories in China, and others. Strong business lobbies emerged in the U.S. and Europe that worked to stabilize relations with Beijing. Trade threats lost their credibility.[20]

Economic ties smoothed China's relations around its periphery. In Hong Kong, the business community supported retrocession to Chinese control in 1997, believing that economic ties with the mainland would do more for Hong Kong than political reforms. In Taiwan, cross-strait trade and investment built up an incentive to oppose independence. Trade and investment prospects contributed to South Korea's shift of diplomatic recognition from Taipei to Beijing in 1992. In the 2000s, Australia put new emphasis on good relations with China as its prosperity became increasingly tied to Chinese ore and energy purchases and mining investments. China's rise as a manufacturing–assembly center for the more advanced Asian economies created the first period of Asian economic integration in history, supporting China's assurance strategy in the region.[21] China's need for raw materials made it a key customer and hence a key diplomatic partner of many countries in Africa, Latin America, and the Middle East.

Economic ties opened the way to strategic access. Governments welcomed China to build roads, pipelines, ports, and railways, extending China's transport network deep into Vietnam, Burma, Nepal, Sri Lanka, Pakistan, Turkmenistan, Uzbekistan, Kazakhstan, and Mongolia. Such projects not only eased access to energy imports and opened China's hinterland to cross-border trade but helped tie neighboring economies more closely to China's and in some cases created logistical facilities with potential military uses.[22]

Robust development gave China enough money to make a dramatic transition from foreign aid recipient to major donor and lender. China had provided development assistance to selected African states in the 1950s, but not until 1982 was a special foreign aid agency created, the Department of Foreign Aid in the Ministry of Foreign Economic Relations and Trade (later renamed the Ministry of Commerce). In the 1990s, the government created three banks with international responsibilities—the China Development Bank, the China Agricultural Development Bank, and the China Exim Bank, the latter charged to create a program of concessional loans abroad. In 2007, the China Development Bank launched the China–Africa Development Fund.[23]

Despite this major initiative, China still does not publish official figures on foreign aid. One scholar estimates that its ODA jumped from $500 million in 1996 to more than $3 billion by 2007. Nevertheless, its ODA to Africa in 2007 approximated only about 20 percent of what the World Bank and the U.S. each provided to the continent as well as less than the ODA provided individually by Germany, Japan, the United Kingdom, and France. Moreover, comparing loans from the World Bank and China's Exim Bank is "like comparing apples and lychees" because most of the former are interest free and repayable over thirty-five to forty years, whereas the latter are interest bearing and repayable in ten to twenty years.[24]

SHARED VULNERABILITY IN GLOBAL SYSTEMS

On the downside, the deep immersion in globalization has posed a whole new category of security challenges for China. Under conditions of advanced globalization, not only China but its friends and enemies alike are subject to global "system effects"[25]—forces that they jointly create but cannot control. The risk is not so much that countries can use economic links purposely to hurt each other, but that they can harm each other unintentionally in the course of trying to manage their own economies. The controversy of the 1970s and 1980s in China over the pros and cons of entering a global economic system that other countries controlled has yielded to worries over immersion in a global economic system that no one controls.

By the time China joined the WTO, the globalized economy was larger and more interdependent than anyone—in China and probably elsewhere—had ever foreseen it would become. International trade as a percentage of world GDP had gone from 38.5 percent in 1980 to 54 percent in 2005; international investment as a percentage of world GDP went from 0.5 percent to 2.3 percent. And both continued to rise thereafter.

Global flows of this magnitude created historically novel pressures on job markets, commodity prices, foreign exchange markets, the environment, and public health, among other domains. And in politics they generated new pressures as well—demands for protectionism in many countries, the antiglobalization movement, and, with respect to China in particular, the fear of a "China threat" to the economic welfare of other economies, both advanced and developing. While producing a new level of mutual vulnerability, intensified globalization made it harder than ever to figure out how to apportion responsibility for solving systemic problems. China faced these challenges with distinctive strengths rooted in its economic and political system, but also with specific weaknesses arising from its position in the world economy.

First, globalization linked job markets across borders. Even though workers could not travel freely to find jobs, many kinds of jobs could be transferred more easily than before to places where they could be done at good quality for low cost. From 1985 through 2004, Chinese township and village enterprises created an estimated 3.5 million new manufacturing jobs per year, filling them mostly with workers who were no longer needed for farm labor as the agricultural economy became more efficient and partly with the 20 million or more new workers entering the job market each year.[26] These workers started out in the 1980s producing clothing, toys, shoes, bicycles, lamps, and power tools. They moved up the technological ladder in the 1990s to produce computers, household appliances, specialty steel, automobiles, and ships. Chinese manufacturers then set their sights on higher-tech global markets, including airplanes, electric and luxury cars, electronics, pharmaceuticals, and environmental technologies.

The rise in Chinese jobs manufacturing for export did not automatically mean a decline in jobs elsewhere. For one thing, as the global economy grew, manufacturing was increasing not only in China, but in other countries as well. In addition, the rise of living standards in China generated new jobs in China's trade partners in agriculture (to supply China with meat, soy beans, apples, and so on), manufacturing (to supply China with parts for assembly), high-tech industry (to sell China airplanes, power stations, precision machine tools, and medical instruments, among other products), intellectual property (movies, music, software, and so on), and services (including legal and financial services). Because of this dynamic, U.S. exports to China increased every year after 2001 even as its trade deficit with China also increased. Third, job markets were changing in other countries through their own internal processes of development independent of whatever was happening in China. In wealthy countries, advances in technology caused productivity to increase, so fewer workers were needed to produce more goods, and workers tended to shift from manufacturing to the service sector. In developing countries, job markets also changed constantly as economies changed.

Yet certain jobs did migrate to China. Most of them had been lost by the West long ago when wage increases made it uneconomical to manufacture low-price products. Such jobs were moving from other Asian economies or countries such as Mexico to take advantage of China's low wages and increasingly reliable quality, creating pressure on other developing economies to find new competitive advantages against not only China, but other rivals. Direct loss of jobs from the advanced countries to China were statistically small, yet they were politically visible, as when factories were packed up and moved from Ohio or Dortmund, Germany, to new sites in China [27] or when communities of Chinese workers moved to Prato, Italy, to take jobs in designer garment factories at wages lower than Italian workers were willing to take.

The impact of the global economy was felt on the Chinese job market as well. Instead of growing, that job market would shrink if overseas markets contracted. Knowing this narrowed policymakers' freedom of action. For example, it meant that even when the value of the U.S. dollar went down, China could not stop buying U.S. Treasury bonds despite their low or negative rates of real return, out of concern for the effect that doing so might have on one of their largest markets. In effect, buying U.S. Treasury bonds was a way of lending money to American consumers to keep buying Chinese goods so Chinese citizens could keep on working—and continue to subsidize American consumers. It was hard for either side to dismount from this merry-go-round.

Looking over the other shoulder, Chinese policymakers had to worry when new exporters such as Vietnam started producing quality products at competitive prices. To be sure, the Chinese export powerhouse depended on more than inexpensive labor—it also depended on labor's quality and reliability; the quality of Chinese ports, telecommunications, and financial services; and efficiencies arising from what is known as "industrial clustering."[28] Yet as Chinese manufacturing wages inexorably increased with the general rise in living standards, they put pressure on manufacturers of price-sensitive products. Such dynamics made it hard for the Chinese government to enforce its own labor laws, which were good on paper, for fear of pushing companies out of business. The pressure of competition also made it difficult for China to rapidly raise the exchange value of the renminbi, even though policymakers wanted to do so in order to control inflation and reduce the price of imported investment goods and energy, because a higher renminbi would increase the price of imports and put more pressure on wages.

Despite these complexities, China's size and rate of growth made it the natural focus of blame for job losses in the West. There were no "made in India" labels on software or "made in Brazil" labels on aircraft for consumers to see, but they saw "made in China" labels on shoes, radios, toys, clothing, and a products that in many cases were not really made but only assembled in China. In the U.S, Europe, and Japan, labor and industry groups demanded more antidumping investigations directed at China than at any other country. Labor rights groups exposed violations in Chinese factories producing for export. The Chinese government tried to manage the political backlash by sourcing imports in a wide range of electoral districts all across the U.S. and Europe and by arguing that its low-priced, good-quality goods enhanced living standards in the West. In the developing world, China sought to position itself as an economic good neighbor. But none of this stemmed the hostility to globalization in general and to China in particular produced by the worldwide acceleration of job shifts.

Second, the rise of globalization meant increased mutual vulnerability in commodity markets. By 2010, China was one of the world's top consumers—and in many cases one of the top importers—of many strategic commodities, including oil, food grains, wool, cotton, rubber, copper, lead, zinc, tin, nickel, aluminia, and rare earths.[29] As global demand surged with global growth, supply interruptions or demand surges produced bumps in the market, when prices rose and supplies proved harder to get. To avoid short-term inflationary effects, the government subsidized the domestic prices of gasoline, electricity, transportation, and fertilizers, among other items. Not only did the subsidies drain the government's coffers, but they promoted wasteful use of commodities, leaving a legacy of financial and environmental damage.

For the longer term, Chinese policymakers tried to guard against commodity shortages in several ways. Under the rubric of "grain security," they tried to keep grain imports at 5 percent of consumption by promulgating policies to preserve arable land, raise per hectare productivity, and use tax relief and subsidies to encourage peasant farmers to produce food grains alongside the more profitable specialty crops. Under the heading of "energy security," they promoted more efficient use of energy; invested in domestic oil and coal production, hydropower (such as the Three Gorges Dam), as well as nuclear, solar, and wind energy; and sought to lock in "equity oil" abroad so that they could count on supplies even in times of global shortage (chapter 7). They purchased shares in copper, iron, and cobalt mines abroad. They placed restrictions on the export of rare earths to preserve supplies for domestic production of electronic products, batteries, and solar panels.

In the face of rapid growth, however, even long-term policies could only slow, not stop, the erosion of commodity security. Expanding factories, roads, airports, and housing chewed up arable land. Water was too scarce to provide the intensive irrigation that green-revolution strains of rice and wheat needed to supply higher outputs per acre. The population was not only growing in size, but changing its diet. As people used their new wealth to buy more eggs, meat, farmed fish, and beer, it took more grain to meet each person's needs. New factories, cars, and airplanes required more hydrocarbon energy than Chinese coal mines and oilfields plus Chinese-owned overseas sources could supply.

Dramatic increases in Chinese demand were often seen elsewhere in alarmist terms as the main factor disrupting world market stability. The actual effects varied by commodity. In petroleum, for example, greater Chinese demand contributed to rising prices for crude oil, but, at least during the period 1995–2004, global production also increased, which softened the effect on prices. In 2004, China accounted for only 8 percent of world consumption, whereas the U.S. guzzled 25 percent of the world's petroleum output. By contrast, the price of a product such as wood pulp (the key input for paper) remained basically constant despite growing Chinese demand during the same ten-year period. In the case of ferrous scrap metal (important in the making of steel), dramatic price increases occurred during the same period, pushed to some extent by China, but also by rising demand in other steel-producing countries such as South Korea and Turkey.

People worried that China's demographic size and the speed of its economic growth (along with the rise of India and some other countries), beyond their impact on prices, had finally brought the earth close to the long-discussed limits of its carrying capacity.[30] Ideas such as a global "limit to growth" and "peak oil" (the danger of oil supplies running out) threatened Chinese security by giving rise to pressure on Beijing to rein in the rising living standards that were crucial to the regime's domestic stability.

A third area of interdependent vulnerability in the global economy involved the management of currency and foreign exchange. For domestic firms to buy and sell from foreign firms, they had to use dollars, euros, yen, or a small number of other international reserve currencies. As China's trade went into a global surplus around 2005, Chinese accounts accumulated large surpluses of these currencies. Because most global trade is conducted in dollars, most of this surplus came in the form of dollars. Only a small fraction of China's foreign trade was conducted on a "currency swap" basis with the use of the Chinese yuan and another nonreserve currency such as the Brazilian real. In the face of this situation, the government had to make two policy decisions: how to treat the exchange rate between Chinese and foreign currencies and how to deal with the foreign exchange reserve generated by the trade surplus.

The government chose to keep control over both the exchange rate and the management of foreign exchange reserves. The People's Bank of China set the exchange rates between the Chinese yuan and the global reserve currencies, and the State Administration of Foreign Exchange managed the reserves. The chief reason to sustain government control of these functions was to prevent changes in the value of foreign currencies from causing inflation in the domestic economy and hence affecting Chinese citizens' welfare and political loyalty. A second reason was to maintain exchange rates at levels favorable to the promotion of Chinese exports. A third was to manage foreign exchange reserves in such a way as to ease political relations with influential officials in Washington and other foreign capitals—for example, by purchasing U.S. Treasury bonds to help the U.S. government manage its fiscal deficits.

But such policies were rife with pitfalls both economic and political. On the economic side, a low yuan-to-dollar (or yen or euro) exchange rate promoted exports at the cost of shifting benefits from Chinese to Western consumers. In effect, by virtue of government-controlled exchange rates, Chinese workers accepted lower wages to subsidize higher living standards for Western consumers. Artificially low yuan values also helped create overinvestment, waste, inflows of speculative capital, stock market and real estate bubbles, and inflationary pressures — all of which required government responses to try to manage and smooth them out.

Likewise, conservative management of foreign exchange reserves saddled the Chinese economy with low (sometimes even negative) returns on huge investments. In 2011, China held the equivalent of $3.2 trillion in foreign exchange reserves — more than any other country. Although the makeup of these reserves was a secret, most experts estimated that about 70 percent of the money was held in dollar-denominated assets during the 2000s, even though the value of the dollar was declining in relationship to other reserve currencies. In 2007, China set up a sovereign wealth fund, the China Investment Corporation, to invest a fraction of the reserves more aggressively for better returns, but the corporation's initial investments performed badly. The total amount of the reserves was in any case too large for a large fraction of it to be managed in this way. Nor could China convert large amounts of its dollars to other currencies without driving down the value of its dollar stake even further while also harming the economic health of one of its chief markets and raising the prices of Chinese products in that market. Through its holdings of U.S. dollars, therefore, China's economic health was to some extent held hostage to the wisdom of financial managers in Washington — a wisdom that China had little faith in after the economic crash that started in the U.S. in 2008.

Exchange-rate controls and foreign exchange reserve management became added counts in the "China threat" discourse centered in but not limited to Washington. Partly in response to pressure from Washington and partly in order to move toward its own long-term goal of making the renminbi an international exchange currency, Beijing in 2005 launched a "managed float" of exchange rates. The yuan rose in value from 8.27 to the dollar in 2005 to 6.36 in 2011, an increase of 23 percent. But the revaluation had no discernible effect on the U.S.–China trade balance, and the slow, irregular pace of the increase failed to mollify critics in Washington, who intermittently threatened trade sanctions if China did not move faster toward a market-determined exchange rate.

MUTUAL VULNERABILITY IN OTHER GLOBAL SYSTEMS

The logic of mutual vulnerability extended beyond the economy to encompass other interconnected spheres of life—most importantly, the environment and public health. Here, too, the new logic applied: even though countries are more likely to hurt one another inadvertently than on purpose, such harms could be serious, and they are increasingly likely because global systems are too complex to control.

Mutual vulnerability in the natural environment is one example of this logic. China is one of the most polluted countries in the world. To a large extent, the pollution is caused by China's production for consumers abroad. There is also much pollution from dumping of electronic waste that has come back to China after outliving its usefulness in the West. In this way, participation in the global economy imposes heavy economic and health costs on the Chinese people.[31]

In turn, some of China's behaviors hurt the environment for people abroad. Poisons dumped by Chinese factories into the Songhua River have more than once reached downstream populations in the Russian Far East. River and ocean dumping has polluted the waters off the Chinese coast and pushed Chinese fisherman farther into the surrounding seas to compete with boats from other countries. Because of prevailing winds, emissions from Chinese factories have reached Korea and Japan as acid rain and "yellow dust." Even soot in Los Angeles has occasionally been chemically traced to Chinese factories. If a nuclear accident on the scale of Japan's 2011 Fukushima reactor disaster were to occur somewhere on the Chinese coast, it might well deliver radiation to more people in Japan, Korea, and Taiwan—depending on which Chinese reactor was involved— than in China itself. Farther away, demand created by China's economic growth contributes indirectly to forest depletion, water pollution, and habitat destruction in Southeast Asia, Africa, and Latin America.

It is in China's long-term interest to help solve such environmental problems. They often arise from inefficiencies, the improvement of which will bring benefits to all. As jobs in polluting industries are lost, new jobs can be created in remediation and green industry, but that kind of transition is painful and expensive and can hurt vocal constituencies. As in other countries, in China the enforcement of environmental regulations lags behind commitment, and there is always the question of who bears the cost. Whereas foreign critics claim that China uses backward environmental standards to subsidize exports and compete for jobs unfairly, the Chinese criticize the use of environmental protection standards by developed countries to erect barriers to Chinese imports.

The grand example of mutual vulnerability in the environment is climate change (global warming) because the movements of the earth's atmosphere mix everyone's pollution together and bring its baneful effects to bear indiscriminately. Burning 2.6 tons of coal per person per year as of 2009, China has become the number one contributor to the production of carbon dioxide and other greenhouse gases. But coal remains the only way to meet a large fraction of China's soaring energy needs. A wholesale switch to renewable sources is not an option. China is developing nuclear power, but nuclear plants are expensive and slow, require sophisticated safety equipment, and pose the risk of environmental damage in case of breakdown. Major hydropower projects such as the Three Gorges Dam entail habitat damage and population displacements and have proven internationally controversial. Any increase in oil and gas use makes China more dependent on international sources of supply, and these fuels carry their own environmental problems, which will worsen as Beijing implements its commitment to develop the domestic automobile industry to supply China's emerging middle class with private cars.

Beijing has shown a willingness to recognize its shared interest in the global commons and to cooperate with evolving world standards. It created the National Environmental Protection Administration (upgraded to a ministry in 2008) as well as local environmental protection agencies and signed a number of international environmental agreements. The government is phasing out the household use of charcoal briquettes for cooking and heating and requires state-owned factories to burn coal more efficiently and install emissions-scrubbing equipment. But China has drawn the line at slowing its pace of development to ameliorate pollution problems that the Chinese argue were created by the developed world. It took the position at the 2009 Copenhagen climate negotiations that China would not take extra measures to slow emissions unless the developed countries drastically slowed their own emissions and gave major aid to China and other developing countries to help cover the cost of emissions cuts there.[32]

China and other countries are also mutually vulnerable in the area of public health. HIV/AIDS came into China from outside. Now there are three epidemics, two of which are linked to cross-border transmission—intravenous drug use along the Burma border and sex work along the east coast (the third epidemic is the blood transfusion epidemic in Henan, which is gradually diminishing as the blood purchase stations are banned and the victims die). No disease that originated in China has so far spread to the rest of the world in a major way. But the spread of Severe Acute Respiratory Syndrome (SARS, 2002) and avian flu (2003) from China to neighboring countries put the world on notice that China might produce disease vectors that under modern conditions would travel quickly to the rest of the world. As a result, international health organizations such as the WHO began to pressure the Chinese authorities to share information more quickly and accurately than they had done in the past, thus leading to another loss—however beneficial in the long run—to China's accustomed autonomy.

A third example of mutual vulnerability lies in the Internet and other forms of new information technology. The Internet took off in China around the mid-1990s and reached some 500 million users in its first decade. Between 2000 and 2009, cell phone subscriptions increased almost sevenfold from seven per one hundred persons to fifty-six, with escalating use of texting and Twitter. The government promoted the use of information technology as a focus of economic growth but also invested major resources in a multilayered control system, the Great Firewall, to prevent information from destabilizing domestic politics. In 2009, the government closed down the Internet for six months in Xinjiang to prevent the spread of antigovernment ideas among the restive population. In 2011, the authorities worked hard to control the spread of information about unrest in the Middle East and the use of the Internet and cell phones to call for a peaceful "Jasmine revolution" in China. The Internet also served as a channel for threats projected outward from China to other users. For example, the Pentagon, Google, and numerous other institutions and individual users outside China reported hacking and phishing attempts and virus attacks emanating from inside China. It was unclear when the hackers were private persons and when they were Chinese government institutions.

Despite all the problems brought by globalization, the policy direction seems irreversible for both China and its foreign partners. A Chinese pullback from global markets would hurt both Chinese and foreign workers and consumers and threaten the stability of both the Chinese and the global economies. Even if foreign powers wanted to stop the economic rise of China, they have no practicable way to do so. The only thing that might decouple China from the global economy would be a global depression or other breakdown that would affect all parties in unpredictable negative ways.

CHINA'S ENGAGEMENT IN INTERNATIONAL REGIMES

In the face of the kinds of mutual vulnerabilities just described, states have responded by creating more—and more complex—international regimes than ever before. International regimes are systems of norms and institutions that regulate interactions in various domains in the international system. Examples range from the UN, which seeks to maintain international peace and security, to the international financial institutions such as the World Bank and the IMF that regulate global finance, as well as to more narrowly focused regimes such as the WTO and systems governing international air traffic, migration, postal traffic, police cooperation, arms proliferation, human rights, and numerous other fields large and small. International regimes include formal provisions at their cores in the form of treaties, conventions, and other agreements. They often establish regulating bodies such as the UN Security Council or the WTO Secretariat. They sometimes also include a penumbra of informal norms about how states should behave within that regime. Most regimes are "intergovernmental" in nature, with states as their chief actors, even if NGOs and other entities also participate in some form. Some regimes are "nongovernmental," with countries being represented by formally private organizations, such as national Olympic committees.

China's entry into the world system caused it to become an active member of virtually all the international regimes in existence—a massive change in posture from the Mao period, when the PRC was a member of almost no international organizations except those that formed part of the socialist camp.[33] Until 1971, the China seat in the UN was held by the ROC instead of by the PRC. After the PRC regained that seat, it began to join other international organizations connected to the UN, such as the WHO and the Food and Agriculture Organization. It started to take an active role in UN bodies related to human rights (chapter 12). It regained the China seat in bodies such as the World Bank, the IMF, the WTO, the Asian Development Bank, the International Olympic Committee, and so on (chapter 8).

One of the most dramatic shifts came in China's participation in the global nonproliferation regime. Under Mao, China rejected all international limits on proliferation of missiles, nuclear weapons, and other weapons of mass destruction, arguing that such restrictions aimed only to consolidate the two superpowers' hegemony. Starting in the mid-1980s and accelerating during the 1990s, China acceded to a host of treaties—including the Biological Weapons Convention (1984), the NPT (1992), the Chemical Weapons Convention (1993), and the Comprehensive Test Ban Treaty (1996)—and it joined long list of additional agreements, institutions, and committees. Through its diplomatic activity, China tried to prevent or roll back the nuclear weapons programs of North Korea and Iran. It announced its support for the idea of nuclear-free zones and for treaties that had been proposed to ban the circulation of fissile materials, to ban the first use of nuclear weapons, to ban the development of antiballistic missiles, and to ban an arms race in outer space. Although the motives for joining different parts of the arms control and nonproliferation regime varied, in general the shift reflected Beijing's judgment that preventing proliferation was good for China's security (chapter 11).[34]

Once the PRC joined an international regime, it complied with its rules about as much as any other member. Complying often required a phase-in period, which could be contentious, as in the areas of nonproliferation and protection of intellectual property rights, because the central government had a hard time enforcing compliance with international rules on bureaucratic agencies and local governments that had an interest in avoiding compliance.[35] China's compliance often involved disputes with other members over the meaning of the rules, as when China, using the WTO Dispute Resolution Mechanism, sued the U.S. over the meaning of the term *dumping* or when China differed with the U.S. over the legitimate ambit of authority for the UN Security Council to intervene in the internal affairs of states such as Serbia or Iraq in pursuit of "international peace and security." Chinese compliance also did not preclude Chinese efforts to change an organization's voting rules or other rules. So China was not blindly compliant, and as its power increased — and its diplomats' sophistication about each regime's rules grew — it sought to become not only a rule follower, but a rule shaper. But in these respects China's behavior was no different from that of other powers, all of whom used their seats at various tables to pursue their own interests.[36] Even when it came to the international human rights regime, China attended the necessary meetings and filed the necessary reports on time even if its actions at home contravened what international NGOs claimed was the covenants' real intent (chapter 12).[37]

For China as for other states, participation in international regimes has been a mixed blessing. It has involved a yielding of autonomy to the shared community of states and sometimes to independent international bureaucrats and to the influence of an ill-defined international public opinion influenced by NGOs and other private actors. Yet to fail to participate would be to forego many of the benefits that globalization offers. Abiding by the rules has not meant giving up the pursuit of national interest, but learning how to pursue that interest under new conditions and in new ways.

LOOKING FORWARD: CHINA AS NUMBER ONE

Once Deng Xiaoping propelled China into engagement with the international economic system, its role in that system has never stopped changing.[38] How much more will change if and when China becomes the largest economy in the world, as it is predicted to do by some time in the 2020s if its economic trajectory stays on course? This expectation might be derailed by domestic instability or global economic shocks, but assuming that China becomes number one eventually, what will it mean for China's place in the world?

China as number one will be different from other economic number ones in history in several ways. First, its lead will not be built on technological preeminence, but on demographic preeminence. To be sure, the Chinese government has invested in research and development as well as in the shortcuts of technical espionage and reverse engineering. Its high-tech and military industries are continuously improving, its export industries are moving up the value chain, and the government has invested in research institutes that are striving to seize the world lead in plant bio-technology, genomics, particle physics, nuclear energy technology, and nanotechnology. But unless the other high-tech nations stop competing, China will not surge ahead of them in a wide range of fields to become the global fountainhead of technology as nineteenth-century England or twentieth-century America did.[39] It will be the biggest economy because it has the largest population. On a per capita basis, however, it will still be relatively poor.

Second, even though China as number one will command enormous financial resources and market power—setting the tune for global commerce and finance because it will have the biggest market—its prosperity will still be interdependent with the prosperity of its global rivals such as the U.S. and Japan. It will not prosper like nineteenth-century colonial powers by exploiting and impoverishing other societies. It will not benefit from setting up an exclusive economic bloc the way the U.S. and the USSR each did during the Cold War. Unlike Spain competing with Portugal in the sixteenth century, Holland competing with Spain in the sixteenth and seventeenth centuries, or Britain competing with France in the nineteenth century, China will not get ahead if its rivals do not. Their economic decline or destruction will not help China. This connection has grown even stronger as globalization has intensified interdependence around such issues as climate change and public health.

Third, although China's economic size will give it an ever-growing appetite for oil and other raw materials, it will not be able to gain commodity security through conquest as the colonial powers did in the eighteenth and nineteenth centuries or through indirect neocolonial control as the U.S. did in the twentieth century. Given the existence of other strong powers competing for resources, neither conquest nor domination is an option. China will have to get hold of commodities through economic means.

Number one status will undoubtedly enhance the influence that China's way of doing business is already having. More young Westerners will flock to China to learn Chinese and the art of "human relationships" Chinese style. Chinese music and films will gain wider appeal; the Chinese renminbi will become an international reserve currency, giving Chinese officials the ability to print money with less risk of inflation. Moreover, China will gain a share of the seignorage privilege that the U.S. and other minters of reserve currencies have enjoyed to get free loans by letting other countries accumulate their currencies.

The program that started in the 2000s to make China a "branding superpower" will most likely expand. China will gain a stronger voice in the World Bank and the IMF and in international negotiations over trade, climate, Internet security, and other issues. And with a larger market, it will have a growing ability to set the rules by which transnational corporations have to act—as it began to do, for example, when it adopted an antimonopoly law in 2008, becoming one of only three markets (along with the U.S. and the EU) that can regulate transnational corporations' ability to merge.

Of course, China itself will change as it rises to number one status in ways we cannot predict. Some say it will democratize. Or perhaps economic success will strengthen its authoritarian system. Either way, whoever is in charge is likely to use the country's newfound economic power to pursue national interest based on the strategic challenges that they face at the time.

11

MILITARY MODERNIZATION

From People's War to Power Projection

Before Deng Xiaoping came to power in the late 1970s, the PLA—as all the branches of China's military are collectively called—was a huge force of 4 million officers and troops, whose fighting experience was limited to land warfare within and in close proximity to China's borders. Its leadership consisted of aging revolutionaries, many of whose fighting credentials dated back to the 1940s or earlier. Its soldiers were drawn mainly from the rural countryside. Many were illiterate. The forces used antiquated weaponry, primitive logistics, and rudimentary communications. The air and naval components were small and backward. The most modern arm was a small nuclear-equipped missile force. Deng Xiaoping summarized the PLA's problems as "bloating, laxity, conceit, extravagance, and inertia."[1]

Changes in the security environment required changes in the military. When Deng came to power, the opening to the U.S. had alleviated but not removed the Soviet threat; the U.S. was still arming Taiwan, confronting North Korea, and promoting the growth of Japanese military power; and competition was heating up with China's neighbors over control of island groups in the South China Sea. Moreover, the early success of Deng's economic-reform program made China increasingly dependent on the security of far-flung sea lanes to carry resources into the country and send manufactured goods to markets abroad. Even as new military missions took shape, other militaries in the region were modernizing. The PLA needed new capabilities just to keep up.

Even so, Deng gave priority to economic rather than military reform in the first decade of his rule. He told his generals that military modernization required money and technology that could be provided only by economic growth. But even in this first phase he pushed the military to make changes. In the first years of the PRC and again during the Cultural Revolution in the late 1960s, the armed forces had been closely involved in all aspects of the economy, with soldiers growing food and officers running local government and managing factories. Deng began to move the military out of the economy and civilian governance, as well as reduce military manpower. He initiated a retirement system for officers, began to restore the system of professional military education, and reshaped PLA doctrine away from the outdated concept of "People's War" to a new concept of "local war under modern conditions," which pointed to the need to confront neighboring armies in geographically limited but technically demanding conflicts.

That these efforts were not enough was driven home by a series of strategic shocks starting in 1989. The Tiananmen incident in that year and the collapse of Communist regimes in Eastern Europe and the Soviet Union in 1990–1991 highlighted the need to improve the capabilities of the domestic security and paramilitary services and to cement the military's political loyalty to the regime. The stunning victory of the U.S.-led coalition forces over the Iraqi military in the Gulf War in 1990–1991, broadcast on global television, awakened the Chinese generals to the existence of a new technological horizon in warfare: the Americans' Revolution in Military Affairs. The revolution centered on the use of information technology to coordinate large, complex operations and to deliver violence with precision, capabilities far beyond the PLA's reach at that time. In 1995–1996, the U.S. surprised China by dispatching two aircraft carrier strike groups to the vicinity of the Taiwan Strait (chapter 9), which led the Chinese to conclude that they needed a real military option — not just an empty threat — to solve the Taiwan problem in case their political–economic strategy failed and that the military option would have to include the ability to deter or defeat an American intervention. The U.S. deployment helped China's naval strategists argue that the nation faced an important new strategic frontier at sea and would have to expand its maritime forces to achieve security.[2]

MILITARY REFORM AND RESTRUCTURING

In response to these shocks, Deng launched a more expensive and arduous second phase of military modernization, which his successors continued to pursue after his death. It involved every element of military organization from doctrine to weaponry.

REVISING DOCTRINE

Military doctrine tells an army what kinds of war it should prepare to fight and how to fight them. It starts with an appraisal of the security environment, identifies potential enemies and their capabilities, and assesses the adversary's and one's own strong and weak points. The most authoritative articulations of PLA doctrine are found in documents issued by the CMC. The most important of these documents are the Military Strategic Guidelines (MSG, *Junshi zhanlue fangzhen*). Amendments and new MSGs are promulgated infrequently, usually only when major changes in the security environment or nature of warfare demand it. In the Mao period, the generals were told to prepare either for an invasion by the U.S. or the Soviet Union or both or for a nuclear conflagration between the two superpowers that would inflict severe collateral damage on China. An invasion would lead to a protracted war of attrition on Chinese soil, during which all of Chinese society, with the PLA at its core, would seek to wear down the invading enemy. A superpower war would also require a massive PLA, living close to the people, to wait out the nuclear holocaust so that China with its huge population could rise from the ashes.

Mao characterized these two scenarios under the common rubric of "early, major, and nuclear war." To prepare for either eventuality, the PLA had to be large, dispersed, low tech, and politically integrated with the people. It would draw on its pre-1949 experience as a guerrilla army, sustain itself as self-sufficiently as possible without complex logistics, cultivate good relations with the masses, and stand ready to wait out and wear out the enemy. Soldiers would operate as fish among a sea of civilians. A vast rural militia, divided into three levels (ordinary, basic, and armed), would assist the guerrilla fighters and harass the enemy. The population would practice civil defense, "digging tunnels deep and storing grain everywhere." The core idea was defense in depth ("luring the enemy deep") to trade space for time. Mao referred to this strategy as "People's War." "[I]f the United States with its planes plus the A-bomb is to launch a war of aggression against China," he said, "then China with its millet plus rifles is sure to emerge the victor."[3]

Under changed strategic circumstances, Deng Xiaoping saw war as less likely and less total, but if it occurred as more technologically demanding. He said that the main world trends for the 1980s and beyond were "peace and development." If war took place, it would not be on Chinese soil, but in a limited geographic area on China's periphery, such as the Taiwan Strait, the South China Sea or East China Sea, Vietnam, or Korea. The enemy—the U.S., Japan, or other neighbors—would command advanced technology. The war would be brief and would end not with the total destruction of one side's forces, but with decisive blows that would deliver a psychological victory. The PLA was instructed to prepare to "fight a quick battle to force a quick resolution."

In keeping with these ideas, the CMC in 1985 adopted a new MSG to prepare for "local war under modern conditions." This MSG was then modified in 1993 to replace "modern conditions" with "high-technology conditions" and again in 2002 to read "local war under conditions of informatization." In all these formulations, what was meant by "local war" (*jubu zhanzheng*, also translatable as "partial war" or "limited war") was that the war would occur in a limited area, extend for a limited time period, have limited aims, and require less than full military mobilization. By "modern," "high technology" and "informatization," the CMC referred to the need for China to be able to contend with the U.S. and its allies with their advanced logistics, comprehensive real-time battlefield information systems, and precision weapons targeting. In this context, the CMC recast Mao's concept of "active defense" from a tactical and operational tenet to a strategic-level principle. Rather than wait for an adversary to attack, the PLA would prepare to strike first outside its borders if necessary to prevent an impending attack or a sharp degradation of its ability to enforce territorial claims.

There was a strong chance that such a war would be fought in large part at sea, so the navy needed new capabilities to operate at significant distances from China's coast and block interference by high-tech navies such as those of the U.S. and Japan. Chinese officers saw the key to the Revolution in Military Affairs as information technology—computers, satellites, sensing and targeting devices—that would provide instant communication among scattered military units. In this area of specialization—information operations and information warfare—their strategy focused on acquiring niche capabilities that would impede, hamper, and perhaps even defeat the U.S. military in the Taiwan Strait. The PLA aimed to disable U.S. space satellites, sabotage computer networks, and hit U.S. bases and ships in the western Pacific with ballistic missiles in order to implement what U.S. military analysts dub "anti-access" and "area denial" strategies.

In a major speech to the CMC in 2004, Hu Jintao articulated a set of four broad mission areas for the PLA, quickly dubbed the New Historic Missions. These missions were, first, "providing an important guarantee of strength for the party to consolidate its ruling position"; second, "providing a strong security guarantee for safeguarding the period of important strategic opportunity for national development"; third, "providing powerful strategic support for safeguarding national interests"; and fourth, "playing an important role in safeguarding world peace and promoting common development."[4] The speech permitted Hu to put his stamp on military doctrine and hence lay claim to the stature of his predecessors, each of whom had made contributions to the evolution of PLA strategy. His list of missions highlighted the continuing importance of First Ring security for the Chinese armed forces, the growing importance of territorial disputes in the Second Ring, the need to provide secure access to resources for China's economic growth, and the imperative of maintaining a deterrent capability that would prevent other powers from launching a major war against China.

STREAMLINING FORCE STRUCTURE

To prepare for a new kind of war required a smaller, more educated, and better-trained PLA with expanded air and naval components. The government conducted three rounds of demobilization to reduce and upgrade the force. Between 1985 and 1996, an estimated 1.1 million troops were taken out of service. From 1996 to 2000, an estimated half a million more uniformed personnel were demobilized. The third round of cuts occurred between 2003 and 2005 and removed a further 200,000 personnel. These cuts, spread out over twenty years, reduced the size of the PLA by almost half. As of 2012, the PLA had approximately 2.25 million men and women in uniform, making it still the largest army in the world, but by a much smaller margin than previously. The government mounted a huge national effort to find jobs for the demobilized officers and troops. Many were assigned to the newly reestablished People's Armed Police (discussed more fully later). Others were posted to specialized security units, local governments, schools, and enterprises. The task was especially challenging because the manpower reduction focused on those who were illiterate, undereducated, and underskilled and who were therefore hard to place in new jobs. But it was carried out without disruption, testimony to the regime's organizational effectiveness.

Most of the PLA's ground forces had previously been organized into units called "armies," each comprising three large-scale infantry divisions, and all similarly equipped regardless of their different missions and locations. The 1980s reforms created new units called "group armies" (*jituan jun*) of between 30,000 and 50,000 men that are about half the size of the former armies, currently are composed typically of brigades (approximately 3,000 to 5,000 strong) rather than divisions (8,000 to 10,000), and include a more flexible mix of infantry, armor, and artillery formations. Each military region (MR) was assigned at least one rapid-reaction unit, or "fist force," and such units were supposed to be able to reach any destination within China's borders within forty-eight hours. The two-day window is necessary because the units usually rely on road or rail transportation; China still lacks airlift capabilities adequate to the task.

The PLA reserves were reconstituted in the 1980s and revamped in the 1990s to back up and supplement the regular PLA in time of war. There are approximately 510,000 reservists, most of whom have not served on active duty but who have technical skills needed in the force. The reserves are distinguished from the militia by a higher level of readiness and integration with the regular military. Reserve units conduct training exercises with regular PLA forces, and individual reservists are groomed to serve as replacements in regular PLA formations.

The PLA is backed up by a militia of 8 million. In the early reform period, the militia had become inactive as rural men and women focused on expanding agricultural output and engaging in sideline production for personal gain. But in the 2000s it was revived and extended to urban areas. In addition to serving as an adjunct to the regular military and reserves in wartime, the militia helps to maintain domestic order; assists in border patrol; helps guard roads, railways, and bridges; and participates in disaster relief after earthquakes, floods, and snowstorms.

Another important step in streamlining the PLA was reducing the number of MRs to seven from eleven in 1985. Fewer MRs meant fewer headquarters, which reduced bureaucratic bloating. With the demise of the Soviet Union, the three northern MRs (Beijing, Shenyang, and Jinan) saw reductions in the manpower of main-force units. Since the late 1990s, six group armies have been redistributed among the Beijing MR (crucial for political stability), the Shenyang MR (facing Korea), and the Jinan MR (facing Japan). There has been no change in the number of group armies garrisoning the Chengdu MR, which includes most of the Tibetan Autonomous Region as well as Yunnan and Sichuan provinces and faces Burma, or in the number garrisoning the Lanzhou MR, which covers the Xinjiang Autonomous Region, westernmost Tibet, and other provinces and which faces Central Asia. Nor has there been any change in the number of group armies stationed in the Nanjing and Guangzhou MRs in the south.

With the military pared down in size, ramped up in technology, and focused on more specialized skills, the government created separate formations with primary responsibility for domestic security tasks. In 1983, a paramilitary force that had gone out of existence during the Cultural Revolution, the People's Armed Police (PAP), was reestablished with the task of controlling major outbreaks of civil disorder. Its roster eventually came to include as many as 1.5 million troops, many transferred from the PLA during the demobilization of the 1980s. In addition to riot-control forces, the PAP has units specializing in border security, firefighting, and guard duty for gold mines, forests, hydroelectric facilities, and high-level government officials. In training and equipment, the PAP stands between the more lightly armed Ministry of Public Security and the more heavily armed PLA, serving as a gendarmerie. It operates under a dual chain of command, responsible to both the CMC and the civilian State Council.

PROFESSIONALIZING PERSONNEL

At the end of the Mao era, many Chinese officers had served for decades and had little formal education and few modern military skills. Deng complained in 1980 that some of them could not even read maps. Around that time, he instituted a system of retirement ages and raised educational standards for promotion. By 2000, the percentage of PLA officers with some college education had risen from 10 percent to 75 percent. The average age of CMC members dropped from seventy-five in 1989 to sixty-three in 2003, and average ages declined by comparable amounts in the lower echelons.[5]

During the Cultural Revolution, some two-thirds of the PLA's education and training establishments shut their doors. During the 1980s and 1990s, the professional military education system was restored and overhauled from the top down. At the apex were two universities. The National Defense University, modeled on its U.S. namesake, was established in 1985 in Beijing, and it came to be nicknamed the "cradle of generals." The National Defense Science and Technology University, located in Hunan Province, was reopened in 1978 and reorganized in 1999. Below these two institutions, dozens of military academies and technical schools were reestablished. The PLA also tapped into civilian universities through an ambitious reserve-officer training program that has attracted thousands of bright young people with desirable specialties to military service. Moreover, a small but significant number of officers were allowed to expand their horizons by going abroad—some to study, others for visits as part of delegations, and others on peacekeeping and, most recently, antipiracy missions. The leadership that has emerged from this system is well educated, with a substantial engineering and armaments background and a fondness for high-tech weaponry.

In 1999, the PLA began to expand the size and role of its noncommissioned officer (NCO) corps. NCOs form the backbone of most modern militaries, playing key roles in training, disciplining, and mentoring the rank and file, thereby freeing up higher officers from most of the mundane day-to-day responsibilities of supervising enlisted personnel. PLA leaders concluded, after studying the system in the U.S. armed forces, that a strong cadre of professional and experienced NCOs is crucial for combat effectiveness in the modern era. The expansion of the NCO corps allowed the

PLA's officer corps to be downsized, with 70,000 officer billets reportedly redesignated for NCOs. At the enlisted level, China continues to rely on a conscription system, with quotas for each military district. Conscripts serve for a minimum of two years. The PLA has found it challenging to retain the best enlisted personnel beyond their conscription period.

To upgrade the skills of those in uniform and improve their ability to work together, the PLA improved training, with more realistic force-on-force and live-fire exercises. It began to conduct specialized exercises such as search and rescue, counterterrorism, and amphibious operations. It has conducted combined arms training and has also attempted joint exercises, so far with limited success.[6] In the long run, seamless coordination among branches and services will be necessary for the kind of complex military operations that would be required, for example, for an attack on Taiwan. The consensus of outside observers is that standards have significantly improved but remain deficient compared to the best militaries in the region or to U.S. capabilities. Foreign military attachés invited to observe PLA exercises compliment the troops more frequently on their bravery, fitness, and drilling than on their operational skills.

The PLA also began to conduct multinational exercises with other countries. The first such exercise China undertook on foreign soil was a bilateral two-day counterterrorism exercise held in Kyrgyzstan in 2002 with approximately three hundred troops backed up by armored vehicles and helicopters. The first multinational exercise on Chinese soil was held in Xinjiang under the auspices of the SCO in 2003. It involved Chinese and Kyrgyz forces as well as Russian, Kazakh, and Tajik observers. Small-scale exercises have been conducted with the militaries of other countries, including India, Pakistan, Thailand, and the U.S. The largest and most ambitious multinational exercise to date was Peace Mission 2005, held on Chinese soil with approximately 8,000 Chinese troops and almost 2,000 Russians, including air force and marines. Such exercises have multiple purposes: they provide valuable experience to the troops, build trust with neighbors, and send a signal of determination to potential rivals.

BOOSTING THE BUDGET

Modernization meant freeing the PLA from its traditional interpenetration with the civilian economy. During the pre-1949 era, PLA soldiers had been guerilla fighters trying to live off the land without placing an undue burden on the local peasantry. Under Mao, the country's economy was completely oriented toward national defense, and society was perpetually primed to mobilize in the event of invasion. The PLA and the militia were organically inseparable from and enmeshed in the economy, with the country on a permanent war footing. Even in the 1980s, because of budgetary stringency, in the context of economic liberalization Deng had allowed the PLA to commoditize some of its assets—such as land, airports, and personnel—so as to make money from a wide range of ventures such as factories, hotels, and transport facilities. But in the mid- and late 1990s, when the government had enough money to increase the defense budget, Deng and his successor, Jiang Zemin, forced the army to divest itself of such commercial ventures. By the end of the century, the PLA no longer had a business empire, nor did it engage directly in military production, and civilian defense industries took over the conduct of most foreign arms sales. However, military units continued to operate farms to meet their own food needs and sold some produce, with the profits going to benefit the unit.

The government compensated the army for the loss of self-generated income with an increased budgetary allotment. Under Mao, the PLA had received a relatively modest amount of money from the central government, never exceeding 17 billion renminbi or more than 25 percent of central-government expenditures in the period after the Korean War. After 1989, the military budget started to see significant annual increases. There may have been several reasons for the timing of these increases—the need to reward the military for its loyalty during the Tiananmen crisis, increasingly tense relations with Taiwan and the U.S., initial awareness of the Revolution in Military Affairs, and the greater availability of funds because the economy was growing and because changes in the tax system started to bring a larger proportion of GDP into the central government's coffers. Starting in 1990, the officially announced defense budget has risen in double digits virtually every year, more than doubling from 1989 to 1998, more than doubling again between 1998 and 2003 and yet again between 2003 and 2008. In 2010, the defense budget officially reached 532.1 billion renminbi.[7] Although these increases were much less dramatic than they appear when adjusted for inflation, they have been significant, especially since the late 1990s. The division of budget increases among the service arms is not known, but it appears from the buildup that followed that the navy got a disproportionate share, followed by the air force and the missile service, with the land forces getting a lesser share of the increase.

Real military spending is larger than the publicly budgeted amount because the defense budget does not include certain large expenditures that are found in other countries' comparable budgets. These expenditures include foreign arms purchases, research and development, testing of weapon systems, pensions, and the costs of the reserves. In addition, the national defense budget is supplemented with funding provided by provincial and local governments in those localities where the troops are billeted, and China's defense dollar buys more than those of other countries because of the lower price of labor and food in the Chinese economy. Most analysts consider that a more accurate estimate of total defense spending on a comparable basis to other countries' defense budgets would be double the official figure. In 2009, for example, according to a U.S. Department of Defense estimate, the official level of the Chinese defense budget expressed in U.S. dollars was about $70 billion, and the actual total of military-related spending was about $150 billion.[8]

Although China's defense spending has risen to second in the world after that of the U.S., there is still a big gap between China's spending even at its estimated actual level and U.S. defense spending at about $690 billion in 2010. Also, China provides entirely for its own defense, whereas the U.S. military has the support of close allies such as Australia, the United Kingdom, Germany, and Japan, whose own defense budgets are among the largest in the world after those of the U.S. and China. All that said, the real measure of each military's fighting strength is the fit of its resources to the missions it has to perform.

UPGRADING WEAPONRY AND EQUIPMENT

A significant part of the budget increases went to upgrading weapons and equipment. The pattern of arms acquisitions provides insight into the evolution of Chinese strategy. Top priority has been given to building up the PLA Navy. Starting in the 1990s, China's shipbuilding complex began to produce a dozen new classes of ocean-going vessels with advanced weapon systems, including four types of submarines, five types of guided-missile destroyers, and three types of guided-missile frigates. The acquisitions enabled the navy to make the initial transition from a coastal defense force to an ocean-going, or blue water, force. Of particular concern to the U.S. has been the development of over-the-horizon radar and electronic warfare capabilities, which contribute to a capability to deter or prevent the U.S. from intervening successfully in a war over Taiwan. Leading strengths of the PLA Navy include diesel-powered submarines and antiship cruise missiles, which can damage or sink an American aircraft carrier. The navy acquired four Russian-built Sovremenny-class destroyers equipped with "Sunburn" antiship cruise missiles, as well as Chinese-made Luyang-class destroyers equipped with radar to help guide its Chinese-made Hai Hongqi-9 anti-air missiles. It also upgraded and enhanced the capabilities of its patrol boats operating in littoral waters and of its amphibious ships designed for the task of landing troops on Taiwan.

Other acquisitions indicate that the navy is preparing for expeditionary maritime missions: recent ocean-going additions include a hospital ship and replenishment oilers. In addition, it is actively working to commission an aircraft carrier. The first is likely to be the *Varyag*, purchased in 1998 from Ukraine, renovated in Dalian, and taken on sea trials in 2011. It will probably serve as a training vessel for the foreseeable future as Chinese crews and naval aviators learn to operate this complex system of systems. In addition to expanding its surface fleet, the PLA Navy has enhanced its submarine force with advanced weapons and sensors. As of 2010, the fleet consists of a handful of nuclear attack submarines and more than fifty diesel subs (ballistic missile submarines are discussed later in this chapter). These appear aimed at enabling China to enforce its maritime territorial claims and to protect the sea lanes in the western Pacific. A large new naval base on Hainan Island completed in the late 2000s signaled Beijing's intent to continue a robust submarine program and a commitment to defend its claims in the South China Sea.

The PLA Air Force has engaged in a wholesale modernization of its inventory. It retired some 70 percent of its air fleet between 1990 and 2010, amounting to approximately 3,500 aircraft, and acquired several hundred advanced fighter planes more capable of defending Chinese territory. In 2011, China tested a prototype of a fifth generation J-20 stealth fighter. It is also developing fighter jets capable of operating from an aircraft carrier. It has midair refueling capabilities, but they remain limited because of the small size of the tanker fleet and limited number of appropriately fitted aircraft. The air force is upgrading its H-6 bomber fleet and arming it with land attack cruise missiles. Its ability to transport ground forces beyond—or even within—China's borders remains a weak point. For example, most of the 1,600 Chinese troops who participated in Peace Mission 2007 with Russia were transported by rail from Xinjiang, requiring some two weeks to travel 6,000 miles to the site of the exercise (the circuitous route was necessary because Kazakhstan denied the Chinese forces transit). All provisions, logistics, and security were provided by their Russian counterparts. Moreover, in the spring of 2008 the PLA was desperately short of fixed-wing and rotary aircraft (especially the latter) to come to the relief of earthquake victims in Sichuan when roads were impassable or completely destroyed. Although some troops, equipment, and supplies were airlifted or parachuted in, the lion's share of rescue personnel and supplies were brought in by vehicle or on foot, with inevitable delays in reaching the disaster zones. The air force has reportedly ordered thirty-four additional Il-76 transports from Russia, but they have been slow in coming, and it has had to make do with about twenty Il-76s and various Y-8 aircraft. In addition, China has worked hard to improve its air defenses—a continuing priority for an air force that has long anticipated battling a foe with vastly superior airpower. The PLA Air Force has acquired one of the world's largest surface-to-air missile forces and is enhancing its system for detecting attacks, including the use of a small number of airborne early-warning and control aircraft—a less-sophisticated version of the American airborne command-and-control system.

As for the ground forces, they have also acquired new hardware, although it has attracted less attention than the other services' new weaponry. Notable additions have included third-generation Type-99 main battle tanks, which are gradually being introduced to group armies throughout China, as well as armored personnel carriers and infantry fighting vehicles. A new generation of artillery and multiple rocket launchers is also being introduced.

The Second Artillery is in charge of China's ballistic missile forces, which include both nuclear and conventional warheads, deliverable by intercontinental ballistic missiles (ICBMs), intermediate-range ballistic missiles, medium-range ballistic missiles, and short-range ballistic missiles. The greatest expansion has taken place in China's arsenal of short-range ballistic missiles, which numbered as many as twelve hundred by 2011. By virtue of sheer numbers, improved accuracy, and greater mobility, these conventionally armed rockets pose significant challenges to Taiwan and potentially also to countries around China's periphery.

Cyber operations, which fall under the purview of the General Staff Department, have been a focus of growth in PLA capabilities. Hacker attacks emanating from China have hit businesses, NGOs, individuals, and government offices around the world, including in the U.S., Germany, Taiwan, and the United Kingdom. It is difficult to know which of these attacks were launched by private hackers and which by Chinese military or intelligence agencies, but the best guess is that the attacks represent wholesale cyber espionage and are the surface manifestation of a larger effort directed at building the capability to disrupt Internet operations in case of a conflict with U.S. or other advanced forces that are highly dependent on information technology. Unlike in the U.S., where space programs are spearheaded by a civilian agency (the National Aeronautics and Space Administration), in China a good chunk of space exploration, including the manned space program, belongs to the PLA's General Armaments Department. Although China and ninety-six other states are bound by the provisions of the Outer Space Treaty of 1967, which commits signatories to pursue only "peaceful purposes" beyond the earth's atmosphere, the vaguely worded provisions can be interpreted liberally. As the U.S. and other countries utilize space assets for military purposes, so too China is developing its capabilities to compete with rivals on this new military frontier. In 2003, Lieutenant Colonel Yang Liwei successfully orbited the planet, making China only the third country in the world to send a human into space. In 2008, China launched the *Shen Zhou 7* with a crew of three. Although the military applications of the manned flight program are unclear, many aspects of China's space program have defense dimensions, including its satellite program, with its launch of navigation satellites and remote-sensing satellites, the development of improved launch rockets, and construction of a new satellite launch center on Hainan Island. China's capabilities were demonstrated by the 2007 destruction of an aging weather satellite in orbit approximately six hundred miles above the earth with a ground launched ballistic missile. Because advanced militaries—especially that of the U.S.—depend heavily on satellites for intelligence and communication, this act signaled that China was working on capabilities to blind the American military in case of a conflict.

In the mid-1980s, Beijing launched the High-Technology Research and Development Plan with a focus on national-priority high-tech projects, including military programs. The initiative, personally approved by Deng Xiaoping, is better known as "Project 863," named after the year and month of its conception. Spearheaded by a group of top civilian scientists and senior military leaders, the effort has since its inception reportedly provided tens of billions of U.S. dollars worth of funding to more than ten thousand projects. Two of the initial seven research areas, space technology and lasers, were undertaken by military researchers. One project in the former area produced the *Shen Zhou* space module, and another project in the latter area achieved significant progress in synthetic aperture radar, which can provide high-resolution images invaluable for satellite surveillance, reconnaissance, and precision-guided munitions.

In 1998, the PLA created the General Armaments Department and charged it with acquiring high-tech weapons indigenously. To handle research, testing, development, and evaluation of new systems, the government reconstituted a civilian-administered entity, the Commission on Science and Technology in National Defense, and then in 2008 renamed it the State Administration for Science, Technology, and Industry for National Defense (SASTIND), demoted it from ministry level to bureau level, and merged it into the new superbureaucracy, the Ministry of Industry and Informatization. As a result, SASTIND has relatively great autonomy from the military chain of command, which ensures that research, testing, development, and evaluation processes are kept separate from procurement. SASTIND oversees a military–industrial complex of ten large defense–industrial corporations that employ at least 2.5 million civilian workers.[9]

Improvements in the country's industrial base have allowed the PLA to produce more of its own advanced equipment. Globalization reduced the effectiveness of rules and regulations used by the West to limit the flow of sensitive technologies to the PRC.[10] A mix of technology transfer through access to foreign commercial technology, technical assistance from Russia and Israel, espionage, and domestic research and development allowed China to attain near world levels in aerospace, information technology, telecommunications, and shipbuilding. It has been successful in indigenous military production in many areas such as ballistic missiles and anti-ship cruise missiles as well as in modern systems such as fighter aircraft, frigates, submarines, main-battle tanks and armored personnel carriers.

Despite its achievements, the defense establishment has been slow to research, develop, mass-produce, and deploy in a timely fashion high-tech Chinese-made weapon systems to meet all of the PLA's needs. The military–industrial complex has long been forced to purchase high performance aircraft and naval vessels from Russia or to coproduce them with Russia under license in China. In many cases, although the basic frame is built in China, the electronics and other high-tech components must be imported. The bottom line is that although indigenous military production capabilities have improved significantly in recent decades, it will still be necessary for China to continue to import some kinds of full systems and many component systems for the foreseeable future.

STRENGTHENING MECHANISMS
OF CCP CONTROL OVER THE ARMY

The PLA's allegiance to the CCP remains strong, but civil–military relations have become more complex, and mechanisms of civilian control and coordination are underinstitutionalized, especially at the apex. The CMC (chapter 2) is less a mechanism for party control than an arena for the military to lobby the party on behalf of the PLA's institutional interests. The central mechanism of civilian control is the quasi-formalized post of paramount leader, the one civilian in a position to exercise control. Paramount leaders of the post–Long March generation, such as Jiang Zemin and Hu Jintao, have had to work hard to earn the respect and allegiance of senior soldiers. They have largely succeeded by supporting sustained budget increases, championing aggressive defense modernization, cultivating relationships with senior military leaders, and making their own highly publicized contributions to PLA strategy and doctrine.[11]

Throughout the military, allegiance to the party is reinforced by the political commissar system, party committees within military units, and disciplinary inspection commissions. At each level of command—MR, group army, fleet, and below—a commander is paired with a political commissar, the former with a chain of command running through the General Staff Department and the latter with a chain of command running through the General Political Department. The commander and the commissar exercise joint leadership.

What is called "political work" in the PLA is less about substantive indoctrination of soldiers on the finer points of Maoism and more about hammering home the sacred link between the party and the army. The core of the so-called New Historic Missions articulated by Hu Jintao in 2004 was notably not new: the PLA's first and most important mission has always been to defend the party against all enemies. The CCP defines national security as including regime security and the national interest as including the party's interests.

With military modernization, a sense of PLA corporate identity distinct from that of the CCP has emerged, along with increasingly separate service identities, as the navy, air force, and Second Artillery rise in influence vis-à-vis the ground forces. There are signs that some within the military aspire to evolve from an army loyal to a particular party to an army loyal to the state, an identity that some soldiers consider more modern and cosmopolitan. But this desire has not yet manifested itself in any concrete act of disloyalty to the CCP. Despite this loyalty, party leaders find the ideas of "statification" (*guojiahua*) and depoliticization (*feizhengzhihua*) dangerous enough to condemn them openly in the official media.

The military's ethos and organization make it almost unthinkable that the PLA might mount a coup d'état or other political intervention against the will of a united party leadership. The only post-1949 incident that qualifies as a coup was the 1976 arrest of the Gang of Four. This incident occurred during a leadership succession crisis in the immediate aftermath of Mao's death and was carried out at the behest of a section of the party leadership. This kind of political split in the civilian leadership has been rendered less likely by the post-Deng institutionalization of leadership transitions. Also arguing against the likelihood of a coup is the fact that the broad security apparatus is organized in such a complex manner, with so many overlapping agencies and competing chains of command, that it would be difficult for any military or security leader or organization to plan a coup without being discovered.

CORE MISSIONS

All these defense modernization efforts were configured to prepare the PLA to perform three specific missions today and a possible fourth in the future. Within China's borders, the PLA must be able to participate with other agencies to maintain domestic stability. At the borders, the PLA must be prepared to defend the country's territorial integrity, which means defending the territory that the PRC already holds from being attacked and preventing moves by rival claimants to consolidate control over territory that the PRC claims but does not hold, including Taiwan. Beyond the borders, the PLA is charged with maintaining the capability to deter nuclear attack by the U.S. or any other nuclear power. As these three sets of capabilities are consolidated, the PLA is likely to aspire to a fourth mission of projecting power into regions beyond China's immediate periphery. How future leaders define the fourth mission will depend on their assessment of the geostrategic challenges China faces at that time.

THE FIRST MISSION: DEFEND CCP RULE

The PLA's first mission is to serve as the ultimate backup for other security forces to protect the ruling regime against domestic challenges. Standing on the first line of defense for internal security is the Ministry of Public Security. Its functions include population registration, neighborhood policing, crime control, firefighting, and traffic control. The ministry also has specialized units that surveil and suppress political dissidents (the so-called *guobao* or national security police) and that control the Internet (euphemistically referred to as the Public Information Network Security Supervision Bureau). Its total personnel reportedly number 1.7 million. If one takes this figure as accurate, then China's police manpower per capita is less than 50 percent that of the U.S., in part because civil order functions are separately delegated to other groups, including locally hired adjunct "contract police" and the PAP.[12] According to Ministry of Finance figures, in 2010 China spent more on public security than it did on national defense. The comparison is only indicative, because the official defense budget does not include all national defense spending, and China's public-security budget does not include internal security expenditures by provincial and local authorities. Moreover, most government entities and corporations have their own security forces, and this additional manpower serves to supplement the Ministry of Public Security's relatively modest size.

Alongside the Ministry of Public Security is the Ministry of State Security, which is charged with both espionage and counterespionage functions — a single entity combining the intelligence duties of the CIA and the counterintelligence duties of the FBI. There are no known figures for this ministry's manpower or budget.

The third line of defense against civil disorder is the paramilitary PAP, which is deployed around the country and coordinates with both local government agencies and the MR commanders. PAP troops undergo training similar to that of the PLA but are differently equipped, with batons, rubber bullets, electric cattle prods, shields, tear gas, and armored cars. In addition to these organizations, major domestic security roles are performed by the party and state discipline-inspection commissions, whose key job is to investigate officials who are suspected of corruption, and by a variety of specialized guard forces and security services that protect key economic institutions, key party and state offices, and top leaders.[13]

The PLA serves as the final line of domestic defense. The role of fallback internal security force is deeply rooted in PLA history. The PLA was founded as a revolutionary army whose mission was to defeat the KMT's armed forces in a civil war. In the last stage of the civil war in the late 1940s, it made the transition from a guerilla force to a regular infantry. After victory, its major mission was to subdue the CCP's remaining internal enemies: scattered KMT units that remained on the mainland, landlord militias, clan armies, bandits, and armed minority fighters in Tibet and elsewhere, some of whom were aided by the KMT and the U.S. The PLA was later called upon to control internal migration and unrest associated with tumultuous events such as the famine triggered by the Great Leap Forward (1958–1962) and the chaos unleashed by the Cultural Revolution (1966–1976).

Following the first phase of the Cultural Revolution, Mao ordered the military to step in and directly run the country. The party and government apparatuses had been destroyed in political strife. Some 2 million soldiers became the leaders and main staff of what were called "revolutionary committees," which assumed the day-to-day administration of township, county, municipal, and provincial jurisdictions and of communes, factories, and schools across the country.[14] At this point, Mao's government was virtually a military regime. The military served not only as an instrument of state control over society, but also as Mao's instrument of control over the administrative machinery and as the main tool in his personal power struggles with his rivals. The two power instruments that Mao never relinquished throughout his turbulent political career were his chairmanship of the CMC and his direct control of the Zhongnanhai guard corps, which provided security for all the top leaders and could arrest any of them at Mao's behest.

Deng Xiaoping's and his successors' power continued to rest to some extent on a military base, although not as exclusively as Mao's had done in the late phase of his career. After Mao's death, a group of generals and some civilian party leaders decided to arrest Mao's wife and other close colleagues—the so-called Gang of Four—and these generals played a large role in supporting Deng's rise to power. Deng gradually moved the military out of day-to-day politics and tried to reduce its role in maintaining civil order by reviving the PAP. The military nevertheless remained the ultimate bulwark of regime survival. The civilian authorities called in the PAP to suppress demonstrations in Lhasa in 1989 supported by the PLA. They employed PAP units later that year to disperse crowds in Beijing but finally had to call in the PLA to suppress the Tiananmen demonstrators. The PAP has been strengthened since 1989 and is routinely called upon to deal with disturbances in locales across China. In particularly seriously cases, such as the 2008 unrest in Lhasa and the 2009 disturbances in Urumqi, the PAP is still backed up by the PLA.

Starting in the 1980s, the PLA's domestic security role was codified in legal documents. The 1982 Constitution allowed the State Council or the NPC Standing Committee to impose martial law but gave no further guidance about the operations of troops to maintain martial law. In 1996 and 1997, the NPC adopted the Law on Martial Law and the National Defense Law, respectively. The former specified the circumstances that would necessitate the imposition of martial law (in case of "serious turmoil, riots or disturbances that endanger national unity, security, or public security"). The latter highlighted that the PAP had the primary mission for maintaining order but said that the PLA "may assist in maintaining public order according to the law." The decision whether to deploy the PLA after receiving a request from civilian authorities is vested in the CMC, a provision that in effect keeps ultimate power in the hands of the top party official, who also chairs the CMC. Once deployed, troops used to maintain martial law are authorized to ban assemblies, marches, demonstrations, strikes, and other crowd activities; to control news and communications; to restrict travel, impose curfews, ban public access to certain areas; and to take a wide variety of other measures, including, if necessary, shooting people identified as threats.

In 2004, a constitutional amendment replaced the legal term *martial law*, burdened with negative baggage from 1989, with the more innocuous-sounding *state of emergency*. Three years later the NPC adopted the Emergency Response Law. The law defines emergencies broadly enough to include not only nonpolitical events, but also threats to social stability. With respect to the PLA's role, the law authorizes the military as necessary to set up security cordons and checkpoints; control traffic and communications; guard key installations; control fuel, power, and water supplies; and use force to quell resistance.

The prominence of the PLA's internal mission shows in its deployment. The ground forces make up approximately 70 percent of total manpower. Even though each of China's seven MRs faces a potential battlefront directly across its border, most troops are not deployed close to the borders but are distributed widely across the landscape in camps located in and around China's major population centers. Within each major municipality, a garrison command maintains liaison with local civilian authorities and coordinates units stationed in and around the city, including PAP units, reserve units, and militia units. (In comparison, U.S. ground forces compose about 53 percent of total manpower. U.S. forces are deployed in a wide variety of locales across the fifty U.S. states and dependent territories as well as overseas but are geared to undertake or support missions overseas rather than at home.)

The two most powerful group armies are stationed not on the borders, but close to the political center of the country, the Thirty-Eighth Group Army in the Beijing MR and the Thirty-Ninth Group Army in the Shenyang MR; the majority of the other group armies are located in densely populated eastern China. By contrast, the vast western areas of the country—the Lanzhou and Chengdu MRs, which include Xinjiang and Tibet—are relatively lightly garrisoned. Although each of these MRs has some units deployed close to its international borders, their largest units are located near their own major population centers. Xinjiang is also home to the Xinjiang Production and Construction Corps, a military-cum-civilian organization that both serves as a garrison and functions as an agricultural and industrial productive force. The corps has an estimated 2.5 million personnel, of which 100,000 are reportedly organized into a militia force. It reports jointly to the PRC central government and the government of the Xinjiang Autonomous Region and is not included in the official PLA manpower count.

Even though the expansion of the Ministry of Public Security, the Ministry of State Security, the PAP, and other specialized forces has left the PLA with a more limited domestic security role than it had in the Mao era, the internal security mission remains sufficiently important and wide ranging to constitute a "domestic drag" that constrains the military from further reducing manpower and to decrease the energy and resources it can devote to its technologically more demanding missions beyond China's borders.

THE SECOND MISSION: TERRITORIAL DEFENSE

The PLA's second mission is to protect national territory from foreign challenge. Because of the length and contested nature of China's borders and its formidable array of potential enemies, this mission is complex. It has taken three forms: deterring or defeating a foreign attack or invasion; preemptively striking at forces on the other side of the border that seem poised to attack PRC territory; and upholding China's position with respect to territory that the PRC claims but does not control.

First, during the Cold War the PLA had to be prepared to deal with potential attacks or invasions, even though in the end they did not occur. On at least four occasions, such attacks seemed possible. During the Korean War, Beijing feared nuclear or conventional attack by U.S. forces. Then, in the Taiwan Strait crisis of 1958, China faced Matador surface-to-surface missiles capable of carrying nuclear warheads, which the U.S. had shipped to Taiwan the previous year. During the Vietnam War, the U.S. Air Force made regular incursions into Chinese airspace, with an ever-present possibility of further escalation. Most threatening of all was the possibility of a large-scale Soviet invasion of Northeast or North China in the 1960s (chapter 2).

Any of these attacks would have been hard to resist if they had materialized. The Americans had a large air force and strategic nuclear weapons; the Soviets had tank forces and both strategic and tactical nuclear weapons. The backward Chinese forces had no way to stop such forces at the border. Instead, Mao's strategy of a People's War spoke bravely of making advantages out of China's weaknesses—low technology, high population, large territory, peasant masses, undereducated officer corps, poor internal communications and transport, and lack of allies. Despite the rhetoric, it is doubtful that Mao regarded these weaknesses as ideal strengths; they were simply the resources he had to work with. He may even have exaggerated the likelihood and scale of a possible invasion to keep domestic political tensions high in support of his project of continuous internal revolution and to justify the militarization of the economy and society. In any case, his strategy did help to deter any possible American and Soviet attacks or invasions. Both superpowers were afraid of getting bogged down in a country so large and ungovernable and with a reputation for "absorbing conquerors."

With the end of the Cold War, the risk of attack diminished, but the defense-in-depth mission continues to occupy an important place on the PLA's agenda. The potential future enemy—most likely the U.S. reacting to a PRC assault on Taiwan, but in the longer run possibly Japan, India, or even Russia in some future scenario—is considered less likely to invade with ground troops and more likely to use air power to strike air and naval bases, missile sites, and other targets deep within Chinese territory. The military regions accordingly give great attention to training in the use of anti-aircraft artillery and developing integrated air defenses. Through a nationwide system of National Defense Mobilization Commissions, established in 1994, local governments and their counterparts in the military regions coordinate the militia with PAP and PLA forces in training to resist attack or invasion.

Second, China has on four occasions tried to prevent the anticipated invasion of territory it controlled by striking at an enemy just beyond its borders. These wars have taken place on land and, thanks to Chinese pre-emption, have taken place on a neighbor's territory or on contested land controlled by the other side rather than on the Chinese side. The first such case occurred when U.S. forces were moving northward on the Korean Peninsula toward the Chinese border in late 1950. Beijing did not wait to find out if the American forces would cross the border and so launched a preventive attack across the Yalu River. In 1962, China fought a border war with India that was triggered by Indian probes on contested territory held by China; Chinese forces attacked Indian-held territory, then pulled back to the original line of control. In 1969, China fought a series of border clashes with Soviet troops. In the first engagement, orchestrated by Beijing, Chinese forces ambushed Soviet troops. By acting in a provocative yet measured manner, China sought to signal to the Soviet Union its readiness to fight despite its relative military weakness and the political upheaval of the Cultural Revolution.[15] In 1979, China sent forces into Vietnam, partly in response to a series of clashes along the two countries' disputed border, although the invasion also had other purposes (chapter 6).

All four episodes required projecting conventional land forces over short distances. The terrain was rugged and remote and was not conducive to campaigns employing armor formations or large-scale maneuvers. The Chinese displayed little in the way of mechanization, no naval dimension and, with the exception of Korea, no use of airpower. Chinese tactics were characteristic of early- to mid-twentieth-century land warfare: infantry massed at the point of attack, with concentrated artillery support where available, utilizing stealth and the element of surprise to gain the advantage.

Today, the possibility of challenges to Chinese land borders have been reduced but not eliminated. Relations between Beijing and New Delhi have thawed, and confidence-building measures have lowered tensions. But their territorial disputes remain unresolved (chapter 6), and border incidents occur periodically.[16] China is sensitive over its border with North Korea, which has been extremely porous in recent years. China and North Korea are unlikely to clash over border issues as long as they remain allies, but tensions may rise if relations fray. And Beijing must stand ready to conduct at least a limited military intervention into North Korea should it become necessary to do so to protect China's interests if the Pyongyang regime collapses.

Other land borders must also be protected against infiltrators and refugees, including those with the three Central Asian states that adjoin Xinjiang and with Burma and Laos. Primary responsibility for border security in peacetime lies with the Ministry of Public Security and the PAP, but the PLA plays an important support role. Each military region must maintain the capability to deal with more serious contingencies by responding either defensively or preemptively. Limited interventions in countries around China's periphery are conceivable if core interests—such as the safety of Chinese citizens or access to energy resources—come under threat. It is for these reasons that confidence-building measures with SCO members have not required the elimination of forces near the borders, only pullbacks.

The third dimension of the military's territorial protection mission requires it to assert or enforce PRC claims over disputed territories. The first example of such a mission was the invasion of Tibet in 1951, which established control over a large and strategically crucial piece of territory over which the PRC claimed sovereignty.

The other cases of protecting territorial claims have taken place at sea. The primary example is the buildup of a capability to coerce or conquer Taiwan, which we discuss in the next section. Another important priority has been to push back against what China believes are illegitimate incursions by U.S. Navy and Air Force craft into its territorial waters. The PRC takes the position that the UNCLOS forbids another power to conduct military surveillance anywhere within China's 200-nautical-mile EEZ or along its continental shelf, which according to Beijing extends all the way west past Okinawa. The U.S., which has not ratified the convention but says it observes its provisions, holds that the convention gives it the broad freedom to conduct surveillance operations throughout these same waters.[17] This disagreement has generated frequent episodes of friction and occasional confrontations. In two of many examples, a Chinese fighter jet collided with an American EP-3 surveillance plane flying some 75 miles away from the Chinese coast in 2001, leading to the death of the Chinese pilot and an emergency landing of the American aircraft on Hainan Island; and a PLA Navy submarine surfaced dangerously close to the aircraft carrier USS *Kitty Hawk* in 2006.

The mission of enforcing maritime territorial claims is undertaken not just by the PLA Navy, but by an array of other entities, including the Coast Guard, the State Fisheries Administration, the State Oceanographic Administration, and the Marine Surveillance Service (sometimes aided as well by commercial vessels that may be under PLA Navy command). In order to assert Chinese claims, Chinese maritime forces clashed with Vietnamese forces in 1974 and 1988, confronted Filipino forces in the 1990s, conducted maneuvers in the vicinity of the Senkaku Islands in the 1990s and the 2000s, and conducted a range of operations in the South China Sea in the early 2000s. On many occasions, Chinese ships threatened or clashed with Japanese, Vietnamese, and Filipino naval or commercial vessels. China was not the only state to behave this way: the maritime services of other countries engaged in similar behavior toward the ships of other claimant states. But it was the state with the widest claims and the one with the largest set of maritime security forces among regional states.

China's behavior toward its territorial claims has been assertive but not expansionist. In light of the fact that the Qing dynasty covered a much larger sweep of territory than the PRC does today, Beijing could potentially lodge claims to irredenta throughout the Russian Far East, Central Asia, Korea, and Southeast Asia, but it has not done so. To be sure, it took maximum advantage of the newly enacted UNCLOS, which came into force in 1994, to lodge sometimes implausibly expansive claims in all its surrounding seas, but it was not alone in this way of interpreting the UNCLOS. Some see signs of Chinese expansionism in the new Chinese historiography on the ancient state of Koguryo in what is now Korea (chapter 5). But it is unlikely that Beijing is using this body of historical writing to build a case for a territorial claim. To lodge new claims against Korea or any other neighboring state would be inconsistent with China's larger strategy of trying to stabilize its borders and reassure its neighbors.

THE SECOND MISSION, CONTINUED: TAIWAN

Within the second mission of protecting national territory, the PLA's most important task is to prepare to enforce China's claim to Taiwan in case the government's long-term peaceful strategy fails to work. Until the Taiwan problem is resolved, the PLA considers Taiwan its primary war-fighting scenario. Preparation for this task has absorbed the lion's share of the military modernization effort since the mid-1990s.

Starting in 1950, when the U.S. interposed its forces in the Taiwan Strait, Chinese strategy toward Taiwan had been nonmilitary in emphasis. The two Taiwan Strait crises in 1954–1955 and 1958 were not attempts to take the island, but efforts to signal Beijing's determination not to abandon its claim to sovereignty. But the third Taiwan Strait crisis in 1995–1996 persuaded Chinese leaders that they needed a military option in case political trends in Taipei and Washington continued to move against them (chapter 9). This determination was expressed in Article 8 of the 2005 Antisecession Law, which stated, "In the event that the 'Taiwan independence' secessionist forces should act under any name or by any means to cause the fact of Taiwan's secession from China or that major incidents entailing Taiwan's secession from China should occur or that possibilities for a peaceful reunification should be completely exhausted, the state shall employ nonpeaceful means and other necessary measures to protect China's sovereignty and territorial integrity." The PLA was charged with preparing for this task.

The challenge is daunting. The first obstacle is posed by geography: Taiwan is an island, and therefore the relatively straightforward option of overland invasion is not available. Winning control of the air, securing sea access across the turbulent 100-mile-wide Taiwan Strait—which is characterized by idiosyncratic tides and frequent bad weather—not to mention conducting amphibious landings on Taiwan's rocky shores are all significant operational challenges.

Second, the PLA would face the resistance of ROC forces. Despite personnel reductions, Taiwan's military remains one of the twenty largest armed forces in the world, with some 270,000 active-duty troops and a defense budget of some $10 billion. It is defended against missile attack with several hundred sophisticated, U.S.-built PAC-2 and PAC-3 surface-to-air missiles. To protect Taiwanese air space it possesses more than 50 French Mirage fighter jets, approximately 150 U.S. F-16s, and 130 Indigenous Defense Fighters. The navy continues to develop more advanced versions of its own Hsiung-Feng III antiship missile and to acquire from the U.S. electronic warfare and early-warning/reconnaissance planes. The ROC Navy possesses a modest but capable force of U.S. and French-built destroyers (4) and frigates (22), missile boats (61), and a handful of diesel submarines.

In the 2000s, adverse domestic and international trends weakened ROC preparedness. At home, the KMT-dominated legislature refused to pass an arms budget submitted by the DPP administration. Abroad, PRC pressure on the U.S., France, and other suppliers reduced their willingness to supply advanced arms to Taiwan. At the same time, ironically, many in Taiwan felt a diminished sense of threat, which undercut public support for more robust self-defense efforts, as reflected in a substantial decline in the level of Taiwan's defense spending—more than 50 percent between 1993 and 2005 when adjusted for inflation. The sense of security is grounded in the assumptions either that China is all bark and no bite or that if China does attack, the U.S. will come to the rescue. U.S. military experts have criticized the Taiwan leadership for lacking a clear defense strategy and the military for lax training and weak attention to professionalism.[18]

Since 2008, under the Ma Ying-jeou administration, the ROC government has pursued both a more conciliatory approach toward China and a "hard ROC" defense policy. Although problems remain in Taiwan's preparedness—difficulties in acquiring desired weapons systems, the transition from a conscripted to an all-volunteer force, and the continuing vulnerability of key facilities—the ROC can be expected to impose high costs on an attacking Chinese military.

Third, the PLA expects to have to deal with an American intervention, which despite a U.S. policy of "strategic ambiguity," is understood by most Washington decision makers to be mandated by the 1979 TRA and other policy statements. At a minimum, this intervention would presumably include the dispatch of aircraft carrier strike groups and aircraft from U.S. bases in the Asia-Pacific to repel an attack on Taiwan. Nor can the PLA overlook the possibility of significant escalation of such a battle beyond the confines of the Taiwan Strait to a wider conflagration that involves parts of the mainland or embroils neighboring countries allied with the U.S. or both.

Facing these obstacles, the PLA has prepared itself to use a mixture of elements from four generic strategic options if it has to attack Taiwan.[19]

Blockade. The PRC might declare that Taiwan is in a state of rebellion and thus might exercise the right it claims as the sovereign power to forbid all air and sea transport to and from the island. Simply announcing a blockade or quarantine around the island would have a major psychological impact, potentially resulting in a massive outflow of capital and a plunge in the Taipei stock market. To make a blockade threat credible, the PLA's most potent assets are its missiles and submarines, which would remain largely unseen but very threatening. China could mine Taiwan's major ports of Kaohsiung, Keelung, Tsoying, and Suao or otherwise bottle up military and commercial vessels in these ports with relative ease. Such a move would require only modest actions by China and incur no immediate casualties on either side. With luck, it might produce quick and easy victory.

However, a blockade might stiffen the Taiwan population's resistance and degenerate into a protracted test of wills across the strait. During this interval, the Taiwan air force and navy might attack the blockade forces or escort planes and ships across the blockade lines, daring the PLA to inflict the first casualties and incur global condemnation that would undo years of diplomatic effort to reassure China's neighbors of its benevolent intentions. If the crisis were to drag on for more than a few days, the Americans would almost certainly enter the fray. The PLA would then have to use its electronic warfare capabilities, antiship missiles, and submarines to attack the U.S. aircraft carrier strike groups, thus courting escalation in the possible form of American attacks on missile and air bases on the mainland. If Taiwan resistance and U.S. involvement defeated the embargo, China would face the difficult decision of whether to back down or escalate.

Missile attacks. To reduce these risks, the PLA might precede a blockade with a series of missile strikes on Taiwan, using the more than one thousand short-range missiles it has put in place in various locations in the Nanjing MR across the strait. The missiles are conventional tipped; a nuclear attack on the island would incur more damage to the island, to China's reputation, and to the mainland itself than it would be worth militarily. The missiles would presumably be targeted at airfields, naval bases, and infrastructure facilities. Despite Taiwan's missile defense capabilities, the sheer volume of missiles the Second Artillery might rain down on the island would almost certainly overwhelm them. Precision missile attacks on a dozen or so runways might ground the ROC air force (unless runways can be rapidly repaired) and destroy navy vessels at anchor before they have a chance to move and, by destroying infrastructure, demoralize the Taiwan leadership and population enough to bring surrender. The only fully effective American response would be an attack on the missile batteries on Chinese territory, which would be an act of war that the Americans might be reluctant to undertake. If U.S. military support were not able to arrive swiftly, Taiwan's will and capability to fight might rapidly erode. And if China were to gain rapid control of the air, this action could pave the way for an amphibious invasion.

However, PRC missile attacks might stiffen the resistance of people in Taiwan, create a strong international reaction, and give the U.S. Air Force and Navy reinforcements time to arrive. These reactions might consolidate Taiwan's will to resist and generate international support for Taiwan independence. The ultimate outcome might be defeat for the PRC.

Amphibious landing. If a blockade or missile attack did not produce surrender, the PLA would face the prospect of launching an amphibious invasion of Taiwan. China is developing this capability, acquiring appropriate equipment such as fighter jets to clear the airspace and amphibious landing craft to deposit the troops, and since 1999 the PLA has conducted training in joint operations and amphibious operations. China might reduce the chances of American intervention by choosing an auspicious moment marked by tension in U.S.–Taiwan relations, a favorable atmosphere in U.S.–China relations, or American engagement in crises elsewhere. Given the civilianization of Taiwan's population and potential Taiwanese isolation, a single successful beachhead might spell a quick end to the battle.

However, amphibious operations are among the most complex in warfare, putting tremendous strain on logistics, communication, jointness of operations, and the tactical flexibility of officers in the field—all of which remain weak points of Chinese military organization. The defending side enjoys an inherent advantage because it has to mass forces only where the enemy tries to land. A failed amphibious assault might spell the permanent end of China's claim to Taiwan.

Decapitation. A fourth instrument the PLA leadership might consider— we do not know if it is doing so because planning for this option would produce little observable evidence—would be an unconventional operation targeting Taiwan's top leadership. Many senior military and security officers in Taiwan come from mainlander backgrounds, and senior officials and businesspeople have occasionally been arrested for espionage. Mainland agents have no doubt smuggled themselves onto the island over the years in the guise of students, fishermen, or spouses of local people. The increasing flow of personnel between the two sides for business, tourism, and study since the 1980s must have helped the PRC enlarge its network of agents on the island. These forces might mount an attack on the ROC's top leadership and take over the island at low cost, with minimal casualties, and with little or no damage to Taiwan's infrastructure.[20]

Of course, such operations almost never go according to plan. The cost of trying and failing might be diminished by denying any connection with the plotters, but there is a high risk that such denials would be proven to be false. It is unknown whether the PLA and their civilian superiors think such an option is worth planning for.

Although the PLA is likely preparing for at least the first three of these four options, this does not mean that Chinese soldiers are eager to implement any of them. Any combination of the four military strategies presents not only tremendous military difficulties, but grave political risks, including those of turning the Taiwan public irrevocably against any form of unification with the mainland, spurring a U.S. shift to a policy tilted more to containment than engagement, contributing to the remilitarization of Japan, driving most of Southeast Asia into the arms of the U.S., and putting India decisively on its guard against China. Policymakers still prefer and indeed expect the political, diplomatic, and economic prongs of their strategy to work. For the time being, the military options serve more as supports for the other three prongs than as operational intentions.

Yet these options are not empty threats. According to some analysts, a shift has taken place in the balance of military power across the strait because ROC preparedness has not kept up with the growth of the Chinese military. Although the U.S. military claims to be ready, the cost of intervention to the U.S. has undeniably gotten higher. The PLA has the capability, if not to defeat the U.S., then at least to put its carrier strike groups and other assets seriously at risk—in the words of Thomas Christensen, to "[pose] problems without catching up."[21]

Moreover, Beijing is convinced that it enjoys an asymmetry of motivation over the U.S. with respect to Taiwan. China has passed a tipping point in its ability to ensure that there is no low-cost option for the U.S. to intervene in a Taiwan military confrontation. And it may be nearing a second tipping point—the ability to use military action to create an irreversible momentum before the U.S. can get to the fight. By raising the cost of a potential conflict to both Taiwan and the U.S., the PLA adds to the credibility of its preferred strategy to win control over Taiwan peacefully.

THE THIRD MISSION: NUCLEAR DETERRENCE

China has developed a small but capable nuclear-tipped ICBM force whose sole function appears to be to deter nuclear attack, most prominently by the U.S., but potentially by India, Russia (if relations were to sour), or Japan or Taiwan (if either were to develop a nuclear option). All of China's effective nuclear arsenal is land based; as of 2012, the two classes of submarines that might theoretically be used to launch ICBMs do not appear operational.

Mao made the decision to go nuclear with Soviet help in 1955. After the Soviet Union reneged on its promise to provide plans and technology, he launched a project for self-sufficient development of the bomb. The first Chinese atomic bomb test took place in 1964; China demonstrated the capability to launch the bomb on a missile a few years later.[22] Mao's nuclear strategy was unclear, probably even to him. Nuclear weapons were a symbol of determination, a mark of national prestige, and in these ways a (relatively) cheap substitute for military modernization. But the small arsenal was not much of a deterrent to superpower attack. Indeed, it functioned more as an inducement to attack. Both the Americans (in 1963) and the Soviets (in 1969) gave serious consideration to bombing the Chinese nuclear weapons program at Lop Nor in Xinjiang to block its further development. Had such an attack taken place, it is unknown whether China had developed a second-strike capability against the Soviet Union. It certainly did not have one against the U.S.

By 1981, China had developed the capability for an ICBM strike against the continental U.S. By the early twenty-first century, it possessed an estimated forty ICBMs capable of reaching U.S. territory. The number has remained relatively stable for some time, suggesting that China does not seek to expand the size of its ICBM arsenal, but it is moving forward to harden silos, to use solid fuel, which provides quicker launch times, as well as to build entirely new types of ICBMs capable of being mounted on mobile launchers, with improved guidance, and smaller warheads. Once the PLA Navy's upgraded strategic nuclear submarine force is operational, as many as five Jin-class nuclear submarines will enhance the country's second-strike capability.

Although the deterrent intent is clear, Beijing's calculus of deterrence is not. The PRC has never produced an official articulation of its nuclear doctrine. The most accepted view among outside analysts is that it intends to exert what is called "minimum deterrence"—that is, to mount a force just large and survivable enough to prevent a better-armed power from initiating a nuclear attack.[23] But others argue that China seeks to create what is called a "limited deterrent," one that is large enough to deter the launch or escalation of war in any form—not only nuclear—by an adversary. For example, limited deterrence might prevent the U.S. from entering a war in the Taiwan Strait. There is also, in theory, the potential for nuclear weapons to be used for actual war fighting in Korea or Taiwan or as "coercive diplomacy" against India or even the U.S., but these possibilities seem remote. China officially adheres to a no-first-use pledge. Although there is debate within the Chinese military establishment about the merits of this approach and whether it should be reinterpreted, the pledge costs China nothing and promotes a positive image.

China has long opposed any U.S. defense program that threatens to undermine its nuclear second-strike capability. Beijing's reliance on a relatively small nuclear arsenal and missile force helps explain its consistent opposition over the years to the Strategic Defense Initiative ("Star Wars") launched by Ronald Reagan and to its successors, "national missile defense" and "theater missile defense." Any of these programs potentially threatens the deterrent function of China's strategic force against the U.S. China is also concerned that enhanced missile defense for Japan, even if justified on the basis of a North Korean ballistic missile threat to that country, erodes Beijing's capability to hold at risk American targets in Japan. Finally, China worries that a theater missile defense deployed in Japan with American cooperation might be used to defend Taiwan from missile attack. Such considerations help explain why in 1999 China proposed a "prevention of an arms race in outer space" treaty that would ban the weaponization of space.

Proliferation: A road not taken. In theory, Beijing might also make strategic use of its missiles and nuclear weapons by proliferating such technologies to countries or nonstate actors that are unfriendly to Washington, but it does not seem to be doing so. The export of missile and nuclear weapons technology and sometimes of the weapons themselves did play a role in Chinese foreign policy from the 1970s through the 1990s. However, the motives appear to have been a mix of regional power politics (strengthening Pakistan against China's rival India by aiding its nuclear weapons program), diplomatic bridge building (consolidating friendships with North Korea by selling missiles, with Iran by selling dual-use nuclear technology and antiship missiles, and with Saudi Arabia by selling intermediate-range ballistic missiles), and commercial profit (by selling a nuclear reactor to Algeria and attempting to sell short-range ballistic missiles to Syria). Some of China's nuclear technology transfers to North Korea and other states may have passed through a network run by Pakistani nuclear official Abdul Qadeer Khan without Chinese knowledge.

Instead of developing these relationships into a proliferation strategy, China has acceded step by step to the bulk of the international arms control and disarmament regime and has complied in large part, although not perfectly, with its obligations. Starting in the 1970s, the U.S. began to bring pressure to bear on China to stop proliferating nuclear and missile technology. To respond to these pressures, China developed a cadre of experts in the complex area of arms control and nonproliferation. Presumably under these experts' advice, China began attending the UN Conference on Disarmament in 1979 and officially joined the following year. In

1995, China issued its first white paper on arms control and disarmament and subsequently included pronouncements on nonproliferation in its biannual defense white paper. In 1997, the Ministry of Foreign Affairs created the new Department of Arms Control and Disarmament. In 1984, Beijing signed the Biological Weapons Convention; in 1992 the NPT; in 1993 the Chemical Weapons Convention; and in 1996 the Comprehensive Test Ban Treaty. In 1994, China tightened its commitment to observe the Missile Technology Control Regime guidelines that forbid the export of middle-range missiles. In 1996, it promised to restrict nuclear cooperation with Pakistan, and in 1997 it promised not to initiate any new nuclear-cooperation efforts with Iran. In 1997–1998, it established a series of domestic regulations to tighten its control over its exports of nuclear materials and joined the Zangger Committee, whose member states agree to strict controls on nuclear exports.

By the turn of the century, China had acceded to all the main arms control treaties.[24] Its policy can be attributed to several reinforcing motivations. First, Beijing needed to accommodate U.S. arms control demands in order to achieve its goals in Washington, including renewal of most-favored-nation trading status, a lifting of the U.S. ban on nuclear power plant exports to China, and a lifting of post-Tiananmen sanctions on technology transfer and diplomatic summits with China. Second, China benefited from an international ban on certain weapons that it did not want to use or to see used, such as chemical and biological agents. Third, China recognized the benefit of gaining a place at the table in international arms control negotiations and saw that positions in favor of nonproliferation and disarmament strengthened its rhetorical position as an advocate of peace and nonintervention. Fourth, as China's interests in the Middle East and other distant regions of the world intensified, Beijing began to appreciate the danger to its own interests of regional destabilization. Finally, it came to see that arms control and arms reduction agreements might help constrain Washington's technological edge in areas such as outer space, make it harder for rival states such as India to develop weapons systems that China already possessed, and encourage the states with the biggest nuclear arsenals, Russia and the U.S., to reduce them to sizes closer to that of China's own arsenal.

As late as the 2000s, the U.S. imposed sanctions dozens of times on Chinese companies, including state-owned enterprises, for proliferation transgressions, most often involving the sale of nuclear and missile technology to Pakistan and Iran. China's role in enabling North Korean proliferation is ambiguous: Beijing seems to permit Pyongyang's ballistic missile shipments to other countries to transit Chinese territory. Despite these problems, China appears to have strengthened its system of export controls and made progress in complying with its obligations under the various arms control regimes, particularly regarding nuclear technology and material.[25]

THE FOURTH MISSION: BEYOND TAIWAN

If and when the Taiwan issue is settled, China's military position will look very different.[26] China will possess whatever remains of the impressive military capabilities created for the battle over Taiwan. The primary obstacle to the projection of naval and air power south and east from the mainland will be gone. Depending on the nature of its arrangement with the Taiwan authorities, the PLA may be able to use Taiwan's ports and airfields to extend the reach of its navy and air force 200 miles farther out into the western Pacific. The PLA might be able to cooperate with—or even absorb—the ROC's armed forces, including its fighter planes and pilots, antiship and other missiles, frigates, and advanced communications technology. In all, as PRC strategists would see it, the American policy that intentionally or not had done the most to contain China militarily for many decades would at this point come to an end.

How China uses this opportunity will be influenced by the way in which the Taiwan problem is settled. If it is settled by force, many PLA and Taiwan assets will be destroyed. China's neighbors and the U.S. will likely view China as dangerous and will come together more strongly to resist Beijing's next moves. If the Taiwan question is settled peacefully by negotiation—the outcome that PRC strategy aims for—the PLA assets that were built up for the attack on Taiwan will be fully available, and China's neighbors and the U.S. are likely to accept the leap forward in China's strategic position as inevitable and legitimate.

Because China's security needs are so large, there are many ways that China's future leaders can construct the fourth mission. There have already been some signs of what shape it might take.

First, the PLA has already begun to give attention to non-war-fighting tasks beyond its borders that produce political influence and foster goodwill. For these operations, it has adopted the name "Military Operations

Other Than War" (MOOTW), coined by the U.S. military, but has interpreted the concept even more broadly than the U.S. does to encompass significant domestic duties consistent with PLA traditions. With the lessening of tensions in the Taiwan Strait since 2008, military leaders have seized upon this concept as a means of reminding the CCP and the Chinese citizenry of the PLA's central place in China's rise. The MOOTW concept helps to justify continued sizeable defense outlays even as the likelihood of war has decreased, promotes a positive image for the PLA to counter foreign perceptions of a growing Chinese military threat, contributes to dealing with nontraditional security threats, and provides valuable peacetime operational experience.[27]

Second, China may decide that it needs to use force to influence the distribution of power in neighboring regions. It has already done so once in its history, when it invaded Vietnam in 1979. This attack had a second-mission purpose: it was in part a response to Vietnamese probes along the two countries' contested border. But it also had a fourth-mission purpose: to frustrate what China saw as a developing Soviet encirclement. Future Chinese leaders may want to undertake similar ventures in various places around the country's periphery. For example, unrest, civil war, or state failure in Korea, Burma, or Central Asia may draw China in to evacuate its citizens, protect its investments in oil fields or gas pipelines deemed vital to national security, prevent flows of refugees, or stabilize local regimes. Or the PRC might intervene to prevent another major power—the U.S., India, or Russia—from taking advantage of a crisis or change of government somewhere on China's periphery.

Third, China might want to intervene farther away, in the Fourth Ring, to protect economic interests and concentrations of personnel. Since 1992, China has deployed more than 17,000 personnel to participate in nineteen peacekeeping missions around the world (chapter 7). Although these units are small, they have developed some initial expertise in operating at great distances from the homeland. In 2006, the Foreign Ministry chartered four aircraft to pick up some four hundred PRC citizens and Hong Kong compatriots stranded in the Solomon Islands by civil unrest. In 2009, China deployed two destroyers and a supply ship to participate in a multinational mission to protect Chinese and other countries' oil tankers and other merchant shipping as they entered and exited the Gulf of Aden. In 2011, it used several PLA Air Force transports as well as dozens of chartered commercial aircraft and ships to evacuate some thirty thousand Chinese construction workers from strife-torn Libya. All these missions were modest in scope and limited to the protection of economic interests and personnel. But as China's investments increase in the Fourth Ring, there may be more locations where such missions become necessary, and if relevant PLA assets are available, they may be put to use.

Fourth, China's energy imports and the rest of its foreign trade depend on sea lanes that reach to China all the way from the Middle East and the coast of Africa to the west and the North and South American coasts to the east. Most vulnerable to disruption—as well as closest to China—are the Straits of Malacca, Sunda, and Lombok, through which all traffic from the west must enter the South China Sea. Of course, ships might circumnavigate this body of water, but travel time would be lengthened by many days. For its sea-lane security, China depends on the U.S. Navy, aided by the maritime services of the littoral states (Indonesia, Malaysia, and Singapore) and Australia. The PLA Navy might provide assistance to the littoral states in their security operations if it were invited to do so. Passing across the Indian Ocean, Chinese shipping depends on the U.S. and Indian navies for protection. It would not be realistic for China to replace these other navies, but Chinese policymakers may see reasons to try to play a role in the protection of their own routes of commerce, as they are doing in the antipiracy mission in the Gulf of Aden. The Chinese navy might increase its influence in the Indian Ocean by using what are now purely commercial ports that China is building in Kyaukphyu in Burma, Hambantota in Sri Lanka, and Gwadar in Pakistan (chapter 6)—a series of facilities that U.S. analysts have labeled the "string of pearls."[28]

But none of these "pearls" compares in magnitude or sophistication to the U.S. military base maintained on the Indian Ocean island of Diego Garcia, nor are they nearly as numerous as the ports to which the U.S. Navy has access throughout the Middle East, South Asia, and Southeast Asia.

Fifth, the Chinese navy may seek to expand its reach into the western Pacific and beyond. A grand strategic vision along these lines was articulated in 1982 by the then commander of the PLA Navy, Admiral Liu Huaqing. In a first phase, by 2000, he suggested, the PLA Navy would extend its area of operations in the near seas to reach the "First Island Chain," comprising the Kuril Islands, Japan, the Ryukyus, Taiwan, the Philippines, Borneo, and Natuna Besar. In the second phase, by 2020, the PLA Navy would extend its operational reach to the "Second Island Chain," reaching beyond the First Island Chain to the Bonins, the Marianas, and the Carolines. Finally, by 2050, China would become a global sea power on a par with the U.S. Navy. Liu insisted that the goals of this strategy were defensive, to protect China from coastal attack and to defend its maritime territorial claims. To date, the PLA Navy's activities and actual presence beyond the East China and South China seas have been in keeping with the timeline Liu projected. For the foreseeable future, military power projection into the Pacific will likely entail a largely symbolic presence — showing the flag through periodic port visits and humanitarian assistance on modest scale.

Nothing in publicly articulated PLA doctrine gives a clear answer to the question of what the fourth mission will be. The U.S. has long urged China to be more transparent on this point. U.S. defense secretary Donald Rumsfeld famously challenged the Chinese on this point in 2005 by asking, "Since no nation threatens China, one must wonder: Why this growing investment? Why these continuing large and expanding arms purchases? Why this continuing robust deployment?"[29] Since 1998, Beijing has produced biannual defense white papers designed in part to answer its neighbors' concerns about the future mission. But they do not provide complete answers. It is probably too early for Chinese leaders themselves to know what kind of fourth mission will be most necessary — and most feasible — for the PLA to perform.

CHINESE MILITARY MODERNIZATION IN PERSPECTIVE

The evolution of the PLA's fourth mission will not take place in a vacuum. Other militaries in the region are also improving technology, increasing capabilities, upgrading training, and adjusting strategies. Although no single one of them can stand up to China alone, in the aggregate they present formidable challenges to Chinese power. Japan stands out as a country that has quietly developed a suite of cutting-edge space technologies — rockets, satellites, and spacecraft — that were originally designed for commercial applications but did not make money and moved under military sponsorship. In addition to ballistic missile defense capabilities developed in cooperation with the U.S., Japan is working on reusable launch vehicles (i.e., space planes); multifunctional satellites that provide missile early warning and help with navigation, communication, and targeting; warhead-reentry technologies that can advance the use of missiles in warfare; unmanned aerial vehicles; and technologies for space situational awareness that show concern for possible future conflict in space.[30] South Korea is modernizing its military, including its navy, and starting to focus its efforts beyond the North Korea threat. India is upgrading its navy and its military satellite capabilities, although most of its defense efforts are focused on dealing with Pakistan. Vietnam and other ASEAN states are improving their militaries. The littoral states around the Straits of Malacca, Sunda, and Lombok are building up their navies, reluctant to concede to outsiders too much responsibility for security along their own shores.

Above all, the U.S. continues to improve its capabilities in the region despite the strain imposed by operations elsewhere in the world. During a 2011 visit to East Asia, Secretary of Defense Leon Panetta assured U.S. allies that even after a decade of war in Afghanistan and Iraq, the U.S. "will always maintain a strong presence in the Pacific." Also in 2011, President Barack Obama made even stronger assurances during a visit to Australia, insisting that the U.S. was a "Pacific power and we are here to stay." He backed the rhetoric with the announcement of an agreement to rotate U.S. marines in northern Australia for training and exercises. According to the 2010 *Quadrennial Defense Review*, U.S. defense posture in the Asia-Pacific and elsewhere will remain "forward stationed and [with] rotationally deployed forces, capabilities and equipment; supporting network of infrastructure and facilities; a series of treaty, access, transit, and status-protection agreements and arrangements with allies and key partners." Budget cuts announced in 2012 were designed in such a way as to avoid weakening the U.S. posture in Asia.[31]

Equally important are the innovations coming on line in U.S. doctrine and technology. They include the concept of AirSea Battle, which integrates air and naval capabilities throughout the operational arenas of air, sea, land, space, and cyberspace and appears particularly appropriate for the Asia-Pacific region, and the use of unmanned-aircraft systems, which have proved their worth in operations against terrorists in the Iraq and Afghanistan/Pakistan theaters. These systems significantly enhance the accuracy and expand the reach of U.S. intelligence, surveillance, reconnaissance, and strike capabilities.

In effect, the Asia-Pacific is experiencing a permanent, almost routinized, multilateral arms race. In the Fourth Ring as well, the U.S. maintains a formidable presence, European powers cultivate a presence in their traditional colonies, and newly rising powers continue to build their military strength, among them Turkey, Brazil, Saudi Arabia, and Iran. In this environment of change, episodes of friction among militaries will continue to occur, and shifts will take place in the relative balance of power in various theaters. But China, for all its growing military strength, will not be able to expel other major militaries either from its own region or from regions farther away, except if other nations pull back from their own programs of military development.

Nor will the PLA's first three missions disappear. Domestic security will continue to absorb a significant part of the PLA's effort, and the army will accordingly continue to be deployed overwhelmingly within China's borders. Protection of national territory from invasion and of territorial claims from erosion will remain high on the military's task list. Nuclear deterrence will remain a priority. The fourth mission, whatever it may be, is more likely to focus on areas closer to China's periphery and less likely to develop in a major way in more distant theaters. Even as Chinese military power grows, it is tied down by many nearby challenges. It cannot mount a challenge of geostrategic proportions to the militaries of major rivals unless those rivals make their own decisions to yield.

12

SOFT POWER AND HUMAN RIGHTS IN CHINESE FOREIGN POLICY

China's growing economic and military clout and its skillful rollout of a reassurance strategy in the surrounding regions brought Beijing a surge of "soft power"—that is, the ability to exert influence beyond what a country wields through the use of force and money because of the appeal of its cultural values, its ideas, and the perceived success of its way of doing things.[1] Soft power is a valuable resource in foreign policy because it helps a country gain cooperation from other actors in the international system at low cost. Others may even follow its lead without being asked.

In the first years after the end of the Cold War, the advantages of soft power accrued exclusively to the democratic West, especially to the U.S. with its triumphant model of liberal capitalism. But in the early 2000s, the U.S. seemed to falter, facing trouble in Iraq, Afghanistan, North Korea, Iran, and elsewhere and suffering a financial crisis that seemed to reflect the failings of its individualistic culture. China was less affected by the global economic downturn. Its economy continued to grow, and a robust, cosmopolitan consumer society that had emerged in the 1990s continued to expand. There was some social disorder, but the political system appeared stable. China's way of doing things began to look good to citizens of other countries. China stood for what some called "Asian values," meaning solidarity and cooperation among citizens at home and egalitarian respect among countries in the international system regardless of size and wealth.

Commentators labeled the Chinese model the "Beijing consensus," referring to a supposedly more dynamic, more efficient, and fairer version of capitalism than the formerly dominant "Washington consensus," which now seemed to have gotten the West and its partners into trouble.

But China has not yet surmounted one long-standing vulnerability in the battle of values and ideas: the self-inflicted wound of its pervasive violation of internationally recognized human rights. Although reform and opening brought widening personal freedoms and rising individual wealth, the government acted as if any questioning of its legitimacy might get out of hand and cause a national collapse. It met any perceived challenge to its authority with harassment, threats, beatings, and arrests. Such violations were the ugly twin of China's successful development model, described in chapter 10, for both had their roots in authoritarian one-party rule.

Mao's regime had violated human rights far more extensively than the post-Mao government did, but China in those days was too isolated for the outside world to know or do much about these violations. Once Deng Xiaoping opened China to the world, the country's domestic problems were put on global display. Unfortunately for Beijing's diplomats, this opening coincided with an expansion in the scope and activism of the international human rights system. During the late– and post–Cold War periods, new rights norms were promulgated, UN human rights institutions proliferated, and Western-based NGOs grew more active. The more China's hard power grew, the more its claims to soft power were scrutinized as these outside institutions paid greater attention to its human rights problems, generating a constant challenge to its international prestige, which Chinese diplomats scrambled to counter.

CULTIVATING SOFT POWER

Chinese diplomacy has always used soft power.[2] Beijing's authority was at first extended into what are today the Tibet, Xinjiang Uyghur, and Inner Mongolian autonomous regions by conferring upon local rulers the status of vassals of the Chinese emperor. Imperial China gained special influence in Vietnam, Korea, and Japan because these societies emulated its writing system, Confucian classics, poetry, music, clothing styles, metal-working techniques, and agricultural practices. Foreign envoys were impressed with China's greatness when they were treated with elaborate ceremony and showered with precious gifts.

Even in the 1960s, when China was most isolated, Mao Zedong insisted, "We have friends all over the world" and welcomed a stream of pro-China Communist and leftist party leaders from other countries to visit the fountainhead in Beijing. China used cultural treasures such as the Great Wall, the Forbidden City, and the tomb of the first emperor of the Qin dynasty to impress foreign visitors. Cultural artifacts such as ceramics, calligraphy, and martial arts have always enjoyed worldwide respect, and China's varied and often exotic cuisine is a widely appreciated attraction.

Foreign dignitaries invited to the Middle Kingdom were given royal treatment regardless of the size or significance of the country from which they hailed. One of the first senior American diplomats stationed in the PRC, George H. W. Bush, noted in his diary on June 29, 1975: "China's attention to . . . Third World countries is amazing. In how many big countries do they give such a great stylish welcome to chiefs of state from tiny African countries, for example. The airport is bedecked, downtown is colored [with] banners all over and big signs of welcome in French or English or whatever the language might be. Children, soldiers marching around, dancing enthusiastically, welcoming; all make an impression on the visitor."[3]

Richard Nixon's visit in 1972 triggered a China vogue in the West, with prominent journalists and celebrities writing books after two-week tours to reveal the miracles of pollution-free agriculture, incentive-free industrialization, and acupuncture anesthesia. During the period of the strategic triangle, even veteran practitioners of hard power such as Henry Kissinger and Zbigniew Brzezinski were reduced to giddiness on occasion by the wonders of China. Both confessed in their memoirs to feelings of exhilaration upon arriving there.[4]

China suffered a soft-power deficit for two decades or so after Mao's death. The tragedies of the Mao years were revealed in a genre of novels, poems, and plays called "scar literature." One of the post-Mao leaders, Hu Yaobang, said that 100 million Chinese had had their lives ruined by Mao's Cultural Revolution. In 1981, the Central Committee adopted a resolution summing up the official view that most of what Mao had done in the last ten years of his life was wrong. Pro-democracy and pro-Western ideas gained currency among liberal theorists within the CCP and were discussed by ordinary people in wall posters hung on "Democracy Wall" in late 1978 and early 1979. The mood of liberalization gave rise in 1989 to the nationwide pro-democracy movement and student hunger strike known as the "Tiananmen movement." The regime's violent crackdown on the movement left hundreds of students and workers dead. China's international prestige was at a low point.

But China's soft power in the early twenty-first century rose in conjunction with its economy, underscoring the reality that a significant accumulation of hard power is a precondition for generating appreciable soft power. When China's GDP passed Japan's in 2010 to make it the world's second-largest economy, China's leaders—and its financial officials—became global superstars, welcome everywhere. Two symbols encapsulated the country's surging prestige: the incomprehensibly huge number affixed to its foreign exchange reserves, which passed the $2 trillion mark in 2005 and has kept growing, and the eye- and ear-bursting opening ceremony of the 2008 Beijing Olympics—a grand enactment of vigor, vastness, and vaunting ambition.

Beijing's huge investment in the Olympics—larger than that of any previous host city—was part of a well-considered strategy. Chinese foreign relations experts in the early 2000s had formed the consensus that soft power was a necessary part of comprehensive national power. It would reduce the fear of China's rise and create a more welcoming environment for other forms of Chinese influence. They believed the core of China's soft power should be its culture—including traditional art, literature, philosophy, and the Chinese language—together with its contemporary image as a peace-loving nation standing for harmony at home and abroad.[5] Hu Jintao made this policy official in his report to the Seventeenth Party Congress in 2007: "In the present era, culture has become a . . . factor of growing significance in the competition in overall national strength. . . . We must . . . enhance culture as part of the soft power of our country."[6] The Central Committee reinforced the point in 2011 with a lengthy, formal decision on "deepening reform of the cultural system."[7]

The Chinese foreign ministry funded "China Year" exhibitions and activities in various countries. China sent cultural artifacts on loan to museums around the world. In 2005, Beijing permitted select treasures from the Forbidden City to be displayed in London. The opening of the exhibition was timed to coincide with a state visit by President Hu Jintao. Some of the famous terra cotta warriors normally displayed near the tomb of Emperor Qin Shihuang visited the British Museum and other locales in 2007–2010. Starting in 2004, the Ministry of Education began establishing Confucius Institutes in collaboration with foreign universities and other institutions to teach Chinese language and culture, partly with the help of teachers sent from China on temporary assignment. Reviled in Mao's China as backward and feudal, Confucius was now seen to personify Chinese values of harmony, community, and deference. Within a few years, there were some three hundred such institutes in sixty countries on five continents, including more than two dozen in the U.S., mostly at universities.

Chinese media moved into foreign markets under the combined leadership of the State Council Information Office and the Foreign Ministry's new Office of Public Diplomacy. Long-established publications such as *China Daily, Beijing Review*, and *China Pictorial* as well as similar publications in other foreign languages became glossy and professional. China Central Television, Xinhua TV, and China Radio International broadcast to the world in many languages. The official Xinhua News Agency established an office in New York City's Times Square to compete with the traditional wire services to supply news to global media. The quality of Chinese journalism was upgraded as media workers were increasingly trained at professional journalism programs in Chinese universities. Under the rubric of e-government, many agencies at the central and provincial levels and even some at lower levels established English-language Web sites alongside their Chinese-language sites. All Chinese media were still government or party owned and had to follow directives from the CCP's Propaganda Department, but their look and content were modernized and they were increasingly accepted worldwide as reliable sources of information.[8]

China's universities sought international standing and connections. In 2003, Shanghai Jiaotong University began ranking twelve hundred universities worldwide on an annual basis. The rankings gained widespread attention and spotlighted China's massive investment in its top schools. In the first year of rankings, the best Chinese universities (Peking and Tsinghua) stood tied with four dozen others around the world in ranks 201–250. By the time the 2010 rankings were announced, these two schools had risen to the 151–200 level, and five other Chinese institutions had joined the (expanded) tier of 201–300. As conditions in academia improved, foreign-trained Chinese Ph.D.s returned in large numbers to teach. Chinese institutions welcomed more than a hundred thousand foreign students a year to study the Chinese language or to take academic degrees, the majority from Asia and Africa. Foreign schools set up joint programs on Chinese campuses. The China Scholarship Council, under the Ministry of Education, began to send a couple of thousand Ph.D. students abroad each year to study for one or two semesters before returning home to teach, thus increasing the cosmopolitan character of Chinese academia.

Beijing made skillful use of sports diplomacy. South Korea had pioneered the use of sports for diplomatic purposes in Asia when it used the 1986 Asian Games and the 1988 Seoul Olympics to sprint ahead of North Korea in the rivalry for diplomatic recognition.[9] Taiwan, too, had worked hard to counter its post-1979 diplomatic isolation by participating in the Olympics starting in 1984 under the name "Chinese Taipei" (chapter 9). In 1993, Beijing applied to host the 2000 Summer Olympic Games as part of its attempt to reverse post-Tiananmen Western sanctions, but the bid was rejected at least in part because of NGO pressure over China's human rights record. In 2001, however, Beijing's second bid was successful. The unprecedentedly elaborate hosting of the 2008 Olympics sent the message around the world that China had arrived. The city leveled old neighborhoods, built five-star hotels, malls, new subway lines, and theme restaurants; trained fifteen hundred "civilized bus-riding supervisors"; appointed five thousand antijaywalking monitors; held "queuing awareness days"; and mounted campaigns against spitting and slurping. Factories were closed and traffic restricted to improve the air quality in one of the world's most polluted cities. More than one hundred heads of state and heads of government attended. The lavish opening ceremony bruited the theme of China's national unity and love of peace over its five thousand years of history, while—many observers felt—also signaling this rising power's vigor, pride, ambition, mass power, and group discipline.

Under Mao, talented athletes had gone to special schools run by the military.[10] That system was restored after the Cultural Revolution but was tarnished by a series of doping scandals in international competitions in the 1990s. By 2008, the system had been transferred to civilian authorities. But recruitment and training for international competitions remained major priorities under central-state planning. In 2008, Chinese athletes won one hundred medals, second only to the U.S., and more golds than any other country.

China was even able to export some world-class athletes, albeit with strings attached. National Basketball Association sensation Yao Ming was a product of China's state sports-development system, the country's best basketball player, and the key to China's hopes for basketball glory at the Beijing Olympics. As such, he was beholden to his club, the Shanghai Sharks, and the Chinese Basketball Association, and the decision to allow him to play in the U.S. was carefully weighed. He generated incalculable value as a goodwill ambassador for his native country. So did others, including soccer star Sun Jihai, who in the 2000s played for England's Manchester City club in the Premier League, widely regarded as the world's top soccer league.

Even the traditionally reticent PLA tapped into soft power. Breaking with a tradition of extreme secrecy, China's soldiers increased the volume of exchanges and expanded the number of bilateral and multilateral exercises in which they participated. Besides attending international conferences and symposia, the PLA began to host its own gatherings, among them a series of international conferences on Sun Zi's *Art of War* and a biannual international forum on global security issues. Another innovation was the introduction of an annual course for foreign officers and defense officials at China's National Defense University.

Additional elements of soft power came into being without the government's involvement and sometimes even against its will as indirect products of the cultural vitality that accompanied growing wealth and freedom. Chinese artists' paintings, sculpture, films, novels, and poetry drew growing audiences. The world seldom knew which artist had honored the Propaganda Department's red lines and which was a dissident: indeed, the roles changed over time. For example, the artist Ai Weiwei was engaged to help design the main Olympic stadium (the "bird's nest") for the 2008 games but in 2011 was detained for several months, ostensibly for tax evasion but actually because the government considered his artistic and political statements too challenging. Even when the message was not what the government wanted, the rising prices and growing audiences for Chinese works advanced the respectability of China as a cosmopolitan society and culture.

So, too, with the growing power of the Chinese market.[11] China's large new middle class was at first keen to wear Western clothes, drive Western cars, and eat Western fast food. But the Chinese market grew so large that Western brands began to adapt to Chinese tastes. MacDonald's added taro pie to its menu in Beijing. Kentucky Fried Chicken sold "Old Peking Style chicken rolls." Luxury car designers increased backseat legroom for owners who used drivers and incorporated jade into auto interiors. China became the world's largest market for upscale cars, platinum wedding rings, and high-end cognac. As Chinese tourists appeared in growing numbers in major cities around the world, the hospitality industry accommodated to their needs with Chinese-speaking front desk staff and some Chinese dishes in the coffee shops. Prominent architects produced cutting-edge designs for museums, airports, and other buildings in China that took advantage of low construction costs and met the local taste for a high-modern aesthetic. As China becomes the world's largest market, we can expect advertising, packaging, and design around the world increasingly to reflect the influence of Chinese consumers' taste.

Some commentators believe that the same may be true for social and political values.[12] So far, however, values remain the weak point of Chinese soft power. Unlike the U.S., China has not aspired to convince other countries to emulate its political system. Few other authoritarian countries would be able to do so in any case—they lack the key elements of a robust ruling party, a complex technocracy, and a cadre of ambitious local leaders striving to show both initiative and loyalty to the center. China's foreign relations, even with other authoritarian regimes, depend on mutual interest, not ideological affinity (chapter 7).[13] Even so, other authoritarian regimes have learned some lessons from China, such as methods of Internet control, the use of closed-circuit surveillance cameras, electronic face recognition, and the use of the legal system to limit political challenges. China's successes have undercut the once-flourishing "end of history" belief that democracy is the wave of the future and that all authoritarian systems are doomed to fail.

Despite these soft-power successes, however, China continues to find itself on the wrong side of an important set of international values and institutions—the international human rights regime—that gained growing influence during the years when China was cut off from most of the world under Mao. It was just as this cluster of international norms, institutions, and NGOs entered a phase of more assertive activity that China began its reform era under Deng Xiaoping. Even as human rights conditions in China improved, so did the flow of information to the outside world about abuses. As a result of this confluence of events, Chinese diplomats were drawn into a long battle first to confront and deflect international pressure on human rights issues and then to try to shape the international human rights regime in ways more conducive to the Chinese government's interests.

CHINA AND THE INTERNATIONAL HUMAN RIGHTS REGIME

The idea of human rights has a long history but emerged in its full modern form only with the UN General Assembly's adoption of the Universal Declaration of Human Rights (UDHR) in 1948.[14] The UDHR defined human rights as an inclusive set of norms, embodied in international law, consisting of the legitimate claims of every individual upon states and "other organs of society." Because of the Cold War, the international human rights regime at first developed slowly. Over the course of nearly three decades, the only new step the international community agreed to was the restatement in 1966 of the principles of the UDHR in the form of two international covenants. These two covenants were enacted separately, one on civil and political rights to satisfy the West and one on economic, social, and cultural rights to satisfy the socialist camp.[15]

In the mid-1970s, coinciding with the end of the Mao era in China, the international human rights regime entered a period of normative, institutional, and political expansion. The main impetus for these developments was changing state interests—especially Western states' interest to use human rights norms, first, to challenge the Soviet Union at a time when its power seemed to be increasing under Leonid Brezhnev and then, after the Cold War, to create new global institutions to help stabilize a fluid, uncertain international system of power. In addition, the rise of international human rights was stimulated by the growth of international civil society ("transnational activist networks") under conditions of globalization and by the UN's institutional interests in seeking new missions.

This renewed trajectory of growth started in 1975 with the adoption of the Helsinki Final Act, a treaty signed by a group of Western and socialist states. The treaty met the Soviet demand for recognition of the existing borders in Europe; in return, in Basket III of the agreement, the West extracted Moscow's acknowledgment of its obligation to honor human rights. The accords unexpectedly became a focus of organizing for political freedom in Czechoslovakia, Poland, Hungary, and Russia and in that way contributed to the fall of communism in Europe.[16] In 1977, Jimmy Carter took office as U.S. president and put forward the promotion of international human rights as a theme that could help restore a national sense of mission after the loss of the war in Vietnam. Each subsequent American president for his own reasons continued the crusade for human rights and democracy. Ronald Reagan used the language of rights to support his push to redress the U.S.–Soviet power balance, calling for "a global campaign for freedom . . . [that would] leave Marxism–Leninism on the ash heap of history as it has left other tyrannies which stifle the freedom and muzzle the self-expression of the people."[17] George H. W. Bush presided over humanitarian interventions in response to crises in northern Iraq and Somalia. Bill Clinton built human rights into his foreign policy and called for "democratic enlargement." George W. Bush used the name "Freedom Agenda" to describe a package of policies to promote human rights and democracy worldwide. Barack Obama declared human rights a key goal of his foreign policy.[18]

In Europe, policymakers likewise promoted human rights as part of a broader security policy. Especially in the post–Cold War period, Europe saw itself as surrounded by zones of instability in South and Central Europe, the former Soviet Union, and Africa that it could not pacify by military means. The EU developed a values-driven security policy that tried to leverage its economic and cultural—rather than military—strengths to create regional stability by enticing neighboring countries to conform to European values and helping them achieve economic growth and democratic political stability. Its 1992 Common Foreign and Security Policy identified the promotion of democracy and human rights as a pillar of its security strategy toward neighboring regions.

The EU applied the strategy to China in its 1995 Long Term Policy for China–Europe Relations, which proposed to support human rights in China through project assistance and government-to-government dialogue. The European Commission's 2006 document *EU–China: Closer Partners, Growing Responsibilities* raised a range of issues relating to human rights, religious freedom, and relations with ethnic minorities.[19] These issues were also subjects in long-running negotiations between China and the EU in the 2000s to frame a new Partnership and Cooperation Agreement.

Also starting in the mid-1970s, the U.S. and Western Europe supported the "third wave" of democratization that started in Portugal in 1974 and spread through southern Europe, Latin America, and Asia. This process increased the number of democracies in the world from 39 in 1974 to 76 in 1990. Regime transitions in Eastern Europe and the Soviet Union in 1990–1991 extended the democratization wave, which continued further with still more transitions in Africa. The peak was reached in 2006 with 121 democracies among the world's 194 states.[20]

Another development of the late– and post–Cold War periods was the expansion of the international human rights NGO movement, which began to pay attention to China just as China opened up under Deng Xiaoping. Amnesty International was founded in 1961 but issued its first report on China in 1978, criticizing the government for putting people in prison for political reasons.[21] The Helsinki Accords inspired the formation in 1975 of a New York–based group that later came to be known as Human Rights Watch, which established an Asia division in 1985. The Lawyers Committee for Human Rights (later renamed Human Rights First) was founded in 1978, and the Committee to Protect Journalists in 1981. The first overseas advocacy organization devoted exclusively to Chinese human rights problems, Human Rights in China, was founded in New York in 1989 by a group of Chinese students and scholars. Both the Tibet Information Network in the United Kingdom and the International Campaign for Tibet in Washington, D.C., were established in the late 1980s. Numerous other NGOs concerned in whole or in part with human rights issues in China continued to emerge in the following decades. They were among an estimated eleven thousand human rights organizations all over the world that had emerged by the end of the twenty-first century's first decade.[22] This growth in activism was probably attributable to the increased flow of information and the heightened sense of interdependence produced by economic globalization, which had been accelerating since in the 1970s, and by the willingness of foundations, governments, and individuals to provide financial support for groups that promoted human rights.

NGO activists pushed states to expand the international treaty system covering human rights. Until the early 1980s, the major human rights treaties besides the two covenants (the International Covenant on Civil and Political Rights and the International Covenant on Economic, Social, and Cultural Rights)[23] were those concerning genocide (1951), the status of refugees (1954), and racial discrimination (1969). But in the late– and post–Cold War periods, the roster was expanded with treaties that opened up new subject areas and posed unprecedented expectations for the behavior of states. Among the new treaties were those that dealt with the elimination of discrimination against women (1981), the elimination of religious intolerance (1981), the banning of torture (1987), the rights of children (1990), and the rights of persons with disabilities (2006). In addition, the UN adopted declarations on a range of subjects, including the right to development (1986) and the rights of indigenous peoples (2007). Each of these enactments was promoted by an international network of advocates who used various forms of reason and pressure (and made various compromises) to gain governments' sometimes grudging cooperation.

Yet another cause of the growth of the human rights regime was the increasing activism of the UN bureaucracy. The end of the Cold War stalemate liberated the UN to expand its work in the field of human rights as in other areas. In 1993, the UN created the Office of the High Commissioner for Human Rights, an office that several of the incumbents used to bring high-profile pressure to bear on various countries, including China. Secretary-General Kofi Annan (served 1997–2006) promoted the expanded use of UN peacekeeping operations in part to stop human rights abuses. The Security Council in the 1990s authorized a series of humanitarian interventions in the former Yugoslavia, Somalia, Rwanda, Sierra Leone, and East Timor.[24] The UN created the beginnings of a system of international justice, establishing the International Tribunal for the Former Yugoslavia in 1991 and the International Criminal Tribunal for Rwanda in 1994 and hosting negotiations that led to the establishment of the International Criminal Court in 2002. The UN treaty bodies—committees of experts that are charged with supervising the implementation of core human rights treaties—started for the first time in the 1990s to issue numerous "general comments" or "general recommendations," which often interpreted the provisions of international human rights law more broadly than before. Likewise, the UN "special procedures" (independent experts or working groups appointed to monitor human rights issues in certain countries or issue areas) became more active, and several of them visited or negotiated to visit China for investigations.

Concerns with China were not a primary cause of the growth of the human rights regime, but as China opened up, it attracted the attention of human rights activists and institutions.

CHINA ENGAGES

It was ironic from Beijing's point of view that China became a target of international human rights advocacy just when it had begun to rectify the worst abuses of the Maoist system. In the Mao years, Beijing had occasionally targeted other countries with human rights criticisms—South Africa, Israel, the Soviet Union—without having the spear turned against itself. Now, however, with Deng's opening, information about abuses in China— both past and present—began to flow. Western reporters were admitted to the country; Cultural Revolution victims were rehabilitated; "scar literature" and "reportage literature" revealed stories of past victims; the regime intermittently tolerated public expressions of dissent such as Democracy Wall, and it set up a system of laws and courts whose proceedings were more public than the kangaroo courts of the Mao years. China soon had its own "Sakharov," Wei Jingsheng, who along with other Chinese dissidents was adopted as a prisoner of conscience by Amnesty International. International activists applied to China their then-novel technique of "name and shame." Critical reports flowed from Amnesty International, Human Rights Watch, Western journalists, and the U.S. State Department.

As in so many other areas of international politics at the time, China responded to these pressures with a strategy of engagement—joining the human rights regime, learning its rules, complying when useful, and seeking ways to influence the regime in its own interests. Chinese diplomats took part in the UN Human Rights Commission, the Sub-Commission on

Prevention of Discrimination and Protection of Minorities, and working groups concerned with the rights of indigenous populations, human rights aspects of communications, the rights of children, the rights of migrant workers, and the issue of torture. They promoted the idea of a right to development and attended meetings to draft the international convention on the rights of persons with disabilities. The PRC signed and ratified the international conventions against genocide, mistreatment of refugees, racial discrimination, apartheid, discrimination against women, and torture. In the 1984 Sino–British Joint Declaration on Hong Kong, China agreed to allow the International Covenant on Civil and Political Rights and the International Covenant on Economic, Social, and Cultural Rights to continue in force in Hong Kong for fifty years after 1997, although China itself (like the U.S.) had not at that point acceded to the covenants. By 1991, when the PRC issued its first white paper on human rights, it had acceded to a total of seven of the twenty-five major international human rights conventions in force at that time, one more than the U.S.

At the same time, China articulated a number of theoretical positions designed to push back against what it viewed as Western use of international human rights norms to exert undue influence on its domestic affairs. Chinese strategists found that posing a contrast between Western and Chinese (or Asian) culture or values could be a conversation changer. As a symposium at the Central Party School put it, "The theory that there is one set of universal values serves the idea of the centrality of the West. Therefore, we must emphasize and strengthen the study of the differences between Eastern and Western culture."[25] In the 1980s, Beijing supported the idea of Asian values promoted by authoritarian and semiauthoritarian governments in the region, such as Singapore and Malaysia.

The thrust of the Asian-values argument is that, first, Asia can provide an alternative to the American way of life, which has been overrun by excessive individualism, creating a wave of violent crime, drugs, guns, vagrancy, and immoral behavior. The countermodel relies on the strong hand of a wise and benevolent leadership that promulgates traditional values of obedience, thrift, industriousness, respect for elders, and authority. Promoters of Asian values claim that Asians prioritize economic and social rights over civil and political rights, the community over the individual, and social order and stability over democracy and individual freedom. This argument sometimes provided a rationale for China–ASEAN cooperation against U.S. policies perceived as too assertive in the region, such as the U.S. push to sanction the military regime in Burma.

Second, Chinese spokespersons promoted an interpretation of international law and sovereignty designed to limit the reach of human rights norms. They said that because states, not individuals, are the subjects of international law, it is their own responsibility to determine how to protect the rights of their citizens. The rights of individuals cannot be used as a justification for one state's interference in another state's affairs. Problems that outsiders might label as human rights violations, said Chinese diplomats, are precisely such internal affairs—matters of domestic Chinese law and not the business of foreigners to condemn or to fix. In addition, Chinese spokespersons argued that no culture's concept of human rights has greater claim to be accepted than any other's. Because cultural standards differ, no foreigner has a moral right to judge China. To do so constitutes cultural imperialism.

Third, China mounted a variety of counterattacks on its critics. Official spokespersons pointed to a series of double standards: that the West itself had committed human rights violations more deplorable than those it was criticizing, such as slavery and the Holocaust; that the West continued to be plagued with human rights problems from which it distracted attention by criticizing others; that the West picked China to complain about while ignoring worse violations in countries aligned with itself, such as South Africa under apartheid; that Westerners who said nothing about Mao's violations complained about less severe violations under Deng; and that prosperous Westerners insisted on immediate implementation of advanced modern standards even though China was still a developing country. Chinese spokesmen said that such double standards revealed the accusers' bad faith.

By the end of ten years of engagement with the international human rights regime, China had a place at the table among those interpreting international norms and was skilled at defending itself against criticism, but it did not yet aspire to shape the regime to its own preferences. At home, the leadership was considering political reform; in the international sphere, official media and the government commented favorably on the UDHR in 1988 and signaled the government's intention to sign and ratify the two international human rights covenants in the near future.

THE IMPACT OF TIANANMEN: FROM RAPPROCHEMENT TO CONFRONTATION

The crackdown in Beijing in 1989, shown on international television, changed the tenor of the human rights regime's interaction with China from rapprochement to confrontation.

The Tiananmen crisis occurred at a time when economic and political sanctions were becoming more common as a tool of human rights policy. In the 1970s, the U.S. under Carter had cut military and economic aid to Pinochet's Chile; in 1981, the U.S. sanctioned Poland after the declaration of martial law; many governments imposed sanctions on the South African apartheid regime in the 1980s; and the U.S. imposed a series of sanctions on the Burmese military regime starting in 1988.[26] International human rights NGOs had added political lobbying to their previous major technique of information exposure and moral pressure. Now with respect to China they pressed for concrete actions by governments and international agencies to punish the Chinese regime. In response, the governments of the leading industrial countries (the G7) imposed sanctions. These sanctions included suspension of high-level diplomatic contacts, restriction of exports of military equipment and military-related technologies, and suspension of cultural exchanges, bilateral aid, and loans. Under U.S. leadership, the World Bank and the Asian Development Bank temporarily suspended loans. Negotiations on China's accession to the WTO came to a halt that lasted three years.

The renewal of normal trading rights (most-favored-nation privileges) with the U.S. was threatened annually from 1989 through 1994 by public and congressional desire to push China toward human rights improvements. Armed with information from NGOs, a procession of senior statesmen from the industrial countries made public representations on human rights when visiting China. Beijing's 1993 bid to host the 2000 Olympics encountered international opposition on human rights grounds and was defeated. The world press took the 1995 women's conference in Beijing as an occasion not to celebrate improvements in the status of women in China, but to attack the government for heavy-handed security measures. The fact that China was on the defensive on human rights weakened its ability to block American and French arms transfers to Taiwan and helped motivate Britain to replace a conciliatory Hong Kong governor with one who confronted Beijing on the issue of Hong Kong democratization (chapter 8).

Even though it was a permanent member of the Security Council, China suffered a series of humiliations in UN bodies. In August 1989, the Sub-Commission on Prevention of Discrimination and Protection of Minorities adopted by secret ballot a resolution critical of China. In 1991, Beijing came under fire again when the subcommission voted by secret ballot to request China to respect the human rights of the Tibetan people and asked the secretary-general to prepare a report on the situation in Tibet. In the 1990 session of the Human Rights Commission, Chinese representatives had to sit through the presentation of a secretary-general's report on violations in China based on material compiled by Amnesty International and other groups. The commission debated a resolution to condemn China, although the resolution was ultimately not put to a vote. From that year through 1997, in every year but one, Chinese diplomats had to expend diplomatic resources to defeat unwelcome resolutions presented by the U.S., Japan, and other countries. China's lobbying included state visits and aid projects for countries holding rotating seats on the commission[27] as well as the argument that "what is happening to China today will happen to any other developing country tomorrow."[28]

Thanks especially to the work of international NGOs in presenting relevant information, Chinese human rights problems were repeatedly criticized by UN treaty bodies and special procedures. In 1994, the special rapporteur on religious intolerance recommended that China reduce its numerous restrictions on freedom of religion. In 1997, the Working Group on Arbitrary Detention advised China to incorporate the presumption of innocence into its criminal procedure law, to provide a precise definition of the crime of "endangering national security," to assure that the criminal code would not outlaw any peaceful exercise of fundamental UDHR rights, and to stop sentencing people to labor reeducation without trial. In 1999, when Hong Kong filed its regularly scheduled report with the treaty body supervising fulfillment of the International Covenant on Civil and Political Rights, it criticized the Hong Kong administration for allowing Beijing to interfere with the Special Administrative Region's judicial independence. In 2000, the Committee Against Torture expressed concern about mistreatment of Tibetans and other national minorities and recommended abolition in China of a form of jailing without trial known as "administrative detention." Chinese problems were discussed at one time or another in reports or meetings of the UN's special rapporteur on summary and arbitrary executions, the special rapporteur on torture, and the Working Group on Enforced or Involuntary Disappearances.

For Chinese leaders, this pattern of events revealed a hidden agenda: to weaken China abroad and subvert its political system at home. According to the Ministry of State Security,

> The big socialist country of China has always been a major target for the peaceful evolution methods of the Western capitalist countries headed by the United States. . . . Each American administration has pursued the same goal of peaceful evolution and has done a great deal of mischief aimed at overthrowing the communist Party and sabotaging the socialist system. . . . The phraseology may vary, but the essence remains the same: to cultivate so-called democratic forces within socialist countries and to stimulate and organize political opposition using catchwords like "democracy," "liberty," or "human rights."[29]

From a symbolic issue of international prestige, human rights had become an issue that imposed real economic and diplomatic costs on Beijing.

HUMAN RIGHTS MEETS CHINA'S RISE

The regime's immediate response to Tiananmen was to slow the tempo of reform, increase repression at home, and reduce engagement abroad. Under pressure from Deng Xiaoping, however, in 1992 the leaders returned to the path of reform and opening (chapter 10). The recommitment to globalization helped restore mass support at home and diplomatic influence abroad.

As part of its return to a global role, China intensified its involvement with the international human rights regime. In 1998, it entered into a dialogue with the newly established Office of the United Nations High Commissioner for Human Rights, and in 2000 it signed a memorandum of understanding for a long-term program of technical cooperation on issues such as human rights education, which served government purposes and helped shelter it from public challenges to its human rights performance. Also in 1998, it signed the International Covenant on Civil and Political Rights (although it did not ratify it), and in 2004 it acceded to the International Covenant on Economic, Social, and Cultural Rights. In 2004 as well, the NPC amended Article 33 of the Chinese Constitution to state, "The State respects and preserves human rights."

Using its renewed voice in the international system, China worked to slow the expansion of the international human rights regime and weaken its ability to influence Chinese foreign relations and domestic affairs. In 1990, Beijing helped block a proposal to establish an emergency mechanism that would have enabled the UN Human Rights Commission to come into session following a major event such as Tiananmen. In the preparatory work for the 1993 Vienna World Conference on Human Rights, China gained the backing of most Asian countries for the principles of noninterference in states' internal affairs; nonselectivity (i.e., UN bodies should not single out specific countries for criticism); the priority of collective, economic, and social rights over civil and political rights; national sovereignty; and cultural particularism (the nonuniversality of human rights values across regions). Although rejected by the Western governments at the conference, these arguments were acknowledged in some parts of the final Vienna declaration.

In the fifty-three-member UN Human Rights Commission, China helped create a caucus of non-Western states that made sure that resolutions against China and other rights-abusing states never came to a vote. The commission even went so far as to elect Libya—one of the more flagrant violators of human rights—as its chair in 2003. In response to such actions, UN secretary-general Kofi Annan reorganized the commission in 2006 into a forty-seven-seat Human Rights Council, which he hoped would be more effective. But this body continued to be dominated by a majority of repressive regimes. These states, including China, shaped the ground rules for the new council around a system of "universal periodic review," which treated all countries equally and hence did not target the worst abusers. Each state defined its own human rights aspirations, received recommendations from the council based on the report it submitted, and was free to adopt or reject all recommendations. As one of the first countries reviewed, China submitted a Human Rights Action Plan in 2009, emphasizing its achievements to date and aspirations consistent with its existing political system, and it rejected all the concrete recommendations made by other states at the end of the review.[30]

In its relations with the UN special procedures, China accepted only four visits (two by the Working Group on Arbitrary Detention and one each by the special rapporteur on the right to education and the special rapporteur on torture), set limits on the activities of each visit, and dragged out negotiations or left requests pending from nine other such bodies.[31] It worked with other members of the "like-minded group" of countries in the Human Rights Council to end, shorten, or restrict the mandates of various special procedures.[32]

In relations with Western countries, China diverted the human rights issue into a channel referred to as "quiet diplomacy." Instead of accepting prisoner lists from high-level foreign visitors and accepting public démarches on issues such as censorship, Tibet, and religious freedom, China began to treat such representations as affronts, as when the meeting of a U.S. State Department official, John Shattuck, with Wei Jingsheng in Beijing led to Wei's rearrest in 1993. Businesspeople and scholars in the West increasingly emphasized the importance of maintaining smooth ties with China.[33] As business ties burgeoned, groups such as the U.S.–China Business Council, consulting firms such as Kissinger Associates and Stonebridge International, and think tanks such as the Brookings Institution's John L. Thornton China Center and the Woodrow Wilson Center's Kissinger Institute on China and the United States articulated the importance of not letting human rights issues get in the way of business and strategic interests. The threat of American trade sanctions for human rights violations disappeared in 1994, when Bill Clinton asked Congress to approve the extension of China's most-favored-nation tariff status even though Beijing had not complied with any of the human rights–related conditions that he had put forward a year earlier. This "delinkage" of trade and human rights was made irreversible when Congress approved "permanent normal trading relations" with China in 2001 as part of the agreement for China to enter the WTO. To take the place of the annual trade privileges debate as a venue for airing worries about China, Congress set up two specialized commissions, the China Economic and Security Review Commission and the

Congressional–Executive Commission on China, but these bodies only issued reports and policy recommendations and had no serious potential to threaten Chinese interests.

Beijing rewarded quiet diplomacy with selective prisoner releases, which had the added benefit of weakening the democracy movement by sending its leaders into exile. In 1998, as a price for restoring summit-level meetings with China, Bill Clinton won the right to give an uncensored lecture at Peking University that was broadcast on Chinese TV, using it to say that China was swimming against "the tide of history." By contrast, Clinton's successor George W. Bush said it was best to speak in private with Chinese leaders about human rights issues. For China, the diplomatic cost of hearing such interventions in private was far less than that of hearing them in public. European leaders followed suit. Nevertheless, U.S. presidents continued to find ways to express their commitment to human rights in China. Every president since Clinton has met with the Dalai Lama informally, although George W. Bush went beyond this by publicly presenting the Tibetan spiritual leader with the Congressional Gold Medal—the highest award the legislature can bestow on a civilian—in the U.S. Capitol building in 2007.

One of the West's demands in the 1990s had been that China enter into official dialogues about human rights. China yielded to this demand in the mid-1990s, establishing dialogues with the U.S., Canada, the EU, the United Kingdom, France, Germany, Norway, Sweden, Switzerland, Austria, and Australia. But it shaped the ground rules to its advantage, insisting that the agendas be negotiated in advance, that they concern technical issues rather than current violations, and that the proceedings be confidential. Keeping the dialogues bilateral and separating them in time prevented foreign powers from coordinating. China characterized as unfriendly the occasional attempts to convene meetings of relevant officials from Western governments to exchange ideas about their dialogue experiences (the so-called Berne Process).[34] NGOs could not participate in Western delegations but were shunted off to occasional forums with Chinese academics that occurred prior to the government dialogues. China vetoed the participation of certain Western NGOs even in these forums by walking out or threatening to cancel if they were invited. From time to time, it cancelled dialogues to express protest over other issues, then framed the resumption of the dialogues as a concession made in exchange for an advance in some area unrelated to human rights. By the turn of the century, China had blunted the human rights critics' traditional strategies of name and shame and diplomatic pressure.

ADVOCACY INNOVATIONS

In this changing landscape, human rights advocates searched for new ways to influence China. First, some groups made increasingly sophisticated use of international human rights mechanisms. Human Rights Watch opened offices in Brussels, London, and Paris that, among other functions, assisted the EU and European governments to prepare for their dialogues with China. Its UN specialist provided information and ideas to UN human rights bodies that worked with China. Human Rights in China increased its lobbying and informational services for European foreign ministries as well as the UN treaty bodies and special mechanisms to enable them to more effectively challenge official Chinese claims about China's compliance with international human rights law.[35]

Second, knowing that human rights improvements would be driven chiefly from within China, human rights groups began to use the Internet to communicate directly to the Chinese public. Human Rights in China promoted Internet-based advocacy directed at readers inside China with a Chinese-language biweekly newsletter of banned news and opinion (*Zhongguo renquan shuangzhoukan*), which was disseminated by email and made available online as well as through its Web site. China Human Rights Defenders circulated news of human rights abuses not only overseas in English, but inside China through email news releases and a Web site. Chinese human rights advocates in exile broadcast their views to Chinese audiences over the U.S. government–supported Radio Free Asia. Most dissident organizations in exile set up Web sites, which the Chinese government tried to block with the Great Firewall.

A third advocacy innovation involved working Chinese civil society— an increasingly active and diverse collection of bloggers, lawyers, petitioners, advocates, and demonstrators. China Labour Bulletin experimented with labor rights litigation, finding lawyers and providing support for workers who sued under Chinese law in Chinese courts against employment discrimination, for severance and pension benefits, or for compensation for injuries.[36] Such cases sometimes produced favorable judgments or settlements that might have an impact on other cases through publicity and force of example, even though local CCP authorities control the Chinese courts, and the courts have little power to enforce their judgments—and although in civil law systems such as China's the judgments rendered by one court do not bind other courts. The Committee to Support Chinese Lawyers provided help for lawyers specializing in rights protection (*wei-quan*) who were willing to take the cases of victims of discrimination, land seizure, and other abuses even at great risk to their careers and personal safety. The committee publicized abuse of lawyers' rights, helped with the defense of those rights, and supported capacity building and exchange between Chinese lawyers and lawyers outside China.[37]

Fourth, human rights groups responded to China's increasing importance in the world economy by interacting directly with businesses. In this approach, they were part of a rising trend to connect business and human rights.[38] The National Labor Committee, China Labor Watch, and others issued reports highlighting abuses of labor rights in factories in China that produced for Western markets, trying to use consumer pressure to force firms such as Wal-Mart, MacDonald's, and Disney to get their China-based suppliers to improve labor conditions. Several of the leading human rights groups concerned with China engaged in a series of meetings with Internet firms working in China and other stakeholders to produce a code of conduct to protect user privacy. In October 2008, the organizations jointly launched the Global Network Initiative as a voluntary compact to promote the implementation of international human rights standards, including freedom of speech, in the governance of the Internet.[39]

The Chinese government responded to each kind of advocacy innovation. It exerted far-reaching control of the Internet and other new information technology in China, blocking most citizens' access to information about human rights. It outlawed and repressed independent civil society organizations that challenged the system too directly and in some cases treated their contact with outside supporters as a violation of criminal law. It threatened foreign Internet companies with loss of business if they did not cooperate with Chinese regulations, even though those regulations themselves violated users' rights under international law. In the UN system, in international diplomacy, and in its dealing with international and domestic NGOs, China's goal appeared not to be to get rid of the international human rights regime (which would be difficult and unnecessary), but to cap its growth and expansion, freeze its effectiveness, shade the norms to fit long-articulated Chinese priorities, and shape the institutions so that they would be deferential to China and like-minded states.

SOFT POWER PLUSES AND MINUSES

Despite its successes in building up soft-power resources and fending off human rights criticisms, China remains vulnerable to the international costs of its human rights violations. The controversies surrounding the 2008 Beijing Olympics exemplified this vulnerability. From the moment the games were awarded to Beijing in July 2001, human rights advocates began planning how to use the event to ramp up pressure on the Chinese government. Human Rights Watch and Human Rights in China set up special Web sites tracking the Beijing organizing committee's failure to make good its commitments related to human rights. The Committee to Protect Journalists issued a series of reports on violations of press freedom. Amnesty International's "Olympics Countdown" series tracked violations over the two-year period leading to the games. China Human Rights Defenders issued an "Olympic Watch" series of press releases. The Save Darfur campaign and an offshoot, Olympic Dream for Darfur, pressed Beijing to use its influence in Khartoum to help solve the Darfur problem. Advocacy groups demonstrated along the route of the Olympic torch in Paris and other capitals, clashing with blue-and-white-suited Chinese escorts who were drawn from the student body of the PAP academy. It is not clear that these pressures did anything to improve human rights on the ground either in China or in Darfur, but they did detract from what was otherwise a public-relations success.

China's response to the award of the 2010 Nobel Peace Prize to a prominent dissident, Liu Xiaobo, was another illustration of its vulnerability in the realm of soft power. Having sentenced Liu to eleven years in prison for advocating peaceful change, Beijing could not deter the Norway-based Peace Prize committee from awarding the prize and then endured weeks of ridicule for preventing Liu or his wife from attending the ceremony, for denouncing the prize committee as "clowns," and for openly pressuring other governments not to send their ambassadors to the ceremony.

Human rights violations also remain an ongoing source of insecurity within China's borders. The regime's current level of acceptance among the people depends on performance-based legitimacy, grounded in economic growth, foreign policy successes, and control of the propaganda message. But the system remains permanently vulnerable to citizen rejection in a way that consolidated democratic regimes are not—even those that are far less popular on policy grounds—because citizens are constantly aware that there is an alternative type of regime that is widely considered to be more legitimate. As the Asian Barometer Surveys have shown, when citizens in democratic systems are asked whether they would be interested in changing the current regime—even one that is viewed as performing poorly—for one that is authoritarian, most of them say no. But citizens in China and other authoritarian regimes mostly agree that "democracy is the best form of government." In this sense, authoritarian systems live on sufferance, accepted only so long as they perform.[40] This vulnerability is the core reason why the Chinese regime continues to see human rights promotion as a form of political subversion. The enduring appeal of democratic ideals suggests the limits to China's prospects of enhancing its soft-power standing.

As China rises—and thanks to the skill of Chinese diplomacy and the cooperation of like-minded governments—its efforts to weaken the effectiveness of the international human rights regime have enjoyed some success. As a result, what at one time seemed to be an inevitable progress toward the universalization of human rights values now appears as a more contingent historical struggle with an uncertain outcome. China will have a large role in shaping the future trajectory of human rights both as an idea and as a system of international laws and institutions.

PART V

CONCLUSION

13

THREAT OR EQUILIBRIUM?

China's arrival as a great power is no longer a possibility, but a reality. Thanks to the sustained growth of its economy, China has narrowed the gap in military strength with the U.S. and Japan, made initial investments in projecting soft power, and moved into the Fourth Ring as a major economic and diplomatic actor. It has, as *The Great Wall and the Empty Fortress* predicted, "join[ed] the international regimes that govern trade, human rights, weapons proliferation, and other interactions as much in order to change them as to obey them."[1]

At the same time, China continues to face serious security challenges within its territory and around its borders. The country is surrounded by unreliable friends and potential adversaries. It presses territorial claims that others refuse to recognize. Most of its neighbors view its rise with suspicion. Beijing exerts less influence than it wants to in the regional balance of power and in international regimes. China is still "not a satisfied power."

On balance, however, as *The Great Wall* went on to argue, "these considerations give China stronger interests in favor of than against regional stability, and for rather than against cooperative relations with its potential great-power rivals. They create stronger incentives for China to accept a voice in shaping the global order than to opt out of it." Therefore, "China's strength on mainland Asia does not constitute a threat to regional stability."

But strength can turn threatening. We continue to believe that to prevent this from happening, a balance of power that includes China remains an "appropriate foundation for building a stable post–Cold War regional order." The task for U.S. China policy in the coming decade or more is to construct a new equilibrium of power that meets the interests of the U.S. and its allies without damaging Chinese security.

A CHINA THREAT?

The rise of China so far has been more beneficial than damaging to Asian and Western interests, but it may not continue to be that way.

On the economic front, China has benefited some actors in the West, especially consumers and investors, and hurt others, especially those seeking manufacturing jobs, although many of those jobs had already moved to other developing countries before they moved on to China. It has put heavy new demands on global commodity markets, but much of that demand is to feed production for the West. Its foreign trade has been globally balanced for most of the open-door period, but it has run a large trade surplus with the U.S. Its currency, although undervalued, has appreciated gradually, and it is moving toward full convertibility, although too slowly for its critics and too rapidly for those who fear a challenge to the supremacy of the dollar. China's rise has helped drive economic growth in many Asian economies and in countries in Africa, Latin America, and elsewhere, although in doing so it has taken away some local jobs and stepped up resource extraction in fragile environments. The balance sheet is mixed in any economic relationship, but on the whole the rise of China has contributed to prosperity not only in China, but in Asia, the West, and the world.

On the political front, China has given its citizens more personal liberty, opened its culture to outside influences, encouraged Chinese to go abroad for education and travel, promoted the study of English and other foreign languages, and fostered the rise of a Western-oriented consumer lifestyle among the large urban middle class. China is integrating with the world in many ways, but it has not become a democracy, nor has the state given up its control of the economy and society. The PRC is still an authoritarian regime that in many ways offends Western values. Even though the regime is repressive at home, however, it has not tried to undermine democratic political systems in the rest of the world.

On the strategic front, the rise of China has brought a broad convergence of its interests with those of the West. China has joined world regimes and by and large complies with them. It favors stability rather than revolution in Asia and the Fourth Ring. It stations no troops abroad and is unable to prevent Western powers from deploying their military forces wherever they want. To be sure, China's interests are seldom identical with those of the West, and it often has different ideas about what policies work. Its cooperation comes at some cost. In all important global institutions and regimes, it works to modify the rules to suit its interests. Its goal is to influence, but not to undermine, the world order that the West has created.

On the military front, China remains almost exclusively concerned with missions within and around its own borders. Even though it has acquired economic interests far away from Asia, it has not put in place the means to defend those interests with force. There is no sign that China intends to use military force to seize territory beyond what it already claims, to drive the U.S. out of Asia, or to compete with Western military influence in the Fourth Ring. U.S. alliances in Asia remain robust. But the rise of the Chinese military is presenting new challenges to the existing balance of power in Asia. China is building the capacity to frustrate an American intervention in the Taiwan Strait and to enforce territorial claims against Japan and other U.S. allies or quasi-allies in the East China and South China seas. These developments are changing what was once a one-sided military balance in favor of the U.S. in the western Pacific.

On the ideological front, China has mounted a public-relations effort to improve its image around the world, seeking to show that it is a benevolent, civilized, and peace-loving society that does not deserve the criticism and suspicion leveled against it. This effort is defensive. Chinese spokesmen respond to criticism of their own policies—for example, in human rights—with criticisms of the other side, and to burnish China's image, but China does not try to promote change in other countries' ideologies.

In short, although China today is a dissatisfied country, it has acquired a large stake in the stability of the world order and the prosperity of the West. In pursuit of its own interests, it has often challenged the interests of the U.S. and U.S. allies. But in the post-Mao period these frictions have not expanded into direct economic, political, or military conflicts. In this sense, the engagement policy pursued by the U.S. since 1972 has achieved its key strategic goal.

Despite these considerations, it is possible that China's future leaders may decide to challenge U.S. preeminence. If China's economic growth continues for another decade or two at the rate it has sustained in the past three decades, it will possess enormous resources to build up its military and acquire bases overseas, and it will face an increasing imperative to use force to protect its expanding interests. As China comes to own more assets beyond its borders and to import more resources from the Asia-Pacific and the Fourth Ring, it may decide to project power farther from its shores to protect its interests. Technological diffusion under conditions of globalization might erode the U.S. lead in military and information technology, so that even if the U.S. continues to modernize its military, China might be able to close the gap.

If China were to mount such a challenge to American dominance, it would have to acquire access to military bases in South Asia, Africa, Latin America, and the Middle East, where it has important interests to protect. Within a few decades, the Chinese navy would roam the oceans the way the American navy does now, even patrolling along the American coasts. The renminbi would replace the dollar as the largest international reserve currency. Chinese culture and values would achieve global influence along with Chinese products. The U.S. would have to decide whether and when to resist. If it did, the two countries might go to war.[2]

The potential of this kind of threat is inherent in China's growing power, but not inevitable. The task for the coming decades is to define a role for China that is more constructive than damaging to the interests of other actors. Three factors will determine whether it is possible to do so: changes within China, changes in its regional environment, and changes in U.S. policy.

HOW WILL CHINA CHANGE?

Although China today is a strong country with a strong regime, it is also troubled and fragile. Chinese society is turbulent, questioning, and often angry. A revolution of rising expectations is under way that places growing pressure on the state to run faster to keep ahead of people's demands for both wealth and administrative responsiveness. People have more freedom to express their unhappiness on the Internet and in private. No one believes the regime's current official myth: that the ruling party is legitimate because the people put it in power during the revolution; that it is implementing Chinese-style socialism, which serves all the people; and that the top party leaders have a monopoly on knowledge about what policies are best for society. Few Chinese, even in the leadership, think the system has reached the end of its evolution. There is a pervasive feeling, which we share, that the current political system is a transitional arrangement on the way to something else.[3]

There are three main possibilities for political change. These possibilities do not include a military coup or a Soviet-style ethnic breakup. The former is unlikely because the PLA has an ethos of loyalty to the party, and its complex chains of command make it difficult to organize a coup (chapter 11). The latter is unlikely because the minorities are too small and too tightly controlled by the Han state to break away (chapter 8).

The first possibility is the one that the regime seems to be aiming for: gradual evolution to a new form of rule that might be called "responsive authoritarianism"—an authoritarian system that is efficient, effective, popular, and stable. Such a system might claim to be democratic because of its responsiveness to public opinion, but it would ban open political competition in the name of stability. China would become an enormous Singapore. The current leaders seem to believe they can achieve this kind of stable authoritarian rule by reining in corruption, providing good public services, allowing limited transparency, and engaging in conspicuous if not necessarily authentic policy consultation. The idea makes sense to many Chinese because the Chinese conception of democracy historically places little emphasis on political competition and greater emphasis on the state's service to the people's interests. This conception accepts a heavy concentration of power in exchange for governance that is viewed as effective and just.[4]

But this model is filled with internal contradictions. If the regime wants to avoid open political competition, it has to use repression, and repression generates a sense of injustice. Without increasing repression, civil society is likely to grow and challenge the regime's policies and ideologies. Society will spawn interests too diverse for the regime to adjudicate in the absence of political competition. A growing middle class will continue to generate its own ideas about what it wants. If the regime allows open political debate and competition, one-party rule will eventually founder.

To be sure, such tensions might take a long time to destabilize a regime that is adaptive and resilient. Some evolving version of the current Chinese system might continue to function for a long time to come. As long as the regime stays on this path, the domestic political conditions will continue to exist for economic growth, although not necessarily at the rate of the past three decades, and economic growth would provide the material basis for China's continuing international assertiveness.

The second possibility for internal change is a peaceful transition to democracy. If the country faces a major economic or social crisis, a group within the leadership might try to reach an accommodation with society by opening up the political system to political freedoms and the open competition for power. The CCP leader at the time of Tiananmen, Zhao Ziyang, wanted to do something like this, but he was blocked by conservatives in the leadership. In Taiwan, this kind of opening from the top began in 1986 and served the ruling party well because it has managed to retain power by democratic means for much of the time since the transition to democracy.

Democratization is unlikely to bring a fundamental change in China's foreign policy objectives. Democratic rulers in Beijing will still want to preserve control over Tibet and Xinjiang and assert Chinese authority over Taiwan because these territories are crucial for the defense of China's heartland. A democratic leadership will still want to press its claims to strategic and economic assets in the East China and South China seas; build up the PLA Navy so that it can participate in the defense of the sea lanes that are crucial to the country's prosperity; project influence in neighboring regions such as Central Asia, Korea, and Southeast Asia; maintain the military capability to deter attacks; exercise influence in the far-flung territories where it acquires resources and sells goods; and, in general, pursue much the same national security agenda as the regime follows today.

If democratization is achieved peacefully, China's power assets would not necessarily diminish and might even increase. The economy might become more efficient and more innovative. Some of the country's internal challenges might become less severe. The West would no longer mount efforts to change the Chinese regime, removing a key security worry of the regime today. One source of Taiwanese distrust of the mainland will disappear. Beijing might be able to manage relations with ethnic minorities in

Tibet, Xinjiang, and Mongolia less repressively. Distrust between China on the one side and the U.S., Europe, and Japan on the other around issues of ideology would diminish, removing some sources of friction and making it easier to handle issues such as trade deficits, currency valuation, and the naval balance. These changes would free up military resources for other uses and create new soft-power resources. Thus, a democratic China may in some respects be harder for foreign governments to deal with than the current regime.

On the other hand, if democratic transition causes government authority to weaken, China might face slower economic growth, generate more cross-border population flows and crime, and have a harder time implementing commitments on arms control, public health, and climate change. Beijing may assert itself more impulsively than it does now as the government responds more to public opinion, which is likely to be nationalistic. These developments would present new challenges for the West as well, but of a different kind.

The third possibility is that the Chinese system may be destabilized by an economic stall, inflation, a natural disaster, an environmental or public-health crisis, an international humiliation such as failure in a military clash with another country, a power struggle that splits the leadership, or any combination of these events. Such a train of events would damage the economy, undermine military effectiveness, decimate soft power, and diminish China's ability to conduct a consistent, strategic foreign policy. It might exacerbate problems in Taiwan, Tibet, and Xinjiang, alarm neighbors, and force leaders to give most of their attention to problems at home.

Such a breakdown would remove the possibility of a direct Chinese military and political challenge to U.S. influence in Asia for a long time but would replace this challenge with other problems. It might lead to worse repression against minorities and irrational lashing out against Taiwan, Japan, the U.S., and others. It might intensify refugee, environmental, public-health, and other cross-border issues. The military might be drawn into the power vacuum as the institution best able to hold the country together. In any case, turmoil in China would likely spill over into conflict beyond its borders as other states seek to exploit China's weakness and China struggles to respond. If so, China might become more aggressive about territorial disputes even if it has a reduced capacity to impose its will.

Aside from political changes, other internal problems may change the trajectory of Chinese power. China sits on three time bombs: a demographic time bomb—by 2050, one-quarter of China's population will be older than sixty; a water time bomb—it has the most severe water shortage of any advanced economy; and a climate time bomb—global warming will hurt China more than most countries because its rivers derive most of their volume from the Tibetan glaciers, which are melting. Even in the best of circumstances, if China's economic growth model goes well and does not fall victim to any of these time bombs or to domestic inflation or foreign protectionism, it faces a likely economic slowdown as its economy matures.[5]

In short, China will change. Each scenario for the future carries risks for China's neighbors, but each may also carry advantages. The first scenario would see China's strength and assertiveness increase but provide continuity in the country's foreign policy objectives and strategies, with experienced policymakers in charge. The second scenario would reduce the incentives for China to pursue an ambitious strategy of power expansion and possibly reduce the resources for China to do so, but it would also introduce some elements of unpredictability into China's international behavior. The third would weaken the country but create new kinds of instability in its relations with the rest of the world.

WILL CHINA'S REGIONAL ENVIRONMENT CHANGE?

The second factor that will shape China's future strategic options is the evolution of the political environment around its borders. Thanks to Chinese policymakers' efforts over the past three decades, the international environment is about as favorable for the exercise of Chinese power as it is likely to get. Most of China's border disputes have been settled; most of its neighbors have accepted the economic benefits of engaging with it and have refrained from taking strong steps to resist its rise; China's role is accepted in multilateral organizations in Asia and beyond; and its business is welcomed, if with some ambivalence, everywhere in the world. The surrounding regions are peaceful. Any foreseeable change in the external environment is likely to make things harder rather than easier for Beijing.

China is surrounded by two kinds of countries—unstable ones where almost any conceivable change will make life more difficult for Chinese policymakers and strong ones that have the potential to grow stronger in the future and pose sharper competition for China. In the first group of countries are North Korea, Pakistan, Burma, and the Central Asian states. Regime collapse or war in any of these places would likely draw China in somehow, whether politically or, in the extreme, militarily. Beijing would have to decide either to cooperate with other regional powers (the U.S., Japan, Russia, India) to manage the situation or to compete with them. China may conceivably emerge with more influence at low cost, but it is more likely that, like most states that intervene in unstable neighbors, it would end up expending large resources and achieving unsatisfactory results. In the aftermath, the neighboring regions might be dominated by another power or be continuously unstable or come under Chinese influence at the cost of a heavy long-term commitment of resources. Whatever happens is likely to tie China down more heavily on its immediate periphery than now and thus reduce Beijing's ability to project power beyond its region.

In the second group of countries are India, Japan, Russia, and Vietnam. All have the potential to become more serious competitors than they are now. India's population is growing faster than China's and will be both larger and younger by about 2030. The country has urbanized more slowly than China, so it can potentially enjoy a more protracted growth trajectory as its rural population moves to the cities and takes up more productive work. If India were to make peace with Pakistan—a long shot, to be sure, and one that Beijing makes less likely by Chinese military and diplomatic cooperation with Islamabad—its ability to compete with China in the Indian Ocean, Southeast Asia, and Central Asia will grow. Vietnam is too large for China to dominate, is growing rapidly, and has the capability to cause trouble for China either alone or in cooperation with others. Less likely but conceivable power shifts would involve the resurgence of Russia or Japan through a combination of smart economic policies and smart international strategies. Any of these four countries might multiply its influence over China by strengthening relations with the U.S. China now has stable relations with each of these regimes. Any shift in relative power or deterioration of relations can only make life more complicated for Chinese policymakers.

China has little control over changes in neighboring countries, and any changes that do occur are likely to tie it down even more in the problems of its periphery than it is today, postponing its ability to project power beyond its own region. The best option for China is stability in Asia.

A U.S. DECLINE?

The most consequential change that might occur in China's international environment would be a marked decline in the U.S. power position. Most Chinese strategists and many Western analysts believe that such a decline is taking place. They believe the U.S. is overstretched militarily, has lost its economic dynamism, and is too politically polarized to solve its problems. Although the decline may be masked by Washington's intermittent efforts to reassert power, over time the U.S. will lose the ability to dominate international markets, provide security for the rest of the world, and influence people's ideas of the good life. Assuming Chinese power continues to grow as U.S. power declines, China would pass the U.S. to become the strongest global power, enacting what political scientists refer to as a "power transition."

This development, however, would be a mixed blessing for China. On the one hand, it would be able to take Taiwan with little fuss, take its share of the economic assets of the East China and South China seas on favorable terms, print renminbi as a world reserve currency that other countries would pay a price to hold, establish the principles that it prefers for various international regimes, and gain wide acceptance for its way of doing business.

But China would not easily replace the U.S. as a global superpower with enough reach and influence to preside over a stable world system. Power transition is not the crossing of two straight lines. The descending power may decline slowly. The ascending power would have to undertake a long climb up an increasingly steep hill to translate economic strength into global military and political reach. One hegemon would not neatly replace another. To take over from the U.S. as a global policeman, China would have to stretch its economic and military resources to the breaking point and would be doing so from a less favorable geostrategic position than that which the U.S. has enjoyed.

In the initial stage of a power transition, six big powers—the U.S., China, Europe, Japan, India, and Russia—would be engaged in a complex balancing game with great risk of instability. To protect its interests, China would pay an increasing price and bear increasing burdens, likely without proportionate gain in most of its security concerns. It is of course conceivable that other countries in the international system would quickly bandwagon with China and help China to become the dominant power. But it is more likely that some or all of the other large powers would band together to resist China. Already in the 1990s, the U.S. began to supplement its engagement strategy toward China with a "hedge" or balancing strategy, strengthening the military and political assets needed to constrain the exercise of Chinese influence. As Beijing asserted its influence more forcefully in the 2000s, this U.S. strategy found a wide welcome among China's regional neighbors. China's continuing rise in the 2010s led the U.S. to pivot even more sharply to Asia as it drew down its forces in Iraq and Afghanistan. China's neighbors are likely to continue to prefer to work with Washington instead of Beijing because the U.S. is located outside the region, has a reputation for providing public goods, and is a familiar partner.

China, by contrast, is close enough to be threatening, and its neighbors consider its strategic goals to be unclear. Unlike the U.S., it has few natural allies among the world's stronger powers. For Japan, India, Russia, and the U.S., it is physically too close to their security zones to be an attractive partner. For the U.S., Japan, India, and Europe, it is an unlikely partner because it does not share their individualistic political values and democratic, free-market political systems. It seems unlikely that most of China's smaller neighbors—including the ASEAN and Pacific powers—would tilt to China either, unless China's power were to surpass their aggregate power by such a large amount that they have no other choice or unless China were to promote policies that these other countries perceive as being as much in their own interests as in China's, which would be a hard balance for Beijing to strike.

Fourth Ring countries have not yet started to balance against China because they have much to gain and nothing to lose at this point from an increasing Chinese role in their regions. But should China extend military power into the various regions within the Fourth Ring and attempt to influence their strategic landscapes, then some Fourth Ring powers can also be expected to balance against Beijing.

For all these reasons, if China's rise continues, it will climb a sharpening curve. The higher it goes, the more energy it will need to convert each unit of power into an increase in security. It would cost more to consolidate the advantages of preeminence than it would have cost to rise to that position. And if China fails to replace the U.S. as a global policeman, it is hard to see another candidate who can do so. Along with the rest of the world, China might have to suffer the consequences of a general decline in global security. This prospect is not necessarily more attractive for Beijing than the cooperative balance-of-power security regime it might be able to construct with a strong U.S. China therefore has no interest in an American decline. Even if it thought it did have this interest, it has no practical way to promote such a decline, and there is no sign that it is trying to do so.

ESTABLISHING A NEW EQUILIBRIUM

The better alternative both for China and for the U.S. and its allies would be to enhance Chinese security by creating a new equilibrium of power that maintains the current world system, but with a larger role for China. China would remain what geography has made it: a large, heavily populated land power. It would focus on raising the living standards and quality of life of its people and on protecting its environment.

China has good reasons for choosing this course. Even as the country's military grows, it will continue to need to invest in domestic security and territorial defense, which will make it hard to project force on a large scale far from its borders. Its security policy will still have to concentrate on the immediate periphery, stabilizing land borders, protecting the coasts, and upholding claims to valuable resources in nearby seas. In a crisis, disorder around its borders might tempt a Chinese military response, but, from China's point of view, intervening militarily even in its own neighborhood would be a distant second best to trading peacefully. Likewise, China will persist in its Taiwan policy of peaceful unification through economic integration and try to avoid war. Farther away, China will cooperate with other naval powers to protect the sea lanes and will rely on diplomacy to help maintain regional stability.

Even when China becomes the world's largest economy, its prosperity will remain interdependent with the prosperity of its global rivals, including the U.S. and Japan. The richer China becomes, the greater will be its stake in the security of the sea lanes, the stability of the world trade and financial regimes, nonproliferation, the control of global climate change, and cooperation in public health. No fundamental conflict need emerge between Chinese and U.S. strategic interests.[6]

The U.S. should encourage this choice by drawing policy lines — military, economic, and political — that meet its own needs without threatening China's and by holding to them firmly. As China rises, it will push against American power to find the boundaries of Washington's will. As it does so, Washington must push back to establish boundaries for the growth of Chinese power.

American interests in relation to China are uncontroversial and should be affirmed — a stable and prosperous China, peaceful resolution of the Taiwan issue, freedom of navigation in the surrounding seas, the security of Japan and other Asian allies, an open world economy, and protection of human rights.

Two areas are especially important. First, the U.S. must maintain its military predominance in the western Pacific, including the East China and South China seas. This predominance will be difficult for China to accept because this area of the oceans is the closest to it and contains territorial features that it claims as part of its own territory. To maintain this predominance, the U.S. will have continually to upgrade its military capabilities, maintain its regional alliances, and act so as to maintain its credibility when facing challenges. While doing so, Washington must reassure Beijing that these moves are intended to create a balance of common interests rather than to threaten or contain China. Mechanisms for managing interactions and building trust between defense establishments are essential if crises are to be resolved and military confrontations avoided.

Second, the U.S. needs to push back against Chinese efforts to remake global regimes in ways that do not serve the interests of the U.S. and its allies. In regimes as diverse as arms control, trade, finance, and climate change — and in virtually all others — China has its own priorities. Although

China's attempt to pursue its interests in global regimes is legitimate, so too is the U.S. interest in making sure that these regimes continue the remarkable evolution they have enjoyed since the end of World War II and especially since the end of the Cold War. This is so above all in the case of the human rights regime, a set of global rules and institutions that in the long run bear major consequences for the construction of the type of world order that the U.S. has promoted since the time of Franklin Delano Roosevelt.

These core American interests do not threaten China's security. In the First Ring, China needs stability in the midst of rapid social and cultural change, ethnic reconciliation with its minorities, and peaceful resolution of the Taiwan issue. Even though the current political system has improved many Chinese citizens' livelihoods, it has failed to achieve these political goals. The U.S. should continue to work for a more stable China in the long run, which means among other things a China that respects its people's human rights.

In the Second Ring and Third Ring, the U.S. and its allies can accept a degree of expanded Chinese military, economic, and diplomatic influence around its borders that falls short of dominance. Defining a balance of American and Chinese roles that maintains stability in these regions will take time and require negotiation and even friction, but this goal is achievable. The hardest of China's Second Ring relationships to stabilize will be that with Japan. A strong U.S. defense commitment to Japan remains crucial to helping China and Japan find their way eventually to a balance in which both sides can be secure.

In the Fourth Ring, economic competition, for all its harshness, should not be confused with strategic conflict. China should be afforded open access to the resources it needs to support its own people and to play its role in the interdependent world economy. At the same time, China must not be allowed to deny or restrict other states' access to resources or to dictate the terms of global economic interaction.

Resisting China's rise is not a realistic option. The attempt to do so would require a break in mutually beneficial economic relations and enormous expenditures to encircle China and would force China into antagonistic reactions. And the effort would fail because China is already too strong. Such a policy would have unpredictable consequences for Asia's stability and prosperity. There is no effective political support for such a policy in the U.S. or among U.S. allies in Asia. Although many Chinese policymakers think the U.S. is pursuing this strategy, it is not doing so, and it should not.

But it is not necessary to yield too much to China's rise. China has not earned a voice equal to that of the U.S. in a "Pacific Community" or a role in a global condominium as one member of a "G2." China is not going to "rule the world" unless the U.S. withdraws from it.[7]

China's rise will be a threat to the U.S. and the world only if the U.S. allows it to become one. Therefore, the right China strategy begins at home. The U.S. must resume robust growth, continue to support a globally preeminent higher-education sector, continue to discover new technologies, protect intellectual property from espionage and theft, deepen trade relations with other economies, sustain military innovation and renewal, nurture relationships with allies and other cooperating powers, and by example, earn the respect of people around the world for American values. As long as the U.S. holds tight to its values and solves its problems at home, it will be able to manage the rise of China.

NOTES

INTRODUCTION

1. Andrew J. Nathan and Robert S. Ross, *The Great Wall and the Empty Fortress: China's Search for Security* (New York: Norton, 1997).
2. Ibid., xi.
3. Richard M. Nixon, "Asia After Viet Nam," *Foreign Affairs* 46, no. 1 (October 1967), 121.
4. The phrase "rule the world" comes from Martin Jacques, *When China Rules the World: The Rise of the Middle Kingdom and the End of the Western World* (London: Allen Lane, 2009).
5. On Chinese military power, see, among other sources, Andrew Scobell, *China's Use of Military Force: Beyond the Great Wall and the Long March* (Cambridge: Cambridge University Press, 2003); and David Shambaugh, *Modernizing China's Military: Progress, Problems, and Prospects* (Berkeley: University of California Press, 2002).
6. For instance, see Nicholas R. Lardy, *Integrating China Into the Global Economy* (Washington, D.C.: Brookings Institution Press, 2002).
7. For instance, see Elizabeth Economy, *The River Runs Black: The Environmental Challenge to China's Future* (Ithaca: Cornell University Press, 2004); Bates Gill, Jennifer Chang, and Sarah Palmer, "China's HIV Crisis," *Foreign Affairs* 81, no. 2 (March–April 2002): 96–110; Shanthi Kalathil and Taylor Boas, *Open Networks, Closed Regimes: The Impact of the Internet on Authoritarian Rule* (Washington, D.C.: Carnegie Endowment for International Peace, 2003).
8. For instance, see Evan S. Medeiros and M. Taylor Fravel, "China's New Diplomacy," *Foreign Affairs* 82, no. 6 (November–December 2003): 22–35; Evan S. Medeiros, *China's International Behavior: Activism, Opportunism, and Diversification* (Santa Monica, Calif.: RAND, 2009).

9. For instance, see Rosemary Foot, *Rights Beyond Borders: The Global Community and the Struggle Over Human Rights in China* (Oxford: Oxford University Press, 2000); Joshua Kurlantzick, *Charm Offensive: How China's Soft Power Is Transforming the World* (New Haven: Yale University Press, 2007).

10. For instance, see Michael Pillsbury, *China Debates the Future Security Environment* (Washington, D.C.: National Defense University Press, 2000).

11. Also see, among others, Lu Ning, *The Dynamics of Foreign Policy Decisionmaking in China* (Boulder: Westview, 1997); Andrew J. Nathan and Bruce Gilley, *China's New Rulers*, 2nd ed. (New York: New York Review of Books, 2002); and Zhang Liang, comp., *The Tiananmen Papers*, trans. Andrew J. Nathan and Perry Link (New York: PublicAffairs, 2001).

12. Robert Jervis, "Cooperation Under the Security Dilemma," *World Politics* 30 (1978): 167–214.

13. For instance, see Stephen D. Krasner, ed., *International Regimes* (Ithaca: Cornell University Press, 1983); Robert O. Keohane, *After Hegemony: Cooperation and Discord in the World Political Economy* (Princeton: Princeton University Press, 1984).

14. For instance, see Michael Yahuda, "The Limits of Economic Interdependence: Sino–Japanese Relations," in Alastair Iain Johnston and Robert S. Ross, eds., *New Directions in the Study of China's Foreign Policy*, 162–185 (Stanford: Stanford University Press, 2006); Allen S. Whiting, *China Eyes Japan* (Berkeley: University of California Press, 1989).

15. Other works that combine realist and constructivist approaches to China–Japan relations are Ming Wan, *Sino–Japanese Relations: Interaction, Logic, and Transformation* (Washington, D.C., and Stanford: Woodrow Wilson Center Press and Stanford University Press, 2006), and Richard C. Bush, *The Perils of Proximity: China–Japan Security Relations* (Washington, D.C.: Brookings Institution Press, 2010).

16. John J. Mearsheimer, *The Tragedy of Great Power Politics* (New York: Norton, 2001).

17. Thomas J. Christensen, "Posing Problems Without Catching Up: China's Rise and Challenges for U.S. Security Policy," *International Security* 25, no. 4 (Spring 2001): 5–40.

18. Arthur Waldron, *The Great Wall of China: From History to Myth* (Cambridge: Cambridge University Press, 1990).

19. Last names come first in Chinese, and only a small number of them have two syllables.

1. WHAT DRIVES CHINESE FOREIGN POLICY?

1. In 1989, the military regime changed the traditional British colonial name "Burma" to "Myanmar." The country's name has been in contention ever since. We use "Burma" throughout.

2. There are thirty-three states plus the twelve microstates.

3. Alistair Iain Johnston, "Is China a Status Quo Power?" *International Security* 27, no. 4 (Spring 2003): 5–56; Edward S. Steinfeld, *Playing Our Game: Why China's Rise Doesn't Threaten the West* (New York: Oxford University Press, 2010).

4. Michael R. Chambers, "Explaining China's Alliances: Balancing Against Regional and Superpower Threats," Ph.D. diss., Columbia University, 2000.

5. On the wedge strategy, see Gordon H. Chang, *Friends and Enemies: The United States, China, and the Soviet Union, 1948–1972* (Stanford: Stanford University Press, 1990).

6. Michael B. Yahuda, *China's Role in World Affairs* (New York: St. Martin's, 1978), 11.

7. Barry Naughton, "The Third Front: Defence Industrialization in the Chinese Interior," *China Quarterly* 115 (September 1988): 351–386.

8. J. Du and Y. C. Ma, "Climatic Trend of Rainfall Over Tibetan Plateau from 1971 to 2000," *Acta Geographica Sinica* 59 (2004): 375–382, cited in an Intergovernmental Panel on Climate Change report at http://www.ipcc.ch/publications_and_data /publications_ipcc_fourth_assessment_report_wg2_report_impacts_adaptation _and_vulnerability.htm, accessed June 16, 2010.

9. Wolfram Eberhard, *China's Minorities: Yesterday and Today* (Belmont, Calif.: Wadsworth, 1982): 8–10; Ying-shih Yü, "Minzu yishi yu guojia guannian" (Ethnic Consciousness and the State Concept), *Mingbao Yuekan* 18, no. 12 (December 1983), 3.

10. Joseph Fletcher, "Ch'ing Inner Asia c. 1800," "Sino–Russian Relations, 1800–62," and "The Heyday of the Ch'ing Order in Mongolia, Sinkiang, and Tibet," in John K. Fairbank, ed., *The Cambridge History of China*, vol. 10 (Cambridge: Cambridge University Press, 1978), 35–106, 318–350, 351–408.

11. A recent estimate of Overseas Chinese in the world is 39,089,000 (as of December 31, 2008), from Overseas Compatriot Affairs Commission, ROC (Taiwan), *Overseas Compatriot Population Distribution* (n.d., periodically updated), at http://www.ocac. gov.tw/english/public/public.asp?selno=8889&no=8889&level=B, accessed July 6, 2010. The classic work on the early phase of the PRC's overseas Chinese policy is Stephen Fitzgerald, *China and the Overseas Chinese: A Study of Peking's Changing Policy, 1949–1970* (Cambridge: Cambridge University Press, 1972). For a discussion of the Overseas Chinese as a liability in PRC diplomacy, see Robert S. Ross, "Ethnic Chinese in Southeast Asia: Political Liability/Economic Asset," in Joyce K. Kallgren, Noordin Sopiee, and Soedjati Djiwandono, eds., *ASEAN and China: An Evolving Relationship* (Berkeley: Institute for East Asian Studies, University of California, 1988), 147–176.

12. Fletcher, "Ch'ing Inner Asia," "Sino–Russian Relations," and "The Heyday of the Ch'ing Order"; Owen Lattimore, *Pivot of Asia: Sinkiang and the Inner Asian Frontiers of China and Russia* (Boston: Little, Brown, 1950), 103–151.

13. Eberhard, *China's Minorities*; Edward Friedman, "Reconstructing China's National Identity: A Southern Alternative to Mao-Era Anti-imperialist Nationalism," *Journal of Asian Studies* 53, no. 1 (February 1994): 67–91; Emily Honig, *Creating Chinese*

Ethnicity: Subei People in Shanghai, 1850–1980 (New Haven: Yale University Press, 1992).

14. Thomas S. Mullaney, *Coming to Terms with the Nation: Ethnic Classification in Modern China* (Berkeley: University of California Press, 2011); June Teufel Dreyer, *China's Forty Millions: Minority Nationalities and National Integration in the People's Republic of China* (Cambridge, Mass.: Harvard University Press, 1976), 141–146; David Yen-ho Wu, "The Construction of Chinese and Non-Chinese Identities," *Daedalus* 120, no. 2 (Spring 1991): 159–179; Dru C. Gladney, *Muslim Chinese: Ethnic Nationalism in the People's Republic* (Cambridge, Mass.: Council on East Asian Studies, Harvard University, 1991).

15. Frank A. Kierman Jr. and John K. Fairbank, eds., *Chinese Ways in Warfare* (Cambridge, Mass.: Harvard University Press, 1974); Jonathan N. Lipman and Stevan Harrell, eds., *Violence in China: Essays in Culture and Counterculture* (Albany: State University of New York Press, 1990); Alastair Iain Johnston, *Cultural Realism: Strategic Culture and Grand Strategy in Chinese History* (Princeton: Princeton University Press, 1995); Andrew Scobell, *China's Use of Military Force: Beyond the Great Wall and the Long March* (New York: Cambridge University Press, 2003).

16. John King Fairbank, ed., *The Chinese World Order: Traditional China's Foreign Relations* (Cambridge, Mass.: Harvard University Press, 1968); Mark Mancall, *China at the Center: 300 Years of Foreign Policy* (New York: Free Press, 1984).

17. Fletcher, "Ch'ing Inner Asia," "Sino–Russian Relations," and "The Heyday of the Ch'ing Order"; Lattimore, *Pivot of Asia*; Morris Rossabi, *China and Inner Asia from 1368 to the Present Day* (London: Thames and Hudson, 1975).

18. Morris Rossabi, ed., *China Among Equals: The Middle Kingdom and Its Neighbors, 10th–14th Centuries* (Berkeley: University of California Press, 1983); Joseph F. Fletcher, "China and Central Asia, 1368–1884," in Fairbank, ed., *The Chinese World Order*, 206–224.

19. David C. Kang, *China Rising: Peace, Power, and Order in East Asia* (New York: Columbia University Press, 2007), chapter 2; and David C. Kang, *East Asia Before the West: Five Centuries of Trade and Tribute* (New York: Columbia University Press, 2010).

20. On the origins of the new security concept, see Alastair Iain Johnston, *Social States: China in International Institutions, 1980–2000* (Princeton: Princeton University Press, 2008), 172–173. The quote is from Ministry of Foreign Affairs, People's Republic of China, "China's Position Paper on the New Security Concept (July 31, 2002)," at http://www.mfa.gov.cn/eng/wjb/zzjg/gjs/gjzzyhy/2612/2614/t15319.htm#, accessed March 19, 2010.

21. On the origins of the peaceful-rise concept, see *Peaceful Rise: Speeches of Zheng Bijian, 1997–2005* (Washington, D.C.: Brookings Institution Press, 2005). The quote is from Hu Jintao's report to the Seventeenth Party Congress, October 15, 2007, translated at http://www.china.org.cn/english/congress/229611.htm#11, accessed February 1, 2009.

22. Information Office of the State Council, People's Republic of China, *China's*

Peaceful Development (Beijing: Information Office of the State Council, September 2011), part III, translated at http://news.xinhuanet.com/english2010/china/2011 -09/06/c_131102329.htm, accessed January 27, 2012.

23. Su Xiaokang and Wang Luxiang, *Deathsong of the River: A Reader's Guide to the Chinese TV Series "Heshang,"* introduced, translated, and annotated by Richard W. Bodman and Pin P. Wan (Ithaca: East Asia Program, Cornell University, 1991).

24. Now these most-favored-nation clauses are common in world trade and have come to be called "normal trading relations." What is exceptional today is not granting but withholding most-favored-nation status, as America threatened to do from China during the 1990s because of human rights concerns; see chapter 12.

25. William A. Callahan, *China: The Pessoptimist Nation* (Oxford: Oxford University Press, 2010).

26. Information Office of the State Council, People's Republic of China, *China's National Defense in 2006* (Beijing: Information Office of the State Council, December 2006), translated at http://www.china.org.cn/english/features/book/194421.htm, accessed July 6, 2010.

2. WHO RUNS CHINESE FOREIGN POLICY?

1. For an overview of the structure, see Kenneth Lieberthal, *Governing China: From Revolution Through Reform*, 2nd ed. (New York: Norton, 2003).

2. Andrew J. Nathan, *Chinese Democracy* (New York: Knopf, 1985).

3. Dr. Li Zhisui, with Anne F. Thurston, *The Private Life of Chairman Mao* (New York: Random House, 1994).

4. Roderick MacFarquhar, *The Origins of the Cultural Revolution, 2: The Great Leap Forward 1958–1960* (New York: Columbia University Press, 1983).

5. "On Questions of Party History," *Beijing Review* 27 (July 6, 1981), 29.

6. Li, *Private Life*.

7. Ezra F. Vogel, *Deng Xiaoping and the Transformation of China* (Cambridge, Mass.: Harvard University Press, 2011); Zhao Ziyang, *Prisoner of the State: The Secret Journal of Premier Zhao Ziyang*, trans. and ed. Bao Pu, Renee Chiang, and Adi Ignatius (New York: Simon and Schuster, 2009).

8. Bruce Gilley, *Tiger on the Brink: Jiang Zemin and China's New Elite* (Berkeley: University of California Press, 1998).

9. Zong Hairen, "Zhu Rongji in 1999: Visit to the United States," *Chinese Law and Government* 35, no. 1 (January–February 2002): 36–52.

10. Andrew J. Nathan, "A Factionalism Model for CCP Politics," *China Quarterly* 53 (January–March 1973): 34–66; Andrew J. Nathan and Kellee S. Tsai, "Factionalism: A New Institutionalist Restatement," *China Journal* 34 (July 1995): 157–192.

11. Robert S. Ross, "From Lin Biao to Deng Xiaoping: Elite Instability and China's U.S. Policy," *China Quarterly* 118 (June 1989): 265–299.

12. Paul H. Kreisberg, "China's Negotiating Behavior," in Thomas W. Robinson and

David Shambaugh, eds., *Chinese Foreign Policy: Theory and Practice* (Oxford: Clarendon Press, 1994), 453–477; Richard H. Solomon, *Chinese Negotiating Behavior: Pursuing Interests Through "Old Friends"* (Washington, D.C.: United States Institute of Peace Press, 1999).

13. Gao Wenqian, *Zhou Enlai: The Last Perfect Revolutionary* (New York: PublicAffairs, 2007).

14. Andrew J. Nathan, "China's Changing of the Guard: Authoritarian Resilience," *Journal of Democracy* 14, no. 1 (January 2003): 6–17.

15. "Lee Teng-hui" is the conventional spelling of this name. Other correct spellings are "Li Teng-hui" (Wade-Giles) and "Li Denghui" (pinyin).

16. Thanks to Zong Hairen for this information. Some of the CLSGs involved in foreign affairs are discussed in Qi Zhou, "Organization, Structure, and Image in the Making of Chinese Foreign Policy Since the Early 1990s," Ph.D. diss., Johns Hopkins University, 2008.

17. John W. Garver, *China & Iran: Ancient Partners in a Post-Imperial World* (Seattle: University of Washington Press, 2006); Evan S. Medeiros, *Reluctant Restraint: The Evolution of China's Nonproliferation Policies and Practices, 1980–2004* (Stanford: Stanford University Press, 2007).

18. Martin K. Dimitrov, *Piracy and the State: The Politics of Intellectual Property Rights in China* (Cambridge: Cambridge University Press, 2009).

19. Public security is a powerful separate domain and also quite federalized, leading to a lack of channels to consider the international impact of arrests. Examples in which the public-security apparatus has apparently overlooked the foreign affairs costs of its actions are the cases of Nobel Peace Prize winner Liu Xiaobo, blind amateur lawyer Chen Guangcheng, AIDS activist Hu Jia, and (in an earlier time) the arrests of U.S.-based scholars Song Yongyi, Li Shaomin, and Wang Fei-ling. Of course, some of these acts may have been approved by the center and intended to send a message. It is hard to know.

20. Scott W. Harold, "Freeing Trade : Negotiating Domestic and International Obstacles on China's Long Road to the GATT/WTO, 1971–2001," Ph.D. diss., Columbia University, 2008.

21. Ann Kent, *Beyond Compliance: China, International Organizations, and Global Security* (Stanford: Stanford University Press, 2007).

22. Alastair Iain Johnston, *Social States: China in International Institutions, 1980–2000* (Princeton: Princeton University Press, 2008).

23. A. Doak Barnett, *The Making of Foreign Policy in China* (Boulder: Westview, 1985); David Shambaugh, "China's National Security Research Bureaucracy," *China Quarterly* 119 (June 1987): 276–304; Carol Lee Hamrin and Suisheng Zhao, eds., *Decision-Making in Deng's China* (Armonk, N.Y.: M. E. Sharpe, 1995); Lu Ning, *The Dynamics of Foreign Policy Decisionmaking in China* (Boulder: Westview, 2000); David M. Lampton, ed., *The Making of Chinese Foreign and Security Policy* (Stanford: Stanford University Press, 2001); David Shambaugh, "China's International Relations Think Tanks: Evolving Structure and Process," *China Quarterly* 171

(September 2002): 575–596; Bates Gill and James Mulvenon, "Chinese Military-Related Think Tanks and Research Institutions," *China Quarterly* 171 (September 2002): 617–624.

24. U.S. Defense Security Service, *Technology Collection Trends in the U.S. Defense Industry 2007* (Alexandria, Va.: Defense Security Service Counterintelligence Office, 2006).

25. Zhang Liang, comp., Andrew J. Nathan and Perry Link, eds., *The Tiananmen Papers* (New York: PublicAffairs, 2001).

26. Andrew Scobell, *China's Use of Military Force: Beyond the Great Wall and the Long March* (Cambridge: Cambridge University Press, 2003); Andrew Scobell, "Military Coups in the People's Republic of China: Failure, Fabrication, or Fancy?" *Journal of Northeast Asian Studies* 16 (Spring 1995): 25–46.

27. James Mulvenon, "China: Conditional Compliance," in Muthiah Alagappa, ed., *Coercion and Governance: The Declining Political Role of the Military* (Stanford: Stanford University Press, 2001), 329–30.

28. According to the memoirs of Admiral Liu Huaqing, it was then party secretary and CMC vice chair Zhao Ziyang who pressed for resolute action in 1988, undoubtedly with Deng's support. See Liu Huaqing, *Liu Huaqing huiyilu* (Beijing: Jiefangjun chubanshe, 2004), 535–544.

29. On the issuance of No. 1 Order, see John W. Lewis and Xue Litai, *Imagined Enemies: China Prepares for Uncertain War* (Stanford: Stanford University Press, 2006), chap. 3; on the events of 1971 and 1976, see Scobell, "Military Coups in the People's Republic of China."

30. On the PLA's rhetoric and actions, see Andrew Scobell, "Is There a Civil–Military Gap in China's Peaceful Rise?" *Parameters* (Summer 2009) 39, no. 2: 4–22.

31. On Chinese soldiers' attitudes and mindsets, see Scobell, *China's Use of Military Force*; on the underinstitutionalization of civil–military relations, see Andrew Scobell, "China's Evolving Civil–Military Relations: Creeping *Guojiahua*," *Armed Forces & Society* (Winter 2005): 228–230.

32. Andrew J. Nathan and Bruce Gilley, *China's New Rulers: The Secret Files*, 2nd ed. (New York: New York Review Books, 2003).

33. The quotes in this paragraph come from ibid., 137–143.

3. LIFE ON THE HINGE

1. Dean Acheson, "Crisis in China—an Examination of United States Policy," *Department of State Bulletin* 22 (January 23, 1950), 116. The speech was delivered on January 12, 1950, before the National Press Club in Washington, D.C.

2. Mao Tse-tung, *Selected Works of Mao Tse-tung*, 5 vols. (Peking: Foreign Languages Press, 1961), 4:415.

3. Nancy Bernkopf Tucker, *Patterns in the Dust* (New York: Columbia University Press, 1983).

4. The four Nordic states and Israel recognized the PRC in 1950.

5. "Mao Zedong and Dulles's 'Peaceful Evolution' Strategy: Revelations from Bo Yibo's Memoirs," introduction, translation, and annotation by Qiang Zhai, *Cold War International History Project Bulletin* 6–7 (Winter 1995–1996): 228–231.

6. Deborah A. Kaple, *Dream of a Red Factory: The Legacy of High Stalinism in China* (New York: Oxford University Press, 1994); Hua-Yu Li, *Mao and the Economic Stalinization of China, 1948–1953* (Lanham, Md.: Rowman and Littlefield, 2006).

7. Zhang Shuguang, *Economic Cold War* (Stanford: Stanford University Press, 2001).

8. Nicholas R. Lardy, "Economic Recovery and the 1st Five-Year Plan," in Roderick MacFarquhar and John K. Fairbank, eds., *The Cambridge History of China*, vol. 14 (Cambridge: Cambridge University Press, 1987), 179.

9. Steven I. Levine, *Anvil of Victory: The Communist Revolution in Manchuria, 1945–1948* (New York: Columbia University Press, 1987), chaps. 1–2.

10. Alexander V. Pantsov with Steven I. Levine, *Mao: The Real Story* (New York: Simon and Schuster, forthcoming).

11. Gordon H. Chang, *Friends and Enemies: The United States, China, and the Soviet Union, 1948–1972* (Stanford: Stanford University Press, 1990).

12. Using the technique of "Pekingology"—that is, close scrutiny of esoteric texts—Donald Zagoria was able to trace the signs of the emerging Sino–Soviet split in the public communiqués of socialist camp meetings starting in 1956; Donald Zagoria, *The Sino–Soviet Conflict, 1956–1961* (Princeton: Princeton University Press, 1962). Leading recent works are Lorenz M. Lüthi, *The Sino–Soviet Split: Cold War in the Communist World* (Princeton: Princeton University Press, 2008), and Sergey Radchenko, *Two Suns in the Heavens: The Sino–Soviet Struggle for Supremacy, 1962–1967* (Washington, D.C., and Stanford: Woodrow Wilson Center Press and Stanford University Press, 2009).

13. The negotiations over nuclear cooperation are discussed in John W. Lewis and Xue Litai, *China Builds the Bomb* (Stanford: Stanford University Press, 1988).

14. Frank Dikötter, *Mao's Great Famine: The History of China's Most Devastating Catastrophe 1958–1962* (New York: Walker, 2010).

15. "Minutes, Conversation Between Mao Zedong and Ambassador Yudin, 22 July 1958," *Cold War International History Project Bulletin* 6–7 (Winter 1995–1996): 155–159.

16. Quoted in Quan Yanchi, *Mao Zedong yu Keluxiaofu* (Mao Zedong and Khrushchev) (Huhehot, China: Nei Menggu renmin chubanshe, 1998), 139.

17. Michael MccGwire, *Military Objectives in Soviet Foreign Policy* (Washington, D.C.: Brookings Institution Press, 1987), 164; Raymond L. Garthoff, *Détente and Confrontation: American–Soviet Relations from Nixon to Reagan* (Washington, D.C.: Brookings Institution Press, 1985), 208.

18. In 1969, a Soviet diplomat in Washington asked a State Department official what the U.S. reaction might be if the Soviets bombed the Chinese nuclear test site at Lop Nor. Patrick Tyler, *A Great Wall, Six Presidents, and China: An Investigative History* (New York: PublicAffairs, 1999), 67.

19. Thomas Robinson, "China Confronts the Soviet Union: Warfare and Diplomacy on China's Inner Asian Frontiers," in Roderick MacFarquhar and John K. Fairbank, eds., *The Cambridge History of China*, vol. 15 (Cambridge: Cambridge University Press, 1991), chap. 3.

20. Alexey D. Muraviev, *The Russian Pacific Fleet: From Crimean War to Perestroika*, Papers in Australian Maritime Affairs no. 20 (Canberra: Department of Defence Seapower Center, 2007), 28, table 1.

21. Chang, *Friends and Enemies*, chap. 8.

22. Evelyn Goh, *Constructing the U.S. Rapprochement with China, 1961–1974* (Cambridge: Cambridge University Press, 2005); Michael Lumbers, *Piercing the Bamboo Curtain: Tentative Bridge-Building to China During the Johnson Years* (Manchester: Manchester University Press, 2008).

23. Robert S. Ross, ed., *China, the United States, and the Soviet Union: Tripolarity and Policy Making During the Cold War* (Armonk, N.Y.: M. E. Sharpe, 1993); Lowell Dittmer, "The Strategic Triangle: An Elementary Game-Theoretical Analysis," *World Politics* 33, no. 4 (July 1981): 485–515.

24. Henry Kissinger, *Years of Upheaval* (Boston: Little, Brown, 1982), 233.

25. Zbigniew Brzezinski, *Power and Principle: Memoirs of the National Security Adviser, 1977–1981* (New York: Farrar, Straus, Giroux, 1983), 412.

26. On Chinese views of Gorbachev's mistakes, see David L. Shambaugh, *China's Communist Party: Atrophy and Adaptation* (Berkeley: University of California Press, 2008), chap. 4.

27. These figures are from the Stockholm International Peace Research Institute Arms Transfers Database, updated March 31, 2009, at http://www.sipri.org/contents/amstrad/at-db.htm, accessed April 1, 2009.

28. Bobo Lo, *Axis of Convenience: Moscow, Beijing, and the New Global Politics* (Washington, D.C.: Brookings Institution Press, 2008), chap. 8.

4. DECIPHERING THE U.S. THREAT

1. On the range of Chinese views of the U.S., see Carola McGiffert, ed., *Chinese Images of the United States* (Washington, D.C.: Center for Strategic and International Studies, 2005).

2. Andrew Scobell, *China and Strategic Culture* (Carlisle, Pa.: Strategic Studies Institute, U.S. Army War College, 2002), 2. This conception was derived from Allen S. Whiting, *China Eyes Japan* (Berkeley: University of California Press, 1989).

3. Scobell, *China and Strategic Culture*; Andrew Scobell, *China's Use of Military Force: Beyond the Great Wall and the Long March* (New York: Cambridge University Press, 2003), chap. 2.

4. See, for example, Zhang Liang, comp., Andrew J. Nathan and Perry Link, eds., *The Tiananmen Papers* (New York: PublicAffairs, 2001), 338–348.

5. See the quotations and analysis of the views of China's fourth generation of leaders

in Andrew J. Nathan and Bruce Gilley, *China's New Rulers: The Secret Files* (New York: New York Review Books, 2002), chap. 8.

6. John Mearsheimer's theory of offensive realism has attracted even greater attention in China than it has in the U.S. He has been invited to China, and his book *The Tragedy of Great Power Politics* (New York: Norton, 2001) has been translated into Chinese. Western realism is compatible with premodern Chinese understandings of political behavior. See Alastair Iain Johnston, *Cultural Realism: Strategic Culture and Grand Strategy in Chinese History* (Princeton: Princeton University Press, 1995).

7. See, for example, "China Condemns US Two-Faced Human Rights Report," *People's Daily Online*, May 20, 2004, at http://english.peopledaily.com.cn/200405/20 /eng20040520_143933.html, accessed December 10, 2008; and "Opinion: US Two-Faced Stance on Taiwan Damaging," *China Daily*, December 5, 2003, at http:// www.chinadaily.com.cn/en/doc/2003–12/05/content_287410.htm, accessed December 10, 2008.

8. See Michael Pillsbury, *China Debates the Future Security Environment* (Washington, D.C.: National Defense University Press, 2000).

9. Except when there is an active war going on within the territory of another combatant command.

10. U.S. Department of Defense, *Base Structure Report Fiscal Year 2007 Baseline* (Washington, D.C.: Department of Defense, 2007), 6, at http://www.defenselink.mil/pubs /BSR_2007_Baseline.pdf, accessed November 8, 2008.

11. Official figures from U.S. Pacific Command, at http://www.pacom.mil/about /pacom/shtml, accessed September 19, 2010.

12. Qian Wenrong, "What Has Influenced Bush?" *Shijie zhishi* (World Knowledge) (September 2005), 43, cited in Susan L. Craig, *Chinese Perceptions of Traditional and Nontraditional Security Threats* (Carlisle, Pa.: Strategic Studies Institute, U.S. Army War College, 2007), 49.

13. Wolfgang K. H. Panofsky, "Nuclear Insecurity," *Foreign Affairs* 86, no. 5 (September–October 2007): 109–118; Keir A. Lieber and Daryl G. Press. "The Rise of U.S. Nuclear Primacy." *Foreign Affairs* 85, no. 2 (March–April 2006): 42–54. Another five thousand nuclear weapons are in reserve.

14. Harold James, "The Enduring International Preeminence of the Dollar," in Eric Helleiner and Jonathan Kirshner, eds., *The Future of the Dollar* (Ithaca: Cornell University Press, 2009), chap. 2.

15. Daniel W. Drezner, "Bad Debts: Assessing China's Financial Influence in Great Power Politics," *International Security* 34, no. 2 (Fall 2009): 7–45.

16. Key treaties to which the U.S. has not acceded include the International Covenant on Civil and Political Rights, the Convention on the Elimination of All Forms of Discrimination Against Women, the Convention on the Rights of the Child, and the Rome Statute that created the International Criminal Court.

17. Zhang Baijia and Jia Qingguo, "Steering Wheel, Shock Absorber, and Diplomatic

Probe in Confrontation: Sino–American Ambassadorial Talks Seen from the Chinese Perspective," in Robert S. Ross and Jiang Changbin, eds., *Re-examining the Cold War: U.S.–China Diplomacy, 1954–1973* (Cambridge, Mass.: Asia Center, Harvard University, 2001), 173–199.

18. Evan S. Medeiros, *Reluctant Restraint: The Evolution of China's Nonproliferation Policies and Practices,1980–2004* (Stanford: Stanford University Press, 2007).

19. For authoritative discussion of these texts, see Richard C. Bush, *At Cross Purposes: U.S.–Taiwan Relations Since 1942* (Armonk, N.Y.: M. E. Sharpe, 2004). Quotations relating to Taiwan in this paragraph and the following paragraphs are drawn from this work.

20. Some specialists have argued that "recognizing" the Chinese government as the sole legal government of China and then "acknowledging" its position that Taiwan is a part of China were not necessarily the same as recognizing Chinese sovereignty over Taiwan. However, there has been no exploitation of this ambiguity in U.S. diplomacy, so it is a nonissue for practical purposes.

21. Under this framework, the U.S. government's interests are handled by an ostensible NGO that is government funded, staffed, and directed, the American Institute in Taiwan. Taiwan created a counterpart entity—which, after subsequent renaming, became the Taipei Economic and Cultural Office—to perform the duties of the ROC's former embassy and consulates in the U.S.

22. Zhu Chenghu, ed., *ZhongMei guanxi de fazhan bianhua ji qi qushi* (Changes in the Development of China–U.S. Relations and Their Trends) (Nanjing: Jiangsu renmin chubanshe, 1998), 194.

23. Yong Deng makes this point in *China's Struggle for Status: The Realignment of International Relations* (New York: Cambridge University Press, 2008), chap. 4.

24. Because China was a "nonmarket economy," under U.S. law most-favored-nation status was extended on an annual basis and subject to congressional review until China's entry into the WTO in 2001 gave it "permanent normal trade relations" with the U.S.

25. James Mann, *The China Fantasy: How Our Leaders Explain Away Chinese Repression* (New York: Viking, 2007).

26. Analysts' views were obtained in interviews by Andrew Scobell, Shanghai and Beijing, May–June 2008; Beijing, October 2008 and October 2009.

27. Robert D. Zoellick, "Whither China: From Membership to Responsibility? Remarks to National Committee on U.S.–China Relations," September 21, 2005, at http://www.ncuscr.org/files/2005Gala_RobertZoellick_Whither_China1.pdf, accessed August 10, 2010.

28. U.S. Department of Defense, *Quadrennial Defense Review Report* (Washington, D.C.: U.S. Department of Defense, February 6, 2006), 29–30, at http://www.defense link.mil/pubs/pdfs/QDR20060203.pdf, accessed August 11, 2010.

29. White House, *The National Security Strategy of the United States* (Washington, D.C.: White House, March 2006), at http://georgewbush-whitehouse.archives.gov /nsc/nss/2006/sectionVIII.html, accessed August 11, 2010.

30. For analyses of the consistency between the Bush and Obama administration policies, see Zhu Feng, *A Return of Chinese Pragmatism*, PACNET no. 16 (Honolulu: Center for Strategic and International Studies Pacific Forum, April 5, 2010); Zhao Yang, "China Is More Confident, but by No Means 'Arrogant,'" *Nanfang ribao* (Southern Daily), online edition, May 13, 2010, at http://www.nanfang daily.com.cn, accessed May 20, 2010; "The US Pursuit of Hegemony Unchanged," *Study Times*, June 7, 2010, at http://www/studytimes.com.cn:9999/epaper/xxsb /html/2010/06/07/07/07_46htm, accessed June 20, 2010.

31. James B. Steinberg, "China's Arrival: The Long March to Global Power," speech at the Center for a New American Security, Washington, D.C., September 24, 2009, at http://www.cnas.org/node/3415, accessed January 16, 2012.

32. White House, *National Security Strategy of the United States* (Washington, D.C.: White House, May 2010), 43, at http://www.whitehouse.gov/sites/default/files/rss _viewer/national_security_strategy.pdf, accessed August 11, 2010.

33. U.S. Department of Defense, *Quadrennial Defense Review Report* (Washington, D.C.: U.S. Department of Defense, February 2010), 60, at http://www.defense.gov /qdr/qdr%20as%20of%2029jan10%201600.pdf, accessed August 11, 2010.

34. Thomas J. Christensen, *Useful Adversaries: Grand Strategy, Domestic Mobilization, and Sino–American Conflict, 1947–1958* (Princeton: Princeton University Press, 1996); Michael H. Hunt, *Ideology and U.S. Foreign Policy* (New Haven: Yale University Press, 1987).

35. Feng Changhong, "How to View U.S. Strategic Thinking," in McGiffert, ed., *Chinese Images of the United States*, 40.

36. Li Qun, a prominent official on the Shandong Provincial Party Committee, quoted in Andrew J. Nathan, "Medals and Rights: What the Olympics Reveal, and Conceal, about China," *The New Republic*, July 9, 2008, 46.

37. Scobell, *China and Strategic Culture*, 16–18.

38. Quotations from Chinese leaders here and in the next paragraph are drawn from Nathan and Gilley, *China's New Rulers*, 235–238.

39. Wang Jisi, "Building a Constructive Relationship," in Morton Abramowitz, Yoichi Funabashi, and Wang Jisi, eds., *China–Japan–U.S.: Managing Trilateral Relations* (Tokyo: Japan Center for International Exchange, 1998), 22.

40. Zhou Mei, "Chinese Views of America: A Survey," in McGiffert, ed., *Chinese Images of the United States*, 65.

5. THE NORTHEAST ASIA REGIONAL SYSTEM

1. Saadia M. Pekkanen and Paul Kallender-Umezu, *In Defense of Japan: From the Market to the Military in Space Policy* (Stanford: Stanford University Press, 2010); Andrew L. Oros and Yuki Tatsumi, *Global Security Watch: Japan* (Santa Barbara: Praeger, 2010).

2. Many Western scholars have asked this question. Among them are Susan L. Shirk, *China: Fragile Superpower* (Oxford: Oxford University Press, 2007), chap. 6; Ming Wan, *Sino–Japanese Relations: Interaction, Logic, and Transformation* (Stanford: Stanford University Press, 2006); Alan Whiting, *China Eyes Japan* (Berkeley: University of California Press, 1989); Michael Yahuda, "The Limits of Economic Interdependence: Sino–Japanese Relations," in Alastair Iain Johnston and Robert S. Ross, eds., *New Directions in the Study of China's Foreign Policy*, 162–185 (Stanford: Stanford University Press, 2006). All argue that the Sino–Japanese relationship is essentially determined by elite or popular attitudes or both to the extent that popular dislike of each other, especially China's of Japan, limits development of the relationship in defiance of national interest.

3. Richard C. Bush, *The Perils of Proximity: China–Japan Security Relations* (Washington, D.C.: Brookings Institution Press, 2010).

4. The Japanese "side" refers to its side of a line drawn down the middle of the East China Sea, which Japan says should be honored by both countries because the EEZs that each can claim in that sea under the UNCLOS overlap.

5. On the Japanese grand strategy, see Richard J. Samuels, *Securing Japan: Tokyo's Grand Strategy and the Future of East Asia* (Ithaca: Cornell University Press, 2007).

6. Article 9 continues: "[L]and, sea, and air forces, as well as other war potential, will never be maintained. The right of belligerency of the state will not be recognized." It is in keeping with this provision that the Japanese military forces are called the Self-Defense Forces.

7. The U.S. has not taken sides in Japan's territorial disputes with China, Russia, and Korea but takes the position that the Treaty of Mutual Cooperation and Security creates an obligation for the U.S. to help defend any territories held by Japan, which include the Senkaku Islands.

8. See, for example, Thomas U. Berger, *Cultures of Antimilitarism: National Security in Germany and Japan* (Baltimore: Johns Hopkins University Press, 1998); Andrew L. Oros, *Normalizing Japan: Politics, Identity, and the Evolution of Security Practice* (Stanford: Stanford University Press, 2008).

9. See, for instance, Christopher W. Hughes, *Japan's Remilitarisation* (New York: Routledge, 2009).

10. Richard Samuels, "'New Fighting Power!' Japan's Growing Maritime Capabilities and East Asian Security," *International Security* 32, no. 3 (Winter 2007–2008): 84–112.

11. Thomas J. Christensen, "China, the U.S.–Japan Alliance, and the Security Dilemma in East Asia," *International Security* 23, no. 4 (Spring 1999): 49–80; Wu Xinbo, "The End of the Silver Lining: A Chinese View of the U.S.–Japanese Alliance," *Washington Quarterly* 20, no. 1 (Winter 2005–2006): 119–130.

12. Karl W. Deutsch, *Political Community and the North Atlantic Area: International Organization in the Light of Historical Experience* (Princeton: Princeton University Press, 1957).

13. Wan, *Sino–Japanese Relations*, chaps. 2–3.

14. This point is well developed in Wan, *Sino–Japanese Relations*, chap. 3.

15. Here we differ with Susan L. Shirk's *China: Fragile Superpower*, chap. 6, which sees the government's policies as driven by popular sentiment.

16. Chae-Jin Lee, *China and Japan: New Economic Diplomacy* (Stanford: Hoover Institution Press, 1984), 35.

17. Andrew Scobell and John M. Sanford, *North Korea's Military Threat: Pyongyang's Conventional Forces, Weapons of Mass Destruction, and Ballistic Missiles* (Carlisle, Pa.: Strategic Studies Institute, U.S. Army War College, 2007). Pyongyang also developed chemical and biological weapons programs. Discerning Pyongyang's intentions and strategy is an inherently speculative exercise. See, for example, Andrew Scobell, *North Korea's Strategic Intentions* (Carlisle, Pa.: Strategic Studies Institute, U.S. Army War College, 2005).

18. For a firsthand account of this episode, see Charles L. Pritchard, *Failed Diplomacy: The Tragic Story of How North Korea Got the Bomb* (Washington, D.C.: Brookings Institution Press, 2007), chap. 2. North Korea denied that its official made this statement, but in 2009 Pyongyang asserted that it did possess an experimental program in highly enriched uranium.

19. Andrew Scobell, *China and North Korea: From Comrades-in-Arms to Allies at Arm's Length* (Carlisle, Pa.: Strategic Studies Institute, U.S. Army War College, 2004), 11–13; Yoichi Funabashi, *The Peninsula Question: A Chronicle of the Second Korean Nuclear Crisis* (Washington, D.C.: Brookings Institution Press, 2007), 266, 271.

20. On China's interests and priorities, see Avery Goldstein, "Across the Yalu: China's Interests and the Korean Peninsula in a Changing World," in Alastair Iain Johnston and Robert S. Ross, eds., *New Directions in the Study of China's Foreign Policy* (Stanford: Stanford University Press, 2006), 131–161; David Shambaugh, "China and the Korean Peninsula: Playing for the Long Term," *Washington Quarterly* 26, no. 2 (Spring 2003): 43–56.

21. Scott Snyder, *China's Rise and the Two Koreas: Politics, Economics, Security* (Boulder: Lynne Rienner, 2009), 9, 98, 112. For more in Chinese investments, see Jae Cheol Kim, "The Political Economy of Chinese Investment in North Korea: A Preliminary Assessment," *Asian Survey* 46, no. 6 (December 2006): 898–916.

22. Daniel Gomà, "The Chinese–Korean Border Issue: An Analysis of a Contested Frontier," *Asian Survey* 46, no. 6 (November–December 2006): 867–880.

6. CHINA'S OTHER NEIGHBORS

1. Microstates are those with a population of five hundred thousand or less. The twelve microstates of Oceania are the Solomon Islands, Kiribati, the Marshall Islands, Nauru, Palau, Tuvalu, the Cook Islands, the Federated States of Micronesia, Niue, Samoa, Tonga, and Vanuatu.

2. Steven I. Levine, "China in Asia: The PRC as a Regional Power," in Harry Harding,

ed., *China's Foreign Relations in the 1980s* (New Haven: Yale University Press, 1984), 107.

3. Zhang Qingmin and Liu Bing, "Shounao chufang yu Zhongguo waijiao" (Summit trips abroad and Chinese diplomacy), *Guoji zhengzhi yanjiu* (International politics research), no. 2 (2008): 1–20.

4. David Shambaugh, ed., *Power Shift: China and Asia's New Dynamics* (Berkeley: University of California Press, 2005); Evan S. Medeiros, Keith Crane, Eric Heginbotham, Norman D. Levine, Julia F. Lowell, Angel Rabasa, and Somi Seong, *Pacific Currents: The Responses of U.S. Allies and Security Partners in East Asia to China's Rise* (Santa Monica, Calif.: RAND, 2008). We therefore disagree with those who see China as able to drive the U.S. out of Asia, such as Aaron L. Friedberg in *A Contest for Supremacy: China, America, and the Struggle for Mastery in Asia* (New York: Norton, 2011).

5. So does Taiwan, which occupies the Pratas Islands. However, so long as both China and Taiwan adhere to the "one China principle," discussed in chapter 8, their claims reinforce rather than conflict with one another.

6. For a guide to who claims what, see http://www.southchinasea.org/maps/US%20 EIA,%20South%20China%20Sea%20Tables%20and%20Maps.htm, accessed October 8, 2010.

7. Andrew Scobell, "China's Strategy Toward the South China Sea," in Martin Edmonds and Michael M. Tsai, eds., *Taiwan's Maritime Security* (New York: Routledge Curzon, 2003), 42–43; and Andrew Scobell, "Slow Intensity Conflict in the South China Sea," e-note distributed by the Foreign Policy Research Institute, Philadelphia, August 16, 2000.

8. Allen S. Whiting, "ASEAN Eyes China: The Security Dimension," *Asian Survey* 37, no. 4 (April 1997): 299–322.

9. Bates Gill, *Rising Star: China's New Security Diplomacy* (Washington, D.C.: Brookings Institution Press, 2007), 4–5.

10. Geoffrey Till, *Asia Rising and the Maritime Decline of the West: A Review of the Issues: IQPC/Asia Rising*, S. Rajaratnam School of International Studies (RSIS) Working Paper no. 205 (Singapore: RSIS, July 29, 2010).

11. For this and several other details on economic relations, see Tamara Renee Shie, "Rising Chinese Influence in the South Pacific: Beijing's Island Fever," *Asian Survey* 47, no. 2 (March–April 2008), 315.

12. Fergus Hanson, *China: Stumbling Through the Pacific* (Sydney: Lowy Institute for International Policy Brief, July 2009), 3–4.

13. Anthony Van Fossen, "The Struggle for Recognition: Diplomatic Competition Between China and Taiwan in Oceania," *Journal of Chinese Political Science* 12, no. 2 (2007), 135.

14. Jian Yang, "China in the South Pacific: Hegemon on the Horizon?" *Pacific Review* 22, no. 2 (May 2009): 139–158.

15. Brantly Womack, *China and Vietnam: The Politics of Asymmetry* (New York: Cambridge University Press, 2006).

16. Nicholas Khoo, *Collateral Damage: Sino–Soviet Rivalry and the Termination of the Sino–Vietnamese Alliance* (New York: Columbia University Press, 2010).

17. King Chen, *China's War with Vietnam* (Stanford: Hoover Institution Press, 1987); Robert S. Ross, *Indochina Tangle: China's Vietnam Policy, 1975–1979* (New York: Columbia University Press, 1988).

18. For an alternative interpretation emphasizing Asian leaders' preferences as the chief determinant of regional security relationships, see Amitav Acharya, *Whose Ideas Matter? Agency and Power in Asian Regionalism* (Ithaca: Cornell University Press, 2009).

19. Benedict Anderson, *Imagined Communities: Reflections on the Origin and Spread of Nationalism* (London: Verso, 1983).

20. Donald K. Emmerson, ed., *Hard Choices: Security, Democracy, and Regionalism in Southeast Asia* (Stanford: Walter H. Shorenstein Asia-Pacific Research Center, 2008).

21. Wu Xinbo, "Chinese Perspectives on Building an East Asia Community in the Twenty-First Century," in Michael J. Green and Bates Gill, eds., *Cooperation, Competition, and the Search for Community: Asia's New Multilateralism* (New York: Columbia University Press, 2009).

22. Zou Keyuan, "The Sino–Vietnamese Agreement on Maritime Boundary Delimitation in the Gulf of Tonkin," *Ocean Development and International Law* 36 (January–March 2005): 13–24.

23. Hideo Ohashi, "China's Regional Trade and Investment Profile," in Shambaugh, ed., *Power Shift*, 71–95.

24. Richard Cronin and Timothy Hamlin, *Mekong Tipping Point* (Washington, D.C.: Stimson Center, 2010), at http://www.stimson.org/images/uploads/research-pdfs /Mekong_Tipping_Point-Complete.pdf, accessed May 18, 2011.

25. John W. Garver, *Protracted Contest: Sino–Indian Rivalry in the Twentieth Century* (Seattle: University of Washington Press, 2001).

26. George Perkovich, *India's Nuclear Bomb: The Impact on Global Proliferation* (Berkeley: University of California Press, 1999), 196–197.

27. Shirley A. Kan. *China and Proliferation of Weapons of Mass Destruction and Missiles: Policy Issues* (Washington, D.C.: Congressional Research Service, May 2011).

28. Mathieu Duchâtel, "The Terrorist Risk and China's Policy Toward Pakistan: Strategic Reassurance and the 'United Front,'" *Journal of Contemporary China* 20, no. 71 (September 2011): 543–561.

29. Robert D. Kaplan, *Monsoon: The Indian Ocean and the Future of American Power* (New York: Random House, 2010); Christopher J. Pehrson, *String of Pearls: Meeting the Challenge of China's Rising Power Across the Asian Littoral* (Carlisle, Pa.: Strategic Studies Institute, U.S. Army War College, 2006).

30. Jonathan Holslag, *China and India: Prospects for Peace* (New York: Columbia University Press, 2010).

31. On "great-power dreams," see Andrew Scobell, "'Cult of Defense' and 'Great Power Dreams,'" in Michael R. Chambers, ed., *South Asia 2020: Strategic Balances and*

Alliances, 342–348 (Carlisle, Pa.: Strategic Studies Institute, U.S. Army War College, 2002); on views of analysts, see Jing-dong Yuan, "India's Rise After Pokhran-II: Chinese Analyses and Assessments," *Asian Survey* 41, no. 6 (November–December 2001), 992–993, 998.

32. Mohan Malik, "The Shanghai Cooperation Organization," in Sumit Ganguly, Joseph Liow, and Andrew Scobell, eds., *The Routledge Handbook of Asian Security Studies*, 72–86 (New York: Routledge, 2010).

33. Human Rights in China, *Counter-Terrorism and Human Rights: The Impact of the Shanghai Cooperation Organization: A Human Rights in China Whitepaper* (New York: Human Rights in China, March 2011), at http://www.hrichina.org /content/5199#IVDii, accessed May 19, 2011.

34. Gardner Bovingdon, *The Uyghurs: Strangers in Their Own Land* (New York: Columbia University Press, 2010), 140.

35. Kevin Sheives, "China Turns West: Beijing's Contemporary Strategy Towards Central Asia," *Pacific Affairs* 79, no. 2 (Summer 2006): 219–222; Hasan H. Karrar, *The New Silk Road Diplomacy: China's Central Asian Foreign Policy Since the Cold War* (Vancouver: University of British Columbia Press, 2009), 58–66.

7. CHINA IN THE FOURTH RING

1. Gabriel B. Collins, Andrew S. Erickson, Lyle J. Goldstein, and William S. Murray, eds., *China's Energy Strategy: The Impact on Beijing's Maritime Policies* (Annapolis: Naval Institute Press, 2008) ; Erica S. Downs, "The Chinese Energy Security Debate," *China Quarterly* 177 (March 2004): 21–41; Bo Kong, *China's International Petroleum Policy* (Santa Barbara: Praeger Security International, 2010); *China's Thirst for Oil*, Asia Report no. 153 (Brussels: International Crisis Group, June 9, 2008), at http://www.crisisgroup.org/~/media/Files/asia/north-east-asia/153_china_s _thirst_for_oil.ashx, accessed July 21, 2011; Daniel H. Rosen and Trevor Houser, *China Energy: A Guide for the Perplexed* (Washington, D.C.: Peterson Institute for International Economics, May 2007), at http://www.iie.com/publications/papers /rosen0507.pdf, accessed August 3, 2011.

2. John W. Garver, *China & Iran: Ancient Partners in a Post-imperial World* (Seattle: University of Washington Press, 2006); International Crisis Group, "The Iran Nuclear Issue: The View from Beijing," Asia Briefing no. 100, February 17, 2010, at http://www.crisisgroup.org/home/index.cfm?id=6536&l=1, accessed March 23, 2010.

3. Barry Sautman and Yan Hairong. "Friends and Interests: China's Distinctive Links with Africa," *African Studies Review* 50, no. 3 (December 2007): 75–114.

4. Quoted in Robyn Dixon, "Africa Holds Attractions for China Leaders; Beijing's Hunger for Raw Materials and Political Recognition Has Its Top Officials Crisscrossing the Continent Like No One Else to Cement Ties," *Los Angeles Times*, January 31, 2007.

5. Thomas Lum, Hannah Fischer, Julissa Gomez-Granger, and Anne Leland, *China's*

Foreign Aid Activities in Africa, Latin America, and Southeast Asia (Washington, D.C.: Congressional Research Service, February 25, 2009).

6. Deborah Brautigam, *The Dragon's Gift: The Real Story of China in Africa* (Oxford: Oxford University Press, 2009).

7. Joel Wuthnow, "Beyond the Veto: Chinese Diplomacy in the United Nations Security Council," Ph.D. diss., Columbia University, 2011.

8. Information Office of the State Council, People's Republic of China, *China's National Defense in 2010* (Beijing: Information Office of the State Council, March 2011); Bates Gill and Chin-Hao Huang, "China's Expanding Presence in UN Peacekeeping Operations," in Roy Kamphausen, David Lai, and Andrew Scobell, eds., *Beyond the Strait: PLA Missions Other Than Taiwan*, 99–125 (Carlisle, Pa.: Strategic Studies Institute, U.S. Army War College, 2009).

9. Sam Sheringham, "Chinese Invade the Caribbean in an Attempt to Isolate Taiwan," Bloomberg News Service, March 11, 2007.

10. Wuthnow, "Beyond the Veto," 43–45.

11. For examples, see Ann Kent, *Beyond Compliance: China, International Organizations, and Global Security* (Stanford: Stanford University Press, 2007), and Rosemary Foot and Andrew Walter, *China, the United States, and Global Order* (Cambridge: Cambridge University Press, 2011).

8. PROBLEMS OF STATENESS

1. Taylor Fravel, *Strong Borders, Secure Nation: Cooperation and Conflict in China's Territorial Disputes* (Princeton: Princeton University Press, 2008).

2. Katherine Palmer Kaup, *Creating the Zhuang: Ethnic Politics in China* (Boulder: Lynne Rienner, 2000), chap. 8.

3. Uradyn E. Bulag, *Nationalism and Hybridity in Mongolia* (Oxford: Clarendon Press, 1998).

4. Thierry Mathou, "Tibet and Its Neighbors: Moving Toward a New Chinese Strategy in the Himalayan Region," *Asian Survey* 45, no. 4 (July–August 2005): 507–509.

5. Melvyn C. Goldstein, with the help of Gelek Rimpoche, *A History of Modern Tibet, 1913–1951: The Demise of the Lamaist State* (Berkeley: University of California Press, 1989); Melvyn C. Goldstein, *Tibet, China, and the United States: Reflections on the Tibet Question* (Washington, D.C.: Atlantic Council, 1995); Elliot Sperling, *The Tibet–China Conflict: History and Polemics* (Washington, D.C.: East–West Center, 2004).

6. In international law, an "association" is a union of two sovereign states in which one of them agrees to yield certain attributes of sovereignty to the other.

7. The Dalai Lama's speech can be found at http://www.dalailama.com/messages /tibet/strasbourg-proposal-1988, accessed August 15, 2010.

8. The memorandum can be found at http://www.savetibet.org/policy-center/topics -fact-sheets/memorandum-genuine-autonomy-tibetan-people, accessed August 15, 2010.

9. Tashi Rabgey and Tseten Wangchuk Sharlho, *Sino–Tibetan Dialogue in the Post-Mao Era: Lessons and Prospects*, Policy Studies no. 12 (Washington, D.C.: East–West Center, 2004), 6.

10. President Bill Clinton, "Conditions for Renewal of Most-Favored-Nation Status for the People's Republic of China in 1994, " Executive Order 12850 of May 28, 1993, *Federal Register*, vol. 58, no. 103, June 1, 1993, at http://www.archives.gov/federal-register/executive-orders/pdf/12850.pdf, accessed January 19, 2012.

11. Melvyn C. Goldstein, "The Dalai Lama's Dilemma," *Foreign Affairs* 77, no. 1 (January–February 1998): 83–97.

12. The speaker was Zhang Qingli, and his statement can be found at http://www.chinatibetnews.com/GB/channel4/31/200803/19/78973.html, accessed August 15, 2010.

13. "Declaration on Principles for Relations and Comprehensive Cooperation Between the People's Republic of China and the Republic of India," June 25, 2003, at http://www.fmprc.gov.cn/eng/wjdt/2649/t22852.htm, accessed January 12, 2012.

14. S. Frederick Starr, ed., *Xinjiang: China's Muslim Borderland* (Armonk, N.Y.: M. E. Sharpe, 2004).

15. James A. Millward, *Eurasian Crossroads: A History of Xinjiang* (New York: Columbia University Press, 2007).

16. A vivid account is given in Rebiya Kadeer, with Alexandra Cavelius, *Dragon Fighter: One Women's Epic Struggle for Peace with China* (Carlsbad, Calif.: Kales Press, 2009).

17. Arienne M. Dwyer, *The Xinjiang Conflict: Uyghur Identity, Language Policy, and Political Discourse*, Policy Studies no. 15 (Washington, D.C.: East–West Center, 2005), 39.

18. Gardner Bovingdon, *Autonomy in Xinjiang: Han Nationalist Imperatives and Uyghur Discontent*, Policy Studies no. 11 (Washington, D.C.: East–West Center, 2004).

19. See the careful study by James Millward, *Violent Separatism in Xinjiang: A Critical Assessment*, Policy Studies no. 6 (Washington, D.C.: East–West Center, 2004).

20. Gardner Bovingdon, *The Uyghurs: Strangers in Their Own Land* (New York: Columbia University Press, 2010).

21. Rémi Castets, "The Uyghurs in Xinjiang: The Malaise Grows," *China Perspectives* 49 (September–October 2003), 39.

22. Andrew Scobell, "Terrorism and Chinese Foreign Policy," in Yong Deng and Feiling Wang, eds., *China Rising: Power and Motivation in Chinese Foreign Policy* (New York: Rowman and Littlefield, 2005), 317; Dru C. Gladney, "China's Minorities: The Case of Xinjiang and the Uyghur People," paper prepared for the UN Commission on Human Rights, Subcommission on Promotion and Protection of Human Rights, Working Group on Minorities, E/CN.4/Sub.2/AC.5/2003/WP.16, May 5, 2003, p. 11. J. Todd Reed and Diana Raschke review the available evidence in minute detail in *ETIM: China's Islamic Militants and the Global Terrorist Threat* (Santa Barbara: Praeger, 2010) and conclude that the ETIM is in fact a terrorist organization with links to al-Qaeda.

23. Christine Loh, *Underground Front: The Chinese Communist Party in Hong Kong* (Hong Kong: Hong Kong University Press, 2010).

24. Andrew Scobell, "China and Taiwan: Balance of Rivalry with Weapons of Mass Democratization," in Sumit Ganguly and William R. Thompson, eds., *Asian Rivalries: Conflict, Escalation, and Limitations on Two-Level Games* (Stanford: Stanford University Press, 2011), 26–43.

25. As we pointed out in chapter 4, the U.S. "acknowledges" the Chinese view rather than "recognizes" that Taiwan is part of China. But having deliberately created and maintained this ambiguity, it has done nothing to promote Taiwan independence.

26. Among other places, MacArthur used this phrase in "Memorandum on Formosa," June 14, 1950, *Foreign Relations of the United States, 1950*, vol. 7: *Korea* (Washington, D.C.: U.S. Government Printing Office, 1976), 162. His argument was that if access to Formosa was not denied to the Soviets, they could use it to threaten U.S. positions in Japan, Okinawa, and the Philippines. But the logic applies equally to the use of Taiwan by American or other forces to threaten China.

27. Quote given in Shirley A. Kan, *China/Taiwan: Evolution of the "One China" Policy—Key Statements from Washington, Beijing, and Taipei*, RL30341 (Washington, D.C.: Congressional Research Service, June 3, 2011), 7.

9. TAIWAN'S DEMOCRATIC TRANSITION AND CHINA'S RESPONSE

1. Andrew J. Nathan and Yangsun Chou, "Democratizing Transition in Taiwan," *Asian Survey* 27, no. 3 (March 1987): 277–299; Andrew J. Nathan, "The Effect of Taiwan's Political Reform on Taiwan–Mainland Relations," in Tun-jen Cheng and Stephan Haggard, eds., *Political Change in Taiwan* (Boulder: Lynne Reinner, 1992), 207–219; Andrew J. Nathan and Helena Ho, "Chiang Ching-kuo's Decision for Political Reform," in Shao-chuan Leng, ed., *Chiang Ching-kuo's Leadership in the Development of the Republic of China on Taiwan* (Lanham, Md.: University Press of America, 1993), 31–61.

2. The poll numbers in these paragraphs were provided by Shiau-chi Shen. They come from surveys conducted by the ROC Mainland Affairs Council, at http://www.mac.gov.tw/mp.asp?mp=3, and by the Election Study Center of National Chengchi University, at http://units.nccu.edu.tw/server/publichtmut/html/wS00/ewS00.html (access dates not available).

3. The overall thrust and key facts in what follows, except where noted otherwise, come from Su Chi, *Taiwan's Relations with Mainland China: A Tail Wagging Two Dogs* (London: Routledge, 2009).

4. Richard C. Kagan, *Taiwan's Statesman: Lee Teng-hui and Democracy in Asia* (Annapolis: Naval Institute Press, 2007).

5. Chiang Ching-kuo said in his statement of December 29, 1978, "The Republic of China is an independent sovereign state with a legitimately established government based on the Constitution of the Republic of China. It is an effective government, which has the wholehearted support of her people. The international status and

personality of the Republic of China cannot be changed merely because of the recognition of the Chinese Communist regime by any country of the world. The legal status and international personality of the Republic of China is a simple reality which the United States must recognize and respect." Quoted in Martin L. Lasater, *The Taiwan Issue in Sino–American Strategic Relations* (Boulder: Westview Press, 1984), 258–259.

6. *The Taiwan Question and Reunification of China* can be found at http://www.china .org.cn/e-white/taiwan/index.htm, accessed August 16, 2010, official translation. We silently correct "straits" to "strait" here and in other quotations.

7. In addition to the phrase *two political entities*, the official English translation contained the term *two governments*. But the relevant part of the Chinese text says only that the two sides are "separately governed" *(fenzhi)*. The term *two governments* does not appear in the Chinese text.

8. Su, *Taiwan's Relations with Mainland China*, 56–58.

9. Taiwan Affairs Office and the Information Office of the State Council, "The One-China Principle and the Taiwan Issue," February 2000, at http://english.gov.cn /official/2005-07/27/content_17613.htm, accessed January 20, 2012, official translation.

10. On the history of U.S. dealings with Taiwan, see Nancy Bernkopf Tucker, *Strait Talk: United States–Taiwan Relations and the Crisis with China* (Cambridge, Mass.: Harvard University Press, 2009).

11. From http://www.taiwandc.org/nws-9920.htm, accessed September 8, 2011.

12. "Premier Zhu Rongji Takes Questions About China's Focal Issues (2000)," March 15, 2000, at http://www.gov.cn/english/official/2005-07/25/content_17144.htm, accessed August 12, 2009.

13. Nancy Bernkopf Tucker and Bonnie Glaser, "Should the United States Abandon Taiwan?" *Washington Quarterly* 34, no. 4 (Fall 2011): 23–37.

10. DILEMMAS OF OPENING

1. Ezra F. Vogel, *Deng Xiaoping and the Transformation of China* (Cambridge, Mass.: Belknap Press of Harvard University Press, 2011).

2. Nicholas R. Lardy, *Foreign Trade and Economic Reform in China, 1978–1990* (Cambridge: Cambridge University Press, 1992).

3. Even though China claimed political sovereignty over Hong Kong and Taiwan, it treated them as separate entities for the purposes of trade and investment policy and statistics, and we do the same in this chapter.

4. "Chairman of Delegation of People's Republic of China Deng Xiaoping's Speech at Special Session of U.N. General Assembly," *Peking Review*, Supplement, April 12, 1974, iv.

5. Barry Naughton, *The Chinese Economy: Transitions and Growth* (Boston: MIT Press, 2007), 377–378.

6. Hong Kong stood so far in the lead in part because it served as a conduit for

investment from Taiwan and elsewhere and as a pass-through for money sent out of China and then back again in order to gain the concessionary benefits available for investments originating abroad.

7. China was a founding member of both organizations, but the China seat had previously been held by the ROC.

8. Many of the data cited here and elsewhere follow Naughton, *The Chinese Economy*.

9. On these struggles, see Zhao Ziyang, *Prisoner of the State: The Secret Journal of Premier Zhao Ziyang*, trans. and ed. Bao Pu, Renee Chiang, and Adi Ignatius (New York: Simon and Schuster, 2009).

10. Juntao Wang, "Reverse Course: Political Neo-conservatism and Regime Stability in Post-Tiananmen China," Ph.D. diss., Columbia University, 2006.

11. Lardy, *Foreign Trade*, chaps. 2 and 3.

12. The Chinese government disputes the U.S. calculation of the deficit, saying it unfairly includes goods shipped from China to the U.S. through Hong Kong, which should be listed in Hong Kong's export statistics, and that it excludes goods shipped from the U.S. to China through Hong Kong. However, even with these corrections, the U.S. would still have run a large trade deficit with China in the years we are talking about.

13. Martin K. Dimitrov, *Piracy and the State: The Politics of Intellectual Property Rights in China* (Cambridge: Cambridge University Press, 2009).

14. Much of the material in this section derives from Scott Harold, "Freeing Trade: Negotiating Domestic and International Obstacles on China's Long Road to the GATT/WTO, 1971–2001," Ph.D. diss., Columbia University, 2007.

15. Joshua Cooper Ramo, *The Beijing Consensus* (London: Foreign Policy Centre, 2004); Stefan Halper, *The Beijing Consensus: How China's Authoritarian Model Will Dominate the Twenty-First Century* (New York: Basic Books, 2010).

16. Richard MacGregor, *The Party: The Secret World of China's Communist Rulers* (New York: HarperCollins, 2010).

17. Vikram Nehru, Aart Kraay, and Xiaoqing Yu, *China 2020: Development Challenges in the New Century* (Washington, D.C.: World Bank, 1997), 29–30.

18. The datum is from Dong Tao, a Credit Suisse economist, quoted in David Barboza, "Some Assembly Needed: China as Asia Factory," *New York Times*, February 9, 2006, at http://www.nytimes.com/2006/02/09/business/worldbusiness/09asia.html, accessed August 8, 2008. Another report said the value of exports to the Chinese economy was as little as 20 percent of the face value of the exported products; see David D. Hale and Lyric Hughes Hale, "Reconsidering Revaluation: The Wrong Approach to the U.S.–China Trade Imbalance," *Foreign Affairs* 87, no. 1 (January–February 2008): 57–66.

19. The subhead for this section borrows a phrase from Jonathan Holslag, "China's Regional Dilemma: An Inquiry Into the Limits of China's Economic and Military Power," Ph.D. diss., Vrije Universiteit Brussel, 2011.

20. Ka Zeng, *Trade Threats, Trade Wars: Bargaining, Retaliation, and American Coercive Diplomacy* (Ann Arbor: University of Michigan Press, 2004).

21. Hideo Ohashi, "China's Regional Trade and Investment Profile," in David Shambaugh, ed., *Power Shift: China and Asia's New Dynamics* (Berkeley: University of California Press, 2005), 71–95; Deng Ziliang and Zheng Yongnian, "China Reshapes the World Economy," in Wang Gungwu and Zheng Yongnian, eds., *China and the New International Order* (London: Routledge, 2008), 127–148.

22. Jonathan Holslag, "China's Roads to Influence," *Asian Survey* 50, no. 4 (July–August 2010): 641–662.

23. Deborah Brautigam, *The Dragon's Gift: The Real Story of China in Africa* (Oxford: Oxford University Press, 2009).

24. Ibid., 179.

25. Robert Jervis, *System Effects: Complexity in Political and Social Life* (Princeton: Princeton University Press, 1997).

26. The number of jobs created by township and village enterprises is taken from Naughton, *The Chinese Economy*, 286, fig. 12.2; the number of new entrants into the workforce is calculated using Naughton, *The Chinese Economy*, 175, table 7.3.

27. James Kynge, *China Shakes the World* (New York: Houghton Mifflin, 2006).

28. See, for instance, Peter Navarro, "The Economics of the 'China Price,'" *China Perspectives* (November–December 2006): 13–27.

29. David Hale, "China's Growing Appetites," *The National Interest* (Summer 2004): 137–147.

30. Lester R. Brown, *Who Will Feed China? Wake-Up Call for a Small Planet* (New York: Norton, 1995).

31. Jonathan Watts, *When a Billion Chinese Jump: How China Will Save Mankind—or Destroy It* (New York: Scribner, 2010).

32. Rosemary Foot and Andrew Walter, *China, the United States, and Global Order* (Cambridge: Cambridge University Press, 2011), chap. 5.

33. Elizabeth Economy and Michel Oksenberg, eds., *China Joins the World: Progress and Prospects* (New York: Council on Foreign Relations, 1999).

34. Other factors included American lobbying and China's "social learning" from other states. Evan S. Medeiros, *Reluctant Restraint: The Evolution of China's Nonproliferation Policies and Practices, 1980–2004* (Stanford: Stanford University Press, 2007); Alastair Iain Johnston, *Social States: China in International Relations, 1980–2000* (Princeton: Princeton University Press, 2008).

35. Medeiros, *Reluctant Restraint*; Dimitrov, *Piracy and the State*.

36. Ann Kent, *Beyond Compliance: China, International Organizations, and Global Security* (Stanford: Stanford University Press, 2007); Foot and Walter, *China, the United States, and Global Order.*

37. Rosemary Foot, *Rights Beyond Borders: The Global Community and the Struggle Over Human Rights in China* (Oxford: Oxford University Press, 2000); Ann Kent, *China, the United Nations, and Human Rights* (Philadelphia: University of Pennsylvania Press, 1999).

38. The subhead for this section adapts the title of Ezra F. Vogel's book *Japan as Number One: Lessons for America* (Cambridge, Mass.: Harvard University Press, 1979).

39. Michael Beckley, "China's Century? Why America's Edge Will Endure," *International Security* 36, no. 3 (Winter 2011–2012): 41–78.

11. MILITARY MODERNIZATION

1. Deng Xiaoping, "The Tasks of Consolidating the Army" (July 14, 1975), in *Selected Works of Deng Xiaoping*, 3 vols. (Beijing: Foreign Languages Press, 1984), 2:27.

2. Particularly useful and comprehensive treatments of Chinese military matters are Dennis Blasko, *The Chinese Army Today*, 2nd ed. (New York: Routledge, 2012); Richard P. Hallion, Roger Cliff, and Phillip C. Saunders, eds., *The People's Liberation Army Air Force: Evolving Concepts, Roles, and Capabilities* (Washington, D.C.: National Defense University Press, 2012); Bernard Cole, *The Great Wall at Sea*, 2nd ed. (Annapolis: Naval Institute Press, 2010); and David Shambaugh, *Modernizing China's Military* (Berkeley: University of California Press, 2002). For more detailed and specialized writings, see the publications of the RAND Corporation and the U.S. Army War College's Strategic Studies Institute, available online at http://www.rand.org and http://www.strategicstudiesinstitute.army.mil, respectively.

3. Mao Tsetung, "The Chinese People Cannot Be Cowed by the Atom Bomb," in *Selected Works of Mao Tsetung*, 5 vols. (Peking: Foreign Languages Press, 1977), 5:153.

4. The text of Hu Jintao's speech has never been made public, but it has been widely cited. See, for example, Daniel Hartnett, *China Military and Security Activities*, Hearings Before the U.S.–China Economic and Security Review Commission, 111th Cong. 1st sess., March 4, 2009 (Washington, D.C.: Government Printing Office, April 2009), 45–55.

5. Figures from Cheng Li, "The New Military Elite," in David M. Finkelstein and Kristen Gunness, eds., *Civil–Military Relations in Today's China* (Armonk, N.Y.: M. E. Sharpe, 2007), 55, 57; and James C. Mulvenon, *Professionalization of the Senior Chinese Officer Corps* (Santa Monica, Calif.: RAND, 1997), 42.

6. Combined arms training involves cooperation among different branches (e.g., infantry, artillery, armor); "joint operations" refers to coordination among different services (i.e., ground, air force, navy, Second Artillery).

7. The increases are calculated using figures for the defense budgets found in the Chinese defense white papers from 2004, 2006, 2008, and 2010 and from Shambaugh, *Modernizing China's Military*, table 4, 188–189. The 2010 figure can be found in Information Office of the State Council, People's Republic of China, *China's National Defense in 2010* (Beijing: Information Office of the State Council, March 2011).

8. *Military and Security Developments Involving the People's Republic of China, 2010* (Washington, D.C.: Office of the Secretary of Defense, 2010), 42–43.

9. Tai Ming Cheung, *Fortifying China: The Struggle to Build a Modern Defense Economy* (Ithaca: Cornell University Press, 2009); Evan Feigenbaum, *China's*

Techno-Warriors: National Security and Strategic Competition from the Nuclear to the Information Age (Stanford: Stanford University Press, 2003).

10. Carla Hills and Dennis Blair, chairs, *U.S.–China Relations: An Affirmative Agenda, a Responsible Course*, Task Force Report (New York: Council on Foreign Relations, April 2007), 47–54.

11. On CMC as a "lobbying group," see Nan Li, "The Central Military Commission and Military Policy in China," in James C. Mulvenon and Andrew N. D. Yang, eds., *The People's Liberation Army as Organization* (Santa Monica, Calif.: RAND Corporation, 2002), 82. On the paramount leader as the key mechanism, see Andrew Scobell, "China's Evolving Civil–Military Relations: Creeping *Guojiahua*," *Armed Forces and Society* 31, no. 2 (Winter 2005), 229.

12. The U.S. ratio was calculated using FBI statistics on law enforcement personnel for 2004 (970,588 for a population of 278,433,063). For the Chinese ratio calculated for 2005, see Murray Scot Tanner and Eric Green, "Principals and Secret Agents: Central Control Versus Local Control Over Policing and Obstacles to 'Rule of Law' in China," *China Quarterly*, no. 191 (September 2007), 664.

13. Xuezhi Guo, *China's Security State: Philosophy, Evolution, and Politics* (New York: Cambridge University Press, 2013).

14. Andrew Scobell, *China's Use of Military Force: Beyond the Great Wall and the Long March* (New York: Cambridge University Press, 2003), chap. 5.

15. China's 1969 action likely had multiple motivations. See Thomas Robinson, "The Sino–Soviet Border Conflicts in 1969: New Evidence Three Decades Later," in Mark Ryan, David M. Finkelstein, and Michael A. McDevitt, eds., *Chinese Warfighting: The PLA Experience Since 1949* (Armonk, N.Y.: M. E. Sharpe, 2003), 198–216.

16. Jonathan Holslag, *China and India: Prospects for Peace* (New York: Columbia University Press, 2010), chap. 5.

17. Richard C. Bush, *The Perils of Proximity: China–Japan Security Relations* (Washington, D.C.: Brookings Institution Press, 2010), 64; Cole, *The Great Wall at Sea*, 22–23.

18. Michael D. Swaine and Roy D. Kamphausen, "Military Modernization in Taiwan," in Ashley J. Tellis and Michael Wills, eds., *Strategic Asia, 2005–06: Military Modernization in an Era of Uncertainty* (Seattle: National Bureau of Asian Research, 2005), 420; Bernard D. Cole, *Taiwan's Security: History and Prospects* (New York: Routledge, 2006).

19. These four options are drawn from *Military and Security Developments*, 51–52.

20. Richard C. Bush and Michael E. O'Hanlon, *A War Like No Other: The Truth About China's Challenge to America* (Hoboken, N.J.: Wiley, 2007), 135–136.

21. Thomas J. Christensen, "Posing Problems Without Catching Up: China's Rise and Challenges for U.S. Security Policy," *International Security* 35, no. 4 (Spring 2001): 5–40.

22. John Lewis and Xue Litai, *China Builds the Bomb* (Stanford: Stanford University Press, 1988).

23. Jeffrey Lewis, *The Minimum Means of Reprisal: China's Search for Security in the*

Nuclear Age (Cambridge, Mass.: MIT Press, 2007); M. Taylor Fravel and Evan S. Medeiros, "China's Search for Assured Retaliation: The Evolution of China's Nuclear Strategy and Force Structure," *International Security* 35, no. 2 (Fall 2010): 48–87.

24. Evan S. Medeiros, *Reluctant Restraint: The Evolution of China's Nonproliferation Policies and Practices, 1980–2004* (Stanford: Stanford University Press, 2007).

25. Shirley A. Kan, *China and Proliferation of Weapons of Mass Destruction and Missiles: Policy Issues* (Washington, D.C.: Congressional Research Service, May 2011).

26. The phrase *beyond Taiwan* comes from Pentagon analyses. For detailed discussion, see Roy Kamphausen, David Lai, and Andrew Scobell, eds., *Beyond the Strait: Chinese Military Missions Other Than Taiwan* (Carlisle, Pa.: Strategic Studies Institute, U.S. Army War College, 2009). This section draws from Scobell's contribution to this volume.

27. Andrew Scobell and Gregory Stevenson, "The PLA (Re)Discovers Nontraditional Security," in Lyle Goldstein, ed., *China and the Challenge of Non-traditional Security Threats* (Annapolis, Md.: Naval Institute Press, forthcoming).

28. Christopher J. Pehrson, *String of Pearls: Meeting the Challenges of China's Rising Power Across the Asian Littoral* (Carlisle, Pa.: Strategic Studies Institute, U.S. Army War College, 2006).

29. Donald Rumsfeld, "Remarks to the International Institute for Strategic Studies," delivered in Singapore, June 4, 2005, at http://www.defense.gov/Transcripts/Transcript .aspx?TranscriptID=3216, accessed November 1, 2011.

30. Saadia M. Pekkanen and Paul Kallender-Umezu, *In Defense of Japan: From the Market to the Military in Space Policy* (Stanford: Stanford University Press, 2010).

31. The Panetta quote comes from a speech given in Japan: "Town Hall Meeting with Secretary Panetta with US Military and Japanese Defense Force Personnel at Yakota Air Base," October 24, 2011, at http://www.defense.gov/transcripts /transcript.aspx?transcriptid=4911, accessed November 20, 2011. The Obama quote comes from a speech to the Australian Parliament: "Remarks by President Obama to the Australian Parliament," November 16, 2011, at http://www.whitehouse.gov /the-press-office/2011/11/17/remarks-president-obama-australian-parliament, accessed November 20, 2011. The third quote and related information comes from *Quadrennial Defense Review Report* (Washington, D.C.: U.S. Department of Defense, February 2010), 62. The AirSea Battle and unmanned-aircraft systems are discussed in ibid., 22, 32–33. This section also draws on Roy D. Kamphausen, "America's Security Commitment to Asia: A Twenty Year Outlook," presentation to the International Institute for Strategic Studies Dialogue, Singapore, April 13–14, 2010.

12. SOFT POWER AND HUMAN RIGHTS IN CHINESE FOREIGN POLICY

1. Joseph S. Nye Jr., *Soft Power: The Means to Success in World Politics* (New York: PublicAffairs, 2004); Joshua Kurlantzick, *China's Charm Offensive: How China's*

Soft Power Is Transforming the World (New Haven: Yale University Press, 2007); David M. Lampton, *The Three Faces of Chinese Power: Might, Money, and Minds* (Berkeley: University of California Press, 2008).

2. Portions of this section are drawn from Andrew Scobell, "China's Soft Sell: Is the World Buying?" *China Brief* 7, no. 2 (January 24, 2007): 7–10, and from Andrew J. Nathan and Andrew Scobell, "Human Rights and China's Soft Power Expansion," *China Rights Forum*, no. 4 (2009): 10–23.

3. George H. W. Bush, *The China Diary of George H. W. Bush: The Making of a Global President*, ed. Jeffrey Engel (Princeton: Princeton University Press, 2008), 341.

4. Henry Kissinger, *White House Years* (Boston: Little, Brown, 1979), 1056; Zbigniew Brzezinski, *Power and Principle: Memoirs of the National Security Adviser, 1977–1981* (New York: Farrar, Straus, Giroux, 1983), 213.

5. Bonnie S. Glaser and Melissa E. Murphy, "Soft Power with Chinese Characteristics: The Ongoing Debate," in Carola McGiffert, ed., *Chinese Soft Power and Its Implications for the United States: Competition and Cooperation in the Developing World* (Washington, D.C.: Center for Strategic and International Studies, 2009), 10–26, at http://csis.org/files/media/csis/pubs/090305_mcgiffert_chinesesoftpower_web.pdf, accessed December 9, 2010; Joel Wuthnow, "The Concept of Soft Power in China's Strategic Discourse," *Issues & Studies* 44, no. 2 (June 2008): 1–28.

6. Hu Jintao, *Hold High the Great Banner of Socialism with Chinese Characteristics and Strive for New Victories in Building a Moderately Prosperous Society in All Respects: Report to the Seventeenth National Congress of the Communist Party of China* (October 15, 2007), at http://news.xinhuanet.com/english/2007–10/24/content _6938749_6.htm, accessed December 10, 2010.

7. "Zhonggong zhongyang guanyu shenhua wenhua tizhi gaige tuidong shehuizhuyi wenhua dafazhan dafanrong ruogan zhongda wenti de jueding" (Decision of the CCP Central Committee on some important questions concerning deepening the reform of the cultural system and promoting the great development and great flourishing of socialist culture), October 18, 2011, at http://economy.caijing .com.cn/2011-10-26/110933747.html, accessed January 22, 2012; an official English translation was not available at the time this document was consulted.

8. Anne-Marie Brady, *Marketing Dictatorship: Propaganda and Thought Work in Contemporary China* (Lanham, Md.: Rowman and Littlefield, 2007).

9. Victor D. Cha, *Beyond the Final Score: The Politics of Sport in Asia* (New York: Columbia University Press, 2009).

10. Susan Brownell, *Beijing's Games: What The Olympics Mean to China* (Lanham, Md.: Rowman and Littlefield, 2008); Xu Guoqi, *Olympic Dreams: China and Sports, 1895–2008* (Cambridge, Mass.: Harvard University Press, 2008).

11. Karl Gerth, *As China Goes, so Goes the World: How Chinese Consumers Are Transforming Everything* (New York: Hill and Wang, 2010).

12. For example, Martin Jacques, *When China Rules the World: The Rise of the Middle Kingdom and the End of the Western World* (London: Allen Lane, 2009).

13. Stephanie Kleine-Ahlbrandt and Andrew Small, "China's New Dictatorship Diplomacy," *Foreign Affairs* 87, no. 1 (January–February 2008): 38–56.

14. The remainder of this chapter is a condensed and updated version of Andrew J. Nathan, "China and International Human Rights: Tiananmen's Paradoxical Impact," in Jean-Philippe Béja, ed., *The Impact of China's 1989 Tiananmen Massacre* (London: Routledge, 2010), 206–220.

15. Paul Gordon Lauren, *The Evolution of International Human Rights: Visions Seen* (Philadelphia: University of Pennsylvania Press, 1998).

16. Daniel C. Thomas, *The Helsinki Effect: International Norms, Human Rights, and the Demise of Communism* (Princeton: Princeton University Press, 2001).

17. Ronald Reagan, "Promoting Democracy and Peace," speech before the British Parliament, London, June 8, 1982, in *U.S. Department of State, Current Policy*, no. 399 (June 1982), 4.

18. Among other sources, see Julie A. Mertus, *Bait and Switch: Human Rights and U.S. Foreign Policy*, 2nd ed. (New York: Routledge, 2008).

19. European Commission, *EU–China: Closer Partners, Growing Responsibilities* (n.d.), at http://eur-lex.europa.eu/LexUriServ/site/en/com/2006/com2006_0631en01 .pdf, accessed January 22, 2012.

20. Larry Diamond, *The Spirit of Democracy* (New York: Times Books, 2008), appendix, table 2.

21. Ann Marie Clark, *Diplomacy of Conscience: Amnesty International and Changing Human Rights Norms* (Princeton: Princeton University Press, 2001); Amnesty International, *Political Imprisonment in the People's Republic of China: An Amnesty International Report* (London: Amnesty International, 1978).

22. This number is provided by the Human Rights Organizations Database of Human Rights Internet, at http://www.hri.ca/organizations.aspx, accessed January 22, 2012.

23. The UDHR is not a treaty, but most international lawyers consider it to be part of customary international law. Covenants—such as the International Covenant on Civil and Political Rights and the International Covenant on Economic, Social, and Cultural Rights—are treaties.

24. Thomas G. Weiss, *Humanitarian Intervention: Ideas in Action* (Cambridge: Polity Press, 2007), 43. Additional humanitarian interventions were undertaken during the same decade with the approval of bodies other than the UN, such as the intervention in Liberia authorized by Economic Community of West African States Monitoring Group and the intervention in Kosovo authorized by NATO.

25. Quoted in Jeremy T. Paltiel, *The Empire's New Clothes: Cultural Particularism and Universal Value in China's Quest for Global Status* (New York: Palgrave Macmillan, 2007), 144.

26. Aryeh Neier, "Economic Sanctions and Human Rights," in Samantha Power and Graham Allison, eds., *Realizing Human Rights: Moving from Inspiration to Impact*, 291–308 (New York: St. Martin's, 2000).

27. Human Rights Watch, "Chinese Diplomacy, Western Hypocrisy, and the U.N. Human Rights Commission," March 1, 1997, at http://www.unhcr.org/refworld /docid/3ae6a7d94.html, accessed June 11, 2009.

28. Chinese delegate Wu Jianmin at the UN Human Rights Commission in April 1996, quoted in "Loss for U.S. on Rights," *New York Times*, April 24, 1996.

29. From a document included in Zhang Liang, comp., Andrew J. Nathan and Perry Link, eds., *The Tiananmen Papers* (New York: PublicAffairs, 2001), 338.

30. *National Human Rights Action Plan of China (2009–2010)*, at http://news.xinhua net.com/english/2009–04/13/content_11177126.htm, accessed June 11, 2009; "Human Rights Watch Statement on UPR Outcome Report of China," June 11, 2009, at http://www.hrw.org:80/node/83727, accessed June 11, 2009.

31. As listed in "Country Visits by Special Procedures Mandate Holders Since 1998," n.d., at http://www2.ohchr.org/english/bodies/chr/special/countryvisitsa-e .htm#china, accessed June 11, 2009.

32. See various diplomatically worded press releases, reports, and position papers issued by the International Federation for Human Rights at http://www.fidh.org/-Human -Rights-Council-, accessed June 11, 2009.

33. See James Mann, *The China Fantasy: How Our Leaders Explain Away Chinese Repression* (New York: Viking, 2007).

34. U.S. Commission on International Religious Freedom, "The Many Faces of China's Repression: Human Rights, Religious Freedom, and U.S. Diplomacy in China," January 31, 2007, at http://www.uscirf.gov/index.php?option=com_content&task =view&id=1785&Itemid=1, accessed August 25, 2008.

35. For example, see Human Rights in China's submissions to UN treaty bodies and special mechanisms at http://hrichina.org/public/contents/category?cid=22042& lang=iso%2d8859%2d1, accessed June 11, 2009.

36. "An Introduction to CLB's Labour Rights Litigation Work," n.d., http://www.china -labour.org.hk/en/node/100020, accessed June 11, 2009.

37. For more on the Committee to Support Chinese Lawyers, see http://law.fordham .edu/ihtml/center3.ihtml?imac=1658, accessed May 27, 2009.

38. For an overview of developments in the link between business and human rights, see the Web site of the Business and Human Rights Resource Centre at http://www .business-humanrights.org/Home, accessed January 22, 2012.

39. For an overview of the Global Network Initiative, see http://www.globalnetwork initiative.org/index.php, accessed January 22, 2012.

40. Yun-han Chu, Larry Diamond, Andrew J. Nathan, and Doh Chull Shin, eds., *How East Asians View Democracy* (New York: Columbia University Press, 2008).

13. THREAT OR EQUILIBRIUM?

1. The quotes from Andrew J. Nathan and Robert S. Ross, *The Great Wall and the Empty Fortress: China's Search for Security* (New York: Norton, 1997), are on pp. xiv and 229–230.

2. Aaron L. Friedberg, *A Contest for Supremacy: China, America, and the Struggle for Mastery in Asia* (New York: Norton, 2011); Martin Jacques, *When China Rules the World: The Rise of the Middle Kingdom and the End of the Western World* (London: Allen Lane, 2009); John J. Mearsheimer, *The Tragedy of Great Power Politics* (New York: Norton, 2001); Arvind Subramanian, *Eclipse: Living in the Shadow of China's*

Economic Dominance (Washington, D.C.: Peterson Institute for International Economics, 2011).

3. Yu Liu and Dingding Chen, "Why China Will Democratize," *Washington Quarterly* 35, no. 1 (Winter 2012): 41–63.

4. Andrew J. Nathan, *Chinese Democracy* (New York: Knopf, 1985); Andrew J. Nathan, "China's Changing of the Guard: Authoritarian Resilience," *Journal of Democracy* 14, no. 1 (January 2003): 6–17; Andrew J. Nathan, "China's Political Trajectory: What Are the Chinese Saying?" in Cheng Li, ed., *China's Changing Political Landscape: Prospects for Democracy* (Washington, D.C.: Brookings Institution Press, 2008), 25–43; Andrew J. Nathan, "China Since Tiananmen: Authoritarian Impermanence," *Journal of Democracy* 20, no. 3 (July 2009): 37–40.

5. Salvatore Babones, "The Middling Kingdom: The Hype and the Reality of China's Rise," *Foreign Affairs* 90, no. 5 (September–October 2011): 79–88.

6. For example, see Robert S. Ross, "The Geography of the Peace: East Asia in the Twenty-First Century," *International Security* 23, no. 4 (Spring 1999): 81–118; Michael D. Swaine, *America's Challenge: Engaging a Rising China in the Twenty-First Century* (Washington, D.C.: Carnegie Endowment for International Peace, 2011).

7. Zbigniew Brzezinski, "From Hope to Audacity: Appraising Obama's Foreign Policy," *Foreign Affairs* 89, no. 1 (January–February 2010): 16–30; Henry Kissinger, *On China* (New York: Penguin Press, 2011); Jacques, *When China Rules the World*.

ACKNOWLEDGMENTS

This book would not have been written without a generous research grant from the Smith Richardson Foundation. We also thank the Weatherhead East Asian Institute at Columbia University and the George H. W. Bush School of Government and Public Service at Texas A&M University for financial support.

We are grateful to the coauthor of *The Great Wall and the Empty Fortress*, Robert S. Ross, and to its publisher, Steve Forman of W. W. Norton, for permission to embark upon a second edition, which evolved into this book. Steven I. Levine was involved in drafting some of the chapters in the early stages of the first edition, and some of his distinctive language survives into this book. He also gave valuable comments on the whole manuscript. The following individuals provided much appreciated comments or other help with various chapters: Robbie Barnett, Michael Beckley, Dennis Blasko, Richard Bush, Chang Kuei-min, Roger Cliff, Cortez Cooper, Paul Godwin, David Kang, Hua-Yu Li, Frank Miller, Andrew Oros, Joanne Estrallita Ou, Alexander Pantsov, Morris Rossabi, Tetsuo Shibata, Shiau-chi Shen, Su Chi, Larry Wortzel, and Zong Hairen.

We also thank Victor Alfaro, Rouben Azizian, Alice Ba, Rommel Banlaoi, Samuel Berkowitz, Jae Ho Chung, Yong Deng, Bruce Dickson, Charles Hooper, Roy Kamphausen, Heung Kyu Kim, Taeho Kim, Heino Klink, Mohan Malik, Evan Medeiros, Lyle Morris, Ren Mu, Ian Storey, and Suisheng Zhao. We appreciate the help of numerous experts inside China who agreed to be interviewed by Andrew Scobell, but who must remain anonymous. In addition, Scobell thanks Professor Zhu Feng of Peking University for graciously hosting him during an extended research visit to China in 2008.

We are indebted to a group of resourceful research assistants who made significant contributions at various phases of this project: Serena Ho, Chiu-yi Ko, Brandon Krueger, Cynthia Lee, Daniel Paluch, Nicholas Reves, Cristine Salo, and Gregory Stevenson. We are grateful to students in Andrew Nathan's Chinese foreign policy class in spring 2011, who caught typos and made other suggestions and corrections.

INDEX